# The Changing Politics of Finance in Korea and Thailand

T0352651

*The Changing Politics of Finance in Korea and Thailand* represents a systematic attempt to explore the causal relationship between financial market reform and financial crisis in an interdisciplinary and comparative perspective. It examines the political underpinnings of financial policy change and provides an in-depth analysis of market liberalisation processes and their impact on the economic turmoil of 1997–98 in Korea and Thailand.

In the early 1980s Korea and Thailand embarked on a process of financial liberalisation, against a backdrop of intensive external economic and political pressures. The two countries followed divergent approaches to financial market reform and achieved different results in the major areas of external and domestic liberalisation. Different as they were, market reforms in Korea and Thailand did not bring about the promised benefits to their national economies. During the early and mid-1990s the decade-long liberalisation efforts produced critical macro-economic and structural problems that contributed to the onset of the financial crisis. The central proposition of this book is that liberalisation differences and reform policy failures had important endogenous sources. The common crisis stemmed from divergent reform patterns and originated from dissimilar institutional deficiencies and political constraints.

The book will be essential reading for both policy-makers and academics concerned with national economic governance in an era of globalisation.

**Xiaoke Zhang** is Research Fellow at the Amsterdam School for Social Science Research and the Department of Political Science, University of Amsterdam. He is co-editor of *International Financial Governance under Stress* (2002). His research focuses on comparative political economy, with specific reference to East Asian newly industrialising economies.

# Routledge/RIPE Series in Global Political Economy

Series editors: Otto Holman, Marianne Marchand (*Research Centre for International Political Economy, University of Amsterdam*), Henk Overbeek (*Free University, Amsterdam*) and Marianne Franklin (*University of Amsterdam*)

This series, published in association with the *Review of International Political Economy*, provides a forum for current debates in international political economy. The series aims to cover all the central topics in IPE and to present innovative analyses of emerging topics. The titles in the series seek to transcend a state-centred discourse and focus on three broad themes:

* the nature of the forces driving globalisation forward
* resistance to globalisation
* the transformation of the world order.

The series comprises two strands:

The *RIPE Series in Global Political Economy* aims to address the needs of students and teachers, and the titles will be published in hardback and paperback. Titles include:

**Transnational Classes and International Relations**
*Kees van der Pijl*

**Gender and Global Restructuring**
Sightings, sites and resistances
*Edited by Marianne H. Marchand and Anne Sisson Runyan*

**Global Political Economy**
Contemporary theories
*Edited by Ronen Palan*

**Ideologies of Globalization**
Contending visions of a New World Order
*Mark Rupert*

**The Clash within Civilisations**
Coming to terms with cultural conflicts
*Dieter Senghaas*

**Global Unions?**
Theory and strategies of organized labour in the global political economy
*Edited by Jeffrey Harrod and Robert O'Brien*

**Political Economy of a Plural World**
Critical reflections on power, morals and civilizations
*Robert Cox with Michael Schechter*

*Routledge/RIPE Studies in Global Political Economy* is a forum for innovative new research intended for a high-level specialist readership, and the titles will be available in hardback only. Titles include:

1. **Globalization and Governance***
   *Edited by Aseem Prakash and Jeffrey A. Hart*

2. **Nation-states and Money**
   The past, present and future of national currencies
   *Edited by Emily Gilbert and Eric Helleiner*

3. **The Global Political Economy of Intellectual Property Rights**
   The new enclosures?
   *Christopher May*

4. **Integrating Central Europe**
   EU expansion and Poland, Hungary and the Czech Republic
   *Otto Holman*

5. **Capitalist Restructuring, Globalisation and the Third Way**
   Lessons from the Swedish model
   *J. Magnus Ryner*

6. **Transnational Capitalism and the Struggle over European Integration**
   *Bastiaan van Apeldoorn*

7. **World Financial Orders**
   An historical international political economy
   *Paul Langley*

8. **The Changing Politics of Finance in Korea and Thailand**
   From deregulation to debacle
   *Xiaoke Zhang*

*\*Also available in paperback*

# The Changing Politics of Finance in Korea and Thailand

## From deregulation to debacle

Xiaoke Zhang

Routledge
Taylor & Francis Group

LONDON AND NEW YORK

First published 2003
by Routledge
2 Park Square, Milton Park, Abingdon, Oxfordshire OX14 4RN

Simultaneously published in the USA and Canada
by Routledge
711 Third Avenue, New York, NY 10017

*Routledge is an imprint of the Taylor and Francis Group, an informa business*

First issued in paperback 2015

Typeset in Baskerville by
Prepress Projects Ltd, Perth, Scotland

*British Library Cataloguing in Publication Data*
A catalogue record for this book is available from the British
Library

*Library of Congress Cataloging in Publication Data*
Zhang, Xiaoke.
  The changing politics of finance in Korea and Thailand :
from deregulation to debacle / Xiaoke Zhang.
    p. cm. – (Routledge/RIPE studies in global political
economy)
  Includes bibliographical references and index.
    1. Finance–Korea (South) 2. Finance–Thailand. 3. Financial
crises–Korea (South) 4. Financial crises–Thailand. 5. Financial
institutions–Deregulation–Korea (South) 6. Financial
institutions–Deregulation–Thailand. I. Title. II. Series.

HG187.K6 Z47 2002
332′.095195–dc21                                    2002028476

ISBN 978-0-415-29862-9 (hbk)
ISBN 978-1-138-81181-2 (pbk)

**To my parents**

# Contents

*List of illustrations*                                                    xi
*Series editors' preface*                                                 xiii
*Acknowledgements*                                                         xv
*Acronyms and abbreviations*                                             xvii

1  Introduction                                                             1

**PART I**
**The political logic of comparative financial policy**                   19

2  Interests, institutions and financial policy                           21
3  Institutional variations in Korea and Thailand                         43

**PART II**
**The political economy of financial liberalisation**                     71

4  Financial liberalisation in Korea                                      73
5  Financial liberalisation in Thailand                                  105
6  Liberalisation differences: focused comparison                        134

**PART III**
**The political economy of financial crisis**                            149

7  Financial crisis in Korea and Thailand                                151
8  Findings, lessons and implications                                    182

*Notes*                                                                   194
*Bibliography*                                                            204
*Index*                                                                   230

# Illustrations

## Figures

2.1  A schematic presentation of the theoretical framework     42
7.1  Private capital inflows in Thailand, 1990–96     153

## Tables

2.1  Key dimensions of private-sector organisational structures     32
3.1  Aggregate concentration ratios by sales for top 50 and 100
    manufacturing enterprises (percentages), selected years     44
3.2  Combined sales of largest business groups as percentage of gross
    national product (GNP), selected years     45
3.3  Deposit money bank concentration ratios (percentages), 1980–90     49
3.4  Bank loans to manufacturing (percentage of total bank loans),
    selected years     52
3.5  Institutional variations of financial policy-making in Korea and
    Thailand     69
4.1  Main economic indicators in Korea (percentages), 1970–96     74
4.2  Main business indicators in the Korean manufacturing sector
    (percentages), 1979–86     78
4.3  Main features of foreign exchange and capital controls in Korea
    prior to financial liberalisation in the late 1980s     88
5.1  Main economic indicators in Thailand, 1970–96     106
5.2  Key changes in the Thai foreign exchange and capital regime     117
6.1  Cross-country differences in reform approaches and outcomes     135
6.2  Trend of major interest rates in Korea and Thailand
    (percentages), 1982–95     138
6.3  Market shares of financial institutions in Korea and Thailand
    (percentages), 1975–95     139
6.4  Ratios of gross capital flows to GDP in Korea and Thailand
    (yearly averages), 1981–95     140
6.5  Index of international financial policy openness in Korea and
    Thailand (yearly averages), 1981–95     140

6.6  Institutional variations and corresponding reform approaches
      and outcomes                                                      141
7.1  External debt in Thailand, 1990–96                                153
7.2  Bank lending by sector in Thailand (percentages), 1986–95         154
7.3  BIBF lending and foreign liabilities of banks in Thailand,
      1993–96                                                          157
7.4  Foreign debt in Korea, 1993–96                                    168
7.5  Sources of external funds raised by the Korean corporate sector
      (percentage of total external financing), 1985–97               169
7.6  Corporate leverage in Korea and other East Asian newly
      industrialised economies (NIEs) (percentage, arithmetic
      means), 1988–96                                                  170
7.7  Main indicators of financial institution soundness in Korea,
      1993–97                                                          171
8.1  Institutional failures and financial crisis in Korea and Thailand  183

# Series editors' preface

In the first half of the 1990s, it was widely assumed that the twenty-first century was to be the century of Asia. It still may be. But the financial crisis that swept across much of East and Southeast Asia in 1997 and 1998 has fundamentally changed the parameters of Asia's further ascendancy. *The Changing Politics of Finance in Korea and Thailand* by Xiaoke Zhang is a welcome and important contribution to the study of this major episode.

There is of course no lack of analyses of the causes and consequences of the Asian financial crisis, neither in general terms nor in terms of specific country studies. In the plethora of more comprehensive studies of the Asian crisis the emphasis is either on the role of market failure (from a neo-classical perspective) or on the impact of the external environment (which Zhang calls system-oriented perspectives). Both perspectives neglect the importance of domestic factors when tracing the trajectory of financial sector reform and crisis.

As Zhang argues, the 'developmental state' approach and the 'political structure' perspective correct this fundamental deficiency. The variables identified by these approaches (state strength, regime form, etc.), however, are too broad to be able to capture the complexities of the policy process in concrete cases.

Zhang identifies two sets of variables that do allow for a detailed and specific analysis. He argues that the structure of private-sector preference formation (and especially the distinctive preferences and practices of the financial and industrial sectors), on the one hand, and the interests and practices of specific state institutions (governments, departments, central banks), on the other hand, determine how external systemic pressures and general weaknesses of state and political structure are differentially transformed into policy reforms. This ultimately explains how the financial crisis of the late 1990s manifested itself throughout East and Southeast Asia. Zhang develops his perspective in a thorough comparative analysis of the Thailand and South Korean cases. He meticulously traces the trajectory of financial sector reforms in both countries from the early 1980s onwards, and is thus able to considerably refine the picture emerging from the more sweeping analyses of the crisis to date. At the same time, his rigorously applied method of focused and structured comparison allows him to formulate conclusions and insights that are applicable to a wider range of economies.

Zhang concludes that the success of financial reforms hinges not just on changes within the financial sector itself or on the reduction of the state role in general terms. He shows, rather, that corporate sector restructuring (including ownership structures), the creation and strengthening of (what he calls) a Weberian bureaucracy relatively insulated from particularistic interests, the strengthening of key state institutions (the central banks especially) and a thorough democratisation of the political and policy-making processes are (mutually reinforcing) preconditions for strong and effective national economic governance. These insights are of undeniable relevance to all of those concerned with the prospects for sustainable economic growth in the region.

Zhang's book is also important because of the crucial theoretical and methodological issues it raises. We mention just two of those issues here.

On the theoretical plane, Zhang's meticulous study contributes to our understanding of how 'domestic' and 'systemic' factors are mutually constitutive, and even more so in the global age. 'External' factors can only really become operative through (and in that sense only exist in) the agency of 'domestic' actors, whereas, vice versa, domestic factors (structures, institutions and agents alike) are embedded inextricably within transnational spheres.

Methodologically speaking, particularly in the age of transnationalisation, Zhang's sophisticated combination of comparative and international political economy methods provides a stimulating example of the much-needed cross-fertilisation of distinct methodological traditions.

The RIPE Series in Global Political Economy is very pleased to add this lucidly written book to its list. It is highly recommended to all students of political and economic development, of global finance, of East and Southeast Asia, and of comparative and international political economy.

Otto Holman, Marianne Marchand, Henk Overbeek, Marianne Franklin

# Acknowledgements

I wish first to thank Jeffrey Harrod and Sandro Sideri, my advisers at the Institute of Social Studies in the Hague, who supported my doctoral research, out of which this book grew. While refining and revising the manuscript, I received valuable guidance from Geoffrey Underhill. His comments and suggestions, I hope, are adequately reflected in the pages that follow. I acknowledge my great debt to Chung-In Moon, Louis Pauly and Routledge's anonymous reviewers, who offered detailed and trenchant comments on the successive drafts of the manuscript. I am also grateful to Leo Douw, Raymond Feddema, George Irvin, Marianne Marchand, Kurt Radtke and Rob Vos for giving important suggestions at different times in the writing of this book.

While carrying out field research for this book, I received financial assistance from the Institute of Social Studies, the Netherlands Fellowship Programme and the Amsterdam School for Social Science Research. I extend my appreciation to the central bankers, government officials, corporate executives, business leaders, private financiers and academicians in Korea and Thailand who consented to take the time to discuss their views with me and to generously share their knowledge. Interviews with them have rendered more accurate and comprehensive my analysis of financial policy change in the two countries.

In Korea and Thailand, the hospitality of many individuals and institutions was helpful. I benefited from the assistance of the Thailand Information Centre of Chulalongkorn University, the Research Division of the Bangkok Bank, the Central Library of Yonsei University, the Research Department of *The Korea Herald* and the School of Economics of Seoul National University. I owe a large debt to Suthiphand Chirathivat, Director of the European Studies Programme of Chulalongkorn University, and his assistants, who helped me in my search for data on Thailand and provided a variety of logistical support. Equally, I want to extend special thanks to Yung-Hwan Jo, Soo-Haeng Kim, Moo-Soo Kwon, Seong-Hwan Oh and Jae-Bok Woo, who not only assisted with arrangements for the field work but also helped me to understand the political process of financial policy-making in Korea.

In the process of researching this book, I have drawn upon the works of country specialists in Korea and Thailand. I wish to single out those academicians whose research and scholarship have exerted shaping influence on my analysis of the institutional underpinnings of financial policy. Scott Christensen, Anek Laothamatas, Pasuk Phongpaichit and Ammar Siamwalla, with whom I had interesting talks about political and economic developments in Thailand, deserve special mention. In Korea, I benefited from discussions with Sung Hee Jwa, Tae-Soo Kang, Pyung-Joo Kim, Sang-Kee Min and Suk Heun Yoon. This would have been a lesser book had it not been for the insights that all of them generously imparted to me.

I am thankful to the following people at the Institute of Social Studies and the University of Amsterdam, who have assisted me in my research in many ways: Ank van den Berg, Melanie Comman, Jose Koman, Maureen Koster, Hans Sonneveld, John Steenwinkel, Helen Kooijman-Tibbles, Dita Walenkamp and Els van der Weele. The editors of *RIPE Series in Global Political Economy* of Routledge, particularly Marianne Franklin and Otto Holman, provided critical remarks, valuable editorial support and essential encouragement in my efforts to revise and finalise the manuscript. Their advice helped to enhance the overall quality of the book and to bring the manuscript to final completion.

Finally, I wish to express my deep gratitude to Meng Hong, my wife, for her love and support. The birth of our son, Meng-Jie, while preventing the earlier completion of the book, has brought enormous delight to my academic research. My biggest debt of all is owed to my parents, who not only gave me life but also taught me the meaning of it. It is to them that I dedicate this book.

Xiaoke Zhang
Amsterdam

# Acronyms and abbreviations

| | |
|---|---|
| ADBI | Asian Development Bank Institute |
| *AF* | *Asian Finance* |
| AFC | Association of Finance Companies (Thailand) |
| AFSC | Act on the Undertaking of Finance Business, Securities Business and Credit Foncier Business (Thailand) |
| *AREAER* | *Annual Report on Exchange Arrangements and Exchange Restrictions* |
| ASC | Association of Securities Companies (Thailand) |
| ATM | automated teller machine |
| *AWSJ* | *Asian Wall Street Journal* |
| BAAC | Bank for Agriculture and Agricultural Corporation (Thailand) |
| BBC | Bangkok Bank of Commerce |
| *BBMR* | *Bangkok Bank Monthly Review* |
| BIBF | Bangkok International Banking Facilities |
| *BK* | *Business Korea* |
| *BP* | *Bangkok Post* |
| *BPER* | *Bangkok Post Economic Review* |
| BOI | Board of Investment (Thailand) |
| BOK | Bank of Korea |
| BOT | Bank of Thailand |
| CBA | Commercial Banking Act (Thailand) |
| DJP | Democratic Justice Party (Korea) |
| DLP | Democratic Liberal Party (Korea) |
| *EIUCR* | *Economist Intelligence Unit Country Report* |
| EPB | Economic Planning Board (Korea) |
| FCDC | Foreign Capital Deliberation Committee (Korea) |
| FCIA | Foreign Capital Inducement Act (Korea) |
| FECA | Foreign Exchange Control Act (Korea) |
| *FEER* | *Far Eastern Economic Review* |
| FEMA | Foreign Exchange Management Act (Korea) |
| FDI | foreign direct investment |
| FKI | Federation of Korean Industries |
| FTI | Federation of Thai Industries |

| | |
|---|---|
| GATT | General Agreement on Tariffs and Trade |
| GDP | gross domestic product |
| GNP | gross national product |
| HCI | Heavy and Chemical Industrialisation (Korea) |
| IFCT | Industrial Finance Corporation of Thailand |
| IMF | International Monetary Fund |
| KDB | Korea Development Bank |
| KDI | Korea Development Institute |
| KFB | Korea Federation of Banks |
| *KH* | *The Korea Herald* |
| *KT* | *The Korea Times* |
| MERI | Management Efficiency Research Institute (Korea) |
| MOFE | Ministry of Finance and Economy (Korea) |
| MRR | minimum retail rate |
| NBFI | non-bank financial institution |
| NESDB | National Economic and Social Development Board (Thailand) |
| NIE | newly industrialised economy |
| NIF | National Investment Fund (Korea) |
| OECD | Organization for Economic Co-operation and Development |
| PIBF | Provincial International Banking Facilities (Thailand) |
| *SEAB* | *Southeast Asia Business* |
| TBA | Thai Bankers' Association |

# 1    Introduction

During the 1980s, many developing countries entered upon a process of financial liberalisation in which government controls over market operations, resource allocation and capital flows were removed or loosened. The driving force behind this wave of neo-liberal orthodoxies stemmed mainly from the traumas of the oil price shock and the ensuing economic crisis, which forced fundamental reorientation of development strategies across developing countries and thrust the issue of financial reform onto their policy agenda. Coupled with the economic crisis was a cross-national ideological crusade against state interventionism that found its most explicit and forceful expression in the Washington consensus. International financial agencies, such as the World Bank and the International Monetary Fund, and major industrial powers exerted strong political pressures upon the governments of developing countries to expand the role of market forces.

Intensive external economic and political pressures, however, did not generate uniform national reactions to financial policy reform in developing countries. In some cases, such as the Southern Cone countries of Argentina, Chile and Uruguay, financial liberalisation was carried out in an extensive and radical manner. Reformist political leaderships took sweeping steps to privatise state-owned banks, free interest rates and eliminate restrictions on capital flows. Contrary to what had been expected by proponents of financial liberalisation, reform efforts in the Southern Cone ended in chaotic financial markets, massive inflation and worsening external imbalances, leading to the reversal of the liberalisation process. The disastrous outcomes raised the question about the appropriate economic and institutional conditions under which financial reform strategies should be designed and implemented.[1]

In the retreating shadow of the extensive failure of the Southern Cone experiments with financial market reform, many East Asian newly industrialising economies (NIEs) embarked on the liberalisation of their financial markets in the early 1980s. Unlike their Latin American counterparts, however, the East Asian NIEs did not opt for an expeditious and across-the-board approach to financial reform. For different but interrelated economic and political reasons, the cautious and gradual line of action typified the experience of many governments with financial liberalisation. Reform implementation did not take a linear direction, but constituted a circuitous, complex and protracted process. Much to the surprise of regional and international policy analysts, however, this process took a dramatic twist during the second half of 1997, when many of the East Asian NIEs were stricken by the worst-ever financial crisis in the post-war economic history of the region.

## Objectives of the study

Like many of their neighbouring economies, Korea and Thailand opted for a gradual pattern of policy responses, particularly in the initial stages of financial reform. Despite this qualified similarity, however, the two countries differed sharply in both reform approaches and outcomes. Korea adopted a gradual and piecemeal approach to the liberalisation of interest rates and credit controls, but took a more liberal position on the deregulation of entry barriers. Thailand was more inclined towards the removal of direct financial controls, but consistently refused to open the way for new entry into the banking sector. In Korea, the government limited the role of commercial banks to implementing industrial policies, but gave greater freedom to non-bank financial institutions (NBFIs), such as finance companies, merchant banking corporations and securities firms, to mobilise savings and develop the financial system. In Thailand, by contrast, the authorities placed more emphasis on expanding the role of the banking system in service diversification and financial development. Whereas Korea did not move to lift foreign exchange and capital restrictions until long after it had undertaken important reform measures on the domestic side, Thailand, which had maintained relatively relaxed controls over its external financial transactions, further deregulated the remaining controls while liberalising the domestic financial market.

Not surprisingly, reform outcomes in the major areas of financial liberalisation varied considerably between the two countries. While Thailand succeeded in deregulating almost all types of interest rates within a relatively short period, Korea followed a lengthy and erratic course in the freeing of interest rates. In Korea, preferential bank loans still accounted for almost half of domestic credit in the early 1990s, despite insistent attempts by the government to reduce them. The reduction of preferential credit involved only minimal effort on the part of the Thai government because such credit had never amounted to any significant share of total bank lending. Furthermore, one important area in which Korea liberalised more rapidly was the lowering of entry barriers into financial markets and the tremendous growth of NBFIs. In Thailand, by contrast, the oligopolistic structure of the banking industry prevailed, and the role of the NBFI sector as a whole remained relatively insignificant. Finally, Korea's belated and selective move towards capital decontrol resulted in many rules on external financial transactions remaining strict; Thailand, on the other hand, because of its more liberal stance on capital liberalisation, achieved greater financial openness.

Different as they were in terms of approaches and outcomes, financial market reforms in Korea and Thailand did not bring about the promised benefits to the national economies. The decade-long reform efforts not only failed to improve the efficiency and soundness of the financial systems but also produced serious problems of financial policy management. During the mid-1990s, a number of critical micro-economic difficulties came together to generate growing structural weaknesses in financial and corporate sectors in the two countries. The accumulation of these structural weaknesses accompanied, and was compounded by, the emerging macro-economic difficulties during the same period. The combined effects of structural and macro-economic problems contributed to the collapse of investor confidence, triggered capital flight and massive currency depreciation and generated the financial and economic crisis.

The major analytical objectives of this study are twofold. First, it seeks to explain the differences in financial reforms pursued by Korea and Thailand since the early 1980s. Why did the two countries, operating under similar international economic and political constraints, diverge so markedly in their approaches? In what ways did they differ so as to generate contrasting reform patterns? Second, the study explores the causal relationship between financial liberalisation and crisis. Why did market reform efforts in the two countries fail to achieve their stated objectives? And how did the failed course of financial liberalisation create structural problems and macro-problems that eventually led to the crisis? Addressing these questions raises a critical case for political economy analysis. This study intends to provide a comparative examination of the political incentives and constraints that set limits on financial policy-making and to identify the causes of different liberalisation patterns and the crisis in Korea and Thailand.

A comparative research on the financial reform and crisis experiences of Korea and Thailand is important for a number of reasons. The economic achievements and development patterns of the Northeast Asian NIEs, such as Korea and Taiwan, and their Southeast Asian counterparts, such as Malaysia and Thailand, have been subject to intensive analysis for nearly two decades. There have been many comparative political economy studies of the Northeast Asian NIEs (Castells 1992; Chu 1989; Deyo 1987; Haggard 1990; Vogel 1991) and of the Southeast Asian economies (Doner 1991; Hawes and Liu 1993; MacIntyre and Jayasuriya 1992; Robison 1989). The number of cross-regional works on these two cohorts is also growing (Booth 1999; Doner and Hawes 1995; Leipziger and Thomas 1993; MacIntyre 1994). Comparative efforts, however, have largely focused on trade and industrial policy reforms and on the causal effects of these reforms on economic growth. Despite the important relationship between development and finance, relatively few systematic comparisons within or between these two groups of industrialising economies have been made in the political economy of financial policy-making in general and financial liberalisation in particular.[2]

Furthermore, in existing comparative studies on financial development in Northeast and Southeast Asia, Korea and Thailand have figured prominently, mainly because they differed in the extent to which governments intervened in financial markets, particularly in the 1960s and 1970s. While the Korean government exercised extensive controls over credit allocation and capital flows, its Thai counterpart mandated few preferential credit requirements and maintained relatively relaxed controls on capital movements. These differences have been generally attributed to cross-country variations in state structures (Choi 1993; Doner and Unger 1993; Haggard and Maxfield 1993a). Did differences in the previous patterns of financial development in Korea and Thailand affect their subsequent financial reform trajectories? Is the existing approach to accounting for variations in financial policy in the two countries applicable to the explanation of disparities in their reform strategies and outcomes? If not, what would be the alternative explanatory framework? The relative paucity of comparative studies on financial liberalisation between Korea and Thailand, and indeed between Northeast and Southeast Asia, has left these questions largely unanswered.

A final reason for interest in this comparative research, which has become increasingly relevant to theoretical thinking and financial policy-making with the outbreak of the Asian financial crisis, concerns the possible causes of the crisis and its linkage to financial liberalisation. It has been widely recognised in the extensive literature on the Asian crisis that poorly regulated financial liberalisation was the primary cause. The structural weaknesses and macro-economic difficulties created by the ineffectively executed financial liberalisation have been a dominant theme of virtually all the analyses of the financial turmoil in Korea and Thailand (Alba *et al.* 1999; Cho 2001; Hahm and Mishkin 2000; Vajragupta and Vichyanond 1999). What initially hampered financial liberalisation processes has not been systematically examined in these analyses however; nor have the policy channels through which financial liberalisation contributed to the various micro- and macro-problems been convincingly explored. More important, little attention has been given to the extent to which political and institutional factors affected the design and implementation of liberalisation strategies and constrained the ability of governments to rectify the flawed line of financial policy management in the period prior to the crisis.[3]

This study seeks to fill these conceptual and empirical gaps and also to produce theoretically informed accounts of the political dynamics of financial policy change and of the causal linkage between financial liberalisation and crisis in the Northeast and Southeast Asian economies. While those two issues are examined in this study, the analytical focus, for the most part, is on the process of financial policy-making and liberalisation in Korea and Thailand between the early 1980s and the mid-1990s. The theoretical framework to be developed is designed primarily to explain the political sources of different liberalisation patterns. The analysis of financial liberalisation is privileged not only because it is important in its own right but also because it can help to illustrate the alternative causes of the financial crisis. To explore the linkage between liberalisation and crisis, the divergent patterns of financial market reform and their institutional underpinnings should be granted analytical primacy.

## Theoretical considerations

An appropriate point of departure for examining the principal research questions of this study is with the consideration of extant theoretical perspectives on the changing nature of national economic policies. Several important lines of analysis have been developed to account for policy change in developing countries in general and in the Northeast and Southeast Asian NIEs in particular. Prominent among these lines of analysis are the neo-classical, the international system, the developmental state and the political structure approaches. Although these approaches offer some important insights into the dynamics of economic policy-making, they, each for different reasons, are insufficient to account for cross-national variations in policy choices revealed in the financial liberalisation processes of Korea and Thailand.

The neo-classical perspective tends to view economic policy-making as the resolution of technical issues and the rational choice of policy-makers, and explains policy change as a function of market conditions.[4] Neo-classical assumptions have been of particular importance in the design and analysis of financial policies in the developing world. What typically characterises a developing economy, neo-classical theorists claim, is financial repression in which the government exercises pervasive controls over financial prices, credit allocation and the operations of financial institutions; government intervention distorts financial markets and adversely affects saving and investment decisions. Moreover, in a financially repressed economy, political factors are likely to influence the allocation of financial resources, leading to unproductive, rent-seeking activities. For these problems, neo-classical policy prescriptions are to reduce government controls and to allow market forces to resume their reign.[5]

From the early 1970s, the neo-classical paradigm appeared to have dominated theoretical thinking on financial policy and reform in developing countries. The paradigm was not seriously challenged until the rise of the Northeast Asian NIEs, which undeniably achieved rapid economic development in repressed financial systems. The fall-back argument made by neo-classical analysts (Balassa 1990–91; Fry 1995) that economic growth would have been even greater had those NIEs not intervened in their financial markets cannot easily dismiss the empirical observation and theoretical implications embodied in it. The paradox posed by the Northeast Asian experience has prompted both economists and political scientists to explore alternative explanations of the relationship between finance and development. Attention has been focused on whether the state should intervene and, more importantly, on the conditions under which state intervention can contribute to optimal outcomes (Haggard and Maxfield 1993a; Lee and Haggard 1995).

Several important studies on financial development in Korea and Taiwan show that state intervention contributed to economic development in those two economies (Amsden 1989; Park 1993; Wade 1985). This was achieved because financial controls provided the governments with an efficient tool for proscribing undue competition among financial intermediaries and reducing market instability, guiding the allocation of investment resources among industrial sectors and orienting private firms towards long-term economic activity. The neo-classical position also seems to be at odds with the successful case of economic development in Southeast Asia. The Thai financial system, which is often depicted as less repressed than those in Northeast Asia but which is far from liberal and market-oriented by conventional standards, accompanied sustained economic growth in Thailand during much of the post-war period (Corsepius and Fischer 1988; Easterly and Honohan 1990). In their efforts to advance reasons why state intervention led to relatively efficient outcomes, some scholars emphasise the institutional factors that insulated economic officials from distributive pressures and committed the governments to development goals (Lee 1992, 1995: ch. 5; Lee and Haggard 1995; Wade 1990: ch. 7 and 8).

What these studies highlight is that market imperfections inherent in developing countries' financial systems may leave ample room for government intervention, and that the success of such intervention is likely to depend on elaborate institutional structures. One important fact that neo-classical scholars tend to neglect is that financial markets are complicated socio-economic institutions rather than neutral resource-allocating mechanisms. This complexity generates a corresponding state action not only in allocating resources but, more importantly, in improving the workings of markets (Moran 1990). This point is well illustrated in the recent Asian financial crisis, for which hasty financial liberalisation without adequate banking regulation has partly been blamed. Financial repression may not impede economic development if the proper institutional structures in which state intervention is organised are established. Similarly, financial liberalisation does not necessarily lead to the improved efficiency of financial systems if the necessary state action is not taken and supervisory institutions are weak (Lee and Haggard 1995; Wade 1998; Weiss 2000).

Neo-classical theorists often fail to appreciate the important role that states play in financial markets in providing institutions that facilitate and stabilise transactions but that are not created automatically by the markets themselves. Equally significant, they tend to overlook the essential role that states play in the financial reform process that requires the creation of institutional conditions for the emergence and operation of free-market financial systems. Pre-existing, non-market arrangements that impeded free-market competition are unlikely to disappear once financial markets are deregulated. These arrangements will continue to distort financial prices and thwart the development of more efficient financial systems until they are deliberately dismantled by states. 'There was nothing natural about *laissez-faire*', Karl Polanyi (1957: 139) argued, 'free markets could never have come into being merely by allowing things to take their course … *laissez-faire* itself was enforced by the state.'

The recent liberalisation experiences of developing countries have also raised the question about the sequence in which financial reforms should be implemented. The neo-classical formula for that sequence requires that domestic financial reform be attempted only after trade liberalisation has aligned domestic prices with international prices, and that domestic financial reform precede foreign exchange and capital decontrol (Edwards 1984; Johnston 1991; McKinnon 1982, 1991: ch. 1). However, the actual sequencing of reform measures pursued in developing countries has not followed neo-classical descriptions and prescriptions – their timeframe for various aspects of financial liberalisation has varied substantially. In Korea, financial deregulation was almost synchronous with, but largely unrelated to, import liberalisation (You 1992). Thailand maintained a relatively liberal foreign exchange regime and moved to lift the remaining capital controls while liberalising domestic financial markets. The issue of reform sequencing is political as much as economic in nature. The order in which trade barriers and financial market restrictions are removed, for instance, is contingent on which reform measures are likely to generate greater political opposition (Cole and Slade 1991).

It is argued here that the determinants of financial reform timing and direction are not merely technical issues – they reflect, in the final analysis, political processes involving bargaining, compromise and even fierce struggle among a wide range of actors and groups. Financial policy is not formulated in a political vacuum, and policy-makers do not conduct rational calculations of costs and benefits involved but respond to political pressures coming from winners and losers created by the reform process. State action or inaction, circumscribed by those pressures mediated through specific institutional settings, shapes the pattern of financial liberalisation. In accounting for the reasons why states pursue certain reform policies and why reform measures are sequenced differently across different countries, the political and institutional dimensions of liberalisation should be taken into account. Neo-classical scholars who attempt to deal with the sequencing order, and indeed the whole issue of financial reform without understanding these dimensions, are unlikely to explain satisfactorily the dynamics of policy change and different reform trajectories.

This brief critique of the neo-classical model suggests the importance of integrating economics with politics to understand the essence of financial policy and reform. The alternative perspectives that emphasise the interactions between economic and political forces and policy change can thus offer a better approach to examining the central research questions of this study. One such perspective focuses on the external environment as the primary explanatory factor. This system-centred perspective views policy choices as the product of interrelations among nation-states in the international system (Cardoso and Faletto 1979; Wallerstein 1976, 1979), as the product of economic shocks and market pressures (Andrews 1994; Stallings 1992) or as the product of external political demands and ideological influences (Helleiner 1994; Kahler 1990, 1992; Remmer 1986). Essentially, these theories explain the changes in the preferences and behaviour of domestic actors and the shifting pattern of national policies as responses to the constraints and opportunities that international economic and political forces create.

The systemic explanations would suggest that financial policy change and reform differences in Korea and Thailand stem necessarily from the effects of external environments. To some extent, this systemic reasoning is quite valid. As will be illustrated in the following chapters, international economic constraints and political pressures were important in generating the strong impetus for continuous financial liberalisation in the two countries. During the early 1980s in particular, external economic shocks and associated financial difficulties precipitated initial reform efforts in the two countries. Pressures leading to policy change also emanated from international institutions, foreign governments and transnational firms that pushed for liberal reforms either as improving the prospects for development or as ensuring market access. While these forces might not operate equally across all the stages of financial reform, a secular trend towards financial globalisation provided a constant stimulus to the liberalising process.

The explanatory power of systemic variables is undeniable, but it falls short of completely accounting for differences in financial reform in Korea and Thailand. There are several significant limits to the nature and direction of financial policy change that can be explained without reference to the second-image or domestic factors. As will be discussed in the following chapters, the economic crises that generated the initial move towards financial reform in Korea and Thailand had their origins in the flawed lines of industrialisation strategies and macro-economic management that had prevailed in the 1970s. External economic shocks served to bring these policy errors to the fore and heightened the need for policy reform. Similarly, divergent reform approaches and outcomes observed in the two countries reflected differences in their pre-existing patterns of financial policy and regulatory intervention that set the parameters within which the governments formulated and implemented reform measures.

Furthermore, policy differences cannot be effectively explained without an explicit analysis of domestic institutions. Scholars working within the system-centred framework emphasise the effects of integration into the international economy on the policy preferences and behaviour of domestic actors. In Korea and Thailand, expanded international economic ties and business opportunities made many corporate and financial firms identify their interests with economic openness. Often, they allied themselves with transnational actors in forming an important source of support for liberalising reforms. Internationally driven changes in preferences and political coalitions, however, cannot be equated with policy outcomes without intervening variables or the role of domestic institutions. As will be elaborated in the next chapter, the key to understanding why reform strategies and outcomes varied between Korea and Thailand lies with an examination of how institutions mediate in the linkage between the interests of state and societal actors and financial policy choice. The impact of external forces must be examined in interaction with different domestic structures in order to explain divergent responses to similar international forces.

Finally, systemic influences rarely affect national policy in such identical ways that they do not allow for alternative responses. It is generally clear that countries do have different policy options over how to deal with their interactions with the external environment. This suggests that systemic factors cannot, by themselves, account for policy differences between countries similarly situated in the international system. Being both small and open economies, Korea and Thailand were equally exposed to external economic constraints and political pressures. Following the logic of systemic reasoning, we would not expect Korea and Thailand to adopt different reform approaches and to achieve divergent policy outcomes. As noted earlier, however, the two countries differed dramatically on both counts. To explain why they responded differently to the basically similar external influences requires that more attention be focused on explanatory factors at the domestic level of analysis. Systemic variables affect national policies only through their impact on various actors and groups operating within specific domestic political and institutional settings.

The developmental state model – which has been advanced largely in response to the limitations of the neo-classical perspective and system-oriented approaches, particularly the dependency paradigm – focuses explicitly and positively on the role of state institutions in the policy process.[6] The model views economic policy and reform as highly constrained by domestic political structures and emphasises the institutional position of the state, specifically its independence from social actors in pursuit of policy objectives. In the developmental state portrait, political autonomy is also accompanied by Weberian bureaucracy: policy-making is centralised in super-ministerial agencies staffed by highly educated and competent technocrats who are firmly committed to corporate goals and are well equipped with policy instruments. The institutional capacity enables technocrats to control the behaviour of private business and to ensure private compliance with the requirements of economic development.

While the developmental state model has provided a powerful tool for explaining the political dynamics of industrial transformation, it has several empirical and analytical limitations. In assessing the viability of the model, we focus on three observations that are relevant to the subsequent analysis of financial reform experiences in Korea and Thailand.[7] The first observation relates to the strength of the state and its autonomy from societal forces. While highlighting the significance of the state as an autonomous actor, developmental state theorists tend to ignore the fact that the state and society evolve together and that the autonomy of the state is defined with reference to the social milieu in which it is embedded. In overstressing state autonomy, they focus narrowly on the one-way causal connection between state power and social capacities. This study argues that societal forces bear directly on the exercise of state power just as much as states intimately affect the behaviour of social actors. Economic policy-making processes cannot be meaningfully interpreted without encapsulating the role of the state in the process of social and economic transformations; policy change is the result not merely of state action but of state–society interactions. The fundamental issues to be addressed here, i.e. why states pursue different policies and why they differ in their roles and effectiveness, cannot be discussed adequately without looking at the social determinants of policy.

Furthermore, not only is state autonomy relational but it is also variable over time. The model is correct in arguing that the ability of the developmental states to assert their ordering over society stems from distinctive institutional attributes. However, it tends to take these institutional attributes largely as given without systematic effort to explore the underlying socio-economic forces that mould or change them. It is important to emphasise that the institutional structures of states are the products of a confluence of historical forces. To appreciate the changing nature of state strength, it is necessary to understand the historical dynamics that shape and reshape these institutional structures. In much of Northeast and Southeast Asia, the transition to democracy and economic liberalisation throughout the 1980s and 1990s witnessed an increase in the capacity of popular forces to organise for political purposes. This eroded the institutional bases that had shored up state autonomy and reduced state power. The implication is that institutional structures of the state are time-bound and state autonomy must be placed within a larger historical framework.

Developmental state theorists also seem to suggest that the ability of states to intervene in the economy can be sustained over time. The important point is that both state autonomy and capacity are not only determined by institutional settings but are also directly linked to prior state action and policy decisions. Although effective state intervention in economic processes may initially grow from autonomous state bureaucracies, that same intervention is likely to lead to diminished state strength because it provides access for social groups to penetrate the state apparatus (Rueschemeyer and Evans 1985). Prior commitments to direct intervention may also undermine state autonomy because affected societal interests will mobilise to press state authorities to maintain such commitments; strong states may turn out to be weak if they cannot extricate themselves from previous interventions (Ikenberry 1986: 133–6). As will be shown below, although direct intervention in the allocation of credit generated engagements that the Korean state found difficult to break (Haggard and Moon 1990), the lesser degree of state intervention in Thailand enhanced the flexibility of state action and facilitated withdrawal from regulatory involvement in financial markets.

The second observation concerns the purported institutional features of Northeast Asian states. The developmental state model tends to view the NIE states as monolithic and unitarian. Not only were Korean and Taiwanese bureaucracies insulated and cohesive, being immune to all sorts of bureaucratic malpractices, they were also uniformly effective in policy formulation and implementation across issue areas. There are at least two problems with this supposition. First, it is empirically inaccurate. Detailed case studies have demonstrated that corruption and clientelism are far from absent in many aspects of the developmental states (Bello and Rosenfeld 1990; Kang 2002; Kim 1986). Although the Northeast Asian bureaucracies exhibit considerable corporate cohesion, they are not so homogeneous as statist scholars depict. Bureaucratic conflicts over economic policy were not uncommon, coalition calculations operated in seemingly insulated bureaucracies and policy preferences differed within the NIE states (Cheng 1990; Kim 1993; Noble 1987).

The second problem with the developmental state argument about the institutional features of states is conceptual. As noted earlier, the financial reform process in Korea and Thailand has revealed marked dissimilarities in the approaches and outcomes. The unitary assumption of state strength is of little utility here and proves problematic in both within- and cross-national analyses of policy change and differences. If the Korean state, for example, is uniformly effective in policy implementation, why was progress in major areas of financial liberalisation so varied? If the Thai state is as weak and ineffective as it is generally described in the comparative literature (MacIntyre 1993: 257–60; Unger 1998: 76–80), how was it able to initiate important reform measures and achieve rapid progress in some areas of liberalisation? To understand the observed reform divergence within and between Korea and Thailand, one needs to differentiate the institutional structures of states and allow for variations in the role and efficacy of states over time and across issue areas.

The third and final observation relates to the role of the private sector. Almost all statist accounts of Northeast Asian NIEs paint a passive picture of the private sector in both economic and political arenas. It has long been established in the structuralist and neo-classical political literature that state autonomy cannot be derived solely from institutional structures without considering the independent economic resources of societal groups (Lindblom 1977; Przeworski and Wallerstein 1988). In both Northeast and Southeast Asian NIEs, governments have not only relied upon private businesses for adequate flows of information but have harnessed their entrepreneurship and managerial expertise to achieve economic goals. More importantly, private entrepreneurs have had independent policy preferences and the capacity to resist bureaucratic intervention. Empirical studies have suggested that domestic capital took independent policy initiatives in industrial restructuring and played an important role in resolving collective action problems that plagued economic development (Doner 1988, 1992; Doner and Hawes 1995; Kuo 1995; Lew 1992; Shin 1991).

The corollary of negating the important role of the private sector is that business associations have been either misinterpreted or underplayed in the statist literature. As elaborated in several important studies on corporatism, business associations that are organisationally co-ordinated and possess informational and productive resources are regarded as critical partners by states in achieving their policy goals. This, in turn, increases the influence of business associations on the process of policy formulation and their autonomy in policy implementation (Atkinson and Coleman 1985; Coleman and Grant 1984). It is true that, in Northeast as in Southeast Asia, states have played an active role in nurturing and promoting the development of business associations. But interactions between the public and private sectors and the increasing delegation of authority from the former to the latter have increased the influence and organisational capabilities of business associations. Eventually, they have been able to press states for greater policy participation and contend for a more independent role, for better or worse, in the policy-making process.

The final theoretical perspective on the changing nature of economic policy views structural features of the political system as crucial determinants of policy choices and differences. Within the diverse literature on the causal role of political structures, two separate but strong conceptual approaches stand out. The first approach emphasises the differential effects of the two broadly defined political regimes – authoritarian polities versus liberal democracies – on the ability of government decision-makers to manage distributive pressures, establish social bases of support and reorient economic policy (Kaufman 1985; Kaufman and Stallings 1989; Skidmore 1977). The second approach, which focuses on more sharply specified structural variables, is concerned with the impact that party systems have on efficiency in policy formulation and implementation (Alesina 1994; Ames 1987; Haggard and Kaufman 1992, 1995: ch. 5). Reduced to their essences, these two approaches explain policy differences among countries as a function of variations in their political structures.[8]

According to the logic of the political regime approach, one would expect authoritarian structures to impose statist policies on society and more democratic regimes to increase the dominance of societal interests. The corollary of this reasoning is that countries with similar political regimes are unlikely to follow divergent policy patterns. However, empirical studies on the politics of economic adjustment in developing countries reveal no systematic association between regime types and policy reform paths (Nelson 1990; Remmer 1986). Of more relevance to the central concern of this study, the effects of the structural variables identified in the political regime approach are indeterminate. This indeterminacy is borne out by the fact that, although Korea and Thailand had both been largely authoritarian until the late 1980s, they followed divergent reform strategies and achieved different policy outcomes. The two countries have since moved towards greater democratisation, yet their reform approaches and outcomes were far from convergent.

The party system approach modifies the crude regime-type argument and focuses on the institutional and procedural factors that tend to cut across different political regimes. While numerous features of the party and party systems may be important for understanding policy differences, the distinction between cohesive and fragmented party systems and between mass and traditional parties appears to have received more attention (Blondel 1999; Haggard 1997). As argued in the approach, fragmented party systems heighten partisan rivalries, facilitate private access to public policy arenas and weaken the ability of central authorities to initiate policy change. The argument is clearly at odds with the fact that, although the party system in Thailand is more fragmented than that in Korea, the Thai government made more progress than its Korean counterpart in the many areas of financial liberalisation. Equally, political parties in both Korea and Thailand tend to be traditional in that they are not based on a national social cleavage and the bond between parties and their electors is typically clientelistic and localised (Ahn and Junj 1999; King 1999). This broadly similar feature of political parties, however, did not lead to similar reform strategies and outcomes in the two countries.

The existing theoretical approaches, drawn mainly from cross-national studies on the political economy of policy reform in developing countries, appear to have limited application to the comparative analysis of financial liberalisation and crisis in Korea and Thailand. The neo-classical perspective, which reduces policy choices to rational considerations and treats the policy-making process largely as a black box, obscures the political and institutional dynamics of economic policy change. The system-centred approach is limited for the obvious reason that it downplays the importance of domestic factors that can potentially explain why similarly situated countries respond differently to external pressures and constraints. While the developmental state model and the political structure perspective correct the fundamental deficiencies of the neo-classical and system-centred approaches, they both suffer from the following two serious limitations. On the one hand, they do scant justice to the role of socio-economic institutions in the policy process. On the other, the structural variables suggested by the two perspectives – state strength, political regimes and party systems – are so broadly defined that they cannot specify policy differences in a fully satisfactory manner.

## Main propositions

The previous section, in pointing out the limitations of the mainstream theoretical approaches, also suggests an alternative analytical framework for an understanding of financial policy change. The major theoretical propositions developed in this study build on a more nuanced and integrated focus on the political and institutional sources of financial policy choices. They are advanced in two broad sets of variables that are drawn from private-sector preferences for, and public-sector interests in, financial policy and reform and from the institutional structures that shape the assertion of these preferences and interests in the reform process. Variations in financial reform strategies and approaches pursued by Korea and Thailand, to which the above-mentioned perspectives fail to provide an adequate answer, will be explained in terms of these two sets of variables.[9]

The first theoretical proposition concerns the structure of private-sector preference formation on financial liberalisation. It argues that private policy preferences should be the focal point of a comparative analysis of financial

reform experiences in Korea and Thailand. Reform policy choices and differences are, in the first instance, a function of pressures applied by financiers and
big industrialists, who tend to be economically and politically the best endowed
societal actors (Haggard and Maxfield 1993a). These pressures increase with the
preference intensity of the two sectors or groups, which arises from, among other
things, their differential positions in the domestic and international economic
systems, sector-specific industrial characteristics, inter-sector relationships and
legacies of government policy. Depending upon specific reform measures, the
preferences of financiers and industrialists are expected to differ and even to
be antithetic to each other.

Industrial and financial sectors, which have different preferences, are likely
to form coalitions around certain reform policies as a result of those preferences
and to attempt to get their demands projected into the financial policy-making
process. However, private-sector preferences and the alliance formation that
goes with them cannot simply be identified as the source of policy change.
Economic interests provide private actors with an incentive to lobby, but they
have to be organised in order to translate their policy preferences into pressure
upon policy-makers (Frieden 1991a: 22–4). How successfully they can organise
and assert themselves in the policy-making process, or turn their economic
interests into political power, hinges upon two organisational and institutional
variables – industrial structure and finance–industry ties.

The second theoretical proposition posits that the political and economic
interests of governments also heavily impinge on the patterns of financial
policy. Governments are not a monolithic entity, however, and should be disaggregated into their constituent ministries and agencies, specifically central
banks and finance ministries, which are the key state economic institutions that
are expected to exert major influence on the direction of financial liberalisation. However, the interests of central banks and economic line ministries in
financial reforms may not coincide, largely because of their different policy
objectives, bureaucratic culture, ideological orientation and relations with the
private sector (Moran 1990). It is thus hypothesised that the degree of central
bank independence or the balance of authority over financial policy between
central banks and governments influences the way in which central banks or
government ministries and politicians assert their interests and set the basic
line of financial liberalisation policy.

Equally important, central bank–government relations also shape the way
in which private-sector preferences are translated into policy. Among state
economic institutions, central banks are more responsive to the preferences
and demands of the financial community not only because central bankers and
private financiers tend to share basic economic interests and objectives, but also
because they have symbiotic relations. In contrast, economic line ministries,
as well as government politicians, have a much broader set of policy objectives
and have to consider a much wider range of interests and wishes of private
constituencies (Henning 1994; Maxfield 1990). Theoretically speaking, if central banks are independent and enjoy a powerful position *vis-à-vis* other state

economic institutions, private financiers may find it easier to make their voices heard in the financial policy-making process. If central banks are subordinate to governments, and if planning and industry ministries have more authority to set financial policy, the course of financial reform is likely to be influenced by the actions of wider constituent interests.

The theoretical framework to be adopted in this study, which focuses on the political and institutional sources of financial policy change and differences, also defines the key explanatory variables in the analysis of the causal relationship between financial liberalisation and crisis. It is assumed for the purposes of argument that domestic institutional structures and associated political constraints have important bearings on how the financial crisis in Korea and Thailand developed and was managed. This assumption has two major elements. The organisational and political structures of financial policy-making, which privilege the aggregation and articulation of certain particularistic interests, are likely to affect the formulation and implementation of liberalisation measures and to produce problems of policy management. The resulting financial reform errors contribute to structural weaknesses in the financial and corporate sectors and set the stage for the crisis. Equally, the same institutional and political constraints that impair financial liberalisation can compromise the ability of governments to manage the contentious politics of financial restructuring and policy adjustment before the outbreak of the financial crisis.

It should be noted that this theoretical framework is designed to examine the impact of financial reform patterns on the development of the financial crisis in Korea and Thailand. It is not intended to facilitate a more synoptic account of what occurred in the two countries during the 1997–98 period, nor is it supposed to provide an analytical tool for exploring the comprehensive causes of the crisis. In Korea and Thailand, as in the other Asian economies, financial crises, which unfolded in a complicated interweaving of national and international economic and political forces, do not lend themselves to single-factor explanations. As will be shown in the following chapters, however, the theoretical framework serves the central purposes of this study well – the explanation of the causal relationship between financial reform and crisis as well as of cross-national differences in reform approaches and outcomes.

## Research strategy and data

To explain divergent financial reform approaches and outcomes and to illustrate how financial liberalisation led to the crisis in Korea and Thailand, this study employs the method of focused, structured comparison.[10] In this research, the comparative analysis is focused, in that the accounts of divergent reform experiences and institutional differences in Korea and Thailand are converted for present analytical purposes. In the theoretical argument chapters, the focal point is provided by the two sets of explanatory variables built on the organisation of private-sector preferences and state institutions that are important from the theoretical perspectives of this study. In the country chapters, the comparative–historical survey of financial reform experiences in the two countries since the early 1980s is conducted around the four major areas of financial liberalisation identified at the beginning of this chapter.

To gain methodological rigour, the comparison is also structured in that the same question is asked of the two different cases of Korean and Thai financial liberalisation, i.e. how the interaction between private-sector preferences and public-sector interests and different domestic institutions shape the policy behaviour of societal and state actors in such a way that the two countries display divergent liberalisation patterns. Each country chapter is configured to facilitate a detailed and systematic analysis of the relationship between the dependent and explanatory variables through a chronological narrative of the financial reform processes. The empirical evidence on reform approaches and outcomes presented in the country chapters is then examined and compared in terms of the two major theoretical propositions in order to highlight the application of the explanatory variables to the two case studies.

The comparable case method is also used to explore the impact of financial market liberalisation on the development of the financial crisis in Korea and Thailand. The aim is not to present a comprehensive account of the crisis in these two countries, but to examine the two interrelated levels of causal linkages between institutional constraints and poorly regulated reform processes and between these processes and the accumulation of structural and macro-economic problems. This method, which forgoes empirical breadth in favour of comparative depth, permits a focused analysis of the changing effects of the ineffectively executed financial liberalisation within each country over time and a structured comparison of how the crisis developed and was managed across the two countries.

The theoretical arguments are developed by drawing mainly on secondary literature – scholarly accounts of the organisation of the private-sector and state institutions in Korea and Thailand that offer comparative perspectives on the two countries. The secondary evidence is supplemented by a variety of government and central bank documents, policy-oriented publications of international institutions and official statistics. The information on which the country case studies are based comes from multiple sources. As the central objective of this study is to examine the actual influence of private-sector preferences and government interests on the financial policy-making process, it is essential to evaluate the perspectives of policy-relevant societal actors and policy-makers. For this reason, the author conducted more than sixty interviews with central bankers, senior finance ministry officials, private financiers, corporate executives, business leaders and academics in the two countries. The country case studies on financial reform and crisis are also informed by newspaper archival research and a detailed review of unpublished reports, newsletters and other grey materials obtainable from local sources.

## Organisation of the book

The first part of this study is theoretical. It develops the analytical framework for the comparative examination of financial policy change and differences in Korea and Thailand. While the framework to be developed in this part is primarily designed to facilitate the cross-national comparison of reform approaches and outcomes, it also defines the basic parameters for the analysis of financial market liberalisation, policy mismanagement and the financial crisis.

Chapter 2 discusses the policy preferences of financial and industrial sectors for liberalisation measures, and specifies the political and economic interests of central banks and government ministries in the process of financial reform. More importantly, it illustrates the reasons why we should expect the organisation of the private sector and the state to exert significant shaping influences on the articulation of private preferences and programmatic government interests. Chapter 3 explores cross-country variations between Korea and Thailand in the organisation of the private sector and the institutional structure of the state. It then advances the reasons why these organisational and institutional variations should be expected to lead to different reform policy choices.

In the second part of this study, the theoretical arguments are supported by the two country case studies on the process of financial liberalisation in Korea and Thailand. Chapter 4 provides a chronological narrative of financial policy reform in Korea between the early 1980s and the mid-1990s. It reviews the unfolding of financial reform plans and shows how domestic political and institutional constraints shaped these plans. Chapter 5 also proceeds chronologically through the case study of Thai financial policy-making and reform during the same period. Like that on Korea, the chapter focuses on changes in the reform process and explores the political forces behind these changes within the institutional setting of financial policy-making in Thailand. Chapter 6 highlights variations in reform approaches and outcomes between the two countries and illustrates how these different patterns of financial reform were caused by the distinctive combination of institutional variables within each country.

The third and final part examines why the financial crisis broke out in Korea and Thailand and how the governments responded to the crisis with reference to the political economic analysis of the two countries' financial policies and reform offered in the previous chapters. The argument to be developed is that the unsuccessful reform process and the political constraints that compromised the ability of the governments to rectify the flawed line of policy management played catalytic roles in the build-up of various micro- and macro-problems and the final outbreak of the crisis. Although the two countries were hit equally hard by the financial turmoil, the largely undifferentiated turmoil had different causes in each country. The seemingly similar financial crises originated in divergent reform approaches and outcomes and stemmed from dissimilar institutional failures.

Chapter 7 explores how the financial crisis unfolded in Korea and Thailand. In each of these two cases, the empirical analysis is approached in two steps. It begins with a sketch of the different symptoms of the crisis and specific financial difficulties in each country and then links these crisis symptoms and financial difficulties to the different financial reform patterns and institutional arrangements in the two countries. The final chapter presents the major findings on the two levels of causal linkages between institutional deficiencies and problems of financial liberalisation and between these problems and the financial crisis. It also reflects on the implications of these findings for financial policy-making and national economic governance in emerging market economies in general, and in Korea and Thailand in particular.

# Part I

# The political logic of comparative financial policy

# 2 Interests, institutions and financial policy

This chapter elaborates on the analytical framework for financial policy choices, which is drawn from two theoretical propositions. The first proposition focuses on the preferences of industrialists and private financiers as an important explanatory variable. It posits that industrial organisation and finance–industry ties structure the ways in which these preferences are aggregated and articulated. The second theoretical proposition argues that central bank–government relations, or the degree of central bank independence, affect not only which state agencies – central banks or line ministries – assert their interests in the reform process, but also how private-sector preferences are projected into the public policy arena.

The first section of this chapter specifies the preferences of industrial and financial sectors for financial liberalisation on the basis of both deductive reasoning and extant empirical research. It then illustrates how the organisational features of the private sector shape the articulation of sectoral preferences. The second section identifies the interests of central banks, government ministries and politicians, which have a theoretical base and are often revealed empirically. This is followed by an examination of the institutional division of governmental powers over financial policy and its effects on the assertion of different public-sector interests and the expression of private preferences in the financial policy-making process.

## Sectors, private preferences and social constraints

This study takes private-sector preferences for financial policy as its analytical entry point. The basic principle underlying the discussion of social influences is that financial liberalisation, like any other economic policy reform, has differential distributive consequences for different societal groups. To improve the allocative efficiency of the financial system through liberalisation may be desirable for economic development, but the associated costs and benefits are not distributed equally within society,[1] which is the reason why financial market reforms are politically controversial and generate strong anti-reform pressures. Liberalisation programmes are unlikely to be effectively implemented unless governments respond to those pressures and develop an adequate base of social support (Haggard and Webb 1994; Nelson 1992). Although governments may choose to ignore distributive demands in formulating reform policy, such behaviour is normally costly to their efforts to create coalitions for their policy choices and to remain in office (Becker 1983; Waterbury 1989). The approach adopted is to treat policy change as a function of the constraints imposed upon policy-makers by the demands of societal actors and to identify the socio-political parameters within which state actors must operate to achieve their policy objectives.

While the policy impact of social constraints is important, not all social groups are expected to exert shaping influences on financial market policy. One of the central analytical objectives of this study is to identify the preferences of policy-relevant sectors and to explain how they are aggregated and expressed.[2] Financial policy choices are affected in the first instance by the weight of sectoral interests of what are termed 'primary constituencies' in the supply-and-demand theory of economic regulation (see Noll 1985). Primary constituencies are economically and politically the best-endowed societal actors upon whom political elites rely for various modes of support. The most powerful of those constituencies in the financial policy-making process tend to be private financiers and big industrialists (Haggard and Maxfield 1993a; Zhang 2002). The policy preferences of these politically weighty actors wield direct influence on policy outcomes and provide one of the focal points of the comparative analysis.[3]

## Private-sector preferences for financial policy and liberalisation

*Ex ante* assessment of private preferences for financial policy is notoriously difficult. Private sectors and their preferences are complex and cross-cutting. Each financial or industrial sector can be divided into subsectors; each sector or subsector may have its own interests, in particular liberalisation measures. Policy preferences differ across sectors and subsectors, depending upon their positions in the domestic and international economic systems, sector-specific industrial characteristics and inter- or intra-sector relationships. The difficulty of tracing and understanding the relevant divisions and preferences necessitates a disaggregated approach that examines circumstances specific to industrial and banking sectors and their expected responses to financial market reform.[4]

The preferences of industrialists are a function of the susceptibility of their vested or perceived interests to financial policy change. The more likely policy change is to harm or advance their interests, the more incentives they will have to organise political action. In many developing countries, industrial manufacturers benefit from interest rate ceilings and preferential credit schemes. Financial subsidies, at their inception, may represent government attempts to correct inefficient market practices, as assumed by public interest theorists of regulation (Bonbright 1961; Stone 1977), or may reflect rent-seeking by interest groups, as illustrated in the capture model (Peltzman 1976; Posner 1974). Once in place, however, subsidies tend to create vested interests. Privileged borrowers have a strong incentive to guarantee the continuation of financial subsidies and to oppose liberalisation that may lead to increases in interest rates.

Industrial firms' preferences towards the deregulation of financial controls are also a function of the degree to which they depend upon indirect financing (bank credit) as opposed to direct financing (equity issues), or to which their capital structures are leveraged. Generally speaking, industrial firms rely upon two main sources of external finance: bank loans and equities. In most developing countries, however, direct financing plays an insignificant role in corporate development (Singh and Hamid 1992). This is partly because firms are reluctant to go public for political and taxation reasons and partly because equity markets are poorly developed and the problems of adverse selection and moral hazard which impede their operations tend to be prevalent in developing countries (Stiglitz 1989; Stiglitz and Weiss 1981).

Industrial borrowers may have recourse to informal credit markets or curb markets. Despite the neo-structuralist argument that curb markets function more efficiently than formal credit markets in developing countries (Taylor 1983; van Wijnbergen 1983), curb interest rates are much higher than those of subsidised bank credits, and the informal nature tends to be associated with corresponding uncertainties and risks. As the costs of alternative sources of external finance are exorbitant, industrial manufacturers prefer bank loans to equities and have every incentive to seek financial subsidies. In other words, the higher the opportunity cost to industrial borrowers of *not* obtaining preferential credit policies, the more likely they will be to attempt to maintain these policies and the more intense their opposition to financial liberalisation.

As bank loans are the major source of investment finance in most developing countries, those industrial manufacturers whose corporate capital structures are highly leveraged rely heavily upon external credit for corporate development. The more heavily they rely upon external financing, the greater the incentive they will have to lobby and keep preferential policies in place. Their dependence upon external finance *vis-à-vis* internal capital may be determined by such variables as product characteristics, capital intensity of investment projects, the mode of initial capital accumulation and the extent to which manufacturing and financial activities are integrated (Leff 1978, 1979a; Titman and Wessels 1988). For instance, industrial manufacturers who engage in labour-intensive production or who possess their own financial institutions are expected to depend more on their own capital and less on external financing. In this case, their demand for preferential credit and their opposition to interest rate deregulation is thus likely to be weak.

On the positive side, industrial manufacturers, especially those who are highly leveraged, tend to support government efforts to remove impediments to the entry of new institutions into the financial sector and to privatise state-owned banks. In most developing countries, long-term investment resources are typically thin. In such financial systems where bank loans are rationed, industrialists appear to have an insatiable hunger for credit and are constantly hunting for alternative sources. Selective credit policies, although of benefit to large manufacturing firms, also imply the possibility of their being subjected to bureaucratic whims and fickle political judgements. Large manufacturers consequently see the deregulation of entry barriers and bank privatisation as good opportunities to own and control financial institutions. This may allow them to meet their financial needs more flexibly, to limit bureaucratic intervention in their business decision-making and to obtain more economic and political autonomy from the government.

By the same token, industrial manufacturers are also likely to be an important source of pressure for expansion of the business scope of non-bank financial institutions (NBFI). NBFIs, compared with commercial banks, generally face fewer ownership and operational restrictions. Manufacturing firms, especially big industrial groups, may thus be able to buy into the sector or incorporate their own non-bank financial firms. Therefore, they are expected to be strong advocates for deregulation of the regulatory barriers that create functional segments between banks and NBFIs. However, industrial firms that can mobilise much of their needed capital from within or that are not closely linked with the NBFI sector tend to be indifferent to, and may even oppose, the liberalisation measures. This is particularly true when they have close relations with banking institutions which identify their profits with the oligopolistic and segmented structure of the financial sector.

The attitude of industrial firms towards foreign exchange and capital decontrol tends to be mixed. The relaxation of rules governing foreign borrowings by domestic firms provides manufacturers with expanded access to foreign capital (Haggard and Maxfield 1993b: 66; Mathieson and Rojas-Suárez 1994: 338). While the manufacturing sector as a whole may benefit from capital account opening, internationally oriented industrial firms stand to gain more from capital mobility than domestically based ones. Firms with wide transnational economic linkages tend to hold more mobile assets; mobile-asset holders in capital-poor economies can profit from liberalisation of capital inflows and outflows (Frieden 1991b: 433–42; Williamson forthcoming). For instance, they can gain the freedom to invest and greater space for business operations abroad from the deregulation of outward direct and portfolio investment by domestic investors. While capital controls reduce investment options, the increased mobility of liquid capital allows internationally oriented firms to diversify into different economic activities in many countries.

Manufacturers' policy preferences towards capital decontrol should be distinguished between inflows and outflows. Whereas deregulation of outflow restrictions may provide industrial firms with enhanced access to more profitable investment opportunities abroad, capital inflows can harm as much as promote their interests. Empirical studies suggest that capital inflows are often accompanied by either an appreciation of exchange rate and/or rising inflation and can lead to a real exchange rate increase (Kim 1995; Mathieson and Rojas-Suárez 1993). This may hurt the profitability of industrial firms, specifically those in the export-oriented sector. Furthermore, capital inflows in the form of direct and portfolio investment are likely to subject domestic industrial firms to increased foreign competition and to dilute the ownership controls of business groups, many of which tend to be family-dominated enterprises in developing countries (Leff 1978, 1979b).

To the extent that capital inflows pose actual and potential threats to the economic interests of industrial manufacturers, their preferences for financial openings are expected to be inconsistent and selective. Although they welcome the opportunities to source cheaper finance and to expand their production and investment activities abroad, they oppose any liberalisation measures that may lead to rapid capital inflows and foreign direct investment. Their opposition to the entry of foreign investors and financial institutions is likely to be stronger if they have financial subsidiaries, which are understandably keen to keep foreign participants at bay.

The financial sector as a whole supports the liberalisation process for two basic reasons. One reason relates to the recovery of decision-making autonomy, which has long been desired by commercial banks and other financial institutions. Under repressed financial systems, government intervention – generally in the form of high legal reserve requirements, pervasive preferential credit schemes and negative real interest rates – considerably impairs their profitability. High reserve requirements, for instance, raise bank operating costs and impose a discriminatory tax on financial intermediation; credit ceilings reduce efficiency by destroying competition for deposits; and preferential credit policies saddle banks with increasing non-performing assets (Fry 1995: 327–34, 354–6). Naturally enough, the banking sector sees financial reform as an opportunity to limit bureaucratic interference with its operations and to improve its profitability.

The other reason, particularly with regard to preferential credit reduction, is that financiers are empirically shown to have a strong interest in price stability and low inflation (Destler and Henning 1989: 132–4; Epstein and Ferguson 1984; Maxfield 1990: 24, 1991: 424–5). Positive spreads between asset and liability interest rates constitute the basic factor in the profitability of financial institutions. However, cheap credit and loose monetary policy tend to narrow the spreads, particularly in high inflationary settings. Preferential credit schemes, which are connected to interest rate ceilings, not only weaken the performance of financial institutions, as mentioned above, but also lead to monetary expansion (Bascom 1994: 9–22; Haggard and Maxfield 1993a: 301). As loose monetary policy erodes their real interest earnings and inflation reduces their profits, financiers are expected to support the removal of such preferential credit schemes.

With regard to interest rate ceilings, the stance of financiers is generally negative for three possible reasons. In the first place, such ceilings tend to narrow the interest spread of financial institutions and to repress the return to financial investment of liquid asset holders, e.g. financiers. Furthermore, ceilings can make real interest rates significantly negative when inflation accelerates, and can cause rapid portfolio shifts from financial to tangible assets (Fry 1995: 21–2). This may result in the shrinkage of the deposit base of banks and other financial institutions, which may affect their ability to raise loanable funds and affect their lending operations. Finally, loan rate ceilings prevent lending rates from adjusting for rising inflation, and resultant low real interest rates favour debtors (industrial firms) over creditors (financial institutions) because they produce an income transfer from the latter to the former (Akyüz 1991).

This general description of financiers' preferences towards preferential credit and interest rate ceilings should be qualified: their position on the abolition of such credit and ceilings may not be so consistent and clear-cut as depicted above. Private bankers, for instance, may want to keep preferential credit policies in place, partly because their role in implementing these policies brings various profitable quid pro quo responses from governments (Haggard and Maxfield 1993a: 300–1) and partly because they have owner-ship linkages with industrial firms and are thus concerned about the effects of credit reduction on their performance. Similarly, empirical evidence from some developing countries suggests that large private banks have resisted interest rate deregulation (Fischer 1993; Fry 1995: 464; Galbis 1986). For one thing, this may derive from private bankers' desire to contain competition and, for another, this appears to be related to the micro-economic structure of financial markets in which a few banks dominate the sector and collude in fixing interest rates.

Oligopolistic financiers also have a vested interest in regulatory policies that keep domestic financial markets closed to both domestic and foreign competition. Removing barriers to the entry of new financial institutions is likely to undermine existing cartels and the guaranteed profits associated with concentrated market structures (Haggard and Maxfield 1993b: 66). Private bankers are therefore expected to resist the deregulation of entry barriers. By the same token, they also have a stake in the continuation of regulatory restraints that have created functional segmentation of financial institutions and oppose the expansion of NBFIs' business scope. On the other hand, NBFIs, barred from offering many banking services, have every incentive to lobby to get regulatory barriers reduced, particularly if they are not bank affiliates.

Foreign exchange and capital decontrol is a final reform area of significant interest to private financiers. Evidence from both developed and developing countries implies that they are generally champions of free capital mobility (Doner and Unger 1993; Epstein and Schor 1992; Maxfield 1990, 1991; Phong-paichit 1980). Like internationally oriented industrial firms, financiers are holders of completely liquid assets and stand to benefit from capital account opening for at least two reasons. First, capital mobility permits them to gain from investment diversification. Whereas financial institutions in small closed economies whose portfolios are confined to domestic assets tend to have a higher risk exposure, capital account liberalisation opens up opportunities for them to invest in an international portfolio. They can gain security by diversifying their financial investments (Mathieson and Rojas-Suárez 1994: 337–8; Williamson forthcoming). Second, banks favour liberalising capital controls because this could result in the multiplication of intermediation and arbitrage opportunities owing to disparities between domestic and overseas interest rates. As one important study shows (Fischer 1993: 121–3), opening a capital account is unlikely to lead to a convergence of domestic and international interest rates in the short term if domestic financial markets remain segmented and oligopolistic structure is prevalent.

Support of capital mobility on the part of financiers does not mean advocacy of deregulation of barriers to foreign entry. Foreign financial institutions often press hard for greater liberalisation in general, and for the removal of impediments to foreign entry in particular; this is especially visible in the emerging and potentially profitable markets of the East Asian newly industrialising economies (Haggard and Maxfield 1993b, 1996). Just as they are loath to see the arrival of new domestic competitors in order to maintain oligopolistic structures and associated profits, private financiers want to keep foreign institutions at bay. Resistance to foreign entry is expected to be stronger particularly because domestic banks would have to face the prospects of competing with more powerful and efficient foreign rivals. Similarly, domestic NBFIs are eager to prevent the entry of foreign finance and securities firms, which is often accompanied by capital account liberalisation.

It is plain from the above analysis that, although private financiers have a clear interest in low inflation, minimum government intervention and unrestricted capital mobility, there is no constant and linear relationship between these core interests and major liberalisation measures. That relationship tends to depend upon how various multifaceted contextual factors define the costs and benefits associated with the liberalisation process. Not only do the preferences of the financial sector vary across liberalisation measures, but the sector itself is not a monolithic actor. Depending upon specific reform measures, we would expect the convergence or divergence of interests between state-owned and private financial institutions, between commercial banks and NBFIs and between domestic and foreign banks. These differences in policy preferences, defined along subsectoral lines, are of special importance in the following examination of how segments of the financial sector form alliances with industrial firms in the process of financial market reform.

### *Preference aggregation and articulation*

Industrial and financial sectors with different policy preferences are likely to form intra- and inter-sector coalitions around certain reform policies as a result of those preferences, and to attempt to have their distributive demands projected into the financial policy-making process. Private preferences, however, cannot be simply identified as the direct source of policy change. Economic interests provide private actors with an incentive to lobby, but they have to organise to translate their preferences into pressure on policy-makers (Frieden 1991a: 22–4). Also, policy outcomes cannot be derived from the configuration of sectoral coalitions because it tells us little about how effectively these coalitions organise and gain access to policy-making processes. 'Knowing preferences and coalitions is not the same as knowing power,' as Peter Gourevitch (1986: 58) correctly points out. The political process through which power or influence is exercised should be traced convincingly.

Once private actors' preferences are determined, the way in which these preferences are aggregated and articulated politically within domestic institutions has to be examined. In this context, institutions refer to the sector-specific features of industrial organisation and linkages between industry and finance. Political aggregation, or how interests are organised, hinges in the first instance on how unified and cohesive sectoral groups are. It also makes a difference whether or not finance and industry are institutionally related to each other.

### Industrial structure and sectoral collective action

Effective group organisation is typically impeded by the contradictions between individual and collective rationality. These contradictions, according to Olson's (1965) theory of collective action, stem from the attributes of group aggregation and influence as being public goods. The benefits of collective organisation are public because their enjoyment by an additional member adds nothing to the organisational costs once the group has set up a formal organisation, and the costs of excluding any member from those benefits are high. If the benefits are present for any member of the group once they are supplied, they are available for every member. These properties suggest that any potential member of a large group, if they are rational and self-interested, will refuse to pay their share of the costs of creating and sustaining collective action even though they may gain from effective organisation. As a consequence, collective action or group organisation and activities are likely to be undersupplied and subject to free riding.

The problem of free riding, Olson observed, is imputable to two factors. As any cost of providing public goods – group organisation and influence – is privately borne but benefits are jointly consumed, the cost of an individual's contribution towards their provision in a large group is likely to be greater than the gains that accrue to that individual as a result of his or her contribution. In other words, the larger the number of individuals that would benefit from collective action, the smaller the share of the gains from the action that will accrue to the individuals who undertake it. Furthermore, in any large group, collective organisation appears to be independent of an individual's actions; the self-seeking individual would choose to neglect the effect of his or her actions and would have no incentive to contribute. Thus, it follows that 'large groups, at least if they are composed of rational individuals, will not act in their group interest' (Olson 1982: 18).

Small groups, the importance of which Olson stresses in his work, are more likely to provide themselves with collective goods successfully. Each individual in a small group may find that the gains from having the collective good exceed the cost of contributing to its provision. There are individuals who would be better off if the collective good were provided than if it were not provided. In such situations, they might be willing to pay the entire cost of providing the collective good, regardless of what others in the group would do (Olson 1965: 22–36). Moreover, in small groups in which individuals are in close contact with each other, the assumption that one individual's action would have an indiscernible effect on the interests and course of action of others cannot be sustained. Close contact or 'interdependence' can thus give members of small groups an incentive to act in their common interest (Olson 1982: 29–30). From this proposition, Olson concludes that the internal cohesion of interest groups and their ability to provide collective benefits to members tend to increase as the size of the group decreases, and that small and concentrated groups are more likely to succeed in organising themselves for collective action than large and dispersed ones.[5]

The logic of collective action implies that industrial concentration would potentially offer a small-group solution to collective action problems (Stigler 1974). When an industrial sector is concentrated, the number of firms is small and oligopoly tends to prevail. The higher the level of industrial concentration, the greater the entry barriers and the more easily the sector would be able to avoid free riding (Shafer 1994). Equally important, the small-number, or cartelised, industry may also find it easier to detect and deter cheating and therefore to maintain internal cohesion (Osborne 1976). Conversely, in a large-number industry, the level of industrial concentration is low and competition is likely to prevail. The large number of small firms poses no barriers to entry and free riding is prevalent. In such situations, collective action problems are likely to be insurmountable.

Furthermore, industrial and financial sectors with similar policy preferences tend to have a strong incentive to engage in collective activity. However, common preferences or interests are often hard to discover. The identification of common interests requires the provision of adequate information that is highly costly (Arrow 1985). Not knowing each other's preferences, industrial and financial firms would be motivated more by their own conception of self-interest than by a shared perception of the common good, and thereby find it difficult or impossible to organise effective collective action. The costs of identifying common interests and searching for like-minded group members can be substantially reduced if there are only a few firms in the industry. In the small-number industry, firms continuously interact with one another – a process through which they can acquire information about each other's interests, expectations and outlooks. This would ease collective action not only by reducing information costs, but also by alleviating the problems of co-ordinating their actions.

*Finance–industry ties and cross-sector collective action*

Finance–industry ties also have strong mediating effects on the aggregation and expression of private-sector preferences. Such ties may take the form of bank/NBFI lending to industry, finance and industry holdings of each other's equities, interlocking directorates or any combination of the three. As argued in the sociological theory of organisational behaviour, these inter-corporate relations imply the actual and potential dominance of financiers over industrialists or the power of financial hegemony, mainly because of financiers' structural cohesion and loan leverage (Mintz and Schwartz 1986; Scott 1986).[6] The dominant position of financiers, however, should not be exaggerated. On the one hand, they depend upon industrial firms for their lucrative businesses. On the other, industrialists may rely more on capital markets and less on banks for their capital needs, depending upon the attributes of financial systems (Zysman 1983: 70–1).

As discussed in the previous subsection, the preferences of financiers and industrialists towards financial reform measures tend to differ. Close inter-corporate relations, however, may change the intensity and direction of these preferences, particularly on the part of financiers. Heavy bank/NBFI lending to industry and holdings of industrial equities are expected to make financial institutions develop a direct stake in the success of their industrial clients, mainly because the lending operations and profits of the former hinge upon the fortunes of the latter (Glasberg 1989: 6–13). As their future viability varies with the performance of the real sectors of the economy which they would have to improve in their own self-interest, financiers are likely to perceive the welfare effects of financial liberalisation from the perspective of their industrial partners and to support financial policies that promote corporate interests. Empirical studies of developed countries suggest that close finance–industry ties tend to transform private bankers' preferences for tight monetary policy, strongly valued domestic currencies and high interest rates. These preferences render them indifferent to or even supportive of monetary expansion, undervalued currencies and modest interest rates that enhance industrial performance (Epstein 1992; Hall 1984: 26–7, 1986: 236–9; Henning 1994: ch. 5).

Conversely, if finance–industry relations are kept at arm's length, financial institutions are expected to display a low propensity for long-term commitment to and managerial involvement with industrial firms. In the case of limited finance–industry ties, there is an implicit assumption that industrialists depend heavily upon internally generated funds or capital markets for their long-term investment needs and that financiers tend to deal in quick and short-term transactions and seek policy changes in line with their own self-interest. Under these circumstances, financiers and industrialists are unlikely to have common interests and may develop different and conflicting preferences on financial policy. This pattern of inter-corporate behaviour is particularly visible in the UK and the United States, where financiers' ties to industry have been limited and industrialists have traditionally been dependent upon retained earnings and capital markets for much of their investment finance. The arm's-length relationship often leads financiers to define their interests in isolation from those of industry and to seek such financial policy as overvalued currencies and high interest rates that harm the long-term strength of industrial firms (Cox 1986: 35–48; Hall 1984: 34–6, 1986: 250–1; Henning 1994: ch. 6; Moran 1981, 1984).

It should be noted that the financial sector as a whole may not be linked with the manufacturing sector as a whole in real-world situations. The actual relationship between the two sectors is likely to be more complex than is depicted above. Finance–industry relations may develop along not only sectoral but also *subsectoral* lines. Commercial banks, for instance, may only have direct business interests in export-oriented industrial firms; big manufacturers may establish closer ties with NBFIs than with other financial institutions. The degree of integration between finance and industry and the mutability of cross-sectoral and subsectoral relations are determined not only by economically rational considerations but also by socio-political factors, industrial and financial policies and the pattern of economic development. This last point is of particular importance and will be further discussed in the next chapter.

## Organisational structures and collective action: a synthesis

It is conceivable that industrial organisation and finance–industry ties can combine in different ways; different combinations may have differential impacts upon group action. It is thus necessary to look at how these two sets of organisational structures shape, in a collective manner, the capability of financiers and industrialists to aggregate and articulate their policy preferences and to assess their relative effects on sectoral and cross-sector collective action in order of importance. At the risk of oversimplification, Table 2.1 characterises heuristically the possible combinations of these structures. From the table, three propositions can be developed, which help to inform the empirical analysis to be conducted in the following chapters.

In the first place, industrial organisation should be placed at the beginning of the causal effects of institutional structures. Other things being equal, cross-sector collective activities are expected to be much easier to organise and more effective if both the financial and industrial sectors are concentrated and cohesive (cell I) than if the two sectors are both decentralised and competitive (cells V and VI). In the latter case, there is a likelihood that each sector would be fragmented among several competing groups, which would be organised along different subsectoral preferences and policy objectives. This results in the multiplication of interests in the private sector and is likely to doom any attempts to organise coherent and effective intra- and inter-sector collective action, whether or not the two sectors are closely linked to each other. Under the circumstances, financial policy reform is most likely to be determined by the interests and policy objectives of the state agencies that dominate the macro-economic policy-making arena.

*Table 2.1*    Key dimensions of private-sector organisational structures

| Degree of industrial concentration (finance–industry) | Inter-corporate relations | |
|---|---|---|
| | *Close* | *Limited* |
| High/high | Cell I Organisationally coherent and effective at both sectoral and cross-sector levels | Cell II Organisationally cohesive and strong at sectoral but not cross-sector levels |
| High/low | Cell III Asymmetrical dependence and strong organisational capacity at sectoral level | Cell IV Lopsided organisational capacity and efficiency at sectoral level |
| Low/low | Cell V Organisationally fragmented and ineffective translation of sectoral interests | Cell VI Organisationally fragmented and incoherent preference articulation |

Furthermore, if one sector is centralised and cohesive and the other is decentralised and discordant, and if the two are closely linked through the latter's dependence on the former for its performance and profitability (cell III), the centralised sector would be better able to dominate the formation and expression of preferences for financial policy and reform. If the concentrated sector has close ties only with certain segments of the decentralised one, and may thus be able to influence their preference orientation, this is likely to further weaken the organisational capability of the decentralised sector. Finally, if the one sector is more concentrated and better organised than the other, and if the two sectors have limited linkages (cell IV), it is almost certain that the preferences of the former would prevail over those of the latter. In the case that the two sectors are both concentrated and organisationally effective and that they have limited ties with each other (cell II), the resulting effects on the direction of financial policy are expected to be dependent upon the status of the state institutions with which the two sectors are each associated.

## Public-sector interests, state institutions and policy choices

Although the sectoral approach based on the configuration of private-sector preferences is important in understanding how state actions in the reform process are socially constrained, it does not fully explain how financial policy change is initiated and liberalisation processes are pursued. Private-sector preferences do not by themselves produce financial policy reform; state agencies make policy choices and formulate and implement reform strategies in line with their political and economic interests that are partially independent from societal demands (Nordlinger 1981). Equally important, while sectoral and cross-sector collective action may have a significant impact on financial policy and reform, private groups, no matter how powerful, have to act through the government to achieve their policy objectives. Whether they can translate their material interests into policy outputs hinges not only on the organisation of the private sector, but also on the institutional features of the state that define the avenues of private access to the policy-making arena. For these reasons, the role of states as both political actors and institutions should be examined.

Among state institutions, central banks are at the core of financial systems and form key agencies in economic policy-making processes of developed and developing countries. Typically, they act as fiscal agents to governments, as bankers to private financial institutions and as regulators and supervisors of financial activity. More importantly, central banks are responsible for regulating the issuance of the national currency, conducting monetary policies and managing international reserves (Deane and Pringle 1994: 110–26; Ghatak 1995: 63–5). Although all central banks fulfil similar micro- and macro-functions, they tend to differ significantly in their relationship with governments or, more specifically, in the degree of their independence from politicians in carrying out those functions, particularly in conducting monetary and credit policies (Goodman 1992: 6–10).

It should be noted that central banks cannot be completely independent from governments. Central banks are public-sector institutions and need to maintain close working relationships with other government agencies, particularly finance ministries, in order to perform their various functions. Equally, the policy-making authority of central banks may also be limited by a range of socio-economic factors. Increasing financial integration, for instance, appears to have constrained the policy options of central banks in most open economies, with the possible exception of those of central banks in a few of the largest countries (Andrews 1994; Epstein and Grintis 1992; Goodman and Pauly 1993). Central bankers are also not politically isolated from societal actors and groups, specifically the private financial community upon which they depend for a variety of support and to whose demands they are thus more responsive (Collyns 1983: 8–9; Maxfield 1990, 1991; Woolley 1984: 69–87).

While such socio-economic factors may affect the policy-making autonomy of central bankers, the concept of central bank independence, used in this book as in many other studies, relates explicitly to the balance of authority over financial policy between central banks and other state economic institutions (Goodman 1992; Henning 1994). More specifically, central banks are expected to be more independent if the final objective of price stability is explicitly spelled out in central bank laws, and if central bankers are assigned wide authority over formulating and implementing monetary policy. Furthermore, political autonomy in monetary management can be strengthened if the appointment and dismissal of senior central bank officials are not under direct government control and if clear restrictions on central bank lending to governments are set by the central bank and other national legislation. Finally, central banks that are subject to weak executive or legislative control over their budgets and operations would generally have more latitude in pursuing their policy objectives than those that are subject to strong control (Burdekin and Laney 1988; Cargill and Hutchison 1990; Woolley 1977: 160–2, 1985: 321–6).

With regard to the major purposes of this study, the discussion of central bank–government relations is important for two fundamental reasons. First, the state is not a monolithic entity but represents a complex system of different agencies. Different state agencies – central banks and line ministries – are expected to have differential interests in financial policy reform, manifestly because they have diverse histories, dissimilar bureaucratic cultures and values, different constituency bases, and divergent missions and policy objectives (Moran 1990). The degree of central bank independence is thus likely to determine which state agencies can assert their interests in the financial policy-making process. Second, different state agencies have different ties with financial and industrial sectors, whereas central banks may have close relations with the private financial community, e.g. planning and industrial ministries may have more connections with industrial firms. Because of these different business–government ties, the balance of power over financial policy between central banks and government ministries would determine which private sectors are more likely to have their policy preferences translated into actual reform policies. For these two reasons, cross-country variations in central bank independence are likely to have a sharp impact upon the course of financial policy and to bear strongly on reform approaches and outcomes.

### Public-sector interests: central banks versus governments

This subsection posits the economic and political interests of central banks and governments in financial policy and reform. As a whole group, central bankers are typically assumed to be more concerned about price stability than are governments and politicians and to take a conservative and longer term view of the effects of financial policy on macro-economic conditions. Evidence from empirical research on the policy behaviour of central bankers in developed and developing countries lends strong support to this assumption (Collyns 1983; Elgie and Thompson 1998; Goodman 1992; Maxfield 1990, 1991; Simmons 1996; Woolley 1994). Central bankers' conservative attitudes towards financial policy may stem from, among other things, statutory mandates, organisational culture and ethos, and close ties with private financiers. This last factor, which is often given more weight in the explanation of central bankers' preferences, will be elaborated upon in the next subsection.

Empirical studies on the politics of macro-economic policy in developed countries have also demonstrated that the more independent central banks are, the tighter the monetary policy and the lower the inflation is most likely to be (Alesina and Summers 1993; Banaian *et al.* 1986; Beck 1988; Grilli *et al.* 1991; Kurzer 1988). Similar studies of developing countries show a generally positive, albeit inconclusive, correlation between central bank independence and low inflationary practices (de Haan and Kooi 2000; Fry *et al*. 1996: 98–103). An extension of this analysis provides some insight into central bankers' basic views on financial reform. As mentioned in the previous section, financial repression, mainly characterised by pervasive preferential credit and negative real interest rates, is normally associated with monetary expansion. Central bankers are thus expected to be among the most important sources of pressure for financial liberalisation, particularly with regard to the reduction of preferential credit and deregulation of interest rates.

Governments and politicians, by contrast, tend to be less able or willing to commit themselves to price stability and to implement restrictive monetary policy that may be beneficial to the economy in the long run. Although they are aware of the benefits of price stability and low inflation, these are often sacrificed for other policy objectives, such as high economic growth and employment, usually due to electoral politics or partisan interests. The mainstream literature on the political business or electoral cycle suggests that governments with monetary discretion face perceived electoral incentives to renege on their earlier commitments in order to achieve short-term gains – they generally have difficulty in making credible commitments to price stability because of their time-inconsistent preferences (Nordhaus 1975; Tufte 1978; Williams 1990). Similarly, studies based on the partisan cycle or party differences model show that monetary policy frequently shifts to reflect the interests of new ruling parties, which in turn reflect their ideology or the preferences of their core constituency (Hibbs 1977; Woolley 1994: 71–6).

Electoral and political factors aside, toleration of inflation on the part of governments may also result from their own economic interests, specifically from their revenue-collecting needs. Apart from the use of such conventional taxes as income and sales taxes for mobilising public-sector savings, inflation is another form of taxation that can be employed to achieve the same purpose.[7] Difficulties in collecting conventional taxes, particularly in developing countries, and the relative ease of collecting inflation taxes generally lead governments to view inflation as a preferable means of securing resources for themselves, despite the evidence that suggests a variety of negative effects of such a policy upon private investment and incremental efficiency of taxation (von Furstenberg 1980). For similar reasons, governments may also be unwilling to put an end to financial repression, which can act as a discriminatory tax on financial asset holders and thus as an alternative source of revenue (Fry 1995: 18–19; Giovannini and de Melo 1993).[8]

Moreover, planning and industry ministries that are growth oriented and that have close connections to constituent interests in the manufacturing sector are often susceptible to the temptation to use monetary expansion to spur rapid industrial development. Government preferences for financial reform, particularly in the area of credit and interest rate policies, would thus be highly variable and situationally dependent. Although governments may take a leading role in the liberalisation process because of their interest in mobilising more resources for industrial investment, they typically do not have such strong preferences for interest rate deregulation and preferential credit reduction as central bankers. As these reform measures threaten to harm major industrial interests and may even slow down economic growth, at least in the short term, electoral and constituency considerations would render government politicians less likely to implement a liberalisation policy in a coherent and consistent manner.

Entry barrier deregulation and functional de-segmentation are other important areas in which the interests of central banks also tend to diverge from those of governments. Regulatory restraints that prevent new entry and create institutional segmentation often depress competition and reduce efficiency in the financial sector. Both central banks and governments may thus be interested in seeing the elimination of these restraints. Their approaches to deregulation tend to differ, however, when it comes to specific liberalisation measures. Stability-oriented central bankers are more concerned about the rapid arrival of new entrants, fearing that resulting price competition would threaten the solvency of smaller and weaker institutions and compromise their supervisory responsibility. Similarly, central banks wish to proceed with functional de-segmentation gradually and are inclined to give banks more leeway in product diversification and business expansion. This is not only because they rely more upon private bankers for various types of support, but also because the rapid broadening of NBFIs' activities often leads to serious regulatory problems.

Governments, with broader responsibilities, generally have much wider political and economic concerns than merely financial stability (Henning 1994: 62–6). Their interests in the reduction of competitive restraints extend to industrial sector development, economic growth and foreign policy goals. Governments tend to view entry barrier deregulation as an important means to improve the efficiency of the financial system in mobilising more investment resources for industrial development. To the extent that governments bear the brunt of external political demands for greater foreign entry, they are more disposed than central banks to appease foreign financial institutions and their home governments. By the same token, governments are more willing to give NBFIs greater freedom to broaden and diversify their financial services and products. This is particularly true where governments are reluctant to relinquish controls over the banking sector for industrial policy purposes and choose to promote the growth of NBFIs in order to increase competition and efficiency.

In foreign exchange and capital decontrol, as in domestic financial liberalisation, the attitudes of central banks are also dissimilar to those of governments and politicians. Foreign exchange and capital controls, at their inception, may reflect public-sector interests in maintaining policy autonomy, the domestic tax base, continued access to low-cost finance and the ability to promote local industrial development (Alesina *et al.* 1994; Dooley 1996). However, central banks and governments share these interests with substantially different intensities. Central bankers' interests in capital controls tend to be much narrower – they are primarily concerned about the impact of volatile capital flows on inflation control and financial system stability. So long as central bankers are assured that capital mobility will not severely compromise their policy objectives, they are generally indisposed to excessive restrictions on capital movements. Recent studies on the political economy of capital controls suggest a positive link between central bank independence and financial openness (Grilli and Milesi-Ferretti 1995; Quinn and Inclán 1997).

Central banks may have several motives for opposing excessive foreign exchange and capital controls. First, controls often make it easier for governments to effect expansionary economic policy through fiscal and monetary means. To the extent that such policy may lead to price instability and rising inflation, central bankers favour decontrols in the hope that greater capital movements can force more exact fiscal and monetary discipline on government politicians. Second, central bankers oppose exchange controls to the degree that they accord additional policy-making powers to other government agencies, such as finance and planning ministries, and thereby weaken their own authority over financial policy. Third, central bankers' opposition to controls may reflect the preferences of their natural constituency – the private financial community – for free capital mobility. Empirical research grounded in Latin American industrialising economies and major OECD countries shows that central bankers are disposed towards decontrols, although they may be concerned about rapid short-term capital inflows (Epstein 1992; Epstein and Schor 1992; Maxfield 1990, 1991).

Governments may be inclined towards foreign exchange and capital decontrol, particularly in the wake of balance of payments and fiscal crises. This inclination reflects their desire to resolve foreign exchange problems and induce capital inflows by enhancing the credibility of government economic policy and by increasing the confidence of foreign investors and creditors (Haggard and Maxfield 1996). Generally speaking, however, governments are more likely to have interests in maintaining rather than removing exchange controls. While central bankers view decontrols as an opportunity to rein in expansionist politicians, governments tend to use controls to increase their policy autonomy, specifically their freedom to stimulate economic growth and full employment. Governments that want to deploy expansionary economic policy are empirically shown to have a greater proclivity for maintaining capital controls in both developed and developing countries (Epstein and Schor 1992: 153–7; Grilli and Milesi-Ferretti 1995).[9]

To the extent that capital decontrols entail the transfer of policy authority to central banks (Haggard and Maxfield 1996: 42), and thus tilt the balance of power between central banks and governments in favour of the former, government ministries are expected to oppose decontrols in order to prevent these changes. Finally, developing country governments normally use exchange and capital controls to achieve a variety of policy objectives. These may include allocating resources to favoured users, promoting the growth of strategic industrial sectors and domestic entrepreneurship, controlling the behaviour of the business sector and structuring the relations of societal actors with foreign capital (Haggard and Cheng 1987; Mardon 1990; Stallings 1990). As decontrols threaten to strip governments of an important political and economic tool, they are very likely to thwart or procrastinate the liberalisation process.

Political considerations aside, reluctance on the part of governments to implement capital decontrols may also lie in their fiscal implications. As noted earlier in this section, financial repression can behave as a tax and create an alternative source of government revenue. To be effective in collecting such a tax, governments have to couple financial repression with restrictions on capital mobility. Without capital controls, liquid asset holders may be able to bypass domestic financial controls and move their financial assets abroad for more profitable investment opportunities, depriving governments of the ability to tax those assets (Alesina and Tabellini 1989; Giovannini and de Melo 1993). Similarly, capital controls can keep real interest rates artificially low by preventing international arbitrage in the asset market, allowing governments to finance their debts cheaply (Aizenman and Guidotti 1994; Sussman 1991). To the extent that tax revenues from financial repression are not trivial and public debts are substantial, both of which appear to be the case in many developing countries, governments are expected to temporise with capital decontrol.

When the institutional interests of central banks and governments diverge with regard to financial policy and reform, central banks are expected to be under political pressure to emphasise some policy objectives at the expense of others. How central banks accommodate these pressures depends largely upon the degree of their policy-making independence and their relations with governments. It can be hypothesised that financial policy and reform are likely to reflect the interests and policy priorities of central bankers if they operate autonomously from governments and politicians. On the other hand, if central banks are subordinate to governments, and if they and finance ministries are not in basic agreement as to the direction of financial policy, the direction of financial policy and reform tends to be shaped by the interests of government ministries and politicians.

### Central bank status and private preference projection

The degree of central bank independence also affects which industrial sector – finance or industry – is more likely to have its policy preferences projected into centres of financial policy. The causal linkage between government–business relations and economic policy has been prominent in the comparative political economy literature (MacIntyre 1994; Schneider and Maxfield 1997; Wilson 1990). It has been argued in the literature that business–government relations structure the policy behaviour of private actors and shape the way in which they get access to public policy-making processes. While the explanatory approach adopted here accepts the basic contention of this body of literature, it diverges from the standard view of business–government relations and argues that different government institutions are likely to develop ties with different business sectors. More specifically, central banks tend to have closer ties with private financiers, whereas planning and industrial ministries are inclined to maintain more intimate relations with industrial manufacturers. The lines of competition and compromise over financial reform may be drawn not between the integrated state and the unified business sector but between policy alliances of central banks and private financiers on the one hand and government ministries and their constituent sectors on the other. Whether financiers or industrialists can have their preferences translated into actual reform policies depends upon not only the sectoral and cross-sector organisational structures of the private sector but also the relative status of central banks and government ministries within the state hierarchy.

Research on developed and developing countries provides ample evidence of close ties between public and private financiers (Doner and Unger 1993; Henning 1994; Maxfield 1990, 1991; Unger 1998: ch. 4; Woolley 1984: ch. 4). This relationship stems, first and foremost, from the fact that public and private financiers share many basic economic interests and policy objectives. As noted earlier, private financiers are generally averse to cheap credit and unexpected inflation; their public counterparts also place high value on price stability and low inflation. Apart from their independently developed preferences, central bankers' conservative proclivity is guided by their concerns about the negative effects of loose monetary policy and high inflation on the profitability and performance of private financiers (Epstein and Ferguson 1984; Epstein and Schor 1990a: 137–8, 1990b). This is mainly because the historical evolution of central banks and their economic and political status *vis-à-vis* other state agencies are bound up with the position of the private financial community (Goodhart 1988; Goodman 1992; Kurzer 1988). As revealed in two important studies (Epstein 1992; Maxfield 1994), independent central banks are associated with and supported by a robust private financial community, whereas dependent central banks result from poorly developed and weak private financial institutions.[10]

The close linkage between central bankers and the private financial community also reflects a symbiotic and reciprocal relationship between the regulator and the regulated. As noted above, central banks exercise controls over the lending and borrowing operations of financial institutions. While often sharing this supervisory responsibility with finance ministries, central banks are primarily responsible for ensuring the safety and solvency of private banks, the most important component of any financial system. Because financial regulations and monetary policies affect the business activities and performance of banks and other private financial institutions, they are willing to co-operate with regulatory authorities and generally accept their controls and supervisions. In return, private financiers, as the natural constituents of central banks, expect to have various policy advantages, such as lender-of-last-resort protection, competition-controlling regulations and freedoms to undertake product innovations and business expansion (Maxfield 1990: 25–6; Woolley 1984: 74, 83–4).

On the other hand, financial authorities, specifically central banks, may have to rely upon private financiers for a variety of supports. In the process of formulating monetary policy, central banks depend upon the private financial community for current and detailed information about developments in financial markets and about changing economic and business conditions. First-hand information can help central bankers to analyse complex economic situations more quickly and accurately than can government ministries. Policy expertise thus obtained enhances central banks' status among state economic institutions (Cukierman 1992: 393–4; Henning 1994: 64–5). More important, private financial institutions act as an important channel through which central banks' monetary policy affects the real economy – this is generally reflected in their roles of financing and distributing government debts and implementing reserve requirements and central bank credit facilities. Finally, central bankers may mobilise the private financial community to support their policy stance, especially when they have disputes with governments (Goodman 1992; Posen 1993; Woolley 1985: 338–9).

For all of these reasons, central banks are expected to be more sensitive to the preferences and concerns of the private financial community and more responsive to its policy demands than to those of other private sectors. Even when financial institutions are owned or heavily controlled by governments, central bankers are also responsible for supervising their business activities and have to depend upon them for information collection and policy implementation. This places central bankers closer to financial institutions than are government ministries and renders them more concerned about the performance and needs of the financial sector. Other things being equal, therefore, private financiers are more likely to have their policy preferences translated into actual outcomes if central banks are independent from governments and politicians and if they are allied with finance ministries and achieve a hegemonic status in the financial policy-making process (Henning 1994; Maxfield 1990).

Governments, specifically planning and industrial ministries, tend to have close ties to industrial firms. This may originate, at least conceptually, from several socio-economic factors. The policy objectives of planning and industrial authorities are likely to be congruent with the economic interests of industrial firms. As discussed above, both are inclined to favour policy programmes that lead to increased government spending, and both tend to be less concerned about the effects of monetary expansion and high inflation than conservatively oriented public and private financiers. The convergence of interests and objectives may also be reinforced by a process of socialisation through which government officials interact with the same firms in the industrial sector and even move into key positions in these firms. This process may give industrialists the opportunity to influence the policy orientation of the ministries that control them, and results in a significant interpenetration of public and private interests (Haggard *et al.* 1997a: 53–7).

Furthermore, just as central bankers rely upon private financiers for policy support, planning and industrial ministries count on their natural constituency for similar purposes; even efficient and competent economic officials may need assistance from industrial firms in data gathering and industrial planning. Equally important, the manufacturing community provides planning and industrial ministries with a bureaucratic *raison d'être* for their regulatory and supervisory functions, and may prove to be an important socio-political ally in such critical situations as where governments' expansionary economic policies are resisted by central banks. As planning and industrial ministries are closely associated with the manufacturing sector for economic and political reasons, they are more concerned about its needs than those of other sectors. Because of these relations, planning and industrial ministries are typically more responsive to demands from industrial firms than from financial institutions. If financial policy-making is centred in, and dominated by, planning and industrial ministries, therefore, industrial firms are more likely to be able to get their preferences projected into the policy-making process.

Empirical research on countries as diverse as Latin American and East Asian NIEs and major advanced industrial societies offers prominent examples of how the different balance of authority over financial policy between central banks and governments affects the articulation of industrial firms' policy preferences. In France, Japan, Korea and Brazil, for instance, where planning and industrial ministries are powerful in relation to monetary authorities and maintain generally close ties to the industrial community, industrial firms and their interest-representing associations are granted direct entry into official policy arenas and find it easier to have their preferences translated into economic policies (Daniels 1992; Henning 1994: ch. 4; Johnson 1982; Maxfield 1990, 1991; Weiss 1998: 50–9). Although governments in those countries impose tight controls over financial sectors, they usually place greater emphasis on the needs and performance of industrial firms at the expense of those of financial institutions, particularly banks. In Britain, the United States, Mexico and Thailand, by contrast, where industrial ministries are relatively weak in relation to monetary authorities that have close links with the private financial community, industrial firms find it more difficult to make their voices heard in macro-economic policy-making processes. Governments usually follow financial policies that are more advantageous to private financiers than to industrialists (Christensen *et al.* 1993; Daniels 1992; Doner and Unger 1993; Hall 1984, 1986; Maxfield 1990, 1991).

## Conclusions

This chapter has presented an analytical framework for explaining cross-country variations in financial reform approaches and outcomes. As presented in Figure 2.1, the framework is built upon two different but interrelated theoretical propositions. Taken together, they argue that the political sources of financial policy choices lie primarily in the policy preferences of dominant societal actors for, and the interests of central banks and governments in, different reform strategies and measures. While the organisation of the

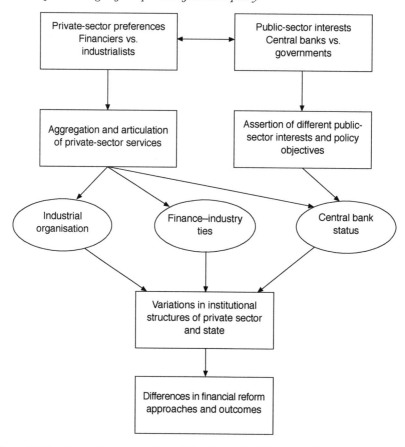

*Figure 2.1* A schematic presentation of the theoretical framework.

financial and industrial sectors shapes the aggregation and articulation of private preferences, central bank–government relations influence not only which sectors are more likely to eventually translate their preferences into reform outcomes, but also which state agencies assert their interests in the reform process. These institutional structures, deeply embedded in and shaped by distinctive national historical developments and socio-political systems, tend to vary across different countries, and cross-country variations provide the key to the explanation of divergent policy-making patterns. In the next chapter, this study examines how Korea and Thailand differ in these two sets of institutional structures and why the institutional differences should be expected to lead to different financial reform approaches and outcomes within the two countries.

# 3 Institutional variations in Korea and Thailand

The theoretical propositions developed in the previous chapter argue that the expression and assertion of private preferences for, and public-sector interests in, the financial reform process are shaped by the organisational structures of the private sector and the state. In this chapter, differences in these structures between Korea and Thailand are compared. The comparison is conducted qualitatively and quantitatively within the limits of comparability of national industrial and financial data. The causes of these institutional differences are also discussed. Comprehensive reviews of these structures and the causes of their differences are far beyond the scope of this study. The focus is therefore on variations in the institutional dimensions between Korea and Thailand and the ways in which the variations lead to divergent policy patterns.

The section that follows compares the industrial organisation and finance–industry relations in Korea and Thailand. The chapter then proceeds to identify in the second section the differences between the two countries in the degree of central bank independence. The third and final section concludes the chapter by integrating these discussions into a focused comparison of financial policy-making institutions in Korea and Thailand and by presenting the hypotheses about how cross-country variations in these institutions should be expected to generate divergent reform patterns.

## Organisational structures of the private sector

As discussed in the previous chapter, financial and industrial sectors that have different preferences for financial policy reform may organise collective action around specific reform measures as a result of those preferences. How effectively they can assert themselves in the financial reform process or turn their economic interests into political power are functions of the sector-specific attributes of industrial organisation and of the ownership and managerial linkages between finance and industry. This section reviews the differences between Korea and Thailand along these organisational dimensions.

## Different attributes of industrial organisation

First, the organisational structure of the manufacturing sector in the two countries is compared. As argued in Chapter 2, the more concentrated an industrial sector, the easier it would be to organise its members for effective collective action. Conventional measures of industrial concentration usually employ the firm as the basic unit of analysis. The aggregate concentration ratio represented by the cumulative share of the *K*th firm in the whole sector is the most common measure, with the top 50 or 100 being the frequently used figure for *K*.[1] Table 3.1 shows that the level of industrial concentration measured in this way differs markedly in the two economies. The aggregate concentration ratios indicated by the sales share of the largest 50 and 100 manufacturing firms were significantly higher in Korea than in Thailand.

Although the firm-based measurement of industrial concentration reveals important differences in the organisational structure of the manufacturing sector in the two countries, the picture is partial and incomplete. In Korea and Thailand, as in many other developing countries, business groups are a dominant organisational feature in the economic system in general and in the manufacturing sector in particular. Industrial concentration on the basis of business groups therefore needs to be compared. Business groups in the two countries – the chaebols in Korea and top non-financial conglomerates in Thailand – have their bases and core business activities in the manufacturing sector, but have also expanded their spheres into trade, transportation, construction, finance and other service industries. Examining the economic concentration of business groups helps to illustrate not only the organisational features of manufacturing industries, but also the extent to which these groups are able to exercise influence on the whole economy.

In Korea, the large-business sector has a dominant and growing share of industrial production. In 1977, the top thirty chaebols accounted for 34 per cent of total manufacturing sales, which increased to 42 per cent in 1994

*Table 3.1*    Aggregate concentration ratios by sales for the top 50 and 100 manufacturing enterprises (percentages), selected years

| Year | Korea | | Thailand | |
|------|--------|---------|--------|---------|
| | *Top 50* | *Top 100* | *Top 50* | *Top 100* |
| 1982 | 37.5 | 46.8 | – | – |
| 1985 | – | – | 8.2 | 11.3 |
| 1987 | 30.9 | 38.9 | – | – |
| 1989 | – | – | 9.7 | 12.1 |

Sources: for Korea, Jeong (1994: 66); for Thailand, the sales figures for the top 50 and 100 manufacturing enterprises are taken from Advanced Research Group (*Thailand Company Information*, Bangkok, 1990) and International Business Research Co (*Million Baht Business Information*, Bangkok, 1990) and these are divided by the total sales figures for the whole manufacturing sector reported by The Thai National Statistical Office (*The Industrial Survey*, Bangkok, various issues).

(Song 1997: 115). This reinforces the conclusion reached in Table 3.1 that the manufacturing sector in Korea is highly concentrated and manufacturing activities are organised around and dominated by a few chaebols. What is more significant about industrial organisation in Korea is not only the high level of concentration of the chaebols' economic power in the manufacturing sector but also their economy-wide dominance. As Table 3.2 illustrates, there are huge differences in the size and economic concentration of business groups between the two countries. The Korean chaebols, relative to Thai conglomerates, are very large and represent a predominant proportion of the total economy.

The differences in the organisational configuration of manufacturing sectors between Korea and Thailand are mainly attributable to the role of the state and the pattern of development strategies. Although the origins of industrial capitalism in Korea can be traced back to the late nineteenth century (Eckert 1991), local business enterprises remained, until the late 1940s, few in number, small in size and weak in capital base. Almost all of today's chaebols owe their position to the specific policies of post-war regimes.[2] Many originated and even thrived under the Syngman Rhee regime in the 1950s. Rhee assiduously fostered close but corrupt networks of interest between private business and his Liberty Party, with a view to building a powerful patronage constituency and squeezing maximum political funds. On their part, business people used these political connections to seek economic rents and to gain favourable concessions from the state in various forms (Jones and Sakong 1980: 269–78; Kim 1976: 466–9).

When Park Chung-Hee came to power through a military coup in May 1961, he tried to crack this collusion between the state and the private sector through aggressive pursuit of anti-business policy, in order to distance his regime from the previous one. Before long, however, Park backed down from his crusade against private business (Haggard *et al.* 1991: 858–960; Haggard and Moon 1993: 65–9). The regime faced a political crisis due to its unconstitutional seizure of power. Park obviously understood that his government had

*Table 3.2*  Combined sales of largest business groups as percentage of gross national product (GNP), selected years

| Groups | Korea | | Groups | Thailand | |
|--------|-------|------|--------|----------|------|
|        | *1983* | *1987* |        | *1979* | *1984* |
| Top 5  | 46.7  | 52.4 | Top 5  | 6.9      | 8.7  |
| 20     | 73.6  | 76.4 | 20     | 13.1     | 14.4 |
| 50     | 84.3  | 88.5 | 51     | 16.7     | –    |

Sources: for Korea, Management Efficiency Research Institute (MERI) (*Korea's Fifty Major Business Groups for 1983 and 1984* 1985) and *Top 50 Business Groups in 1987* (MERI figures as reported in *Korea Business World* September 1988: 72); for Thailand, the corresponding sales figures for the top 5, 20 and 51 non-financial conglomerates are taken from Suehiro (1989: Tables 7.2 and 7.17, Appendices 7 and 8; 1992: Table 9) and these are divided by gross national product figures reported in the International Monetary Fund's *International Financial Statistics Yearbook* (various issues).

to deliver rapid economic growth in order to establish its political legitimacy. To do so, state elites had no choice but to depend upon the proven growth of big enterprises. These enterprises, which had built up their capital and managerial resources under the Rhee regime, now became the most viable economic force for developing the economy. Furthermore, Park and many leading technocrats, who had been trained by the Japanese or who had studied in Japan, decided how to industrialise by copying the Japanese model, which emphasised the role of big business in the development process (Amsden 1989: 51–2; Fields 1995: 50).

The combination of political expediencies and ideological orientations gave birth to the development coalition between the military regime and big business, or the 'sword–won alliance' in the words of Tun-Jen Cheng (1990: 158–9). The alliance was buttressed by some significant institutional changes initiated by Park Chung-Hee: concentration of virtually all economic policy-making powers in a super-ministry, the Economic Planning Board (EPB),[3] and restoration of tight government control over the central bank and nationalisation of commercial banks (Haggard *et al.* 1993a: 309–10). These changes not only institutionalised the state's capacity to pursue the growth-first policy, but also endowed economic bureaucrats with powerful and effective policy instruments with which to foster the growth of big industrial firms.

Collusive ties between the authoritarian state and big business were further consolidated with the launch of the Heavy and Chemical Industrialisation (HCI) plan in early 1973. The plan was a calculated move to overcome the political and economic crisis that threatened the continuation of the Park regime (Haggard 1990: 130–2; Koo and Kim 1992: 132–4; Woo 1991: ch. 5). The government selected six strategic industrial sectors: electronics, machinery, non-ferrous metals, petrochemicals, steel and shipbuilding. More than ever before, the Park regime was willing to entrust large enterprises with this ambitious project and to concentrate resources in their hands in order to promote the targeted sectors within a short time frame. Many of these big enterprises had developed into the chaebols in their fullest form and proved their mettle through impressive economic performance during the first decade of the Park regime. They were deemed the most suitable agents to take on heavy and chemical industrial projects that required immense human resources, large capital investment and huge organisational capacity.

To encourage and guide chaebol investments in the strategic sectors, the government made available a variety of policy privileges in the areas of trade, finance and tax. Most importantly, the government earmarked an enormous amount of policy loans garnered through the central bank's rediscounting facilities, the state budget and the National Investment Fund (NIF). Carrying exceedingly low rates with long maturity, these policy loans accounted for between 55 per cent and 70 per cent of the total domestic bank credit in the second half of the 1970s. More than 70 per cent was channelled into the heavy industrial sector, with the chaebols claiming the dominant share since they were assigned to undertake the strategic projects (Nam 1986: 49–50). The government also guaranteed foreign loans for big enterprises in the selected industries. The share of such loans in total foreign loans increased sharply from 32 per cent in 1973 to 80 per cent in 1979 (Choi 1993: 37–8).

Massive state support to the chaebols led to significant changes in the latter's behaviour and market organisation, which further contributed to industrial concentration. To foster the rapid growth of the strategic industrial sectors, the government committed the chaebols to playing a crucial role in these sectors by ensuring long-term subsidised domestic credit and guaranteed foreign loans. When enormous financial resources were concentrated among a few chaebols, the government was actually forced into the lender-of-last-resort role because the bankruptcy of any of these chaebols would have been devastating to the financial system and indeed to the whole economy. To prevent the failure of heavy and chemical projects that claimed a huge amount of credit, the government had no choice but to assume all potential investment risks (Woo 1991: 170–5).

With their financial risks shared by the government, the chaebols became less cautious in undertaking large-scale, capital-intensive projects, and showed more aggression in moving into new lines of business. By the same token, they felt little need to develop reciprocal obligation networks with non-chaebol firms (Kim 2000a; Whitley 1992: 64–84). Capitalising upon excess capacity in financial resources, the chaebols acquired small- and medium-sized firms with which to complete their own production. Such acquisitions allowed them to make a strategic entry into many key industrial sectors and accelerated their vertical integration. Equally important, in the mid-1970s, the government licensed a small number of general trading companies that were all owned by the largest business groups. Designed to operate as the country's export windows, these trading houses quickly came to control domestic distribution and overseas marketing channels at the behest of their chaebol owners (Fields 1995: ch. 6). As a consequence of this high level of self-sufficiency in production and distribution, the chaebols came to dominate most manufacturing sectors and achieved an unchallengeable position in the economy.

The Thai government has had no policy of fostering the growth of large enterprises as selected agents of development strategy. For more than two decades after the overthrow of the absolute monarchy in 1932, the policy of the constitutional government had been an expressed desire for state-led industrialisation. This strategy began to be reversed in 1958, when Sarit Thanarat came to power. In 1961, the government issued the first 5-year plan, making private initiative and investment the centrepiece of its development strategy. Beyond some trade and fiscal incentives, however, it relied little upon the financial system in carrying out the strategy and made no deliberate efforts to foster the growth of big enterprises to deliver rapid industrialisation (Bowie and Unger 1997: 135–9; Doner and Unger 1993).[4] The adoption of this policy was a function of several ideological, economic and institutional factors.

First and foremost, a strong tradition of fiscal and financial conservatism was long established within the core state economic agencies – the Bank of

Thailand and the Finance Ministry. Educated and trained in the Anglo-Saxon tradition of market economics, the first generation of post-war technocrats who headed those two agencies favoured a minimal state role and were antagonistic towards the rent-seeking and monopoly profiteering that might grow out of collusive government–business relations. This ideological orientation bore sharply upon the state's policies concerning the financial market and the growth of private entrepreneurship (Christensen *et al.* 1993: 22–3; Muscat 1995: 118–21). Unlike the Korean government, which nationalised commercial banks and used them as major tools with which to achieve its development goals, the Thai government formally promised in 1962 to leave banks in private hands. While the Korean government supported the growth of big business by providing guaranteed foreign loans, its Thai counterpart has been prevented by laws enacted in 1958 from guaranteeing private-sector debt (Christensen 1992: 23).

Furthermore, the Park regime fused macro-economic and micro-economic policies and brought their management under the control of a few growth-oriented ministries centred in the EPB. This created an institutional framework conducive to the co-ordinated formulation and implementation of industrialisation strategy. In Thailand, by contrast, macro- and micro-policies were largely separated, and few formal institutionalised linkages existed between macro-economic agencies and line ministries. Their relationship, more often than not, was marked by tension and distrust rather than by co-operation and co-ordination, mainly because of different mind-sets, policy objectives and institutional interests (Christensen *et al.* 1993: 19–29). The lack of connection has restricted the scope of policy instruments that sectoral officials can employ to promote the fortunes of private enterprises.

In perhaps the biggest contrast to its counterpart in Korea, the Thai government did not employ credit allocation as a key policy instrument with which to promote industrial development (Muscat 1995). While there were preferential credit arrangements to channel subsidised loans to some sectors of the economy, these never amounted to any significant share of total bank credit. To the small extent that the government operated subsidised credit facilities, i.e. Bank of Thailand (BOT) rediscount operations and loans guaranteed by the Industrial Finance Corporation of Thailand (IFCT), they were mainly directed towards agriculture and small-scale industry. Between 1960 and 1985, more than 60 per cent of BOT rediscounts and over one-half of IFCT loans were granted to agriculture, agribusiness and textile industries, with small- and medium-sized enterprises being the major recipients (Sibunruang 1986: Tables 7 and 9).

Lacking state support in the form of long-term low-interest loans, business ventures in Thailand were mostly financed through private sources. As a result, Thai entrepreneurs were more risk averse than their Korean counterparts and more cautious about venturing into industrial projects that were large in scale, long in payment period and high in capital intensity. By the mid-1980s Thai industrialists had mainly been engaged in labour-intensive manufacturing, which required relatively little investment finance. In many cases, they managed investment risks by pooling financial resources or by setting up joint ventures through personal networks of families and friends. Large enterprises, particularly in the automobile, electronics and textile sectors, normally had stable relations with domestic subcontractors. Similarly, many also relied upon trading houses for managing their input and output markets. As a consequence, Thai industrial manufacturers tended to be more specialised in their own production areas and were consequently smaller in size.

The sectoral differences in industrial organisation between Korea and Thailand are reversed with regard to the financial sector. Table 3.3 shows that the market concentration of banking institutions differs dramatically in the two countries. In terms of asset holdings, the market share of the largest three Thai banks accounts for more than half of the entire banking system, almost doubling the market share of the largest three banks in Korea. In fact, Bangkok Bank, the largest domestic bank in Thailand and also the largest in Southeast Asia, claimed over 30 per cent of the banking sector's total financial assets throughout the 1980s. It is clear that the structure of the banking sector in Thailand is much more oligopolistic than that in Korea.

In Thailand, the high degree of market concentration only partially reflects the organisational structure of the banking industry. Equally important are the ownership links between commercial banks and the major Sino-Thai banking families. Until June 1992, Thai banking laws stipulated that local commercial banks should have at least 250 shareholders and that no individual, other than a government agency, could own more than 5 per cent of total shares outstanding (Tara Siam 1994a: 70). Notwithstanding this, the ownership of most commercial banks, with the exception of the Krung Thai Bank and the Siam Commercial Bank, was centralised in the hands of a few banking families. By the end of 1995, their control of equity shares in each of these banks ranged from 20 per cent to 44 per cent (*Asiamoney* March 1996: 40–50). In Korea, by contrast, the government had been the dominant shareholder in all nationwide commercial banks before they were privatised in the early 1980s.

These differences in the banking sector's organisational structure in the two countries can mainly be attributed to the divergent government policies towards financial development. Under Japanese rule (1910–45), Korea had a

*Table 3.3* Deposit money bank concentration ratios (percentages), 1980–90

|  | Korea | | | Thailand | | |
|---|---|---|---|---|---|---|
|  | *1980* | *1985* | *1990* | *1980* | *1985* | *1990* |
| Share of the largest three banks | 34.0 | 33.9 | 29.9 | 54.3 | 53.7 | 51.6 |
| Share of the largest six banks | 61.3 | 60.3 | 54.5 | 70.3 | 70.3 | 70.2 |

Sources: for Korea, Bank of Korea (*Annual Report,* various issues), Bank of Korea (*Money and Banking Statistics,* various issues) and Bank of Korea (*Financial System in Korea,* 1983, 1985, 1990, 1995); for Thailand, Bank of Thailand (*Annual Report,* various issues), Bangkok Bank (*Bangkok Bank Monthly Review,* various issues) and Vichyanond (1994).

number of fairly modern and specialised banking institutions that were mostly owned and controlled by the Japanese. When the Second World War ended, these banking institutions were initially taken over by the US government and then transferred to the Korean government in 1948. The immediate post-war period witnessed a severe decline of the banking system because of rampant inflation and the disruption of production and trade that followed the division of the country (Bloomfield and Jensen 1963: ch. 3).

To renovate the banking system, the government planned to privatise commercial banks in 1950, but that plan was derailed by the outbreak of the Korean War. Although the privatisation programme was eventually implemented, the growth of commercial banks was constrained by the eroding effects of high inflation in the wake of the war. Furthermore, the privatised banks were subjected to political interference by the Rhee regime, which mandated low-interest loans to import-substituting industries and used the rents generated by those loans to finance its political activities. Finally, development of the commercial banking sector was hindered by the government's decision to establish the Korea Development Bank (KDB) and the Agriculture Bank as part of its programme of economic reconstruction. During the second half of the 1950s, these two state-owned banks, particularly the KDB, assumed a dominant position in the banking sector while the role of commercial banks was substantially weakened (Cole and Park 1983: 52–4).

On assuming power, the Park regime immediately renationalised the commercial banks in support of its economic development plans. In order to allocate financial resources to strategic sectors, the government not only took control of the existing banks but opened the door to the creation of new institutions. During 1961–67, six specialised banks were established. Between 1967 and 1971, ten local banks, one for each province, were chartered for the purpose of promoting regional development. At the same time, foreign bank branches were allowed in to facilitate foreign capital inflows. Since the government showed no hesitation in creating new banking institutions to carry out its ambitious industrialisation policy, commercial banks found it difficult to achieve dominance in the banking sector. Although they grew more rapidly in the 1960s and 1970s than in the 1950s, commercial banks constantly lost ground to new institutions, particularly the specialised banks [Bank of Korea (BOK) 1995: 33–4; *The Korea Times* (*KT*) 2 September 1986].

Before the outbreak of the Second World War, the Thai banking sector had been dominated by foreign banks: of the twelve banks that conducted business in Thailand, seven were foreign, mostly European, owned. Local banks, with the possible exception of the Siam Commercial Bank, operated on a limited basis and were mainly confined to trade financing. During the war, the Japanese disbanded European banks. Many local entrepreneurs seized upon the vacuum left by European bankers, transferred their capital away from trade and manufacturing and commenced banking operations. As a consequence, eight local commercial banks, mostly of Chinese origins, were incorporated in the 1940s, and ten out of the fifteen domestic banks emerged during that decade (Tara Siam 1994a: 66).

During the following two decades, Thai commercial banks grew rapidly and formed the core of five large Sino-Thai banking groups led by the Bangkok Bank, the Bank of Ayudhya, the Thai Farmers' Bank, the Bangkok Metropolitan Bank and the Union Bank of Bangkok. Their spectacular growth was the result, in the first instance, of the stable macro-economic environment. Particularly important in this respect was the ability of leading financial technocrats to bring the inflation that had been caused by war quickly under control in the early 1950s, and to pursue price stability effectively for much of the post-war period. Furthermore, the major banking groups forged close links with military leaders, relying upon them for political patronage, especially in the 1950s and 1960s. Detailed studies have shown that banks invited these patrons to sit on their boards of directors and offered them free stock in exchange for protection and policy favours (Choonhavan 1984; Hewison 1981, 1989: ch. 6; Suehiro 1989: 245–64). Commercial banks also benefited from the extensive Chinese-dominated business networks in Thailand and across the other economic centres of Southeast Asia. These connections helped Thai bankers to mobilise savings, build commercial alliances and explore new markets (Hewison 1988; Phongpaichit and Baker 1995: 130–2; Suehiro 1993: 45).

Economic factors and socio-political networks aside, it was in the role of the state that the Thai banking sector found its major source of growth and increased concentration. The oligopolistic structure of the Thai banking sector resulted primarily from the state's own policy that severely limited the number of domestic banking institutions and foreign bank branches. To the modest degree that the government did establish new banking institutions, they were highly specialised and often barred from engaging in commercial banking business. This policy reflected both the easy-going approach to industrialisation and the tradition of financial conservatism: money and credit policies would be easier to manage if the banking sector had only a few players.

### *Differences in inter-corporate relations*

Preference aggregation and articulation are also conditioned by the organisational structures of collective action at the cross-sector level. Cross-sector organisational structures, as reflected in inter-corporate relations, take the form of bank/NBFI lending to industry, finance and industry holdings of each other's equities or interlocking directorates. This subsection examines how these inter-corporate relations differ between Korea and Thailand.

Table 3.4 shows that loans outstanding to the manufacturing sector in Korea constantly represented about 45 per cent of total bank loans for almost three decades until the late 1980s. Also, the exposure of Korean banks to the manufacturing sector was roughly three times that of Thai banks before the early 1980s. Equally significant, bank lending was heavily concentrated in big business groups. In 1986, the thirty largest chaebols claimed more than 30 per cent of total bank loans, although that share declined to 20 per cent in 1991 (Sang-Woo Nam 1995: 6–7).

*Table 3.4*  Bank loans to manufacturing (percentage of total bank loans), selected
years

| Korea | *1960* | *1965* | *1970* | *1975* | *1980* | *1985* | *1990* |
|---|---|---|---|---|---|---|---|
| | 38.7 | 40.9 | 45.8 | 57.1 | 54.1 | 43.3 | 42.0 |
| Thailand | *1958* | *1966* | *1974* | *1979* | *1983* | *1988* | *1990* |
| | 10.1 | 16.3 | 18.5 | 17.3 | 21.5 | 25.8 | 25.1 |

Sources: Bank of Korea (*Monthly Bulletin,* various issues) and Bangkok Bank (*Commercial Banks in Thailand*, various issues).

Heavy bank lending to the manufacturing sector, particularly to the chaebols, signified the Korean government's strong commitment to rapid industrial development, as noted earlier. This was also related to the limited extent of domestic capital accumulation in Korea prior to the 1950s. During Japanese colonial rule, economic growth and industrial changes were designed to meet the colonialists' needs, and were largely unrelated to the traditional Korean economy. Large and modern enterprises did exist but were mostly owned and operated by the Japanese. By the early 1940s, colonial ownership constituted over 80 per cent of the paid-up capital of most light industries and more than 95 per cent of heavy and chemical industries (Kim and Roemer 1979: Table 8).

Furthermore, the division of the country that followed the Japanese surrender deprived the South of much of what had been left over by the occupiers, especially in heavy and chemical industries; the ensuing Korean War destroyed almost half the manufacturing facilities that existed in the late 1940s (Kim and Roemer 1979: 33). In such a devastated economic situation, Korean entrepreneurs, who had limited private capital but were entrusted with powerful industrial push, had to rely on substantial external funds. The fact that the stock and other long-term capital markets remained thin and undeveloped until the 1980s resulted in bank credit becoming the major source of industrial financing.

From the early 1980s, in addition to heavy lending to industry, Korean banks began to acquire corporate shares in the manufacturing sector as institutional investors, mainly in chaebol firms. This was encouraged by the government with a view to easing the economic concentration in the hands of a few family-controlled chaebols and to urging these industrial giants to reduce their reliance upon indirect financing. By the early 1990s, the leading nationwide commercial banks owned about 15 per cent of the total shares of chaebol firms (interviews, Seoul, 23 May and 21 July 1997). Heavy lending and considerable holdings of corporate shares naturally made Korean banks develop direct stakes in large manufacturing firms; the soundness of their assets and capital base as well as their investment incomes were contingent upon the performance and fortunes of those firms.

Industry holdings of shares in Korean commercial banks and NBFIs show a different pattern. When government-owned commercial banks were privatised in the early 1980s, there was great concern that big business groups would take control of these banks and turn them into their private coffers. In 1982, the Korean government imposed an 8 per cent limit on the equity shares of a commercial bank that any single shareholder was permitted to own. That limit was tightened to 4 per cent in early 1995. Mainly because of these restrictions, the number of large chaebol firms with shares of over 1 per cent in any of the leading commercial banks fell from nineteen in 1986 to eight in 1994 [*Business Korea (BK)* October 1994: 23; Nam 1994a: 217]. Similarly, average shareholdings by the largest shareholders in each of the six biggest commercial banks dropped from 8.7 per cent in 1986 to 5.8 per cent in 1989 (Nam 1994a: 218).

Other than in the case of commercial banks, no restrictions were imposed on the proportion of equity shares that any shareholders were allowed to own in NBFIs. This enabled the chaebols to acquire prominent blocks of shares in, and extensive ownership of, NBFIs. In 1990, the chaebols owned 63 per cent of securities houses, 42 per cent of insurance companies, 30 per cent of finance firms and 23 per cent of merchant banking corporations (Sang-Woo Nam 1995: 56). Most NBFIs were created in the early 1970s as part of government efforts to divert unorganised curb-market funds into the organised financial market. Allowed to apply higher interest rates and greater managerial and operational autonomy, NBFIs witnessed rapid growth and began to overtake banking institutions in deposit taking and loan allocation in the mid-1980s (BOK 1995: 4). Most NBFIs were actually subsidiaries of the chaebols, and their policy behaviour and preferences were thus heavily influenced by their industrial owners.

Korean commercial banks, by contrast, were not well connected with the NBFI sector in terms of equity investment. In the early 1990s, only 7–10 per cent of the total outstanding NBFI shares was estimated to be owned by nationwide commercial banks (interviews, Seoul, 13 June and 21 July 1997). This was mainly due to two factors. First, commercial banks did not enter the NBFI sector in any significant way until they were privatised in the mid-1980s and government control over their operations was somewhat relaxed. More than 70 per cent of commercial bank-affiliated NBFIs were established after 1985 (BOK 1997: Appendix 2). Second, banks appeared to be unwilling to acquire shares in chaebol-controlled NBFIs. If they wanted to invest in the sector, they preferred to set up their own firms. In early 1997, of all NBFIs in which commercial banks held equity shares, more than 60 per cent were wholly bank owned (BOK 1997: Appendix 2).

All this clearly reveals close but asymmetrical relations between big industrialists and private financiers in Korea. While the latter depend on chaebol firms for the quality of their asset portfolios and capital base because of their heavy lending and holdings of corporate equities, the former are less interested in the performance and profitability of banking institutions, in which they have insignificant and decreasing shareholdings. Close bank–industry ties are also reflected in the fact that not only are almost all banking institutions members of the Federation of Korean Industries (FKI), the peak organisation representing chaebol interests, but there are frequent and formal contacts and consultations between the FKI and the Korea Federation of Banks (KFB). During these interactions, however, it has almost invariably been the FKI and its chaebol members, rather than the KFB, that has held sway over the process of interest aggregation and policy deliberations (interviews, Seoul, 10 and 14 July 1997).

Thai commercial banks have generally maintained an arm's-length relationship with the manufacturing sector, as shown in Table 3.4. For much of the post-war period, banks were largely involved in short-term trade financing rather than in long-term industrial financing. Between the late 1950s and late 1970s, foreign trade accounted for 29–37 per cent of commercial bank credit (Bangkok Bank, *Commercial Banks in Thailand* 1991). Although many Thai banking groups diversified into various industrial sectors in the 1960s and 1970s, they normally established wholly owned manufacturing subsidiaries rather than acquired equity shares in existing firms or non-financial conglomerates.

Thai industrialists appeared to have less need for large amounts of investment finance. They borrowed from commercial banks for the limited purposes of short-term working capital. This partly reflected the fact that Thai economic growth, before the late 1970s, was based upon agriculture and that industrial development was centred on light and agribusiness sectors, as noted earlier. Furthermore, Thai industry's lower dependency upon bank credit resulted from the mode of private capital accumulation prior to the 1950s. Many local industrialists had engaged in long-standing and consistently profitable agro-trade and other commercial activities before commencing manufacturing operations. Internal funds became the major source of finance when Thai manufacturers later embarked upon industrial expansion. Rozental (1970: Table 7.7) showed that in the mid-1960s nearly 90 per cent of initial capital came from internal enterprise sources. Chuansomsook (1983: 31) notes that industrialists' own savings made up 76 per cent of industrial financing in the late 1970s. Finally, industrial dependence on banks was further lessened by easier access to foreign capital, owing to Thailand's relatively liberal foreign exchange regime (Choonhavan 1984).

Relations between Thai bankers and industrialists underwent an important change in the 1970s, when the economy began to switch to a manufactured export-led strategy. While their links with the manufacturing sector as a whole remained limited, commercial banks developed closer ties with some mainly export-oriented industrial sectors, starting with textiles and agribusiness and proceeding to electronics and automobiles. Throughout the 1980s, these industries claimed more than half of the bank loans to the entire manufacturing sector (interviews, Bangkok, 24 January and 18 April 1997). The rapid growth of some Thai industrial conglomerates, such as the Sukree and Saha Union groups in the textile industry, the CP group in agribusiness and Siam Motors, was the result of their close ties with leading commercial banks (Suehiro 1993).

It should be noted, however, that this change has not remoulded the basic pattern of inter-corporate ties in Thailand. In terms of credit allocation or equity investment, bank–industry ties in Thailand have never been as close as those in Korea. Thai banks have generally been reluctant to commit financial resources to large-scale, capital-intensive investment projects. On the other hand, most manufacturers have remained largely dependent upon private capital or equity rather than debt for long-term finance. In a mirror image of this generally distant bank–industry relationship, there have been no formal institutionalised links between the Thai Bankers' Association (TBA) and the Federation of Thai Industries (FTI) – the business organisations that represent the interests of bankers and manufacturers respectively. The TBA normally did not consult its industrial counterpart when formulating its response to changes in government policies (interviews, Bangkok, 25 March and 9 May 1997).

Finally, many NBFIs are affiliated with commercial banks – another important dissimilarity to Korea, where the NBFI sector is largely controlled by the chaebols. Most importantly, Thai commercial banks have extensive ownership linkages with finance and security companies, the major category of NBFIs in Thailand. By the end of 1993, forty-two out of ninety-one finance and security companies were bank affiliates (Tara Siam 1994b: 80). In addition, banks owned the ten largest finance and security companies, which accounted for 43 per cent of the sector's total assets (Tara Siam 1994a: 50). Bank control has also been extended to other categories of NBFIs: five of the eleven life insurance companies and twenty out of the sixty non-life insurance companies are affiliated with local commercial banks; leading banks hold significant stakes in most leasing and factoring companies; and almost all Thailand's mutual fund management companies are in the hands of private bankers (Tara Siam 1994a: 52–60).

## Central bank–government relations

This section examines how Korea and Thailand differ with respect to central bank–government relations or the degree of central bank independence. As the degree of central bank independence has a significant impact upon the nature and direction of financial reform, it is essential that the balance of authority over financial policy between central banks and governments within Korea and Thailand be carefully compared. To achieve greater precision in measuring and comparing the degree of central bank independence, this study adopts a two-step approach, following Goodman (1992) and Elgie and Thompson (1998). The authority of the Korean and Thai central banks – the Bank of Korea (BOK) and the Bank of Thailand (BOT) respectively – over financial policy-making *vis-à-vis* governments and politicians is first assessed by using legal and formal measures. To supplement formal measurement, the important informal aspects of central bank independence will then be reviewed by tracing the evolution of the BOK and the BOT.

## Legal and formal dimensions

The BOK was created in June 1950 as part of the government's efforts to encourage institutional innovation and economic rehabilitation in the immediate post-war period. The Bank of Korea Act, which established the BOK, stipulated that the supreme authority in domestic and foreign monetary policies resided in the Monetary Board of the new central bank (BOK Act 1950: Article 5). In theory, the Board was vested with wide-ranging powers over the basic policies, management and administration of the BOK and was responsible for the general direction and supervision of the financial system as a whole. From its inception, however, the Monetary Board failed to become established as the centre of real financial policy-making and the BOK was unable to fully perform its proper functions, as provided in the original central bank law.

The BOK's authority over monetary management was drastically reduced and government influence was greatly strengthened by the amendment of the Central Bank Act in 1962.[5] With its enactment, much of the policy power originally assigned to the BOK was revoked, the dominant position of the finance minister as chairman of the Monetary Board was established and the government's ultimate responsibility for both domestic and foreign monetary policies was ordained. Most critically, the amended Act empowered the finance minister to request reconsideration of resolutions previously adopted by the Monetary Board; if that request was rejected by the Board with a two-thirds majority, the final decision would be made by cabinet (BOK Act 1982: Article 39). Since the finance minister's view would be ensured a hearing in cabinet, and would be endorsed by the government, this was tantamount to saying that the minister had the final say in the policy deliberations of the Board (Kim 1965: 75–90).

The BOT was established in 1942 under the Bank of Thailand Act and the Royal Decree Regulating the Affairs of the Bank of Thailand. The BOT Act emphasised that 'the general control and superintendence of the affairs of the Bank of Thailand shall be entrusted to a Court of Directors consisting of the governor, the deputy governor, and not less than five other members' (BOT Act: Section 15). The Court, of which the governor and deputy governor were *ex officio* chairman and vice-chairman respectively, not only established key monetary and credit policies but also set basic guidelines for the administration of the central bank (BOT Act: Section 15; Royal Decree: ch. 1). The stipulation actually guaranteed the governor's power and influence over the policy-making process and management of the BOT.

In this subsection, the degree of central bank independence in Korea and Thailand is compared along six legal and formal dimensions: (1) the final policy goals of the central bank; (2) the procedures for appointing and dismissing senior central bank officials; (3) the extent to which the central bank is subject to executive or legislative control over its budgets; (4) responsibility for monetary management; (5) the authority to supervise financial institutions; and (6) the restrictions on central bank financing of government deficits. While the first three dimensions measure the degree of political independence, the remainder form an indicator of economic independence (Elgie and Thompson 1998: 24–6; Grilli *et al.* 1991: 366–70).

*Political independence*

BOK legislation stipulated the maintenance of domestic monetary stability as one purpose of the central bank, but it also set another objective for promoting economic development (BOK Act 1982: Article 3). It is clear that these two objectives contain potential conflict within themselves. As will be shown below, the conflicting policy objectives mainly reflect a widely held belief among political elites, especially after the military government came to power in May 1961, that the main aim of financial policy was to raise the level of production and that maintaining price stability was relevant only when it could facilitate the attainment of development goals (Kim 1965: 16). From the early 1960s, as the financial system was consistently used as an instrument for achieving economic growth, the BOK was unable to formulate its own independent policy objective and to give priority to price stability.

Monetary stability has always been declared the primary objective of the BOT, although it was not explicitly stipulated in the original BOT legislation. 'Stability of the value of the baht is the basis for national reconstruction and development,' Prince Viwatanajai, the first BOT governor, once observed. 'To maintain monetary stability therefore represents one of the most important tasks of the central bank' (BOT 1992: 165). The ability of the Thai central bank to pursue price stability was also secured by the relevant national law. In Section 12 of Thailand's Currency Reserve Act of 1985, there was a clear provision on note issue which required the BOT to maintain currency reserve assets in liquid form for an amount not less than 60 per cent of the total notes issued.

The political independence of the BOK was further weakened by the largely unrestrained appointive and dismissal authority on the part of the government. The BOK governor was appointed by the president for a 4-year term, on the recommendation of the finance minister. On the advice of the governor, the Monetary Board appointed the deputy governor and assistant governors for 3-year terms. The auditor, responsible for inspecting BOK operations, was appointed by the finance minister. Although appointed for fixed terms of office, BOK governors could be dismissed arbitrarily by the government. This is amply evidenced in the fact that, in the BOK's history throughout 1995, only four out of nineteen former governors were able to finish their full terms of office and the average tenure of BOK governors was just over 2 years. The ability of the government to exercise this dismissal authority was an important source of leverage over the central bank.

The governor and deputy governor of the BOT were appointed by the Crown on the advice of the government. The auditors, tasked with examining the books and balance sheets of the BOT, were appointed by the Court of Directors.

Although there was no fixed term for the BOT governor, the government did not appear to take advantage of this lacuna in BOT legislation to exercise its dismissal authority at random. While there was no lack of examples in which BOT governors resigned over policy disputes or other matters, short terms tended to be anomalous. In exceptional instances, such as when the incumbent governor approached the mandatory retirement age, the average length of service of BOT governors was more than 4 years, doubling the average tenure of BOK governors.

The political subordination of the BOK was finally sealed by the broad supervisory authority over it that was granted to the government – in particular, to the Finance Ministry. Under the amended Act of 1982, the authority to appoint the auditor responsible for auditing BOK operations was removed from the Monetary Board and vested in the Finance Ministry (BOK Act 1982: Article 23). Through this appointive power, the finance minister could thus inspect the BOK's affairs and supervise all its operations. Equally important, the central bank was made subject to detailed examination by the finance minister at least once a year and its annual budget had to be approved by cabinet (BOK Act 1982: Articles 7 and 40) – the key provisions that established complete government control and domination over the BOK.

In this final dimension of political status, the BOT also had a stronger position relative to its Korean counterpart. While the BOK was dependent upon government approval of its expenses, BOT budgets were totally separate from government budgets and were not subject to approval by the executive or legislative bodies. BOT budgets and the remuneration of its staff fell under the purview of the Court of Directors but not under the Civil Service Act. This placed the BOT outside normal bureaucratic control and granted it considerable autonomy in its activities (Silcock 1967: 185–90; Unger 1993: 74–5). Equally important, the Royal Decree prescribed that the Court-appointed auditors inspected books, accounts and other documents of the BOT, although they might have to report to the finance minister upon inspection.

*Economic independence*

In the financial policy-making process, it became established practice that the BOK could not act upon the discount rate without the explicit prior approval of the Finance Ministry (the following account draws on author interviews, Seoul, 5 June and 4 September 1997). Changes in minimum reserve requirements also required the consent of the finance minister. Open market operations, insignificant until the early 1980s, were not conducted wholly at the discretion of the BOK – the finance minister's approval was necessary. Moreover, the government had fixed interest rates on deposits and loans of banking institutions before the launch of interest rate reform in the late 1980s. The Finance Ministry often gave detailed instructions to the major commercial and development banks in credit allocation.

The original central bank law granted the BOK full responsibility for formulating foreign exchange policy. With the enactment of the Foreign Exchange Management Act (FEMA) in 1961, however, this function was transferred to the Finance Ministry. The BOK managed the country's international reserves and intervened in the foreign exchange market under the general guidance of the finance minister. Furthermore, control over capital movements was legally established under the Foreign Capital Inducement Act (FCIA) of 1961. The principal agency responsible for enforcing the FCIA was the Foreign Capital Deliberation Committee (FCDC), headed by the finance minister. The EPB and the Trade and Industry Ministry also had influence over general policy regarding capital controls, via their participation in the FCDC (Mardon 1990: 116–18).

Unlike the BOK, the BOT firmly controlled the three primary indirect measures of regulating monetary conditions in the economy – discount rate, open market operations and legal reserve requirements (interviews, Bangkok, 18 December 1996 and 21 March 1997). Before the late 1980s, the BOT had also exercised monetary management through the use of direct policy instruments. It set interest rate ceilings on deposits and loans of banks and finance companies through co-ordination with the Finance Ministry. Credit planning, which determined the overall growth and sectoral allocation of bank credits, was conducted completely at the discretion of the BOT. With the onset of financial liberalisation, these direct means of monetary control gradually became disused.

Just as the BOK was unable to exercise major monetary policy instruments without the explicit endorsement of the government, it was not granted the independent authority over financial regulation. The BOK Act and the General Banking Act specified that the Supervision and Examination Department of the BOK, subject to instructions of the Monetary Board, was responsible for inspecting and regulating banking institutions. As the Finance Ministry dominated the policy agenda of the Monetary Board, however, the BOK exercised these functions in the shadow of the government. More importantly, the development and specialised banks operated outside the control of the BOK but within the jurisdiction of the Finance Ministry.

When the BOT was established, its responsibility for bank supervision, as defined in the BOT Act and the Royal Decree, was confined to determining cash reserve ratio and to examining reports on assets and liabilities which commercial banks were required to submit to the governor. With the enactment of the amended Commercial Banking Act in 1962, most inspection and examination functions previously performed by the Finance Ministry were transferred to the BOT. This transfer of supervisory authority was brought about by the growing complexity of the financial system and, more importantly, by recognition of the policy expertise and integrity of leading BOT technocrats. Furthermore, the Act on the Undertaking of Finance Business, Security Business, and Credit Foncier Business of 1979, and its subsequently amended versions, also placed finance companies under surveillance by the BOT.

Finally, the BOK's economic independence was undermined by the weak and vague legal restrictions on the financing of government deficits. It extended credit to the government in the form of loans or the direct purchase of government bonds. Neither the original nor the amended BOK legislation, however, set limits on the amount of loans and government bonds that the BOK could extend and underwrite. Article 83 of the BOK Act merely provided that the aggregate of all such loans and the direct purchase of government bonds at any time should not exceed the amount of indebtedness which, together with any borrowings by the government from other sources, was duly authorised by the National Assembly. The government appears to have never been bound by this vaguely worded provision because, for much of the post-war period, the National Assembly was unable to exercise this authority to ratify total borrowings by the government and remained largely passive in the budgeting process.

BOT legislation sets explicit limits on the extension of credit to the government. The Royal Decree (Section 12) stipulates that the government may borrow from the central bank in the form of loans and advances to an amount not exceeding 25 per cent of budgeted expenditure, subject to repayment within the first quarter of the following fiscal year. An inter-ministerial agreement between the Finance Ministry and the BOT signed in 1964 set out another strict condition for government borrowing, requiring that such borrowing, both domestic and foreign, should not exceed 13 per cent of total government revenues in any fiscal year (BOT 1992: 204). From the early 1960s, the BOT made consistent efforts to reduce direct lending in the form of loans and advances; a preferred means of financing public spending was through the purchase of treasury bills and government bonds.[6]

### The origin and evolution of the BOK and the BOT

In Korea, a central banking system came into existence during Japanese colonial rule. The Dai-ichi Ginko, an ordinary Japanese bank that had commenced its operations in Korea during the late nineteenth century, was granted the privilege of issuing bank notes, thus becoming a *de facto* central bank for Korea (Ireland 1926: 279–81, 294–5). The Dai-ichi Ginko acted as the central bank until 1909, when its functions were transferred to the newly established Bank of Korea, which was renamed the Bank of Chosen in 1911. Since its establishment, the Bank of Chosen had been in the firm grip of the colonial state and served the financial needs of its imperial expansion in the Russian Far East and China (Grajdanzev 1944: 201–2; Woo 1991: 27–8). Under the circumstances, it could hardly play its role of monetary control in Korea. Some central banking functions were transferred to the Industrial Bank of Chosen. Established and controlled by the colonial administration, the Industrial Bank became the key financial organ for mobilising savings and channelling them into the war effort during the 1930s (Cole and Park 1983: 46). During the last two decades of Japanese rule, the bank played a pivotal role in the colonial state's attempts to push through rapid industrial development in Korea, with the express purpose of turning the colony into 'a base of penetration and war supplies' (Eckert 1991: 87–8).

This legacy of the state's subjugating and deploying the central banking system to its own financial needs and policy interests seems to have been bequeathed to the new government of independent Korea. Woo (1991: 29) notes that many Koreans who had served with the Bank of Chosen and the Industrial Bank went on to take key economic and financial positions in the Korean government. The *modus operandi* of the colonial central banking system inevitably had a sharp impact on the mind-set of these government officials and set an inexorable example for them to follow. This helped to create an ideological environment in the economic bureaucracy that was hostile to the idea of central bank independence. Equally important, the institutional structure that had ordained state control over the central bank, and indeed over the whole banking system, was well suited to serve the economic needs and political interests of state elites.

On the surrender of the Japanese, the new government easily brought the Bank of Chosen under its tight control as the bank had never been an independent institution in the colonial central banking traditions. The Finance Ministry quickly assumed absolute authority over almost every aspect of financial policy-making, leaving the central bank on the sidelines. The finance minister dominated the overall formulation of monetary and credit policies, approved all individual loans over a certain amount, controlled the appointment of most bank directors and officers and exercised powers of bank supervision and examination (Bloomfield 1952: 21–2). The role of the Bank of Chosen in the monetary policy-making process was thus minimal and was mainly concerned with financing government deficits.

During the late 1940s, spiralling inflation, inflamed by dislocation of pro-duction and trade and growing government deficits, devastated the financial system and wreaked havoc with the national economy. In the midst of the crisis, Arthur Bloomfield and John Jensen, two economists from the US Fed-eral Reserve System, were sent in early 1950 to work out a financial reform programme in collaboration with Korean officials. The major intention of this reform programme was to transform the Bank of Chosen into a strong, autonomous central bank (Bloomfield and Jensen 1963: 43–4). It should be noted that this central bank reform was merely political expediency on the part of the government in the face of American pressure and the deteriorating financial situation rather than any change in its basic attitude towards the role and position of the central bank.

During the Korean War, the independent status of the BOK, as laid down in the new central bank legislation, was severely compromised. The BOK was forced to finance the government's war efforts on a massive basis as internal revenue sources disappeared. Despite the principle of an autonomous central bank provided in the new charter, the government exercised *de facto* authority over the BOK from its inception. The central banking system that had been mobilised for the war was redirected towards rehabilitating and reconstructing the war-devastated economy, with the BOK essentially subordinated to the dictates of the state. The central bank played a passive role in real financial policy-making and remained scarcely more than a funding source for government debt financing. During the period 1950–62, borrowings from the BOK accounted for a maximum of 97 per cent and a minimum of 85 per cent of total financing of government debt (Kim 1965: 105).

The financial needs and political interests of the Syngman Rhee regime also accentuated the importance of government control over the central bank. To draw the BOK tightly into the orbit of government control was central to the system of selective credit allocation applied to foster the growth of big business and to pursue import-substituting industrialisation policy. To authorise long-term lending for industrial investment, the government manipulated the existing banks or established new development institutions such as the Korea Development Bank and the Korea Agriculture Bank. The solvent capacity of these banks, however, was always precarious because of their extremely fragile capital base and the highly illiquid structure of their assets. They depended heavily upon the BOK for loanable funds, and the central bank itself thus became the crucial source of industrial financing (Kim 1994).

The Park military regime revised central bank legislation shortly after it came to power in May 1961. Largely in recognition of the actual situation, the legislative changes eventually scrapped the facade of a nominally independent BOK and brought it unequivocally under government control. Park and many of his technocrats were deeply impressed by the organisational leadership provided by the Japanese state in controlling and mobilising the central bank and the financial system for the modernisation of the economy, ever since the Meiji Restoration. The way in which the Industrial Bank of Chosen had been harnessed to the heavy industrialisation drive in Korea in the 1930s remained fresh in their memories. This reinforced a deep-rooted belief among the top political leadership that the primary function of the central bank was to facilitate and finance economic development, and that ultimate responsibility for financial policy, which was so crucial to the attainment of development goals, should lie squarely with the government.

Furthermore, Park explicitly made rapid economic growth his regime's top priority, both as an end in itself and as a means with which to achieve political legitimacy. Throughout the two decades of Park's rule, the issue of political legitimacy was linked inextricably to the fate of the national economy. The fate of the national economy, at least as viewed by Park and his associates, depended upon how successfully the government was able to mobilise financial resources and channel them to selected industrial sectors and chaebol firms. Granting independence to the BOK would have meant surrendering control over financial policies – the central instrument in the overall industrialisation strategy of the Korean state. Although employed in some way in the 1950s, the central banking system was used by the Park government in the 1960s and 1970s with greater intensity to provide low-cost funds to commercial and specialised banks in support of their long-term lending operations.

From the early 1960s onwards, the BOK exercised its monetary management functions entirely within the policy parameters set by the government. Although frequent consultations were held among the BOK, the EPB and the Finance Ministry, the BOK was quite passive in the monetary policy-making process and was almost relegated to the status of a rubber stamp for government decisions. There is ample evidence that important policy measures were formulated under the leadership of the finance minister, the EPB head and the senior economic advisor to the president, to the complete exclusion of the BOK governor. For instance, in June 1962, the BOK governor was not apprised of the decision until the last moment when the government carried out a reform of the won currency (*BK* September 1987: 28). On another important occasion, the central bank had not even been consulted before the Presidential Emergency Decree for freezing loans on the informal or curb market was announced in August 1972 (Ro 1993: 19).

The subordinate status of the BOK also reflected the economic interests of the private sector centred around big chaebol firms. As mentioned earlier in this chapter, private sources of capital were scarce and the financial position of Korean industrialists was fragile in the early post-war period. When the government decided to promote rapid industrial development but could not afford to wait for the slow process of private capital accumulation, it had to encourage firms to borrow heavily. Heavy reliance upon borrowed funds caused big industrialists actively to champion low interest rates, preferential bank credit and loose monetary policy. They therefore had a direct stake in having a subservient central bank that was compliant with the industrial policy objectives of the government (Maxfield 1994). In the 1950s, private economic interests succeeded in penetrating the Rhee administration because of collusive government–business relations. Even during the apparent state dominance of the 1960s and 1970s, the 'sword–won' coalition forged by the Park regime to deliver rapid economic growth made it difficult for the state to ignore the needs and demands of chaebol firms.

From the mid-1980s, capitalising on popular clamour for price stability and on the intensifying trend towards economic democratisation, the BOK began to push for greater policy-making autonomy. In 1987 and again in 1993, all presidential candidates pledged to amend central bank legislation in order to make the BOK more independent. These campaign pledges, however, proved to be empty promises. The long-standing ideological bias for a state-control-led financial system mobilised to spur industrial development was so deeply rooted in the official policy-making process that the notion of central bank independence was still anathema to the government. In the mean time, the Finance Ministry closely guarded its bureaucratic turf and was reluctant to surrender any of its policy power to the BOK.

Following the financial crisis in late 1997, the Korean government moved to grant the BOK more policy-making power. This was not so much because the government realised the crucial importance to financial health of a strong central bank as because central banking reform was an essential part of the International Monetary Fund (IMF)-mandated lending agreement. Facing the danger of national bankruptcy, the government had little alternative but to comply with the policy prescriptions of the Bretton Woods institutions in return for the desperately needed money. Important legislative amendments to BOK law made the governor chairman of the Monetary Board and revoked the right of the finance minister to request reconsideration of resolutions adopted by the Board. These amendments are, however, not expected to quickly change the long-established relationship between the BOK and the government. The powerful Ministry of Finance and Economy still exercises dominant authority over broad macro-economic issues, including domestic and foreign financial policies.

In Thailand, the institutional and ideological origins of the central bank can be traced back to the effects of neo-colonialism and the concomitant politics of national state formation in the late nineteenth and the early twentieth centuries (Samudavanija 1971: 22–37). Facing the imminent threat of European territorial expansion in the mid-1800s, King Chulalongkorn, the fifth monarch of the present dynasty, launched far-reaching administrative and financial reforms in an attempt to maintain internal peace and stability and to defend the existence of Thailand as a sovereign polity. As an important result of these reforms, the Finance Ministry was established in 1890. The power of the Ministry was greatly strengthened in the following decades, during which important legal and institutional changes placed the administration of all government revenue and expenditure under its direct authority (Brown 1975: 319–24). This structure of financial administration centralised in a powerful treasury was continued by the constitutional regime after 1932.

Not only did external factors lead to the creation of a centralised structure of financial policy management, but they also helped to encourage strong preferences for orthodox monetary and fiscal policies among state elites during the period of King Chulalongkorn's reign and beyond. Such preferences stemmed primarily from the determination of the government to preserve national independence in the face of the external threat. Cautious, conservative macro-economic policies were determinedly pursued to preclude any possibility that foreign powers could use financial instability as a pretext for usurping Thailand's sovereignty. The highest priority was therefore given to the strict balancing of government budgets and to the maintenance of high reserve levels to support the baht and to ensure the government's ability to cover its foreign debt obligations (Ingram 1955: ch. 7; Silcock 1967: 174–8).

The economic interests of state elites also reinforced the conservative inclinations of Thai financial policy. The stability of the baht and the soundness of government finance were highly desirable if Thailand was to encourage the development of foreign trade, raise foreign loans and import capital goods essential for its public works projects. Finally, British financial advisors advocated adopting the orthodox financial stance. This was mainly because they viewed an economically stable Thailand as the best guarantee of Britain's trade and investment interests in the country and, more importantly, as an effective buffer between its own and French colonies in Southeast Asia, thus obviating potential military conflict with each other (Ingram 1955: 173). Those financial advisors who had been engaged to advise on economic affairs since the early years of King Chulalongkorn's reign had an influential position in the government and continued to exert influence until well into the constitutional regime.

Similarly to the Finance Ministry, which had been set up in the face of European threats, the BOT was created to protect the country's economic independence against Japanese encroachment. Thailand allied itself with Japan during the Second World War when invasion by Japanese forces became imminent. Shortly after they entered the country in December 1941, the Japanese requested that the Thai government establish a central bank with Japanese advisors and department heads. Fearing that this might become an instrument for Japanese control and exploitation of Thailand's economy, the Thai government fended off the Japanese demand mainly because of Thailand's status as a nominally independent ally and because of the existence of the National Banking Bureau (BOT 1992: 67–8, 79–81; Sithi-Amnuai 1964: 97–8). The functions of the Bureau, which had been established in 1939 as a quasi-central bank affiliated with the Finance Ministry, were thus quickly expanded and upgraded, and the BOT came into being in April 1942.

At its inception, the BOT was meant to inherit the tradition of financial conservatism from the Finance Ministry. It soon became clear that its primary function – to maintain monetary stability – had full and uncompromising recognition by political elites. The ever-present Japanese intention to usurp the country's economic sovereignty made maintenance of financial stability all the more essential. The circumstances that had accompanied the creation of the BOT continued to stress the importance of sustaining the external value of the currency. They also brought to the fore the significance of maintaining internal price stability in the face of wartime inflation caused by Japanese military expenditure, the fixed exchange rate between the baht and yen enforced by the Japanese and shortages of imported commodities (Pocmontri 1980: 31–6).

Ideological heritage alone could not guarantee the BOT's ability to pursue monetary stability, particularly when the circumstances that had given rise to its development changed. The BOT's authority over financial policy-making also derived from its unique relationship with the Finance Ministry. As noted above, the BOT was established on the basis of the National Banking Bureau, which had itself been created as an executive department under the Ministry. The central bank was actually an 'offshoot' of the Finance Ministry, and the two agencies were thus institutionally linked from the outset. Most critically, this institutional linkage was underpinned by a broad coincidence of bureaucratic interests and economic objectives between the two, as the BOT was heir to the financial conservatism long cherished within the Finance Ministry. This enabled them to take similar, if not identical, views on the general direction of financial policy. Institutional interests were sustained by frequent exchanges of personnel at senior levels between the BOT and the Ministry, particularly during the 1950s and 1960s. This practice contributed to the acculturation of working style, professional values and bureaucratic ethos between the two institutions.

A partnership with the Finance Ministry no doubt bolstered the political status of the BOT, especially in its formative years, and endowed it with greater independence from politicians. Quite often, senior Finance Ministry officials acted as a buffer between the BOT and political pressure on financial policy (interview, Bangkok, 20 March 1997), giving the central bank effective freedom of manoeuvre and action unmatched by that of the BOK. Owing to their institutional interests and bureaucratic acculturation, the BOT and the Finance Ministry were often able to form an alliance in the policy-making process. Although there were rifts between the BOT and the Finance Ministry at various times, they were, on the whole, able to work together to formulate and implement financial policy in a coherent manner. The BOT's close relationship with the Ministry, however, was not tantamount to its subordination to the latter. The ability of the central bank to maintain its independence while keeping a policy alliance with the Finance Ministry could be attributed to political support from state elites and close links with a robust private banking community.

In its initial period, the BOT did not contend for control over financial policy in a vacuum. Rather, it operated within a broader socio-political environment that inevitably affected its attempt to build influence in the policy-making process. Political support for central bank independence had, from the start, appeared to be much stronger in Thailand than in Korea. That support reflected, first and foremost, the willingness of Thai political leaders to grant the BOT a full mandate to pursue price stability. Their incentives in encouraging the emergence of a conservative and authoritative central bank derived from the relatively low government budget deficits before and after the establishment of the BOT (Ingram 1955: 236–7). State elites thus had less incentive to use the central bank as a convenient source for financing government spending.

Support for an independent central bank also came from Thailand's most powerful business interests, which were centred in commercial banks. The socio-political bases of central bank strength manifested themselves in the close affinity between the BOT and the private banking community, created and sustained by economic interests, common experiences and institutional linkages. Thai commercial banks, involved mainly in commodity exports and foreign exchange transactions, developed a particularly strong preference for the stable value of the baht and for unrestricted capital mobility. Their interests were also shaped by the orthodox fiscal and monetary policies pursued by state elites long before the creation of the central bank. Nurtured in a stable and conservative macro-economic environment, private bankers identified their economic prosperity with the continuation of financial conservatism. They therefore saw an independent central bank as vital to maintaining that policy stance and safeguarding their economic interests. Shared interests were reinforced by joint and sustained public and private efforts to break foreign control over the Thai financial sector and to promote the growth of local banks before the Second World War (Brown 1988; *The Nation* 6 February 1987; Silcock 1967: 184–5).

Close ties between private and public financiers were further strengthened with the establishment of the BOT. The 1950s and 1960s saw a period of especially active and close interaction between central and private bankers. This was, in the first place, attributed to the BOT's success in having brought wartime inflation quickly under control and to its firm commitment to orthodox financial policies; the BOT thus gained considerable recognition and respect from the private banking community. Further, in the late 1950s, when Puey Ungphakorn was BOT governor, connections between the BOT and private banks began to be institutionalised through the founding of the Thai Bankers' Association (TBA) and the monthly meetings jointly organised by the BOT and the TBA. The institutionalised connections in this context provided formal channels of communication and consultation through which the BOT governors and other senior officials could set forth the central bank's policies, influence the behaviour of commercial banks and seek their co-operation efficiently.

From their early interactions in the policy process, an informal under-standing developed that the BOT would, whenever allowed by political and economic conditions, support private commercial banks in exchange for their co-operation and support in the pursuit of its policy objectives. This helped to enhance private bankers' confidence in the central bank and made it easier for them to support official financial policies, even though the implementation of some of those policies might not be totally compatible with their interests. While tensions between the BOT and private banks did arise at various times, they tended to be outweighed by these long-standing conventions as well as by their shared economic interests and close ties. For most of the post-war period, societal support from the banking community was one of the overwhelming factors that contributed to the independence of the BOT. The very fact that the BOT had a reliable and strong societal ally in the financial policy-making process buttressed its status among state economic agencies.

It should be noted that the independence and prestige of the BOT came under threat in the early and mid-1990s. One important factor behind this change appears to be the on-going process of financial liberalisation and politi-cal democratisation, which not only undercut the ability of central bankers to control the behaviour of private bankers but also increased the macro-economic policy influence of politicians. Equally important, the partnership between the BOT and the Finance Ministry also began to unravel, as more political appointees took the helm of the Ministry. During this period, frequent rifts arose between the two institutions over many important policy issues. As a result, distrust and rivalry gradually replaced close co-operative ties between central bankers and finance ministry officials. Combined with the increasingly outmoded management structure and growing factionalism within the BOT itself (Siamwalla 1997), these changes weakened the institutional strength of Thai central bankers in the financial policy-making process.

For much of the period under discussion in this study – from the early 1980s to the early 1990s – the status of the BOT remained largely intact. Even the above-mentioned changes in the relative position of central and private bankers and in the relationship between the BOT and the Finance Ministry did not completely remould the legal, ideological, social and institutional arrangements that had originally underpinned the position of the BOT. As will be illustrated in the following chapters, these arrangements showed strong historical stickiness and had a significant impact on the direction of Thai financial liberalisation.

## Conclusions

This chapter has shown systematic differences between Korea and Thailand in the organisation of the private sector – industrial structure and finance–industry ties – and in the organisation of the state – the degree of central bank independence and central bank-government relations, as summarised in Table 3.5. On the basis of the theoretical propositions developed in the previous chapter, this concluding section presents the hypothesis about how and why the cross-country variations in these institutional structures should be expected to lead to corresponding differences in the pattern of financial policy-making and reform within the two countries.

The formation and expression of private preferences in Korea are likely to be controlled by the chaebols, and financial policy is likely to be partly influenced by the economic interests of these industrial giants. While the structural concentration and cohesion of the chaebols and their dominant position in the economy facilitate effective group organisation among big industrialists, the more competitive and pluralistic attributes of the financial sector may create collective action problems that plague the relatively decentralised Korean financiers. Furthermore, the close but asymmetrical linkages between bankers and industrialists would enable the policy preferences of the latter to prevail over those of the former. Limited and potentially confrontational bank–NBFI relations may split the otherwise unified private financial community and result in ineffective and vague articulation of preferences within the financial sector. In sum, the organisational structures of the Korean industrial and financial sectors and their effects on private-sector political action correspond to cell III in Table 2.1.

The powerful status of the ministries of finance and of trade and industry within the Korean state is likely to ensure the assertion of government interests in the reform process. Equally important, the close ties between these ministries and the broad industrial community are expected to ease the projection

*Table 3.5* Institutional variations of financial policy-making in Korea and Thailand

|  | *Korea* | *Thailand* |
|---|---|---|
| *Industrial organisation* | | |
| Financial sector | Competitive and pluralistic | Concentrated and oligopolistic |
| Industrial sector | Concentrated/chaebol dominated | Decentralised and competitive |
| *Inter-corporate ties* | | |
| Cross-sector | Close but asymmetrical bank–chaebol ties | Relatively limited bank–industry links |
| Cross-subsector | Close chaebol–NBFI links; limited and potentially confrontational bank–NBFI relations | Increasingly close ties between banks and export-oriented firms; intimate bank–NBFI ties |
| *Central bank status* | | |
| Legal dimensions | Low level of political and economic independence | Higher level of political and economic independence |
| Informal dimensions | Conflictual BOK–Finance Ministry relations; political leaders' preferences for a subordinate central bank; growth-first development ideology; a weak private banking community controlled by government | Co-operative BOT–Finance Ministry ties; political leaders' interests in a strong central bank; strong traditions of financial conservatism; close relations between the BOT and a powerful banking community |

Note
NBFI, non-bank financial institution; BOK, Bank of Korea; BOT, Bank of Thailand.

of the chaebols' preferences for reform measures into the official policy arena. In view of these factors, Korea's financial reform approaches and outcomes are most likely to result from the complementarity or compromise of preferences and interests between big business, government ministries and politicians.

In Thailand, the preferences of the private sector for financial liberalisation are likely to be dictated by commercial banks, and the policy behaviour of official decision-makers in the reform process to be influenced by the demands of private bankers rather than those of industrial manufacturers. This is, in the first place, because the stance of private bankers on financial reform is very unlikely to be guided by the preferences of industrial firms, as they are not closely linked in terms of bank lending to industry or cross-holdings of corporate equities. Moreover, while the highly concentrated and oligopolistic banking sector serves to turn Thai private bankers into an organisationally cohesive and effective group, the more competitive and decentralised structure of the manufacturing sector makes it difficult for industrialists to organise collective action and articulate their preferences in a coherent way. The political power of private bankers, as opposed to that of industrialists, is further strengthened by their control of many NBFIs and their dominant position within the Thai economy. Largely, the Thai corporate and financial sectors are consonant with cell IV in Table 2.1, in terms of organisational features and their impact on the aggregation of private-sector preferences.

Finally, Thai central bankers are more likely to assert their interests in financial reform, by reason that the BOT, allied with the Finance Ministry, exercises hegemony over other state economic institutions in the financial policy-making process. Thai private bankers, who have close links with the Thai financial authorities, are not expected to have any difficulty in getting their preferences translated into actual policy outcomes. In Thailand, therefore, reform policy is assumed to be oriented towards the interests and objectives of central and private bankers.

These hypotheses, derived from the theoretical propositions developed in the second chapter, will be put to the test in the next two chapters, through a detailed empirical analysis of the financial reform experiences of Korea and Thailand since the early 1980s.

**Part II**

# The political economy of financial liberalisation

# 4  Financial liberalisation in Korea

The Korean government moved to liberalise the financial system as an important way to reorient its overall developmental strategy in the wake of the balance-of-payments and fiscal crises of the early 1980s. While the whole process of financial reform in Korea can generally be characterised as cautious and gradual, the approaches to, and sequencing of, the reform displayed their own peculiarities. Korea's distinctive approach to financial reform also led to varied progress in the major areas of liberalisation. Rapid progress was made in the development of the non-bank financial sector and deregulation of entry barriers, whereas interest rate deregulation, policy loan reduction and capital decontrol ran a slow, erratic and selective course.

The explanatory variables, discussed in the previous chapters, focus on the two institutional features of Korean financial policy-making. Private-sector preferences favouring low interest rates, preferential finance and controls over foreign investors were underpinned by the dominant position of the chaebols in the economy, their ownership controls over most non-bank financial institutions (NBFIs) and close bank–industry relations. This structure of private-sector preference formation made it difficult for the banking community to assert its stance on financial liberalisation. Equally important, the subordination of the central bank to the government and the conflictual relations between the central bank and the Finance Ministry hampered the Bank of Korea's (BOK) ability to play a leadership role and to act on its institutional interests in the reform process. It will be shown below that the combination of these two features accounts primarily for the distinctive pattern of Korean financial reform in terms of approaches and outcomes.

This chapter provides a chronological narrative of financial policy reform in Korea since 1980. The first section focuses on the first half of the 1980s and the emergence of a reform policy in connection with the government's response to the economic crisis. The second section outlines the speedier move towards financial liberalisation in the late 1980s, when the country was experiencing economic stability and political transition. The third section analyses renewed efforts to push ahead with financial reform in the early and mid-1990s, which occurred under the new democratic government of Kim Young-Sam. The final section summarises and concludes the chapter.

## Economic crisis and an emerging reform line, 1980–86

After experiencing a long period of rapid growth, Korea faced an economic crisis of major proportions in the late 1970s and early 1980s, as indicated in Table 4.1. External shocks played an important role in the rise of the crisis. Sharp increases in international interest rates and the second oil price hike accelerated balance-of-payments deficits in Korea. Moreover, global economic recession in the wake of the oil shock depressed export growth and aggravated the overall external position. Domestic problems resulting from economic mismanagement were also culpable. The Heavy and Chemical Industrialisation (HCI) plan, while contributing to industrial expansion, gave rise to excess capacity in many manufacturing sectors, weakened the capital structure of the chaebols and caused domestic liquidity to grow speedily (Nam 1986: 46–8). These problems, coupled with a surge in the general wage level (Sakong 1993: 253), created inflationary pressures and eroded the international competitiveness of Korea.

The mounting crisis prompted the Park Chun-Hee government to install stability-oriented technocrats at the helm of the Economic Planning Board (EPB) and to adopt readjustment measures. The result was the comprehen-

*Table 4.1* Main economic indicators in Korea (percentages), 1970–96

| Period | Real GDP growth | Rate of inflation | Current account/ GDP | Real export growth | Budget deficit/ GDP |
|---|---|---|---|---|---|
| 1970–74 | 8.9 | 12.7 | −8.1 | 33.9 | 0.9 |
| 1975–79 | 9.8 | 16.7 | −5.7 | 29.8 | −1.5 |
| 1980 | −3.0 | 28.5 | −11.2 | 11.3 | −2.6 |
| 1981 | 6.9 | 21.3 | −9.5 | 17.6 | −4.0 |
| 1982 | 5.5 | 7.3 | −7.0 | 6.6 | −3.3 |
| 1983 | 10.9 | 3.6 | −3.9 | 16.2 | −0.9 |
| 1984 | 8.6 | 2.2 | −3.6 | 15.7 | −1.1 |
| 1985 | 5.4 | 2.5 | −2.2 | 7.5 | −1.4 |
| 1986 | 12.4 | 2.8 | 6.4 | 19.4 | 0.2 |
| 1987 | 12.1 | 3.5 | 8.0 | 36.4 | 0.4 |
| 1988 | 11.5 | 7.2 | 8.2 | 29.0 | 1.6 |
| 1989 | 6.1 | 5.6 | 2.8 | 3.0 | 0.2 |
| 1990 | 9.0 | 8.6 | −0.6 | 2.8 | −0.7 |
| 1991 | 8.6 | 9.7 | −2.6 | 10.2 | −1.7 |
| 1992 | 4.7 | 7.3 | −1.0 | 8.0 | −0.9 |
| 1993 | 5.8 | 4.8 | 2.1 | 7.3 | 0.6 |
| 1994 | 8.6 | 6.2 | −2.8 | 16.8 | 0.3 |
| 1995 | 8.9 | 4.5 | −3.8 | 30.3 | 0.3 |
| 1996 | 7.1 | 4.9 | −4.9 | 3.7 | 0.1 |

Sources: Bank of Korea (*Economic Statistics Yearbook*, various issues), Economic Planning Board (*Korea Statistical Yearbook*, various issues), International Monetary Fund (*International Financial Statistics Yearbook*, various issues) and United Nations (*Economic and Social Survey of Asia and the Pacific*, various issues; *World Economic and Social Survey*, various issues).

Note
GDP, gross domestic product.

sive stabilisation plan announced in April 1979. While the implementation of the plan was interrupted following the assassination of Park in October 1979, Chun Doo-Hwan, who came to power in May 1980 through a military coup, strongly supported the plan. Chun's endorsement reflected his desire to distance his regime from the policy failures of the Park era and to overcome the economic crisis in an effective manner (Haggard and Moon 1993: 81). Fiscal restraint, monetary control and a wage freeze were implemented in order to dampen inflationary pressure and to restore macro-economic stability. Concomitant with the stabilisation programme was an effort to pursue a more market-oriented development strategy and structural reform of the national economic system. Such an effort was embodied in industrial restructuring, import liberalisation and financial reform (Moon 1988).

The reasons the government moved to liberalise after several decades' stranglehold over the financial system were multifarious. One important factor was that the balance-of-payments and fiscal difficulties associated with the economic crisis of the early 1980s directly restricted the government's ability to sustain the repressive financial regime. As budget deficits widened, foreign debt mounted and reserves shrank, policy-makers found it increasingly difficult to subsidise low interest rates and preferential credit schemes. The desire to reduce the burden of being the lender of last resort thus pushed the government towards financial reform. This desire became an imperative in the early 1980s, when a series of curb-market scandals, precipitated by financial fraud and distress borrowing by chaebol firms, generated a widespread outcry for overhauling the mode of financial policy management [*Far Eastern Economic Review* (*FEER*) 21 May 1982: 50–6; *The Korea Herald* (*KH*) 18 May 1982].

The onset of financial reform reflected not only the severity of external and internal financial constraints, but also the political strategies of the incoming leadership. The structural adjustment programme represented a calculated move on the part of the Chun regime to overcome the political straits in which it found itself. These political straits stemmed from Chun's illegal seizure of power through a military coup and his lack of political legitimacy. By launching the economic liberalisation programme, Chun and his associates hoped to mitigate these negative effects and gain popular support (Haggard and Moon 1993: 83–9; Moon 1994: 145–52). The new regime imputed financial difficulties and curb-market scandals to the collusive ties between the state and big business and attempted to purge the chaebols. Financial reform was in part aimed at weakening the dominance of the chaebols in the economy and undercutting their growing political influence (Jung 1995: 104–7; Lee 1996: 157–9).

To formulate and implement the reform plan, Chun replaced the economic team with reformist technocrats. The government, seeking to reform the economic system as an urgent political imperative, turned to these technocrats and elevated them to positions of importance within the government. Ensconced as the president's chief economic advisors and helmsmen at the EPB and the Finance Ministry, most of them were American-trained economists and were reputed to have professed allegiance to the neo-liberal doctrine (Woo 1991: 190–1). Their dedication to liberalisation, however, was also influenced by their bureaucratic interests. As Byung-Sun Choi (1987: 205–21) notes, the reform measures carried out by economic technocrats signified the EPB's efforts to strengthen its position in the economic policy-making process.

Advocates of financial reform found allies in their desire for liberalisation in the US government, the World Bank and the International Monetary Fund (IMF). As Korea was hit hard by external shocks in the late 1970s, the Americans began to urge the Korean government to scale back state intervention and liberalise the financial market. These demands were very much in conformity with the Reaganite ideology, which was bent on minimising the economic functions of the state (Woo 1991: 182–8). At the same time, American financial institutions lobbied for lower barriers to foreign entry into Korea and were active in seeking diplomatic support for their interests from their home government (Chung 1988: 177–8). The USA was able to exert influence on Korea because the latter depended on extensive defence and economic links with the former; the USA could back up its demands by tying continued military and economic support to financial reform.

The World Bank and the IMF also urged the Korean government to realign monetary and credit policies, restructure industrial incentives and reform the banking sector as routes out of the economic crisis (*FEER* 22 May 1981: 48–9; World Bank 1986). This liberalisation prescription was supported by three standby arrangements with the IMF and two structural adjustment loans from the World Bank for the period from March 1980 to March 1985 (Aghevli and Marquez-Ruarte 1985: 15). All this could not have been more important and fortuitous for the Chun regime, which grappled with grave economic difficulties and legitimacy problems and was thus desperate for financial assistance with which to revitalise the flagging economy.

Despite strong external pressure and the political needs of the Chun government, the financial liberalisation process was slow, uneven and, most of all, limited in scope and degree. Although speedier progress was made in bank privatisation and entry deregulation,[1] the freeing of interest rates was largely thwarted, policy loans remained high in total bank credit and privatised banks continued to be subjected to various forms of administrative guidance. The path of foreign exchange and capital decontrol was just as tentative and halting, with hardly any significant changes to the draconian regime that governed capital movements. The slow and uneven pattern of financial liberalisation was a function of political constraints on financial policy-making.

The Chun government, notwithstanding its authoritarian nature, was not so politically autonomous from private interests as its predecessor. The fundamental reason for this was that the chaebols had emerged as a powerful interest group, mainly because of the state's pursuit of a highly concentrated pattern of industrial development in the 1960s and 1970s. The structural cohesion of large chaebol firms endowed them with institutional resources with which to develop the organisational capacity to protect their interests against the state.

Financial liberalisation was a mixed blessing for the chaebols. While they were likely to benefit from bank privatisation and entry deregulation, they stood to suffer from the elimination of policy loans, interest rate liberalisation and increased foreign competition associated with capital account opening (Choi 1993: 42–3; Dalla and Khatkhate 1995). Their ambivalent position permeated the financial reform process in Korea, partly accounting for its halting and selective nature.

The political constraints on the reform process also came from within the government itself. In the first place, the existing development model based on embeddedness of finance in industrial policy was not discredited within the economic bureaucracy (Amsden and Euh 1993). Although reformist technocrats enjoyed moments of rising authority, particularly in the early 1980s (Haggard *et al.* 1994: 79–80), opponents continued exercising considerable influence over financial policy. Moreover, financial reform, designed to increase the role of market forces as the determinant of economic activity, was bound to deprive the state of the policy instruments with which to control the private sector. Those bureaucrats who wanted to maintain financial controls as an important means of disciplining big business found liberalisation politically painful, particularly when the chaebols became increasingly powerful.

The subordination of the central bank to the government constituted a final determinant of the nature of Korean financial reform. Central bankers supported interest rate liberalisation and preferential credit reduction in order to reduce inflationary pressures. They wanted to strengthen the financial position of commercial banks by removing bureaucratic restrictions, so that the BOK could reduce its burden of providing soft loans and other policy support to banks. They stood for financial reform in general because it promised to give the central bank more policy-making independence and elevate its status within the state hierarchy (interview, Seoul, 4 September 1997). The subordinate position of the BOK, however, made it difficult for central bankers to pursue their reform objectives. The institutional underpinnings of Korean financial liberalisation become more manifest when the liberalisation process is analysed in greater detail.

### Interest rate and credit policy changes

As noted in Chapter 3, the Park government used the financial system as one of its major instruments of development policy, setting low interest rates on loans to favoured industrial borrowers and directing policy loans to selected enterprises and sectors. Preferential credit schemes and an implicit government commitment to be a risk partner in the case of poor performance or the failure of favoured sectors and enterprises, however, caused debt financing to be seen as far less risky than other forms of industrial financing. Although chaebol firms could obtain funds through equity markets and could count on high public demand for their stocks, they did not have much incentive to do so, mainly because of their easy access to cheap bank credits (Cho and Cole

1992). As a result, the corporate sector's ratio of debt to equity became very high in Korea,[2] rendering chaebol firms vulnerable to fluctuations in short-term interest rates and, consequently, strongly opposed to rate liberalisation.

Chaebol opposition was visible from the moment the BOK proposed that commercial banks should be granted more autonomy in determining interest rates in early 1981. Federation of Korean Industries (FKI) leaders rejected the proposal in several policy statements, claiming that banks would push up interest rates and increase production costs. The chaebols' opposition reflected the severe financial difficulties that many of them were experiencing in the early 1980s, as shown in Table 4.2. Echoing the arguments of the large-business sector, the ministries of finance and of trade and industry also asserted that a rate increase would result in higher interest payments, which would in turn contribute, as a cost-push factor, to inflationary pressures (Rhee 1994: 102–3).

Delayed interest rate liberalisation, however, contributed to the worsening of structural problems in the financial sector, which were finally revealed by a series of curb-market crises in 1982. The government was embarrassed by the crises because Chang Yong-Ja, the woman who was held culpable, was distantly related by marriage to President Chun, and was even alleged to have donated part of her profits to Chun's Democratic Justice Party (DJP). The opposition exploited the incident by attacking the government for financial mismanagement and corruption, and demanded that Chun resign. The political fallout from the financial scandals forced the president to dismiss both the prime minister and the finance minister in a swift cabinet shake-up (*FEER* 21 May 1982: 50–6; *KH* 29 May and 2 June 1982).

Kang Kyong-Shik, an economic technocrat with a strong reformist bent, was made finance minister, replacing Rha Woong-Bae, who had close links with the industrial community and had been opposed to rapid liberalisation. Strongly supported by Kim Jae-Ik, chief advisor to the president on economic affairs, the new finance minister implemented a number of important reform measures. In addition to their efforts to privatise the state-owned banks and to deregulate entry barriers to both banking and NBFI sectors, financial

*Table 4.2*   Main business indicators in the Korean manufacturing sector (percentages), 1979–86

|  | *Profit/net assets* | *Profit/net sales* | *Debt–equity ratio* |
|---|---|---|---|
| 1979 | 3.4 | 2.7 | 377.1 |
| 1980 | −0.2 | −0.2 | 487.9 |
| 1981 | 0.0 | 0.0 | 451.5 |
| 1982 | 1.0 | 0.9 | 385.8 |
| 1983 | 3.3 | 2.7 | 360.3 |
| 1984 | 3.4 | 2.7 | 342.7 |
| 1985 | 3.0 | 2.5 | 348.4 |
| 1986 | 4.5 | 3.6 | 350.0 |

Source: Bank of Korea (*Money and Banking Statistics*, various issues).

authorities eliminated interest rate differentials between general bank loans and preferential policy credits, floated the rates on commercial papers and allowed yields on new corporate debentures to fluctuate within certain limits (Koo 1993: 172). However, the impact of these measures on the overall interest rate structure was moderated by a concomitant reduction of bank rates from 16.5 per cent to 10 per cent. This signified the efforts of financial bureaucrats to lower borrowing costs of business firms and to appease the chaebols.

The sharp interest rate reductions made an appreciable dent in the profit margins of banks and undermined their ability to raise loanable funds. From early 1983 onwards, BOK economists began to make a series of policy proposals to the government, emphasising the importance of readjusting the domestic interest rate structure. Meanwhile, the improving economic environment provided favourable conditions for changes in interest rate policy (see Table 4.1). Against the background of these favourable macro-economic trends, the financial position of the business sector witnessed a recovery (see Table 4.2). In early 1984, the Finance Ministry increased long-term deposit rates and allowed commercial banks, within a given band, to charge their borrowers varying interest rates on the basis of their creditworthiness [*Business Korea* (*BK*) March 1984: 17]. This was followed by a 1 per cent increase in loan and deposit rates and the removal of the upper limit on call rates in late 1984 and by deregulating convertible bond yields in mid-1985 (Park 1994: 150).

These reform measures provoked strong opposition from FKI leaders [*KH* 10 July 1985; *Korea Times* (*KT*) 26 December 1984]. Business pressures aside, economic and political constraints also forced the Chun government to withdraw from its commitment to relax direct controls over interest rates. From the second half of 1984 onwards, the Korean economy began to slow down, as indicated in Table 4.1, raising policy-makers' concerns about unemployment. On the political front, public discontent with the Chun government over its continued authoritarian rule and its failure to revive the economy was on the rise before and after the legislative elections of February 1985. Senior politicians in the ruling party thus urged Chun to relax monetary policy in order to boost economic growth (*BK* November 1985: 34; Haggard *et al.* 1994: 94–5). The pro-chaebol elements within the economic bureaucracy also clamoured for investment and export growth to be stimulated through lower interest rates and more preferential credits. A major cabinet reshuffle in early 1986 resulted in policy changes favourable to the business sector.

Just as the government's efforts at interest rate reform were delayed, so its plan to reduce policy loans hardly made any commendable progress. Shortly after his inauguration, Chun devised a credit administrative system aimed at reducing the concentration of bank credits in the hands of big business and at scaling down preferential credit schemes. Preferential finance, which had accounted for 47 per cent of total domestic credit in 1980, was cut to 33 per cent in 1986. The drop partly reflected the rapid growth of NBFIs, whose lending operations were exempt from government control, and partly reflected the declining role of development institutions that had been the main providers of policy loans in the 1960s and 1970s (Park 1996: 254–5). However, the share of preferential finance in total bank credit showed a different trend. It fell from 68 per cent in 1980 to 62 per cent in 1982, yet rose again to 68 per cent in 1983, 70 per cent in 1984 and 71 per cent in 1985 (Choi 1993: 52).

The very political and institutional factors that impeded the government's ability to liberalise interest rates also accounted for this trend. Most critically, the government's previous supply of lavish preferential credits to, and its risky partnership with, the large-business sector made the financial structures of chaebol firms highly leveraged, leaving them very vulnerable to severe external shocks in the early 1980s. Many chaebol firms experienced financial difficulties or even became insolvent, particularly those in the overseas construction, shipping, textile, machinery and lumber industries (*BK* December 1984: 25). The Chun government found itself bound by prior commitments and had to come to the rescue of financially besieged firms, even though the provision of financial relief would only encourage their continued dependence on debt financing (Haggard and Moon 1990).

The government was forced to act as the lender of last resort because the large-business sector, which now produced more than 80 per cent of the country's gross national product (GNP), became so important to the economy that policy-makers simply could not afford to ignore its needs. Moreover, the close links between the large-business sector and the banking system made it impossible for the government to disregard the former's financial difficulties. Banks which had lent heavily to chaebol firms for decades had their fortunes tied up with those of their giant industrial borrowers; the collapse of several of the largest chaebol firms would land their creditor banks in dire trouble. There were also concerns on the part of the government that such a situation would shake foreign creditors' confidence in domestic business firms and financial institutions, giving rise to requests for the early repayment of foreign debts and to reduced availability of foreign funds (Eckert 1993: 105–6).

Furthermore, having realised the real and potential hazards that debt-ridden chaebol firms in a number of problem sectors posed to economic stability, the government began, in early 1984, to implement industrial restructuring programmes. Eight sectors in both labour-intensive and heavy and chemical industries that were plagued by diminishing comparative advantage, surplus capacity and financial distress were designated for restructuring: capital equipment was upgraded, business lines were consolidated by merger and specialised monopolies were created for more efficient export production (Choi 1989; Leipziger and Petri 1994: 592–4). Financial support again played a critical role in the restructuring process, with the BOK and banking institutions providing subsidised credits either to help firms upgrade their industrial structures or to compensate for losses caused by the acquisition of defaulted firms, generally by the largest chaebol firms (Nam 1994a: 207).

Finally, the government mobilised additional financial support to promote the growth of a new range of high-technology industries such as the computer, semiconductor and communication equipment industries. Targeted preferential lending continued to play a key role in this process, although more emphasis was placed on indirect, non-discretionary supports such as staff training and research and development incentives (Yoo 1994). The newly targeted industries received preferential credit in the form of access to bank loans that carried below-market interest rates, if not the super-preferential ones they had once carried over the 1970s. Just as they had been selected and provided with massive subsidised credit with which to undertake the HCI plan, the chaebols again became the main recipients of the new policy loans. Reliance upon the large-business sector for the growth of high-technology industries, as well as industrial restructuring and financial stability, thus made it difficult for the government to reduce the allocation of preferential credit to chaebol firms.

## Deregulation of entry barriers

In early 1982, the Korean government moved to deregulate entry barriers and to establish more commercial banks. This policy initiative primarily reflected the fact that existing commercial banks became increasingly ineffective in mobilising investment funds. By removing entry restrictions, financial policy-makers hoped to improve their operational efficiency. Furthermore, the role of commercial banks relative to that of specialised banks and NBFIs declined significantly during the 1970s. The share of total assets held by commercial banks in the financial sector as a whole shrank from 49 per cent in 1975 to 37 per cent in 1982 (Euh and Baker 1990: 11). The government thus decided to establish more banks to strengthen the position of the commercial banking sector.

The move to deregulate entry barriers also reflected the interests of big business. The chaebols had long wished to own banking institutions in order to facilitate their business expansion and to gain greater financial independence from the government. Bank privatisation might have provided a good opportunity for the chaebols to fulfil their desires. Strict restrictions on ownership and continued government intervention in the operations of privatised banks,[3] however, made it difficult for the chaebols to achieve managerial and ownership dominance within the commercial banking sector. Although the chaebols owned many NBFIs, these institutions were not allowed to tap deposits directly from the public and thus had little flexibility in meeting their rapidly increasing capital needs. In these circumstances, the FKI and leading chaebol groups lobbied financial authorities for new entry in the banking sector, in the hope that they would be able to establish their own banks.

Incumbent banking institutions enjoyed protection against new entrants and developed a stake in policies that kept the banking sector closed to competitive pressure. But the banks and their interest-representing organisation, the Korea Federation of Banks, were passive in the face of policy changes and did not lodge any effective protest against the deregulation decision for two major reasons. First, the Korean banking industry, consisting of different categories of institutions, was characterised by a relatively low level of concentration and a pluralistic structure, with no single category of institutions able to achieve dominance. The collective action problem that typically plagued decentralised political actors made it difficult for Korean banks to organise effectively to press their case. Second, within the business community, it was the FKI and chaebols that exercised predominant influence over the formation and articulation of policy preferences; banks could hardly challenge the stance of industrial giants on entry deregulation.

In the early 1980s, the Finance Ministry licensed two joint-venture commercial banks – the Shinhan Bank and the KorAm Bank. Entry deregulation proved a continuous process in Korea owing to policy-makers' desire to promote banking efficiency, the chaebols' eagerness to gain additional access to investment finance and weak opposition from existing banks. In the mid- and late 1980s, three nationwide commercial banks were chartered, followed by three more in the early 1990s, two of which were created through the merger and conversion of several investment and finance companies. Meanwhile, the two specialised banks, the Korea Foreign Exchange Bank and the Citizens National Bank, were converted into commercial banks. All in all, the total number of nationwide commercial banks increased from seven in the mid-1980s to fifteen in the early 1990s.

Significant changes also occurred with regard to the regulation of foreign entry into the domestic banking sector. Foreign banks were first allowed to open branches in the late 1960s, when the government attempted to expedite the inflow of foreign capital for the promotion of economic development. To facilitate their efforts to bring in foreign capital, the government granted policy privileges to foreign bank branches, although it also restricted their access to BOK rediscount facilities and their branching freedom. Operations of foreign banks were almost risk-free and highly profitable. This was mainly because exchange risks normally associated with foreign capital intermediation were eliminated by the swap system through which foreign bank branches raised won funds from the central bank with foreign currencies and then lent them at a guaranteed margin of at least 1 per cent (BOK 1995: 31–3; Euh and Baker 1990: 21–7). These privileges, together with their greater managerial efficiency and easier access to large pools of foreign funds, contributed to the stable and rising level of profits among foreign bank branches (Park and Kim 1994: 310). As a result, more foreign banks obtained licences to open branches, and their total number increased from only eleven in 1977 to thirty-seven in 1981.

Faced with the large and constant inflow of foreign entrants, domestic banks began to complain about increased competitive pressures and to plead with financial authorities to reduce policy favours granted to foreign banks. The central bank also had misgivings about the flood of foreign entrants and was concerned that intensified competition would pose a direct threat to the stability and solvency of domestic banks, particularly when many of them had to cope with increasingly shaky financial positions in the early 1980s. The government had broader concerns than merely financial stability, however. Its interest in the deregulation of foreign entry extended to economic development, the financial needs and performance of the corporate business sector and the politics of international economic relations, among others. Finance Ministry officials were reluctant to close the door to foreign entry because the presence of foreign banks contributed to the inflow of foreign capital.

Political pressure by foreign banks and their home governments was also an important impetus behind the move to deregulate entry barriers to foreign banks. Banks from advanced industrial countries had long lobbied for lower barriers to foreign entry and for more freedom to expand their business scope in Korea. US-based financial institutions were particularly aggressive in mobilising political and diplomatic support for their interests. Senator Jake Garne, who proposed the Senate bill linking permission for foreign bank operations in the USA to foreign countries' treatment of American banks, visited Korea in the autumn of 1983 and demanded the granting of 'national treatment' for American banks operating in Korea (*BK* June 1984: 35). During his March 1984 visit to Seoul, the US Treasury Secretary, Donald Regan, also pressed the Korean government for equal treatment for foreign banks (*KH* 27 March 1984).

Foreign banks and their home governments were given more or less what they demanded. Between early 1984 and late 1986, the Finance Ministry implemented a series of reform measures to phase out operational restrictions imposed on foreign banks despite opposition by central and private bankers. Foreign bank branches operating in Korea were allowed to expand their working capital and thus their lending and guaranteeing activities, venture into trust businesses, join the Korea Federation of Banks and the clearing house and, most important of all, gain full access to BOK rediscount facilities. The Finance Ministry also permitted foreign banks to act as agencies for selling government bonds and in late 1987 to open, with official approval, more than one branch each. Equally important, the government committed itself to further deregulation of foreign entry; the total number of foreign bank branches in Korea steadily increased to fifty-five in 1987.

## Financial reform through democratic transition, 1987–92

From the mid-1980s, the Korean political system began to witness a fundamental shift in the direction of democracy. In the legislative elections of February 1985, the ruling DJP received only 35.3 per cent of the popular vote, but managed to retain its control of the National Assembly, mainly because of the proportional representation system.[4] Riding on the growing popular dissatisfaction with the Chun regime, opposition forces vigorously campaigned for the end of military rule and political reform. But Chun and hard-liners in the DJP adopted a repressive stance and refused to compromise with the opposition. In the spring of 1987, the DJP officially nominated ex-general Roh Tae-Woo as its presidential candidate, triggering massive anti-government demonstrations. In the face of extensive protests, Chun backed down and agreed to political and constitutional reforms that included direct presidential elections and guarantees of human and political rights (Bedeski 1994: 169–70). However, the failure to co-operate between the two main opposition leaders, Kim Young-Sam and Kim Dae-Jung, enabled Roh to win the December 1987 presidential election.

During the first 2 years of the Roh presidency, the new regime's political priority focused on satisfying growing social demands for equality and fairness. In line with this populist policy, the government set economic stability as the major objective of economic management, and reoriented the overall develop-ment strategy towards balanced growth between different social groups and areas, fair market competition and economic deregulation (Rhee 1994: 234–5). Advocates of more progressive reforms replaced the economic cabinet led by pro-business, expansionist technocrats. The policy changes and institutional shake-up primarily reflected growing public concern about such socio-economic problems as rising inflation, rampant property prices and the widening gap between rich and poor, for which the high concentration of economic power in the chaebols was widely held responsible. The opposition parties capitalised on these problems and appealed directly to those social groups who suffered most under the authoritarian regime. In the circumstances, the progressive development strategy was designed to neutralise the opposition's political tactics and to sustain and broaden the coalition base of the Roh regime.

A key component of the new economic strategy was the acceleration of financial liberalisation. In May 1988, the government announced its comprehensive plan to reform the financial system. This was motivated by policy-makers' political considerations as well as by their desire to promote the growth of the financial industry. Most critically, the plan was intended to squeeze the large-business sector by ending preferential credits; in the same vein, it was to reinstate the abandoned real-name financial transaction system that would force the disclosure of ownership of financial assets and provide a means for more effective taxation.[5] Furthermore, the government planned to liberalise interest rates and to establish a more market-oriented monetary control mechanism in order to regulate the level of systemic liquidity and to fight inflation more effectively.

The decision to accelerate financial liberalisation was also a function of relaxed economic constraints. Korea experienced a strong economic boom over the 1986–88 period (Table 4.1). The notable improvement in macro-economic conditions provided state officials with resources that emboldened them to undertake speedier financial reforms. The emergence of large current account surpluses, for instance, gave financial policy-makers confidence in deregulat-ing a wide array of foreign exchange restrictions. High national savings in excess of domestic investment narrowed the disparity between regulated and curb-market rates and provided a favourable setting for interest rate liberalisa-tion. In addition, the improving balance sheets of financial institutions during boom times encouraged regulatory authorities to remove existing competitive restraints and reduce institutional segmentation.

A final source of pressure for financial liberalisation during this period was the multilateral negotiations on trade in services conducted under the auspices of the General Agreement on Tariffs and Trade (GATT). When the GATT was instituted in 1948, its mandate excluded such highly sensitive and regulated industries as financial services. Prompted by the US government, the GATT Uruguay Round on trade liberalisation, launched in 1986, turned to financial services and banking in particular. This occurred not only because the trade in financial services between industrial countries showed rapid growth, but also because an increasing number of newly industrialising economies, especially those in East Asia, were seen as sizeable prospective markets. These newly industrialising economies (NIEs), including Korea, were thus under bilateral pressure from industrial countries to open their financial markets.

Despite these political and economic stimuli, financial liberalisation did not deviate from the inconsistent and halting pattern. Although the democratic transition set new rules and procedures of engagement between the government and businesses, the previous institutional arrangements that underpinned financial policy-making did not change quickly. Roh Tae-Woo was elected with a mandate to promote socio-economic equality and to curtail the expansion of big business. With the Korean economy overwhelmingly dependent on the chaebols for employment, export prowess and continued growth, however, the Roh regime found it difficult to implement reform measures that would hurt the chaebols' interests. Even as the government faced increasing pressure from the populace to regulate the growth of the large-business sector, its efforts to do so were largely ineffective (Moon 1994: 153–60).

The Roh regime's inability to implement progressive economic reforms in any consistent and arbitrary fashion signified not only the continued dominance of the chaebols in the national economy, but also their ever-growing political influences. Liberalisation of the political climate in Korea, although contributing to the emergence of competing social groups such as labour, did not impair the powerful position of the chaebols to any significant degree. If anything, democratisation expanded the political space in which the chaebols and FKI leaders could operate and enabled them to assert their interests *vis-à-vis* the state even more vigorously. Several striking developments during the Roh years amply evidenced this growing political assertiveness on the part of big business.

In the first place, business leaders became increasingly vocal in expressing their political positions and broke with the long-established convention of refraining from criticising government policy in public. As soon as the Roh regime imposed new regulations and restrictions on the large-business sector, FKI leaders and leading industrialists began to stage formidable counterattacks. They harangued against the reformist, anti-business push at FKI-organised seminars and press conferences. They also accused the government of causing industrial downturns through restrictions on credit allocation and of creating corporate instability through politically motivated chaebol-bashing measures. In a meeting between Roh's DJP and the FKI in October 1988, Chung Ju-Yung, the patriarch of Hyundai, spoke bluntly about the necessity of ending state intervention, protecting business freedom and guaranteeing a market economy under private leadership (*KT* 27 October 1988).

More importantly, the chaebols began to use their formidable concentration of wealth to establish their own political priorities and to advance their policy objectives. In the 1970s and 1980s, chaebol firms had frequently been subjected to numerous and substantial 'secondary taxes' in the form of corporate expenditure on state-sponsored social events and contributions to ruling party politicians (Chang-Hee Nam 1995: 360–2). From late 1988, however, the chaebols began to break away from this clientelist practice and openly warned politicians of potential retaliation through the selective use of financial contributions. FKI leaders declared that in the future they would provide donations only to political parties that were willing to protect business interests, a declaration directed specifically towards politicians who adopted a populist and anti-business position (Moon 1994: 154–5).

Such confidence and independence culminated in Chung Ju-Yung's unprecedented direct move into politics. In late 1991, Chung formed his own political party, the Unification National Party, in an attempt to defy the government's anti-business campaign and to challenge the governing party in the March 1992 general election. In that election, Chung's party won 17 per cent of the popular votes and 10 per cent of legislative seats, becoming the second major opposition party in the National Assembly (Choi and Lee 1995: 46). This significant victory, particularly given that the new party had been formed only several months prior to the election, encouraged Chung to declare himself a candidate in the December 1992 presidential election. Chung's foray into politics demonstrated that the chaebols, a powerful and independent political force, could wield significant influence in a more democratic context.

The transition to democracy not only forced a change in business–government relations but also had a major impact on the *modus operandi* for economic policy-making and on inter-bureaucratic ties. Facing an electoral challenge, ruling-party politicians frequently resorted to the manipulation of policy instruments in order to woo voters. This made it increasingly difficult and politically costly for the government to use coercive measures to achieve policy objectives and forced economic technocrats to operate in a more politicised policy-making setting (Ahn 1990). Moreover, economic line ministries, which had traditionally maintained close links to industrial constituents, had to give greater attention to growing distributive demands. This in turn broadened channels for well-organised social groups, such as the chaebols, to translate their preferences into policy outputs.

Popular clamour for stable growth and democratisation encouraged central bankers to demand more autonomy from the government (*KH* 15 November 1988; *KT* 4 August 1987). The Finance Ministry, however, rejected the call for a change in the existing balance of authority. It contended that the government had ultimate responsibility for the conduct of all economic policies, including financial policy (the following account draws on author interviews, Seoul, 5 June and 4 September 1997; *BK* September 1987: 28–9, May 1988:

25–7, December 1989: 16–17). Supported by the industrial community and conservative elements within the ruling party, the Finance Ministry retained the upper hand in this debate. During the late 1980s, the two institutions were locked in controversy as to who should be in charge of financial policy. The issue was taken to the National Assembly in early 1990 after a series of negotiations had failed to resolve the dispute. Following an intense legislative manoeuvre, campaigners for central bank independence were finally defeated.

The fact that the BOK remained subservient to the government had significant implications for the direction and nature of Korean financial liberalisation. Although a few reform-minded technocrats, such as Il Sakong, were at the helm of the Finance Ministry in the late 1980s, many conservative bureaucrats in the ministry were not convinced that financial reform was desirable. They asserted that Korea had achieved its economic success by making financial markets serve the needs of industry. Moreover, financial bureaucrats were reluctant to relinquish their controls over the financial system and to turn to the free market, fearing for their own futures in a new and changed environment in which their policy knowledge specific to the old system might prove worthless (interview, Seoul, 4 June 1997). The bureaucratic and political interests of the Finance Ministry itself thus cut against financial liberalisation.

### Foreign exchange and capital decontrol

For much of the post-war period, Korea maintained a restrictive foreign exchange regime (see Table 4.3), despite its strong export orientation. Foreign exchange and capital controls, as they were implemented in their most severe form during the 1960s and 1970s, reflected the economic and political interests of the Korean government. In Korea, as in many other developing countries, controls were initially installed to conserve limited foreign currencies for the purpose of economic development. This was reinforced by the authorities' desire to maintain their macro-economic policy autonomy; strict capital controls made it feasible for them to pursue growth-oriented and expansionary economic policies, particularly during the 1970s (Ro 1993). The more important motive for foreign exchange and capital controls was related to the conduct of industry policy. What underpinned Korea's export-led development strategy was the government's allocation of the preferential credit that was garnered from domestic and overseas sources to chaebol firms in the selected strategic sectors (Cho and Kim 1995; Nembhard 1996: ch. 6).

Economic needs aside, there were also ideological and political reasons. The restrictive foreign exchange regime and draconian foreign investment regulations reflected, in part, the economic ideology of the Park government, which was heavily tinged with mercantilism (Coolidge 1981). Further, extensive controls over the operations of foreign investors resulted from the government's efforts to nurture domestic entrepreneurial growth. This in turn stemmed from the Park regime's reliance upon domestic enterprises,

*Table 4.3*   Main features of foreign exchange and capital controls in Korea prior to financial liberalisation in the late 1980s

|  | *Exchange transactions* | *Capital movements* |
|---|---|---|
| Legal restrictions | Residents required to surrender all foreign exchange proceeds from exports to government-controlled banks and not allowed to hold foreign currency deposits with banks until the late 1970s; non-residents subject to restrictions on remittances from their foreign exchange accounts; foreign currencies for import payments sold only to registered traders and manufacturers importing raw materials for the production of exports; all payments for invisibles subject to individual licences and maximum limits | Payments for financial services and capital repatriation subject to limits although remittance of profits and dividends guaranteed by FCIA; foreign loans payable within 3 years governed by FECA and those with longer maturities overseen by FCIA; a positive list system with regard to FDI until 1984; strict limits on foreign holdings of domestic securities; substantial restrictions on direct and portfolio investments by residents; long-term imprisonment or death penalty for illegal overseas transfer of $1 million or more |
| Administrative controls | Foreign exchange for all intended uses approved and rationed through the foreign exchange demand-and-supply plan prepared and administered by the Finance Ministry in accordance with predetermined policy priorities and with a view to restricting undesirable types of foreign exchange spending and to managing the balance of payments | All applications for long-term foreign loans subject to strict government controls and FCDC approval; all FDI applications subject to careful screening by economic ministries and FCDC; extensive controls on foreign investors with regard to ownership, trade behaviour, employment and domestic content; overseas investments subject to stringent reviews |

Sources: Amsden and Euh (1993: 388), Bank of Korea (*Foreign Exchange System in Korea*, 1991, 1993), Cho (1984), Cho and Kim (1995: 46–50), Coolidge (1981), International Monetary Fund (*AREAER*, various issues), Koo (1985), Luedde-Neurath (1984, 1988), Mardon (1990), Nembhard (1996) and Sakong (1993: 102–14).

Note
FCIA, Foreign Capital Inducement Act; FECA, Foreign Exchange Control Act; FDI, Foreign Direct Investment; FCDC, Foreign Capital Deliberation Committee.

specifically chaebol firms, for the economic performance that served as the legitimising basis of its authoritarian rule. Finally, as the government retained the right to control capital flows across the borders, it acted as an intermediary between domestic firms and foreign investors and creditors and thus acquired a political tool for regulating the policy behaviour of private actors (Haggard and Cheng 1987: 110–14).

Initially, the government made efforts to liberalise Korea's international financial flows in the early to mid-1980s, but these were intermittent and the overall process of liberalisation remained tentative and halting. In the late 1980s and the early 1990s, the combination of domestic factors and foreign pressure provided fresh impetus for the deregulation of foreign exchange and capital restrictions. One strong stimulus came from Roh's campaign for internationalisation. While the campaign was motivated by the desire of the new regime to distance itself from its predecessor and to outmanoeuvre the opposition for policy initiatives, it was more than a political strategy. Through internationalisation, political leaders intended to deregulate economic life and to achieve a behavioural reform of government policy-making in order to improve the efficiency and competitiveness of the Korean economy (Moon 1995).

The government also found itself driven by foreign pressure to open the financial market. The rapid accumulation of current account surpluses between 1986 and 1988 created political pressures on the Korean government to liberalise capital account transactions, particularly from its American counterpart. From early 1986, senior officials from the US Treasury and Commerce Departments began to urge Korea to appreciate its currency. This led to several rounds of talks in which US Treasury representatives pressed the Korean government to deregulate capital controls, specifically on the inflow side, in the hope that it would result in exchange rate appreciation. The Americans even threatened to invoke Section 301 of the US Trade Act and to impose retaliatory tariffs on Korea's major export products if the Korean government did not concede to their demands (*BK* October 1987: 14). Political pressures coincided with an array of complaints from American financial companies. These companies had developed an interest in gaining access to the lucrative Korean market, but invariably found the door closed to them (Haggard and Maxfield 1996: 59).

In the face of all these pressures, the Finance Ministry moved to lift some foreign exchange and capital restrictions, but not necessarily in the way that the Americans wished. In 1987 and 1988, the government emphasised the liberalisation of capital outflows; it did not make any significant reduction of capital inflow controls, and even moved to strengthen some of them. The short-term reason for this skewed pattern of foreign exchange and capital decontrol was the concern that capital inflows would complicate macroeconomic management and translate into inflationary pressures (Park and Park 1993: 98–100). Moreover, the government also believed that the rapid entry of foreign investors into the capital market, attracted by the low prices of Korean stocks, would result in the shift of substantial rents, in the form of investment yields, to foreign countries and would lead to undue foreign control over the domestic stock market and Korean firms (Amsden and Euh 1993: 388–9; *KH* 3 December 1988).

The more fundamental reason was the intention of the government and the private sector to maintain capital controls as a key instrument for promoting industrial development and for preventing the rapid appreciation of the won. Despite strong US pressure, the Korean government made only grudging concessions on the exchange rate by allowing the won to appreciate gradually against the dollar by 3.2 per cent in 1986 and by 6.1 per cent during the first half of 1987. Even the slow pace of won appreciation, however, caused a stir among economic and industrial circles. Predicting an appreciation of the won by as much as 10 per cent in 1987, reports from the Korea Development Institute (KDI) warned that such appreciation would cost the Korean industry a maximum of US$1,000 million of export revenues, reduce current account surpluses by at least US$800 million and cause a 1–2 per cent drop in the GNP deflator. Chaebol-affiliated and other private research institutions made an even gloomier forecast (*BK* August 1987: 99).

This would be too heavy an economic cost for an export-oriented country, such as Korea, to bear should the won appreciate as predicted. Manufacturing firms, already feeling the pinch of rising wage levels as a result of aggressive labour actions and swelling overhead costs, due mainly to tight monetary policy, were loath to see their export revenues and profitability further eroded by an appreciating won. The KFI thus saw the appreciation as requiring an immediate response from the government and lobbied hard to contain the value of the won. It also suggested that the government should push trade liberalisation in order to deflect American pressure.[6] Partly in response to the concerns and demands of export-dependent manufacturers and traders, the Finance Ministry was reluctant to loosen its grip on capital movements, particularly on the inflow side.

The government's desire to maintain restrictions on capital movements for the above-mentioned economic and political reasons decelerated what would otherwise have been a quicker appreciation of the won. This led to accusations by the US Treasury Department, in its three reports to Congress in 1989, that the Korean government had 'manipulated' the exchange rate to gain competitive advantages through its continued use of capital controls (Frankel 1992: 8; *KT* 29 April 1989). At the request of the USA, the Finance Ministry agreed to initiate financial policy talks, the first round of which took place in February 1990 and the second in November 1990. As a concession to the USA, the Korean government introduced a more market-oriented exchange rate system in March 1990. The issue of foreign entry into the Korean capital market was addressed by the Finance Ministry's pledge to allow direct portfolio investment in the stock market and to expand the operations of foreign securities companies in Korea in 1991.[7] The revision of the Foreign Exchange Control Act (FECA) in June 1991 also paved the way for the adoption of a negative-list system for foreign exchange management, under which all transactions would be permitted unless specifically prohibited.

These concessions, however, appear to have fallen short of US demands. In its May 1991 report to Congress, the Treasury Department still found that the Korean authorities indirectly manipulated the exchange rate through comprehensive controls over foreign exchange and capital flows (Frankel 1992: 9). In the third round of financial policy talks held in March 1992 at the request of the USA, the Finance Ministry presented a new blueprint for the multi-stage liberalisation of foreign exchange and capital controls to be implemented over the next 5 years. But the blueprint attached the proviso that the implementation of capital liberalisation be contingent on the performance of the Korean macro-economy (*KH* 30 June 1992). As the current account deteriorated and inflationary pressures remained strong throughout 1992, the government again backtracked and lost the political will to proceed with capital decontrol as planned.

### Interest rate liberalisation in a circuitous route

Although interest rate liberalisation constituted a central ingredient of Korea's financial reform programme, progress on this front had generally been piecemeal and spasmodic in the early to mid-1980s. The progressive thrust of socio-economic policy-making of the Roh government – at least during the first 2 years of its rule – provided fresh impetus to interest rate liberalisation. The May 1988 plan envisaged freeing most bank and non-bank lending rates and some long-term deposit rates. In addition, the issuing rates on such marketable financial products as commercial papers, negotiable certificates of deposits and corporate debentures would be completely deregulated (*KH* 27 May 1988). In parallel with this plan, the government intended to reduce the concentration of bank credit in chaebol firms and to curtail the extension of fresh bank loans to the large-business sector.

As in the past, the government's attempt to liberalise interest rates met strong opposition from the chaebols. Throughout the second half of 1988, FKI leaders pressed the Finance Ministry to postpone the liberalisation and to lower interest rates (*BK* September 1988: 25; *FEER* 8 September 1988: 118–19). Joining the chaebols and the FKI in opposition to interest rate liberalisation were some line economic officials. Apprehensive about the impact of higher interest rates on the growth and export performance of the manufacturing sector, the minister of trade and industry cautioned financial authorities against the hasty deregulation (*KT* 29 July 1988). The chaebols and officials in the Trade and Industry Ministry also chafed at the planned reduction of credit allocation to the large-business sector, asserting that this would dampen chaebol firms' investment activities, particularly in high-technology industries (*KT* 23 June 1988).

Political pressure from the chaebols made financial policy-makers cautious about their move to free interest rates, and the liberalisation plan was not put into practice until December 1988. The plan was not allowed to run its full course, however. During the first several months, market interest rates moved steadily upwards from the repressed level, generating a great deal of concern not only among business firms, but also within the economic bureaucracy. These concerns were exacerbated by a slowdown in the economy that started in early 1989 and persisted throughout the year. The country experienced a falling volume of exports for the first time since 1979, despite strong world demand. Its gross domestic product (GDP) growth fell by nearly 50 per cent from the growth level of 1988 and stood at 6.1 per cent (see Table 4.1), an exceptionally low figure in the Korean context. Seizing upon the flagging economic conditions, the chaebols and FKI leaders called upon the government to suspend the process of interest rate liberalisation and pressed for more expansionary monetary and credit policies. Against the backdrop of slower growth and the associated political pressures, the government had no choice but to intervene in the financial market to prevent rising costs of credit and to bring down lending rates.

While the government backtracked on its plan to free interest rates, it made little significant progress in its attempt to reduce the allocation of preferential financing to the chaebols. Not only did some chaebol firms continue to have preferential access to bank credit that was earmarked for the development of high-technology industries, but the large-business sector as a whole also benefited from the government's decision to increase financial support to the fishery industry and agro-industry. This was mainly because the chaebols had highly diversified lines of business, and the allocation of subsidised credit, made by sectors rather than by specific firms, would always benefit some lines of chaebol business (Choi 1993: 39). Equally important, financial policy-makers were still not prepared to face the consequences of the largest chaebol firms going into bankruptcy and would come to their assistance whenever they were in difficulties. A good example in point was the rescue effort made by the government to save the Daewoo Shipbuilding and Heavy Machinery Company, involving a generous debt rescheduling and loan package in early 1989 (*FEER* 23 February 1989: 62–3).

The liberalisation programme launched in late 1988 was reversed in early 1990, when the progressive phase of the Roh administration lost much of its momentum following political realignment between the ruling party and the two major opposition parties. Roh reshuffled his cabinet, ousting the three most important economic ministers, who had been identified with a policy of economic liberalisation and stable growth. The new economic team emphasised its pro-business, growth-oriented credentials by announcing a new set of stimulatory measures designed to boost the investment confidence of the business sector and to pull the economy out of the trough. Interest rates were reduced, credit restrictions imposed on the chaebols were eased and the money supply was allowed to expand (*FEER* 29 March 1989: 56; Haggard *et al.* 1994: 300). As the Roh regime moved in a decidedly more conservative political and economic direction, the liberalisation plan was held in abeyance and no new reform efforts were initiated during the next year.

The issue of interest rate liberalisation was brought onto the government's agenda in mid-1991, when increasing inflation and associated political pressures strengthened the voices of reform-minded technocrats and forced Roh to reinstall a more stabilisation-oriented economic team. The new liberalisation plan, unveiled in August, was to be implemented in four phases. Although the first phase was carried out as scheduled, the second phase – which involved the hard core of interest rate liberalisation, i.e. bank loan rates and long-term corporate debentures – was delayed. Macro-economic conditions were far from propitious as Korea's GDP growth declined sharply in 1992. The tight credit controls that were introduced to control inflation during the second half of 1991 triggered growing bankruptcies and precipitated a fall in investments.

The sagging economy lent the chaebols and the FKI a strong hand in pressing the government to freeze the liberalisation plan and to lower interest rates. Concerned about the effects that rising credit costs would have on international competitiveness and the export performance of the business sector, Finance Ministry officials responded only too readily to chaebol demands and returned to a more regulated mode of interest rate policy. In early 1992, the Finance Ministry instructed banks and NBFIs to reduce some of their key lending rates. It also asked the BOK to lower its rediscount rate in order to bring down market interest rates. Central bankers, under the leadership of Cho Soon, a former EPB minister and an ardent advocate of financial reform, strongly resisted this policy change (*Banker* July 1992: 48–53; *FEER* 4 June 1992: 58). However, backed by Roh and senior politicians in the ruling coalition who were eager to counter the economic slowdown in the face of looming elections, the Finance Ministry again prevailed over the central bank. The BOK was forced to reduce its rediscount rate after Cho was unceremoniously dismissed.

### Desegmentation and intra-sectoral conflicts

During the late 1980s and early 1990s, the Korean government moved more quickly to eliminate functional restrictions on the business scope of financial institutions. Measures were taken in the early 1980s to broaden and diversify the financial services and products offered by banks and NBFIs. These were piecemeal, however, and were not based on any long-term plan to achieve a desired financial structure. The move to liberalise the regulatory barriers that had created institutional segmentation seemed to be guided by policy-makers' desire to increase the efficiency of the Korean financial system. A closer look at the policy process suggests, however, that the major driving force was not so much the economic rationale as the result of interest group politics and associated policy responses from the government.

In Korea, a relatively large unorganised money or curb market had long been coexisting with the organised market. While meeting the needs of business firms for working capital, the curb market not only siphoned off massive funds from the organised market, but also generated financial instability. Reluctant to relinquish control over banks for industrial policy purposes, the government opted to develop NBFIs in the early 1970s in order to control the unorganised money market and to deepen the financial system (Nam 1994b).[8] Authorities granted NBFIs considerable freedom in interest rate setting, portfolio management and lending operations, although they were subjected to prudential regulation (Cho 1994: 121–7). The policy favours helped the NBFI sector to mushroom into the most dynamic segment of the financial market in Korea by the late 1970s. One unanticipated consequence of the government's deliberate efforts to foster the growth of NBFIs, however, was a substantial reduction in the role of banks as intermediaries between public depositors and corporate borrowers. Financial authorities began to redress the unbalanced growth between banks and NBFIs in the early 1980s.

But the Finance Ministry was circumspect in its attempt to change the increasingly asymmetrical structure of the financial system. An efficient way to improve the competitive position of banks might have been to give them the autonomy to set their financial prices and to manage their business operations. But such a strategy was invariably eschewed. On the one hand, the Finance Ministry wanted to maintain stable bank interest rates and was concerned that higher interest rates, as a result of the banks being allowed to set their financial prices, would adversely affect the growth and export performance of the manufacturing sector. On the other hand, to relinquish government control over banks' financial activities would deprive policy-makers of their major industrial policy instrument and make the banking sector an easy prey for the chaebols. The Finance Ministry therefore opted to allow banks to broaden their service offerings and to charge relatively higher interest rates on their new financial products (BOK 1995: 53–4).

Partly because of the implementation of these measures and partly because of a downward adjustment of non-bank interest rates, bank deposits began to increase significantly from late 1985, at the expense of the NBFIs. This increased the conflict between banks and their non-bank competitors that had been brewing since the early 1980s (Choi 1993: 46–9). NBFIs and their interest-representing organisations clamoured for further expansion of their business scope. Given that the chaebols owned most NBFIs and relied increasingly on NBFIs for their financial needs (Cho and Cole 1992: 126), the FKI was supportive of NBFI demands. Banks and the Korea Federation of Banks (KFB) also pressed for a reduction in government interference with their business management and for further deregulation of functional restraints on their financial operations (*KH* 28 May 1987). In response to demands by NBFIs and their chaebol owners, the Finance Ministry permitted the NBFI sector to further diversify its service offerings. When bank deposits began to drop rapidly in the late 1980s, the Finance Ministry also allowed banks to engage in new businesses. This seesaw game between banks and NBFIs, with financial authorities trying to maintain the competitive balance, continued throughout the late 1980s and into the early 1990s.

The intra-sectoral conflicts mirrored differences in the interests of the Finance Ministry and the Bank of Korea and the power struggles between them during this period. Nowhere were these differences and struggles more clearly demonstrated than in the revision of the General Banking Act. In late 1988, the BOK proposed several amendments to the Act with a view to loosening existing restrictions on the management and operations of banks and to helping them to regain their role as the mainstay of the Korean financial system. Central bankers also suggested that banks be allowed to introduce new financial products with higher and more effective yields and to extend into those non-banking business areas that they had previously been prevented from entering (*KT* 26 December 1989).

The Finance Ministry strongly disagreed with the BOK on revision of the Banking Act, as on other major reform issues. In the development of the banking sector, it had interests and policy objectives different from, and even antithetic to, those of the BOK. While aware of the negative impact that the lagging growth of banks had on the conduct of monetary policy, Finance Ministry officials had no intention of loosening their grip on banks or of giving them more operational autonomy. The central bankers' campaign for independence only made the Finance Ministry even more unwilling to make any concessions on this, believing that the BOK sought to enhance its status in the financial policy-making process and to undermine the Ministry's influence and power through revision of the General Banking Act (interview, Seoul, 4 September 1997).

The Finance Ministry's position also reflected the fact that it supervised most categories of NBFIs and relied on them for the execution of its supervisory functions and for the expansion of its regulatory power. It was therefore more concerned about the interests and demands of its direct constituents than about those of other financial institutions. Finally, Finance Ministry officials were eager to promote the development of NBFIs because many of them retired every year into top positions in the sector in a process known as *amakudari*.[9] While the Ministry took some measures to assist the growth of banks, the measures did not alter the fact that it had granted NBFIs more regulatory favours than it had the banks.

It was not surprising that the BOK's proposed amendments to the Banking Act were repudiated by the Finance Ministry even before they were submitted to the National Assembly. In 1989, and again in 1990, the Ministry foiled the central bank's attempts to push its proposal through the legislature. It was not until late 1991, when the Roh government decided to renew its efforts to liberalise the financial system, that the Act was finally revised to include the BOK's proposed amendments, albeit in considerably watered down form. As stipulated in the revised Act, banks remained under tight government control, particularly as regards their interest rates. Commercial banks were allowed to enter the securities business on a limited basis by acting as sales agents and as underwriters of government and public bonds. To mollify securities companies and other NBFIs that complained bitterly about this policy change, however, the Finance Ministry permitted them to offer foreign exchange services in relation to their core businesses.[10]

Although the business scope of the banks was expanded, their performance in general remained lacklustre. The multiplication of new financial products without full deregulation of interest rates appears to have been one major cause. Commercial banks were allowed to issue money market instruments (certificates of deposits, repurchase agreements and commercial bills), but rates on those instruments were kept in line with regulated bank deposit rates and were well below the market rates on similar instruments issued by NBFIs. As a result, the amount of funds that banks were able to mobilise through the issuance of these instruments was very small relative to their total deposits (Park and Kim 1994: 203). Chronic difficulty in mobilising sufficient loanable funds led to an inevitable decline in the growth of bank lending operations. As banks were restrained from determining their financial prices and offering high-yield financial products, their market share compared with that of NBFIs continued to fall.

## New reform initiatives under the new leadership, 1993–96

The process of financial liberalisation in Korea was given fresh impetus by the new democratic government under Kim Young-Sam. As the ruling Democratic Liberal Party's candidate, Kim won the December 1992 presidential election and became the first civilian president in Korea in more than three decades. Soon after taking office, the new president and his associates formulated extensive economic reform programmes. The measures, specified in 'the Five-Year Plan for a New Economy', were announced in April 1993 (*BK* May 1993: 32–5; *FEER* 29 April 1993: 52). Financial liberalisation, part and parcel of the reform package, placed particular emphasis on the early introduction of the long-delayed real-name financial transaction system, full interest rate deregulation, capital account opening and independent central bank control of monetary policy.

Economic reforms entailed a fundamental reorientation of the government's role in economic management and an overhaul of the administrative system. An explicit objective of the 5-year plan was thus to reduce state intervention substantially and to encourage societal participation and initiatives in the economy. To achieve this objective, administrative reforms, including removal of various outmoded regulatory policies and decentralisation of administrative power, were deemed indispensable. Also included in the economic reform plan was a renewed push to restructure the large-business sector. In addition to more aggressive enforcement of the Fair Trade and Anti-monopoly Act, the new government intended to deploy strict tax audits and credit management as supplementary instruments to preventing the chaebols' speculative landholdings and curtailing their horizontal corporate expansion (Choi and Lee 1995). Finally, Kim launched a vigorous anti-corruption campaign during the first half of 1993, which appeared to leave no sector of society unscathed (Lee and Sohn 1994: 2–4).

A combination of political and economic factors at both domestic and international levels seems to have accounted for Kim's strong reformist predilections. In the first place, although Kim was the first fully elected civilian president since 1961, tainted by neither corruption nor authoritarianism, his clean and democratic image was marred by the fact that he had been part of the ruling coalition since 1990, when he led his party into 'an unholy alliance' with Roh's DJP. Furthermore, the fact that Kim won the presidential election as the ruling DLP's candidate made a seemingly unshakeable impression upon the public that he owed his victory to his collaboration with Roh, despite the latter's neutral posture towards both the DLP nomination process and the election itself, and that Kim exercised his presidency under the shadow of Roh

Tae-Woo. The launch of political and economic reforms, Kim and his associates calculated, would be the best way to neutralise this impression and to mitigate the negative consequences of their affiliation with conservative DLP forces.

Finally, the 5 years of democratic rule under Roh bred an unprecedented expansion of civil society. The continuous process of democratisation gave rise to new public interest groups among farmers, workers, urban poor and intellectuals, and significantly broadened the political spaces for societal actors. Taking advantage of the growing influence of mass media and other channels, they were aggressive in protecting and advancing their interests. This development compelled political elites to consider the demands of an increasingly powerful popular constituency for coalition building and election votes and dictated, to a large extent, the political and ideological orientation within the ruling party. Kim's anti-corruption campaign, anti-chaebol measures, economic liberalisation and administrative reforms largely resonated with popular demand for clean government, the equal distribution of social wealth and a more democratic mode of economic policy-making.

The endogenous impulses for the reform were reinforced by intensive bilateral and multilateral pressures on Korea to liberalise its financial system. The final settlement of the lengthy Uruguay Round of GATT talks in 1993 included agreements by participants to liberalise the global trade in services, a sphere in which banking and finance industries represented prominent components. Korea, a signatory to the GATT agreement, would have to commit itself to open its financial sector to substantial foreign participation. Equally important, the USA, playing upon its extensive security links with Korea, applied continuing bilateral pressure on the latter to open its financial sector. In the face of these external challenges, the Kim government began to move away from the defensive mode of foreign economic policy towards active accommodation to external pressure (Moon 1996). The move was epitomised by the government's decision to apply for membership of the Organisation of Economic Co-operation and Development (OECD), which was predicated on the full liberalisation of the financial system.

Despite these strong political and economic stimuli and pressures, however, the overall pattern of financial liberalisation under the Kim government did not deviate greatly from the cautious and selective mode of the Chun and Roh administrations. While the real-name financial transaction system was introduced through an emergency presidential decree, implementation of interest rate liberalisation and capital decontrols again followed a halting and circuitous path. By the end of 1996, the Korean government had not yet completed the final stage of interest rate liberalisation, and kept many capital account transactions on a short leash. In January 1997, in response to growing public criticisms of the government's lack of political will to carry through these important liberalisation measures and to persistent American pressures for capital account opening, Kim Young-Sam decreed, in a rather belated manner, the establishment of a presidential commission for financial reform, in an attempt to boost the slack reform process.

In the early to mid-1990s, as in the 1980s, the institutional features of Korea's financial policy-making, which shaped reform approaches and outcomes, displayed substantial tenacity notwithstanding the drastic socio-political changes brought about by democratisation. Kim had been elected with a mandate to curtail the expanding power of big business and launched a vigorous anti-chaebol campaign. But that campaign lost much of its vigour as the Kim government entered the second half of its tenure because of the chaebols' strong and persistent resistance and because of emerging macro-economic problems, particularly worsening external accounts (Table 4.1). With an economy overwhelmingly dependent on the chaebols for export performance and employment, and the ruling coalition still reliant on big business for political support, even the Kim regime found it difficult to get tough with the chaebols.

While democratisation brought the emergence of countervailing forces *vis-à-vis* the chaebols, Kim's attempt to internationalise the Korean economy imposed inherent limits on his ability to discipline the large-business sector and, paradoxically, enhanced the economic and political power of the chaebols. On the one hand, the globalisation drive helped to develop the knowledge and experience of the private sector to such an extent that it was now more capable than the government of making sound economic decisions, especially in the context of the growing complexity of the economy (Eckert 1993: 106). On the other hand, economic deregulation enhanced chaebol firms' access to alternative sources of finance, broadened their transnational linkages and strengthened their position as crucial agents of international competition (Moon 1996: 10–11). Structurally, these developments reinforced the economic dominance of big business and deepened government dependency on the chaebols for industrial competitiveness and continuing growth.

The institutional setting of financial policy-making within the state also remained largely intact. Riding on a wave of popular demand for central bank independence and on Kim's pledge to amend the central bank law to elevate the position of the BOK, central bankers made another attempt to gain policy-making autonomy from the government in early 1994. As in the past, however, their attempt achieved little, simply because the Finance Ministry did not want to surrender any of its bureaucratic territory. Moreover, government control over macro-economic policy in general and financial policy in particular was strengthened by the merger between the Finance Ministry and the Economic Planning Board in early 1995. Although reform-minded ex-EPB officials and conservative bureaucrats from the former Finance Ministry might not agree on the speed and degree of financial liberalisation within the new Ministry of Finance and Economy (MOFE), they appeared to have common interests in opposing any move towards institutionalising central bank independence.

### Renewed efforts to free interest rates

Interest rate deregulation, as the key constituent of economic and financial reforms, was part of the new government's broader attempt to transfer more policy-making power to market institutions and to reduce the bureaucratic stranglehold over the domestic financial system. The more direct cause for the renewed attempt at freeing interest rates presented itself in early 1993, when the president of Donghwa Bank was arrested for having taken huge bribes from customers in exchange for loans (*FEER* 10 June 1993: 67). Financial irregularities of this sort were not unusual and had long existed in the Korean banking sector. Lax supervision aside, the principal reason rested with the repression of bank interest rates by the government and associated excessive demand for bank loans. This generated heavy competition among lenders and encouraged corruption among bank managers. The political implications of the bank scandal were all the greater as it occurred in the thick of Kim's vigorous campaign to purge the country's economic and political life of corruption.

Less than a month after the bank scandal, the government unveiled a new multistage plan for interest rate liberalisation to be completed by the end of 1997 (*KH* 29 May 1993). This plan was slow in being put into practice, however, owing to bitter divisions on the timing of its implementation within the economic bureaucracy and private sector. On one side, the ministries of finance and of trade and industry, apprehensive about the adverse impact of higher interest rates on the faltering economy, insisted on postponing the first-stage interest deregulation until macro-economic conditions improved (*Banker* July 1993: 58; *KH* 12 August 1993). FKI leaders also called upon financial policy-makers to boost the investment enthusiasm of business firms by reducing lending rates and expanding the money supply. On the other side, reform-minded technocrats at the BOK favoured early implementation of the interest deregulation plan and opposed interest reductions as a way to stimulate economic activities (*KT* 6 March 1993 and 12 August 1993).

Growth-oriented officials and the chaebols gained the upper hand in this policy dispute. The new administration appeared to care more about growth than about stability and was keen to revitalise the country's development potential. During the first quarter of 1993, financial authorities twice reduced bank and NBFI interest rates by a total of 3 percentage points – the deepest interest cut ever made since 1982. The government also committed 1 trillion won in low-interest loans for small and medium-sized business firms and raised the limit on the amount of bonds issued abroad by the largest chaebol firms (*BK* April 1993: 14–15). These measures helped to increase systemic liquidity, dampen demands for bank credits and pull down market interest rates. Combined with the economic recovery in late 1993, this relieved financial officials of their concerns about the negative impact of interest rate liberalisation and, equally importantly, muted the chaebols' objection.

Improved macro-economic conditions and the lack of strong chaebol opposition created a favourable environment for interest rate liberalisation. In November 1993, the government finally succeeded in launching the first stage of interest deregulation. During 1994–95, the Korean economy returned to its rapid growth trajectory, as indicated in Table 4.1. As the government reduced restrictions on overseas borrowings by the large-business sector, chaebol firms gained enhanced access to international financial markets and had sufficient funds with which to finance their investment activities. These factors strengthened financial officials' ability to maintain interest deregulation and to deepen the reform process. It proceeded with the second stage in mid-1994, and had largely completed the projected deregulation items by the end of 1995, freeing interest rates on short-term time deposits and instalment savings and expanding the scope of liberalisation of issuing rates on short-term money-market products.

While the ongoing process of interest rate liberalisation in the early to mid-1990s heralded the end of the era when the Korean state had supplanted the market in setting financial prices and allocating financial resources, it did not signify that government intervention would end soon. The government was unwilling to give banks full autonomy in their operations and management, mainly because of the long-established developmental ideology that was based on financial repression for industry policy purposes and, more importantly, because of the institutional features of Korean financial policy-making that were created by more than three decades of export-led growth. Although the chaebols did not strongly oppose the process of interest rate deregulation, they showed little tolerance of rapid and large increases in market interest rates and often called upon financial authorities to intervene whenever they considered the level of interest rates to be unpalatably high.

There was no lack of examples in which financial institutions were instructed to set or change deregulated interest rates at the discretion of the government. Immediately after the second stage of interest rate liberalisation was implemented in November 1994, for instance, the Finance Ministry summoned senior bank managers and warned them not to hike interest rates 'excessively' (*KT* 26 November 1994). On another occasion, in January 1995, financial authorities rejected the request from commercial banks for a rise in their prime rates in response to climbing deposit rates, on the grounds that the prime rate increase would raise production costs of the manufacturing sector and hamper its overall competitiveness (*KT* 11 January 1995). While financial institutions were, in theory, free to determine most of their financial prices in line with market changes, they would have to seek official approval whenever they intended to make major adjustments to key interest rates.

### Selective and tardy capital decontrol

Capital decontrol was placed high on the agenda of the new government, reflecting the desire of Kim Young-Sam to get Korea admitted into the OECD as a central part of his globalisation strategy. Some government agencies, such as the BOK and the Foreign Ministry, also saw OECD membership as an important way to enhance the prestige and credibility of the country and to speed up the process of financial opening. At the same time, the US government urged the Kim administration to be bolder in capital account liberalisation and maintained strong diplomatic pressures on its Korean counterpart through both bilateral and multilateral channels. Despite foreign pressures and presidential support for capital decontrol to meet OECD entry requirements, however, the scope of external financial liberalisation remained moderate throughout 1993 and 1994; even the modest liberalising measures occurred largely on the outflow side.

This selective pattern underlined government fears about the domestic economic and political effects of uncontrolled capital movements. Financial policy-makers were worried that rapid capital inflows would ignite inflationary pressures and bring about a real appreciation of the won. Even those who favoured greater financial internationalisation to gain OECD membership would have to reckon with the prospects of high inflationary levels and rapid exchange appreciation. To preclude such prospects, the Finance Ministry emphasised liberalising capital outflows. Regulations on overseas direct and portfolio investments were eased and categories of export payments and remittances requiring official approval were cut down. While keeping capital markets largely closed to foreign financial firms and investors, the government allowed Korean banks and chaebol firms greater access to foreign credit markets.

Selective capital liberalisation also reflected the interests of the large-business sector. The chaebols welcomed deregulation of capital outflows because it was likely to expand their scope for overseas operations and provide them with the opportunity to stash away personal fortunes abroad. This proved especially important to big business after the implementation of the real-name financial system (interviews, Seoul, 25 June and 24 July 1997). On the other hand, restrictions on foreign direct and portfolio investments protected chaebol firms from greater foreign competition and stemmed the rapid foreign entry into the capital markets that might otherwise have diluted their managerial and ownership controls. Equally important, the chaebols welcomed enhanced access to foreign funds, which they desperately needed to finance their rapid industrial expansion.

The sequencing of liberalising measures included in the new plan for foreign exchange and capital decontrol, announced in December 1994, incorporated these government and chaebol interests. The plan envisaged a multistage liberalisation whereby the majority of Korea's international financial transactions would be deregulated over the next 5 years, until the end of the century. Moreover, the liberalisation of restrictions on capital outflows was sequenced prior to that of most controls over capital inflows; regulations concerning the opening up of stock and bond markets to foreigners would not be fully removed until 1999. This aroused widespread speculation among international financial analysts that the plan for capital decontrol was sequenced in such a way that the government would be able to temper its pace and contents after Kim Young-Sam stepped down in early 1998 (*Banker* July 1995: 68–71).

Implementation of scheduled liberalising measures was far from smooth and assured. As the country's current account deficit widened during early to mid-1995 because of rapid imports of raw materials and capital goods, liberalisation of payment controls over certain current account transactions and of restrictions on outward investments in foreign securities and real estate was delayed. Although limits on the inflow of short-term capital were eased, long-term investment in Korea remained difficult for foreigners: the ceiling on foreign ownership of a Korean company's shares was grudgingly raised from 12 per cent to 15 per cent; foreigners were allowed only indirect investment in the bond market through bond investment funds; requirements on the opening of branches by foreign securities firms were strict; and regulations on equity participation by foreign investment trusts in their Korean counterparts remained extensive.

Continued controls on the operations of foreign investors and firms provoked an array of complaints from American financial institutions that developed an interest in gaining access to the lucrative Korean capital market. During the first half of 1995, the US government, whether at bilateral meetings or in multilateral financial service negotiations, waged a new round of diplomatic campaigns to extract more concessions on the opening up of the financial market (*KH* 8 February 1995; *KT* 20 April 1995). In October, an OECD mission to Korea found that the level of capital liberalisation was far below the entry requirements set by the OECD and that tight controls over capital flows stood in the way of the country's bid to gain membership (*KH* 20 October 1995).

Kim Young-Sam, who saw Korea's accession to the OECD as a hallmark of his presidency, intended to quicken the process of capital liberalisation to accommodate foreign pressure and to clear the way for membership, but he also had to take domestic politics and public opinion into consideration. Rank-and-file Koreans were at best lukewarm towards OECD membership, if only because the benefits were vague but the costs high. In addition, the tough and pushy attitude adopted by the US government on financial liberalisation aroused strong anti-American sentiment, particularly among student groups, labour unions and nationalistic intellectuals, who opposed further concessions to foreign demands in exchange for OECD admission. Opposition politicians also accused Kim Young-Sam of pursuing personal fame and ambition at the expense of national interests, and warned that blindly seeking OECD membership when Korea's overall economic competitiveness was far below membership levels would have disastrous consequences (*KH* 20 September 1996).

Caught in this two-level game between foreign and domestic pressures, political leaders had to adopt Janus-faced tactics. While the government announced a quicker and more extensive version of capital decontrol in late 1995 to satisfy American and OECD demands, it continued to temporise with the actual implementation of pre-announced reform measures. Although regulations on outward direct and portfolio investments were considerably eased, many limitations on foreign entry into the capital market were maintained. Some liberalising measures were undertaken not so much for reform purposes as for other policy considerations. The ceiling on foreign ownership of Korean stocks was raised mainly to stimulate the bearish stock market. By the same token, the government allowed financial and corporate firms direct access to foreign commercial loans with a view to offsetting shrinking international reserves.

This account of Korean capital liberalisation in the mid-1990s reaffirms the political constraints that sectoral and bureaucratic interests imposed on financial policy reforms. Financial bureaucrats wanted to maintain the political advantage of being able to use capital controls to strengthen the government's regulatory power, manage macro-economic policy and promote industrial growth. The chaebols saw selective capital decontrol as an opportunity to obtain cheap foreign funds and broaden their overseas operations and as a guarantee against foreign competitive pressures. The institutional structures that preordained the dominance of the Finance Ministry among state economic agencies and of the chaebols in private preference formation secured full translation of their interests into the financial policy process.

## Conclusions

In Korea, the main impetuses for the continuous process of financial liberalisation from the early 1980s to the mid-1990s stemmed from changes in policy orientation and government leadership as well as from external political pressure and market forces. The approach to, and sequence of, financial liberalisation displayed their own peculiar patterns. The government maintained general controls over interest rates and credit allocation but allowed increased entry of new domestic and foreign financial institutions; it limited privatised commercial banks to carrying out industrial and credit policies while giving greater freedom to NBFIs to mobilise savings; it continued relatively strong restrictions on capital movements long after having initiated domestic financial reforms. Korea's distinctive approach led to tardy and selective outcomes in interest rate liberalisation and foreign exchange and capital decontrol but to more rapid progress in deregulation of entry barriers and functional de-segmentation.

The structure of private preference formation partly explains these reform approaches and outcomes. Throughout the reform process, major industrial interests centred in the large-business sector favoured entry barrier deregulation and expansion of the NBFI sector but opposed rapid interest rate liberalisation, reduction of preferential credit and removal of FDI restrictions. The ability of the chaebols to translate their policy preferences into actual reform policies was underpinned by their strong organisational resources and dominant position in the economy, their ownership and managerial controls over most NBFIs, their close but asymmetrical ties to banks and their close relations with the ministries of finance and of trade and industry. Whereas all these institutional factors facilitated the aggregation and articulation of the chaebols' preferences, they undercut the ability of the banking community to assert its policy stance on financial liberalisation.

The distinctive pattern of reform strategies and outcomes also underlined the immense programmatic interests of the government that financial liberalisation entailed in Korea. The Korean government, specifically the ministries of finance and of trade and industry, had strong motives for maintaining control over interest rates, credit allocation and capital movements as an instrument not only for macro-economic management and industry policy purposes, but also for structuring and restructuring its relations with the economy and society. These motives were also reinforced by the Finance Ministry's desire to preserve its power and authority in the financial policy-making process. Although central bankers generally favoured financial liberalisation, they were unable to act on their institutional interests, primarily because of the BOK's subordination to the government.

# 5  Financial liberalisation in Thailand

Thai financial liberalisation started gradually in the early 1980s but accelerated during the second half of the decade. In Thailand, as in Korea, external shocks and the associated fiscal and balance-of-payments crises precipitated the adoption of reform measures. Pressure leading to financial liberalisation also emanated from international financial institutions, foreign governments and transnational banks, which advocated the reform either as improving the prospects for economic development or as ensuring market access. While these factors might not operate equally throughout all the stages of financial liberalisation, a secular trend towards greater financial integration appears to have provided a constant impetus.

Thai reform policy was formulated in a regional context that was quite different from that of Korea. Particularly important in this respect were fundamental changes in the political and economic landscape of Indochina over the 1980s. The government viewed these changes as a good opportunity for remoulding and improving diplomatic and commercial links with the Indochinese countries. Consequently, it pushed the idea of a new zone of economic co-operation that would focus on Thailand and span the international boundary lines of the region. Government efforts to turn Bangkok into a regional financial centre became the linchpin of this strategic plan.

External pressures, whether political or economic, did not determine the substance of Thai policy responses; nor did differences in the regional environment preordain the variations in the approach to, and results of, financial liberalisation in Thailand. The direction and content of Thai financial reform primarily reflected the nature of political conflicts over financial policy-making among private actors, government ministries and politicians. The outcomes of those conflicts were shaped by the distinctive configuration of Thai institutions, specifically by the structure of private preference formation, the status of the Bank of Thailand (BOT) and its relations with the Finance Ministry.

This chapter, like that on Korea, proceeds chronologically through the case study of Thai financial policy and reform since the early 1980s, in the following four sections. The first section explores initial efforts to adjust financial policy in the wake of the economic crises of the early to mid-1980s, with particular regard to the structure of interest rates. The second section describes the more rapid and comprehensive move towards financial liberalisation in the late 1980s, when Thailand entered a high-growth period. The third section looks at the continued momentum of the liberalisation programme, including the launching of the Bangkok International Banking Facilities and the opening of the way for new entry in the domestic banking sector in the early to mid-1990s. The final section summarises Thai reform approaches and outcomes.

## Financial policy changes amidst economic crisis, 1980–87

Over the two decades to the late 1970s, Thailand witnessed a relatively strong and sustained economic growth. However, like many other developing countries reliant on commodities for export and dependent on large imports of oil, Thailand experienced tough times in the late 1970s and the early 1980s in the wake of the second oil shock and world-wide economic recession. Table 5.1 clearly shows that the economy was under severe strain during this period, particularly its external accounts. Moreover, the economy was badly hurt by climbing inflation under the combined effects of the near tripling of world oil prices and growing external imbalances. Against the backdrop of the oil

*Table 5.1* Main economic indicators in Thailand, 1970–96

|  | Real GDP growth | Rate of inflation | Current account as percentage of GDP | Real export growth | Debt–service ratio |
|---|---|---|---|---|---|
| 1970–74 | 6.1 | 9.2 | −1.6 | 23.1 | 14.2 |
| 1975–79 | 7.8 | 7.0 | −4.3 | 16.6 | 17.7 |
| 1980 | 5.8 | 19.7 | −6.2 | 17.0 | 15.6 |
| 1981 | 6.3 | 12.7 | −7.1 | 14.1 | 16.5 |
| 1982 | 4.1 | 5.2 | −2.7 | 6.0 | 18.0 |
| 1983 | 5.9 | 3.8 | −7.3 | −4.6 | 20.0 |
| 1984 | 5.5 | 0.9 | −5.1 | 14.1 | 20.8 |
| 1985 | 3.2 | 2.4 | −4.1 | 10.5 | 22.7 |
| 1986 | 4.9 | 1.9 | 0.6 | 20.7 | 20.6 |
| 1987 | 9.5 | 2.5 | −0.7 | 28.8 | 17.1 |
| 1988 | 13.2 | 3.8 | −2.7 | 33.9 | 12.9 |
| 1989 | 12.0 | 5.4 | −3.6 | 27.7 | 10.6 |
| 1990 | 10.0 | 6.0 | −8.6 | 14.9 | 9.1 |
| 1991 | 8.1 | 5.7 | −7.7 | 23.5 | 9.8 |
| 1992 | 7.9 | 4.1 | −5.7 | 14.2 | 10.6 |
| 1993 | 8.3 | 3.4 | −5.1 | 13.3 | 11.0 |
| 1994 | 8.7 | 5.1 | −5.6 | 21.3 | 11.6 |
| 1995 | 8.6 | 5.8 | −8.1 | 25.1 | 11.4 |
| 1996 | 6.7 | 5.9 | −7.9 | −1.3 | 12.3 |

Sources: Bank of Thailand (*Quarterly Bulletin*, various issues), Doner and Laothamatas (1994: 414), Khoman (2000: 42), United Nations (*Economic and Social Survey of Asia and the Pacific*, various issues ), Warr (1993: 54) and Wilbulswasdi (1987: 32, 1995: 17).

Note
GDP, gross domestic product.

price hike and shrinking international trade associated with global recession, Thailand's gross domestic product (GDP) growth rate dropped considerably.

While external shocks were mainly to blame for economic crises, the domestic problem of fiscal and monetary expansion was also a contributing factor. The introduction of brief democratic politics during 1973–76 and associated changes in the relationship between business, politicians and technocrats weakened the hold of conservative economic policies (Doner and Laothamatas 1994: 414–21; Laothamatas 1992a: 32–8; Muscat 1994: ch. 5). Furthermore, the withdrawal of the US military from Thailand when the Vietnam War ended in 1975 sharply reduced the inflow of economic aid and other transfer payments. With the fall of Cambodia to the Khmer Rouge at the same time, this prompted the military to demand more resources to be allocated to defence. From the mid-1970s onwards, successive cabinets had little political incentive to undertake restrictive policies – they leaned towards more expansionary strategies because of increased societal demands on the state, reduced foreign capital inflows and external security concerns.

During this period, public expenditure rose sharply, mainly owing to the rapid growth in defence and development investments. The bulk of these were funded primarily by loans from private sources that were raised internationally, resulting in a greatly increased foreign debt (Hewsion 1987: 64). When the second oil price hike hit Thailand, this growing debt problem became a crisis. To make matters worse, the government kept key inputs, including oil, below world market levels in an attempt to contain inflation. This led to an increase in the public-sector debt, which in turn contributed to the deterioration of external balances (Christensen *et al.* 1993). Realising the heavy price it paid for this implicit strategy of emphasising growth over stability, the Thai government began to take remedial measures in the late 1970s by raising fuel prices and exercising some monetary restraint. These measures were, however, far from adequate in the face of adverse external developments and growing fiscal imbalances. Economic woes thus underlined the urgent need for reform and a new direction for Thai economic policy.

Economic reorientation was facilitated by significant political changes ushered in by the new Prem government in 1980. Although not an elected member of parliament, General Prem Tinsulanonda was favoured by the main political parties as well as by the bureaucracy and military. He retained the premiership for the next 8 years by tactfully balancing the interests of these major political forces. This political equilibrium enabled the prime minister to give economic technocrats greater freedom of manoeuvre and action (Cole *et al.* 1990: 20–5; Doner and Unger 1993: 112–13). Lamenting the disarray into which the economic policy machinery had fallen in the 1970s, Prem initiated important institutional changes, designed not only to improve policy-making efficiency but to insulate state economic officials from broad popular pressure (Suksamran 1990: 140–2). Unlike its predecessors, the Prem government was able to keep major economic decisions out of the hands of elected politicians by filling economic posts in cabinet with specially appointed technocrats. As a result, macro-economic policy now came under the firm control of financial technocrats in the BOT and the Finance Ministry.

Technocratic leverage was further strengthened by the policy advice of the World Bank and the International Monetary Fund (IMF). In the early 1980s, the two institutions began to exert greater influence on the Thai economy as their role increased in alleviating foreign debt and capital formation problems. Loans and aid from the World Bank and the IMF carried conditionality clauses, requiring austerity, stabilisation and structural adjustment. The basic changes demanded of the Thai government were to reduce protection levels, devalue the baht, expand the tax base and lower growth targets (Hewison 1987: 71–6). In 1981, a special World Bank mission to Thailand prescribed abolition of interest rate ceilings, more liberal licensing policy for banks and liberalisation of balance sheet restrictions (Fry 1986: 179–80). While some political parties and populist elements in the military opposed the terms of IMF/World Bank loans, macro-economic technocrats supported much of the deregulatory thrust of that advice because it was in line with policy changes that they themselves intended to pursue (Laothamatas 1992b: 37).

Financial policy adjustments formed the core of the stabilisation programme formulated under the Prem government in the early 1980s. In addition to curbing public-sector deficits through budgetary restraints and tax reforms, the government focused on rectifying external imbalances through two major devaluations of the baht in the first half of the decade, and pegged the baht to a trade-weighted basket of currencies rather than to the US dollar.[1] At the same time, financial authorities readjusted the structure of domestic interest rates to keep it in line with volatile interest rates abroad. The government also moved to strengthen the central bank's supervisory authority following the massive failures of finance companies and commercial banks in the wake of economic crisis.[2] Although financial policy changes made during this period mainly served to restore economic stability, they paved the way for, and had important repercussions on, the next stages of financial liberalisation in Thailand.

### Interest rate adjustments

The rigid structure of domestic interest rates had long existed in the Thai financial system prior to the reform. While the stipulation of interest rate ceilings on deposits and loans by monetary authorities resulted in a certain degree of inflexibility, the rigidity in interest rate adjustment was also linked to the oligopolistic formation of the banking sector. The high degree of concentration in bank ownership led to the cartel-like organisation in which commercial banks collectively, through the co-ordination of the Thai Bankers' Association (TBA) set interest rates below official ceilings. This oligopolistic practice caused domestic interest rates to respond slowly to market conditions – it often took quite some time for all banks to agree upon changes in interest rates to ensure that nobody's interests would be impaired (Muscat 1995: 135–6; Warr 1993: 24).

In the early to mid-1980s, the Thai financial authorities made major interest rate adjustments in the direction of freer specification. The factors that precipitated the first major interest rate change had been emerging since late 1978, when Thailand was confronted with external and internal economic difficulties. Most critically, the large differential between high international interest rates and low domestic rates not only resulted in the slowdown of foreign capital inflows but encouraged interest arbitrage through loan swaps from foreign to domestic sources (Leeahtam 1991: 22–3). At the same time, the net interest earned on time deposits was too low in comparison with the unusually high inflation rate in the late 1970s and early 1980s, discouraging public savings and draining money away from the banking sector into the unorganised market. As capital inflows were decreasing and deposits at financial institutions dwindling, tight liquidity began to emerge and had a negative effect on the Thai economy.

A moderate increase in savings and time deposit rates in mid-1979 failed to address the problems of capital outflows and tight liquidity; the worsening economic situation demanded more drastic measures on the part of financial authorities (Wibulswasdi 1986, 1987). One such measure was to increase loan rates that were legally capped by the Civil and Commercial Code. To get this code amended by the legislature, however, required political sagacity and courage, as this would hurt the interests of the broad business community. In an effort to pre-empt possible opposition against the increase in loan rates, BOT governor Nukul Prachuabmol held a series of meetings with influential politicians and business leaders in late 1979. During those meetings, he explained the severity of tight money and successfully convinced them of the necessity to revise the code (BOT 1992: 280). The Financial Institutions Lending Rate Act, which was passed into law in late 1979, waived the maximum lending rate of 15 per cent that had been maintained for half a century and gave the BOT greater flexibility in setting interest rates in line with changing market conditions. With the newly granted policy-making authority, the BOT initiated three major interest rate hikes over the next 2 years.

With the successful implementation of restrictive monetary policy and other adjustment measures, economic stability appeared to have been firmly restored in the mid-1980s, as clearly indicated in Table 5.1. Partly as a result of the stabilisation process, however, economic growth registered a record low of only 3.2 per cent in 1985. A low interest rate policy was thus needed to stimulate the recession-hit economy. Consultations between central and private bankers were quickly arranged in April 1985 to map out ways by which to reduce local interest rates. During these negotiations, private bankers called on financial authorities to announce an official reduction in ceiling rates on deposits and loans. Financial authorities, however, insisted that banks should take the initiative as they had statutory rights to quote and adjust interest rates below the government-set ceilings. This underlined their desire to see a more competitive and efficient banking system, capable of developing a flexible interest rate structure in accordance with changing market conditions.

Private bankers did not appear to share these views and concerns, and resisted official pleas to lower interest rates on their own. Thai banks were individually reluctant to initiate an interest reduction, particularly on the liability side. This was because, unless deposit rates could be reduced simultaneously by all banks, those that went first would lose their market shares to the others that did not follow suit. This in turn prevented banks from lowering their loan rates as the cost of their funds would rise if they lowered loan rates without cutting deposit rates proportionally. Private bankers and TBA leaders thus insisted that the BOT should make an announcement so that all commercial banks would have to follow the same line of action. Moreover, even if bankers were able to take a uniform action on their own, the discrepancy between immediate cuts in loan rates and the maturity of time deposits would eat into the short-term earnings of banks.

Economic considerations were reinforced by a socio-political factor that weighed heavily on the minds of private bankers. In Thailand, the private banking community, with a high degree of ownership concentration and a dominant position in the economy, was a recurrent target of criticism, especially from populist elements in the army and the rural poor. It is interesting to note that, not long before financial authorities persuaded banks to lower their interest rates, some high-ranking army officers had accused private bankers of becoming fat on savers' hard-earned income and unfairly exploiting poor farmers [*Far Eastern Economic Review* (*FEER*) 10 September 1982: 62–3; *Nation* 18 August 1982]. Banks were thus concerned that any move to cut deposit rates on their own would further tarnish their public image in the eyes of urban and rural depositors.

Given the adverse impact that the voluntary adjustment of interest rates would potentially inflict on their economic and political interests, private bankers stuck firmly by their position. Concerned about the worsening economic recession, financial authorities had to seek co-operation from private bankers by providing them with an array of policy favours in the form of higher rediscount facilities and more freedom to open branches. But such policy favours led to only modest interest rate cuts by banks. Substantial cuts did not materialise until early 1986, when the BOT finally stepped in to reduce ceiling rates on deposits and loans by a big margin. To counteract the adverse effects of the sharp interest rate reductions on banks' profitability and, more importantly, to push them to further lower interest rates, the central bank allowed private bankers to increase their foreign exchange exposure, broaden their investments in non-financial businesses and enhance their access to government bond swaps.[3]

Between May 1985 and April 1987, financial authorities managed to reduce interest rates on deposits and loans by more than 5 per cent and effected a low interest rate policy as an important measure to stimulate economic recovery. For all the difficulties involved in interest rate reductions, the behaviour of both central and private bankers underwent subtle but important changes during this period, paving the way for the advent of a freer system. One significant change was that the BOT, having previously determined all interest rates for commercial banks, now confined itself to setting ceiling rates only and encouraged banks to adjust, collectively or otherwise, the actual levels of each interest rate. The BOT-sanctioned interest rate cut in early 1986 proved to be the last official intervention in the setting of interest rates. For almost 4 years until 1989, when the interest rate structure began to be comprehensively deregulated, private bankers set and adjusted their interest rates both upwards and downwards without waiting for the official decrees, although they sometimes did so with policy incentives provided by financial authorities.

## Deregulation of entry barriers

As noted in Chapter 3, the BOT strictly limited the number of domestic banking institutions and foreign bank branches to maintain the stability of the banking system. The policy led to the creation of a banking industry that was highly concentrated and oligopolistic in its structure and constantly lucrative for the incumbent banks. The 1960s and 1970s were golden years for Thai commercial banks. Operating under stable macro-economic conditions and favourable government policies, they expanded tremendously in size and profits (Muscat 1995: 113; Vichyanond 1994: 31). The sector was among the most profitable industries in the Thai economy, constantly attracting potential entrants, particularly from the manufacturing and commercial sectors.

In early 1978, several groups of industrialists and businessmen tried in vain to establish new banks. Their attempts failed mainly because of the strong opposition from central and private bankers [*Bangkok Post* (*BP*) 13 February and 7 June 1978]. The issue of new bank entry remained shelved until late 1983, when the same groups of industrialists and businessmen again clamoured for banking licences. This time they were joined by many other groups of eager entrants, ranging from businessmen-turned-politicians and retired government officials to private financiers of some leading finance companies and agricultural product traders. Once again, however, the deregulation lobby and its supporters in the government ran into opposition from the alliance of central and private bankers. TBA leaders urged financial authorities to be cautious about granting new banking licences and not to cave in to political pressure. The finance company crisis in late 1983 and the subsequent collapse of the Asia Trust Bank played into the hands of private bankers. Fully aware of the stability mentality of central bankers, TBA leaders made a big issue of the financial debacle, warning that deregulation of entry barriers without putting the trouble-stricken system in order would only invite more problems in future (*BP* 25 November 1983).

Financial leaders were certainly worried about the deteriorating position of some small and weak banks and about the adverse effects of increased competition on the banking sector. If anything, the BOT intended to reduce the number of existing banks via mergers that would weed out ailing institutions, rather than to open up the banking sector to more entrants. Another problem that loomed large in the mind of central bankers was the rapid growth in the country's trade and balance-of-payments deficits during the second half of 1983. To rectify the external disequilibrium, the BOT introduced a strict credit-control scheme to curb the extension of bank loans and stem surging imports. Central bankers feared that, if more banks were established, the amount of credit extension would inevitably rise and nullify their efforts to improve the external accounts.

While central and private bankers allied against industrialists' attempts to enter the banking sector, the finance minister, Sommai Hoontrakul, bore the brunt of mounting political pressure, particularly from some cabinet members and politicians. To placate the pro-deregulation forces, Sommai asked the BOT to prepare guidelines on the establishment of new banking institutions. The Bank of Korea's (BOK) guidelines, however, laid down two strict conditions under which new banks were to be established: they would have to operate on the same lines as the Industrial Finance Corporation of Thailand (IFCT), meaning that they would not be allowed to conduct most commercial banking business, and the government would be the major shareholder in the new banks (*BP* 6 December 1983). The guidelines were designed in such a way that central bankers could be assured that new banks, if established at all, would neither compete directly with incumbent banks nor prove difficult to supervise.

As expected, the guidelines drew negative reactions from the applicants, none of whom was willing to establish banks under such terms and conditions. While some applicants pleaded with the government to revise the formula of the central bank, the odds began to be stacked against them. The prime minister, who was sympathetic to the position of financial technocrats, gave the guidelines his full endorsement during cabinet deliberations. In February 1984, the leading economic advisor to the prime minister publicly suggested that the issue of bank entry deregulation should make way for other more important issues on the government agenda, such as trade deficits and financial crises (*BP* 6 February 1984). Soon afterwards, the financial authorities announced that they would indefinitely postpone their decision on the establishment of new banks and formally closed the whole matter. Industrialists and business-men had suffered a wait of many years and made Herculean efforts in their campaign, only to see their hopes of owning banks dashed once again.

## Economic boom, regime change and speedier reform, 1988–92

The policy reforms undertaken during the first half of the 1980s produced impressive results. Economic growth spurted to 9.5 per cent in 1987 and then maintained double-digit rates until the end of the decade (see Table 5.1). The rapid growth, however, brought to the fore various bottlenecks in the economy. Aside from a growing shortage of skilled labour and of managerial talent, there were strains on the existing infrastructure [*Southeast Asia Business* (*SEAB*) Autumn 1988: 24]. Moreover, Thailand needed to upgrade its industrial structure and to make it more capital and technology intensive in order to cope with the rapid loss of comparative advantages in many labour-intensive industries to other emerging markets in Asia. Considerable investment funds were thus required to finance infrastructural works and industrial upgrading (Chaiyasoot 1995: 164–5). However, the financial system was inefficient in mobilising more investment resources – a tell-tale sign was the widening gap between savings and investment (Wilbulswasdi 1995: 12). The Thai government viewed liberalisation as an important way to improve the overall efficiency of the domestic financial system by increasing the availability of investment funds for industrial development (Kiriwat 1993: 117–20).

Financial leaders also wished to improve the operations of the financial system in line with the changing external environment. Particularly important in this regard were dramatic changes in the political and economic landscape of Indochina. From the late 1980s onwards, not only did the decade-long hostility among neighbouring Indochinese countries ease considerably and their relationships with Thailand begin to normalise, but Vietnam and Laos shifted away from the command economy and moved towards market-oriented systems. The Thai government intended to take advantage of these changes to improve diplomatic and commercial links with the Indochinese countries [*Bangkok Bank Monthly Review* (*BBMR*) April 1989: 172–5; *SEAB* Fall 1988: 22, Winter 1989: 25]. Concomitant with this foreign policy initiative was the ambitious plan of turning Bangkok into a regional financial centre on the Southeast Asian mainland and a provider of financial services for economic reconstruction in Indochinese countries. Financial leaders thus saw a more efficient and competitive domestic financial sector as the centrepiece of this strategic plan.

Another important impetus behind liberalisation was the multilateral negotiation on trade in financial services conducted under the auspices of the General Agreement on Tariffs and Trade (GATT) and increasing bilateral pressure from the USA and Western Europe upon Thailand to liberalise its financial system. Thai financial institutions were expected to adapt to a more competitive environment envisaged after conclusion of the GATT negotiation. Their ability to do so was contingent upon the extent to which they could strengthen their capital bases, modernise their management and boost their efficiency. The government intended to improve the efficiency and flexibility of domestic financial institutions through liberalisation in the hope that they would survive in a highly competitive environment and take advantage of opportunities presented by global market integration (Tivakul and Svetarundra 1993).

Important as domestic economic needs and external pressures were, the more direct impetus for financial reform was the changed leadership of the government and the concomitant political conflicts over financial policy. In the July 1988 election, Chatichai Choonhavan, a retired army general and a prominent politician with business experience, was swept into office as Thailand's first fully elected prime minister for 12 years. The election of

Chatichai represented a mandate for greatly increased participation of private businesses in political affairs (Cole *et al.* 1990: 25–8; Phongpaichit and Baker 1996: 179–80). During the Chatichai years, business interests strengthened their foothold in parliament, and many businessmen-cum-politicians were appointed to important cabinet portfolios that military and bureaucratic elites had regarded as their own turf. On the other hand, technocrats in the National Economic and Social Development Board (NESDB), the country's top planning agency, were pushed aside and the Council of Economic Ministers – a body set up by Prem to screen major policy matters – became marginalised. The prime minister and his deputies increasingly turned to their own teams of personal advisors for policy inputs (*FEER* 19 January 1989: 30–2).

This change in political orientation held immediate ramifications for financial policy-making (the following discussion draws on author interviews, Bangkok, 14 and 28 March 1997; *Asiamoney* April 1990: 49–54; *SEAB* Summer 1989: 35–6). Pramual Sabhavasu, a renowned businessman and deputy head of the Chart Thai Party, was appointed finance minister and became one of the few politicians ever to fill the post. Once in office, Pramual promised to pursue rapid liberalisation of the financial system and attempted to break with the traditionally cautious approach to financial management. The new finance minister's penchant for liberalisation, however, reflected not so much his desire to improve the efficiency of the financial sector *per se* as his partisan interests, personal experiences and strong links to the industrial constituency. Pramual and his Chart Thai colleagues saw themselves as representing the interests of industrialists. His own experience as industry minister and his long background in the construction sector inclined him to be antagonistic towards the local banking community. Financial liberalisation, as viewed by Pramual, was an important means to shatter the dominant position of commercial banks and reduce their power *vis-à-vis* industrial capital.

The new finance minister also took on the central bank. Traditionally, the finance minister and central bankers decided major policy issues together through close consultation and co-ordination. Under Pramual, however, that relationship broke down. Backed by his own team of advisors, he took fiscal and monetary policies into his own hands. Claiming that the BOT had too much independence [*Bangkok Post Economic Review* (*BPER*) July 1989: 17], Pramual attempted to bring it under his control and increasingly intervened in its operations. He bypassed central bankers and asked commercial banks to report their lending and borrowing activities directly to him; he overrode the BOT's prerogative of adjusting interest rates to manage systemic liquidity and control inflation levels; he initiated negotiations with foreign banks over the possibility of allowing them to open full branches in Bangkok without consulting the BOT.

Behind this increasingly sour relationship lay fundamental differences between the finance minister and central bankers in their approaches to financial policy-making and reform. Pramual's aggressive approach to liberalisation did not fit in with the rather conservative posture of the BOT personified in its governor, Kamchorn Sathirakul. While Pramual sought quick results and pushed ahead with selective reform measures for short-term economic and political gains, Kamchorn consistently shied away from drastic changes in the financial system for fear of threatening its stability. Pramual augmented government spending to effect a more expansionary fiscal policy, increased foreign borrowings to finance large infrastructure projects and kept lending rates at a low level to please business interests. This provoked strong opposition from central bankers, who were deeply concerned about the consequence of making financial policy more responsive to political expediencies. The rivalry between the finance minister and central bankers, which had simmered ever since Pramual took office in late 1988, culminated in the abrupt removal of Kamchorn Sathirakul in early 1990.

Confrontation with the finance minister spurred central bankers to wrestle for authority and to manoeuvre for top positions on policy initiatives. The replacement of Kamchorn by his deputy, Chavalit Thanachanan, was hailed by the banking community as bringing new hope in the struggle against the domineering Pramual (*BP* 14 March 1990; *FEER* 15 March 1990: 51). Despite the fact that the new governor was due to retire 6 months later, he was determined to push for a financial policy in line with his own convictions. In the first 10 days after his appointment, Chavalit pushed through the long-delayed plan to raise the ceiling on lending rates and floated the interest rates for most deposit accounts. After 1 month in office, he and his associates initiated sweeping changes in Thailand's foreign exchange regime and elevated its position to Article 8 of the IMF charter, a classification for developed economies that lifted foreign exchange restrictions on current transactions. Three months later, the governor mobilised top BOT brains to put forward a comprehensive programme for liberalisation and development of the financial system [*Asian Finance (AF)* 15 July 1990: 58–60; *Nation* 16 June 1990].

The content of financial policy and the direction of further reforms in the early 1990s carried forward the direction of Chavalit's liberalisation programme, despite drastic and tumultuous political changes. In February 1991, the military, responding to the Chatichai government's attempts to weaken the power base of senior military officials, staged a sudden coup and installed a former diplomat and widely respected businessman, Anand Panyarachun, as prime minister. Following elections held in early 1992, the political parties that supported the military achieved a dominant position in parliament. The coup leader, General Suchinda Kraprayoon, became prime minister even though he was not himself an elected member of parliament. This provoked a massive demonstration in Bangkok and other cities, and was followed by a massacre of demonstrators by soldiers in mid-May. Further conflict and blood-shedding were avoided when Suchinda was forced out of office in disgrace and the King intervened by reinstalling Anand as an interim prime minister to prepare for new elections.

During the first Anand period, the government was given a free hand by the military to manage economic policy. Top military leaders promised to leave the BOT and the Finance Ministry in complete control of fiscal and monetary policies and fully endorsed the liberalisation programme initiated by Chavalit (*AF* 15 September 1991: 73–4; *BP* 26 and 28 February 1991). An important consideration for the military was to ensure that its putsch, routinely condemned by Western countries, should not jeopardise Thailand's economic boom, which was continuously driven by foreign capital inflows. In fact, many senior military officials, who benefited from the economic boom in general and the flourishing stock market in particular, had a direct stake in sustaining prosperity. The sound management of economic policy and financial liberalisation, as seen by the military leaders, were crucial in boosting confidence among foreign investors in the aftermath of the coup and in maintaining the continued inflow of foreign funds (*FEER* 18 July 1991: 31–4).

The interim Anand government reinstated the technocratic apparatus and its leading personalities, and deflected the tendency to subvert economic policy to the whims of politicians that had been so prevalent under Chatichai. Economic management was put into the hands of many of the same technocrats who, at one time or another, had made up the economic team of the Prem cabinet (*FEER* 21 March 1991: 50–1; *Nation* 18 September 1991). Financial technocrats regained their leverage *vis-à-vis* politicians and took the opportunity to accelerate the reform process. Follow-up measures were implemented to dismantle interest rate ceilings and to further loosen foreign exchange controls; new reforms also included the expansion of business activities of financial institutions and the relaxation of constraints on commercial banks' portfolio management (*FEER* 18 July 1991: 45–7).

### Foreign exchange and capital decontrol

Compared with Korea, and indeed with many other developing countries, Thailand had maintained a relatively liberal foreign exchange regime prior to the launch of comprehensive financial liberalisation in the late 1980s. When Chavalit and his associates in the central bank attempted to outmanoeuvre Pramual on reform initiatives, and when a premium was placed on expeditious policy changes, they understandably first took on foreign capital decontrol because significant institutional and political barriers were not expected. Because pre-existing policies and institutional arrangements shaped the parameters within which foreign exchange decontrols were conducted, it is necessary to examine Thai foreign exchange policy over a longer historical perspective.

Until the outbreak of the Second World War, Thailand had virtually no restrictions on foreign trade and capital flows, and its currency was securely linked with, and fully convertible into, the pound sterling (this account is drawn from Mousny 1964: ch. 1; Phongpaichit 1980; Sanittanont 1973). Alliance with Japan during the war caused Thailand's international reserves deposited abroad to be forfeited by the allied countries. Coupled with the disruption of foreign trade, this led to a severe shortage of foreign exchange. Under the circumstances, the government had to resort to exchange controls through enactment of the Exchange Control Act in February 1942. Exchange controls did not terminate with the Japanese capitulation in August 1945, owing to the desire of financial authorities to replenish the severely depleted international reserves, maintain the value of the baht in face of inflation and conserve limited foreign currencies for the need of post-war reconstruction.

The early 1950s saw the first steps in the liberalisation of foreign exchange markets in post-war Thailand; important measures to ease exchange and capital controls followed in the late 1950s and throughout the 1960s, as summarised in Table 5.2. Financial leaders' ability to implement these regulatory changes in the Thai foreign exchange regime was in part a function of improved international reserves (Ingram 1971: 311–14) and financial aids provided by the US government and the World Bank (Doner and Unger 1993: 104; Phongpaichit 1980: 447). Development of the liberal features of Thai foreign

*Table 5.2* Key changes in the Thai foreign exchange and capital regime

| *Current account transactions* | *Capital account transactions* |
| --- | --- |
| *Mid-1950s to late 1960s* | |
| Revoked multiple exchange rate; system allowed payments for imports and invisibles; permitted outward foreign currency transfers under the prescribed amount; no controls on inward foreign exchange remittances; non-residents allowed to open foreign currency accounts with local banks and no limits to transfers from such accounts | Investment promotional privileges made equally available to local and foreign capital in the 1962 Investment Promotion Act; full foreign ownership allowed except in a few sectors; no strict restrictions on profit repatriation; relatively free access to overseas financial markets by domestic firms |
| *Early 1970s to mid-1980s* | |
| More market-oriented exchange rate policy; Thais residing abroad allowed to take more foreign exchange out of the country; raised ceilings for commercial banks to sell foreign currencies to the public | More freedom for domestic industrial firms to borrow abroad; fewer restrictions on outward investment by local firms; relaxed controls on commercial banks' net foreign liability holdings |
| *Late 1980s to mid-1990s* | |
| Foreign exchange transactions authorised by banks without BOT approval; reduced or removed restrictions on the opening of foreign currency accounts by residents with local banks and withdrawal of funds from such accounts | Reduced limits on outward direct investment including those on the acquisition of real estate and investment in stocks; relaxed regulations over foreign equity holdings in industrial firms and participation in the stock market; enhanced access to external funds through BIBF |

Sources: *BP* (various issues), Bank of Thailand (1992: 209–20, 337–8), Bowie and Unger (1997: 142–53), International Monetary Fund (*AREAER*, various issues), Mousny (1964), *Nation* (various issues), Phongpaichit (1980), Sanittanont (1973) and Wibulswasdi and Tanvanich (1992).

Note
BOT, Bank of Thailand; BIBF, Bangkok International Banking Facilities.

exchange policy, however, should not be attributed to economic factors alone. Rather, they had more to do with regime changes, political interests and the ideological proclivities of financial leaders and institutional configuration of economic policy-making processes.

Significant changes in the Thai foreign exchange regime were made in connection with broader economic policy reforms ushered in by the Sarit regime in the late 1950s. For more than a decade after the Second World War, Thailand's development policy had an economically nationalist cast, with particular emphasis on state leadership in the industrialisation process. This strategy began to be reversed in 1958, when Field Marshal Sarit Thanarat came to power. In many of its policy statements, the government reiterated its commitment to the free-market model of development and to the pursuit of a liberal trade and exchange policy. These policy shifts reflected the influence of the US government and the World Bank as well as Sarit's efforts to undercut his political opponents, who relied on state enterprises for the financial resources they needed to foster their coalitional base (Bowie and Unger 1997: 135–9; Hewison 1985: 227; Phongpaichit 1980: 445–6).

Under the favourable regime change, the relaxation of exchange controls became more feasible as a means of expediting the return to the pre-war free market system intended by financial leaders. This intention had an endogenous, ideological base. Leading technocrats in the BOT and the Finance Ministry, who formulated liberal policy reforms, shared policy-making rules inspired by a longstanding tradition of financial conservatism and economic liberalism. These rules favoured open trade practices, non-intervention in financial markets and moderate controls over capital movements. Furthermore, following these principles, the Thai financial authorities pursued a policy that did not attempt in any major way to direct credit allocation within the industrial sector and which did not use controls over foreign capital as a tool to foster the growth of manufacturing firms. Finally, the government shied away from excessive foreign exchange controls, fearing that they would hurt the country's foreign trade and the public revenue (Corden 1967: 166–7).

Financial officials would probably not have been able to act on these interests without the dominant position of the central bank among state agencies. In Thailand, the BOT had overall control over credit and monetary policies and, together with the Finance Ministry, dominated foreign exchange policy formation and execution. In the late 1950s and early 1960s, the roles of financial technocrats in these two key economic institutions were further elevated through an administrative reorganisation initiated under the Sarit regime. As part of this reorganisational process, the balance of authority over economic policy between macro-economic agencies and line ministries of commerce and industry shifted in favour of the former (Bowie and Unger 1997: 137).

The policy preferences of financial technocrats also reflected underlying societal arrangements and private-sector interests. The relatively liberal exchange policy could be reinstalled in part because it had a political constituency. The policy had the support of dominant private actors concentrated in externally oriented financial and commercial activities. Private bankers consistently favoured the unregulated development of domestic financial markets and unrestricted flows of international capital. Their opposition to exchange controls derived from the predominance of trade financing in their portfolios and from their extensive involvement in agricultural exports (Doner and Unger 1993: 105). These naturally increased bankers' direct business interest in the success of the foreign trade sector. Moreover, importers and exporters who stood to gain from prospering international trade were understandably keen to support a free capital payment and transfer system. Driven by common interests, bankers and traders forged a societal coalition and consistently lobbied for relaxation of foreign exchange controls (*BBMR* June 1962: 1–3; Phongpaichit 1980: 444–50).

As Thailand moved into the 1970s, however, its liberal foreign exchange regime was subject to growing stress, against the backdrop of declining US economic and military aid to Thailand, worsening external imbalances and growing demands from some import-oriented industrialists for more restrictions on foreign investors. These economic and political changes, however, did not lead to a rollback of the liberal exchange policy. The socio-political forces – private bankers and exporters who had been nurtured by the open trade and exchange regime in the previous two decades – developed a vested interest in its continued openness. Widespread elite preferences for liberal financial policies were maintained as the dominant status of technocrats in the BOT and the Finance Ministry remained largely intact, despite the increased influence of political parties over the line ministries.

The mid- to late 1980s ushered in a new period of exchange deregulation when Thailand experienced rapid and sustained economic growth that was led by a sharp expansion of manufactured exports. This resulted in a diminishing external debt and rising foreign exchange reserves, which in turn encouraged financial technocrats to further relax restrictions on capital movements, particularly on the outflow side (see Table 5.2). The structure of interests in the private sector also encouraged further exchange deregulation. In the late 1980s, the country's success in exporting manufactured goods was followed rapidly by the export of capital and expertise; many Thai firms, particularly in the export-oriented and service sectors, were eager to move into overseas ventures. These firms, which had grown stronger and more competitive during the economic boom, quickly exhausted local opportunities and hankered for ways to expand their business abroad (Phongpaichit 1996: 372).

Closely following the relocation of their industrial clients' production activities, Thai commercial banks rapidly expanded their overseas networks of branches and representative offices, especially in Indochina [*Banker* June 1993: 29–30; *Economist Intelligence Unit Country Report (EIUCR)-Thailand* 3rd Quarter 1992: 24]. Furthermore, banks increasingly turned to fee-based services to generate more revenue as their income from the traditional banking business of deposit taking and loan extension was being squeezed under the double impact of intensified competition and their reduced role in financial intermediation

(*BPER* 30 June 1992: 25–6). Arranging foreign purchases of domestic securities, managing domestic demand for foreign assets and intermediating in foreign exchange transactions promised to open up opportunities for commercial banks to earn more fee-based income. As existing restrictions on capital movements hampered the expansion of such operations and fee-based businesses, private bankers lobbied financial authorities to remove these restrictions.

Foreign exchange deregulation had thus been in process for quite some time in Thailand and there had been relatively few restrictions on foreign exchange transactions and capital movements prior to the late 1980s. Chavalit Thanachanan decided to reform the foreign exchange regime first, because foreign exchange deregulation would entail fewer legal and institutional changes and would encounter less political opposition. The actual sequencing of liberalisation was based principally upon pre-existing policies as well as on political considerations among policy-makers. Earlier patterns of state action in the foreign exchange policy-making process and the socio-political factors that had forged those patterns shaped the notions held by financial leaders about what was feasible. 'Our road towards a liberalised system must be constructed on a practical ground, that is, to carry out the task that is possible', Chavalit observed when reflecting on the sequence of Thai financial liberalisation, '... our system of exchange control before the relaxation was already quite liberal ... Therefore, this practice was the first to be liberalised' (BOT 1992: 332).

The further reform of the Thai foreign exchange regime unfolded rapidly. In early 1990, Thailand adopted IMF Article 8. This was actually form rather than substance because the country had conformed with Article VIII requirements for years. More significant deregulatory measures followed in the early and mid-1990s to further deepen the process of financial internationalisation in Thailand, as highlighted in Table 5.2. As in the past, this process was underpinned by the powerful interest coalition between private bankers, commercial interests and liberal technocrats and by longstanding institutional arrangements in support of open foreign economic policies (Phongpaichit and Baker 2000: ch. 2).

### Interest rate liberalisation

In early May 1989, Pramual announced that the government was to eliminate the interest rate ceiling on fixed deposits of more than 1 year's maturity (the following account is based on *BP* 11 and 17 May 1989; *FEER* 1 June 1989: 52; *Nation* 12 May 1989 and 15 May 1989). Pramual's reform initiatives struck a chord with many industrialists, who welcomed the move as an attack on oligopolistic banks. Private bankers, on the other hand, were upset because they would face higher operating costs and fiercer competition for deposit mobilisations if the plan were put into effect. TBA leaders accused the finance minister of political manoeuvring and claimed that his decision to free deposit rates without changing lending rates was motivated by his desire to protect the interests of his industrial constituents. The BOT also voiced its reservations about the move and urged the finance minister to modify his reform package and to raise the ceiling rates on both deposits and loans.

The core of contention was not whether interest rates should be liberalised, but when and how that liberalisation should be conducted. As an ambitious politician already in his early sixties, Pramual sought quick political fame by launching expeditious interest rate reform. Regarding himself as the spokesman for the industrial community, he intended to promote the interests of industrialists and was eager to see greater competition and less profit in the banking sector (interviews, Bangkok, 10 and 25 March 1997). Central bankers, by contrast, were more concerned with the stability of the banking sector than with competition. The timing of interest rate liberalisation, in the view of central bankers, was not right when the monetary situation was tight and interest rates were edging upwards. They feared that, if interest rates were to be freed at that time, the fierce search for depositors in the form of competitive increases in deposit rates would reduce interest spread and undermine the position of smaller banks.

Despite the opposition from central and private bankers, Pramual managed to get his liberalisation scheme through the cabinet by dint of his authority and influence derived directly from the dominant position of the Chart Thai Party within the coalition government. But Pramual soon found the effectiveness of his reform dented by the strong efforts of private bankers to control competition among themselves. Immediately after long-term deposit rates were deregulated, almost all commercial banks agreed, co-ordinated by the TBA, to offer 10 per cent and 10.5 per cent interest for 18-month and 2-year deposits respectively. Although some smaller banks later breached the agreement by offering higher than TBA-sanctioned interest rates, the six leading banks stood firm and maintained the cartel. Given that these six banks held more than 70 per cent of the total assets in the banking sector, their decision carried great weight in determining the direction of deposit rates.

In addition to their endeavours to maintain the interest rate cartel, private bankers lobbied the government in late 1989 and early 1990 to have the loan rate lifted. Their efforts were reinforced by the BOT's desire to raise loan rates in order to dampen inflationary pressure. Immediately after Chavalit Thanachanan took over the BOT governorship in March 1990, he and his senior aids embarked upon a comprehensive package of restructuring local interest rates. The package raised the loan rate ceiling for commercial banks from 15 per cent to 16.5 per cent and, more significantly, freed interest rates for all remaining fixed deposit accounts with a maturity of 3–12 months. Changes in BOT leadership and the resolve of the new governor and his colleagues to restore the prominence of the BOT in financial management were crucial to the expeditious revamping of interest rates. Yet if supply-side factors were important, the structure of interests in the private banking community also encouraged the reform process. While private bankers feared increased competition following interest rate liberalisation, they quickly realised that they could benefit substantially from other reform measures. Fee-based incomes accruing from capital decontrol and the expansion of banking business offset the income losses that banks might suffer from rate deregulation and made them more inclined to support the reform package.

The increase in the loan rate ceiling seemed too limited to stall the over-heating economy. In 1990, the Thai economy maintained double-digit growth for the third consecutive year. Inflation hovered around 6 per cent, which was regarded as menacingly high in Thailand; mainly fuelled by unrestrained bank lending, imports surged and the balance-of-payments position worsened (Table 5.1). Meanwhile, with deposit rates rising steadily and loan rates capped, private bankers felt the pinch of increasing operating costs and declining profit margins. Towards late 1990, consensus emerged among financial circles that the only way to tackle the macro-economic ills and to improve the liquidity position of banks was to further increase interest rates. In late November, financial authorities formulated the plan to cool down the economy and raised the loan rate, despite strong complaints and heavy criticism from industrialists, their political patrons and some cabinet members (*BP* 24 and 30 November 1990; *Nation* 28 November 1990).

The increase in loan rates seems to have held back the rising trend of inflation and current account deficits. With higher interest rates, the demand for credits eased and the growth of bank lending declined. This, together with a copious inflow of foreign funds induced by a steady fall in overseas interest rates, reversed the tight monetary situation. With interest rates in a downward trend, the time seemed opportune for the BOT to proceed to the last phase of interest rate liberalisation – dismantling of the loan rate ceiling. If the ceiling were scrapped when liquidity was high and interest rates were declining, downward pressure would mitigate any fierce competition for deposits that might be triggered. The finance minister and senior central bankers drafted the bill for amending the Financial Institutions Lending Rate Act, which would authorise the BOT to scrap the loan rate ceilings for financial institutions. The bill was approved unanimously by the cabinet and was passed into law by the National Assembly in March 1992 and became effective in June, thus winding up the whole process of interest rate liberalisation.

### Deregulation of barriers to foreign entry

In the early 1980s, local businessmen and industrialists had been frustrated in their attempts to establish new banks and, ever since, had been unable to muster the courage to try again. During the second half of the decade, however, central and private bankers came under increasing pressure from foreign financial institutions to lower barriers to entry. In Thailand, financial authorities had long sought to protect the position of domestic banks not only by prohibiting the establishment of new domestic banks, but by restricting the entry of foreign banks. For almost 20 years until 1985, no licence for a bank branch had been issued to a foreign bank, and the only new entrant, Citibank, found its way to a Bangkok branch by acquiring an existing licence. Moreover, incumbent foreign bank branches were faced with operating constraints that affected their ability to compete with indigenous banks.

The mid- to late 1980s saw a surge in foreign direct investment in Thailand by multinational corporations from leading industrial countries and major East Asian newly industrialising economies (NIEs). Banks from these countries wanted to establish branches in Thailand to serve their manufacturing clients. Furthermore, driven by the export-oriented industrialisation strategy, trade between Thailand and its main economic partners multiplied, providing foreign banks with lucrative business opportunities such as trade financing and foreign exchange transactions. Finally, the flourishing stock market opened the way for foreign banks to mediate overseas purchases of domestic securities and to provide other advisory and brokerage services. As the Thai economy boomed, the costs of exclusion from this increasingly prosperous market grew considerably. Between 1984 and 1986, foreign banks lodged more than twenty applications to open branches in Thailand with financial authorities.

Foreign financial institutions were aggressive in securing diplomatic support for their interests. Political pressure was brought to bear on a number of bilateral and multilateral levels. The most direct and strongest source of pressure came from the governments of Thailand's main economic partners, particularly the USA. In the mid-1980s, trade frictions surfaced between Thailand and the USA and quickly intensified. In a series of bilateral talks, the US government pressed its Thai counterpart to open the banking and insurance sectors for more foreign participation, and backed its demands by threatening to revoke privileges offered under the Generalised Systems of Preferences (Phagaphasvivat 1990: 223–9; *SEAB* Winter 1987: 33–4, Winter 1989: 26–7). Moreover, the financial services agenda at the GATT negotiations provided another important source of pressure for financial reform in general and for entry deregulation in particular. The World Bank repeatedly urged the Thai government to license new banks and to lift restrictions on the operations of foreign banks (*EIUCR-Thailand* No. 2 1990: 23).

To ease foreign pressure on the government, financial authorities began, in late 1985, to draw up guidelines for foreign entry into the domestic financial market. These guidelines were prepared so perfunctorily and dilatorily, however, that it took the BOT more than a year to finalise the draft. When the government finally announced them in early 1987, they included the extent to which entering foreign banks contributed to Thailand's economic development and stated that joint ventures with, and foreign equity participation in, existing domestic banks would be favoured over wholly owned foreign bank branches. In addition, the guidelines set very high capital requirements and required foreign banks to take over ailing finance companies in the August 1984 lifeboat scheme as a precondition for market access (*BP* 18 March and 7 July 1987).[4] It may not be surprising that the conditions under which foreign banks could open branches, deliberately made stiff and unattractive, deterred most applicants for banking licences.

Before long, however, the issue of entry deregulation was again thrust back on the government agenda. This time, the pressure came from not only foreign banks and their governments but also the new finance minister, Pramual Sabhavasu. Shortly after his appointment in late 1988, Pramual announced that the government was accepting applications from foreign banks for new branch licences. The new finance minister, together with much of the industrial community, believed that foreign additions would bring in much-needed funds to support industrial development and ease the gap between savings and investment. More foreign banks, the finance minister submitted in several policy statements, would contribute to the government objective of promoting Bangkok as a regional financial centre in Southeast Asia (*Nation* 19 December 1988, 28 January 1989). Equally important, Pramual saw entry deregulation as an effective way to remove domestic bankers from their comfortable and lucrative perch and to strip them of the advantages that they had long enjoyed behind the protection policy.

Pramual's move to open up the banking sector worried central bankers, principally because it would have potential destabilising effects. Their concerns were shared in academic circles. In an unusual move, prominent economists from prestigious Thai universities and the leading think-tank, Thailand Development Research Institute, came out strongly against entry deregulation (*Nation* 27 December 1988, 18 November 1989). Equally, TBA leaders and private banks staged a fierce opposition to the decision to grant new licences and urged the authorities to curb the expansion of foreign banks. Their demands were echoed by employees in the financial sector. The Federation of Bank and Financial Workers Union of Thailand strongly suggested, in its petition to the government, that effective measures be taken to protect the interests of Thai financial firms as well as the welfare of local staff employed by foreign institutions (*BP* 11 October 1989). The enormous opposition from the broad financial community made the cabinet eventually decide to shelve the issue of entry deregulation in early 1990.

### Expansion of financial institutions' business scope

Although the Thai financial authorities had so far successfully kept foreign banks at bay, they knew that they would not be able to shield domestic banks from foreign competition for ever and that it was only a matter of time before political and economic pressure at multilateral and bilateral levels would force open the door. Even without additional foreign entrants, local banks already felt the pinch of growing competition from existing foreign bank branches, which used new technology and instruments to constantly improve their services and broaden their customer base. To strengthen the ability of local banks to contend with the increasingly competitive environment, the authorities moved to break down regulatory barriers that created functional segmentation and to permit local banks to engage in a wider range of businesses.

This move also underlined private financiers' desire to cultivate alternative sources of revenue by offering diversified services. Traditionally, commercial banks and finance companies had relied on interest income as their primary source of revenue. As domestic interest rates were steadily deregulated from the early 1980s, the resulting competition for depositors and customers squeezed interest earnings, and banks found it increasingly difficult to maintain their incremental profits. Anticipating that net interest income from traditional lending activities would diminish over the long term as a result of competitive pressure, banks and finance companies looked for other sources of revenue and started to develop new financial services from which fee-based earnings could be derived (*BPER* 30 June 1990: 20–1; Tivakul and Svetarundra 1993: 26–7). From the mid-1980s, private bankers and TBA leaders lobbied persistently for removing the regulatory restrictions that impeded the development of fee-based and high-margin businesses.

The economic rationales behind the move to broaden the business scope of financial institutions were reinforced by political considerations. Capitalising on the private bankers' strong desire to diversify into new financial services, the BOT sometimes permitted them to engage in more businesses in exchange for their support for its policy changes. In 1986, for instance, commercial banks were allowed to have new businesses, such as leasing, consulting and custodian services, in exchange for their co-operation in the revision of banking legislation; in 1987, when the local financial system was plagued by high liquidity, the BOT permitted banks to sell stock information to the public and to act as agents selling government bonds, in return for their efforts to reduce interest rates; in 1990, to secure bank support for his reform programme, Chavalit Thanachanan proposed the opening up of provident fund management and securities underwriting to commercial banks.

In expanding the business scope of financial institutions, the BOT and the Finance Ministry paid more attention to commercial banks, given that they were the largest and most important part of the financial system and were influential actors in the economic policy process. Throughout the 1980s, greater operating leeway and flexibility were continuously granted to banks rather than to non-bank financial institutions (NBFIs) whenever the BOT modified the regulatory framework to reduce competitive restraints. Aided by favourable policies, commercial banks made significant progress in product diversification and business expansion: not only did they offer most merchant banking, financial advisory and forfeiting services, but they also expanded rapidly into investment banking that had previously been the preserve of finance and securities companies.

In the face of this aggressive expansion, several dozen independent finance and securities companies began to press financial authorities to broaden their operational boundaries and to allow them to compete squarely with banks. Although finance and securities companies enjoyed greater autonomy in fund mobilisation and portfolio management than commercial banks, their business scope was rigidly defined by the regulatory framework sanctioned in the 1979 financial legislation and its 1985 amendments. Finance companies' operations were limited to the areas of commercial lending, hire purchase facilities and consumer and housing finance; securities companies were allowed to engage only in securities trading and underwriting, investment advice and stock brokering. While banks were able to enter the business domain of finance and securities companies, the reverse was hardly possible.

The BOT was cautious about broadening finance companies' business scope and constantly barred them from offering commercial banking products. In fact, many of the new financial services that finance companies were allowed had been operated and therefore dominated by commercial banks for years. One plausible reason for the differential treatment is that the NBFI sector was still recuperating from the financial crises of the early and mid-1980s – many finance and securities companies were redressing managerial malpractices, writing off bad loans and consolidating their capital base. Compared with the banking sector, finance and securities companies showed greater variance in size, breadth of services offered, financial stability and management quality (Vichyanond 1995: 329–33). Under the circumstances, the authorities were concerned that, if they were allowed to expand their services too rapidly and to engage prematurely in some banking business such as foreign exchange trading, serious regulatory problems would arise.

The structure of intra-sector relations within the financial community also impeded the business expansion of finance and securities companies. Almost half the finance and securities companies were affiliated with banks. Although these affiliates operated independently, bank representatives sat on their boards of directors and many key executives had earned their spurs within banks and were understood to take overall direction from bank executives. Moreover, bank-affiliated finance and securities companies relied heavily upon commercial banks for technological support, staff reinforcement and capital back-up. Quite often, banks 'passed on' lucrative business in the area of commercial banking to their affiliates. While independent finance and securities companies demanded deregulation of business boundaries between banks and NBFIs, bank affiliates remained aloof and indifferent (interviews, Bangkok, 25 March and 18 April 1997). This dented the organisational capacities of the Association of Finance Companies (AFC) and the Association of Securities Companies (ASC) and left the NBFI sector poorly positioned to act on its policy preferences.

Commercial banks continued to be able to get their business scope broadened to the disadvantage of NBFIs during the early 1990s, when financial authorities decided to further reduce regulatory barriers. Private bankers, under the leadership of the TBA, pressed hard for permission to engage directly in securities underwriting and investment services – the last major business area reserved for finance and securities companies. The 1992 amendments to the Banking Act relaxed many restrictions, allowing banks to offer financial and information services and act as stock registrars and selling agents for mutual funds. More significant, commercial banks obtained licences for underwriting and trading of debt instruments, despite the strong opposition from the AFC and the ASC. Although permitted to undertake more services, finance companies were kept largely outside the gamut of commercial banking business.

## Financial reform under political transition, 1993–96

In the early to mid-1990s, Thai financial policy-making continued its reform course during a period of political transition. Following two general elections and a bloody massacre on Bangkok's streets, the country eventually reverted to a democratically elected government in September 1992, led by Chuan Leekpai's Democratic Party. Democratic rule was consolidated in the mid-1990s, when the largely fair elections returned the Chart Thai Party, now under the leadership of Banharn Silapa-archa, to power and swept Chavalit Yongchaiyut's New Aspiration Party into office. Despite tremendous initial enthusiasm for democratisation, the governing capacity of all three governments was undermined by institutional constraints inherent in the Thai polity, specifically the recurrent pattern of unstable and shaky cabinets. Thai politics, particularly under the Banharn and Chavalit regimes, seemed in many respects like a return to the old days of the Chatichai administration: corruption in the government, power struggles among coalition partners and bureaucratic ineptitude in solving national problems (*Asia Year Book* 1996: 214–16; King 1997: 160–2).

Despite all these frustrations, Thai politics shifted further away from the balance of power that prevailed within the semi-democratic system of the Prem era. Central to this shift was the political descendancy of the military. Neither Chuan nor Banharn had any experience in the military or bureaucracy. Their prime ministerships signified an eventual departure from the bureaucratic polity in which decisions had been restricted to the patronage needs of military generals and bureaucrats. Following the May 1992 bloodshed, the military was driven onto the defensive. Generals closely associated with the coup were removed from powerful positions in the government; the cabinet repeatedly rejected military requests for further increases in defence budgets. In the mean time, professionalisation was initiated within the armed forces and the new military leadership forswore any further intervention in domestic politics (King 1996: 137–8; Phongpaichit and Baker 1996: 191–2).

Parallel with the weakening position of the military, the role of political parties was strengthened. The Thai political landscape was increasingly dominated by the various parties representing the interests of Bangkok big business, provincial business and the urban middle class (Girling 1996; Phongpaichit and Baker 1996: ch. 8). In both the Chuan and the Banharn governments, many important cabinet posts were typically given to party loyalists, who outnumbered non-political technocratic members. Politicians continued to hold sway in the ministries of agriculture, commerce and industry, which implemented sectoral economic policies and thus provided parties with rent-seeking opportunities. Increasingly, the direction and essence of economic policy were susceptible to the constituency considerations of politicians and to the results of compromises and clashes among various political parties in the governing coalition.

The ascendancy of politicians appeared to be accompanied by the diminishing influence of financial technocrats. The growing weight of political parties in the economic policy-making process aside, several institutional changes played a crucial role. The traditional partnership between the BOT and the Finance Ministry came under threat, as the Ministry became more politicised. During the early to mid-1990s, frequent disputes arose between the two institutions over many important issues, and the inter-agency arrangements for policy co-ordination began to disintegrate. Equally important, financial reform and political democratisation reduced the ability of central bankers to shape the behaviour of financial institutions and broadened the political space of the private banking community (Unger 1998: ch. 4).

The content of financial policy and the direction of its changes in the mid-1990s, however, carried forward the orientation and objectives of the Anand years with substantial continuity. Despite their expanded role, political parties had relatively modest influence over macro-economic issues owing to the lack of clear policy positions on the part of party leaders. With few exceptions, they tended to be deficient in refined understanding about financial policy and remained fragmented and discordant on such policy; their initiatives generally involved sectoral policies and distributive matters rather than broad economic strategies. This in large part reflected the absence of strong and clear ideological orientation among Thai political parties and their competitive and fragmented organisational features (Christensen 1991; Doner and Laothamatas 1994). As a result, they were not sufficiently sophisticated to formulate any long-term vision or plan for financial policy and reform, and were at an intellectual disadvantage *vis-à-vis* financial technocrats.

In late 1992, the BOT formulated a 3-year plan (1993–95) for further deregulation and development of the financial system, with emphasis placed on foreign exchange and capital decontrols (Duriyaprapan and Supapongse 1996; Wibulswasdi 1995). The reform course was given another strong push in early 1995, when the authorities announced a financial master plan for the coming 5 years (*Asiamoney* July/August 1995: 37–8). Although comprehensive in scope and clear in articulation, these wide-ranging financial sector reforms were flawed in several important aspects: the oligopolistic banking structure persisted, the growth of different financial institutions remained uneven and enforcement of prudential rules was weak. By the time the financial crisis gripped Thailand in mid-1997, the consequences of these policy failures became manifest.

## Bangkok international banking facilities

Significant foreign exchange and capital decontrol effected in the late 1980s and early 1990s led to increasing financial openness in Thailand. This trend was reinforced by the launch of the Bangkok International Banking Facilities (BIBF) in March 1993. Licences to operate offshore banking business were issued to forty-seven local and foreign banks among fifty-two applicants. BIBF licencees were allowed to engage in out–out operations, out–in transactions and other related offshore banking business.[5] Towards the end of 1994, the BOT also invited existing foreign BIBF banks to apply for Provincial International Banking Facilities (PIBF) licences, which would allow each successful applicant to open two provincial offices. The underlying agenda of the PBIF was to permit foreign banks to pursue limited expansion programmes beyond their head offices in Bangkok and, more importantly, to encourage the spread of financial services and development to provincial and rural areas.[6]

The ongoing political and economic changes in Indochina were an important impetus behind the establishment of the BIBF. In the late 1980s and early 1990s, with the political climate further improving and market reforms gathering momentum in Indochinese countries, the Chatichai administration had pioneered closer diplomatic and commercial links with those countries. The Anand and Chuan governments continued the strategy by pushing ahead with the idea of a free trade area in the region. Official policy was accompanied by private initiatives to push across the borders to the opening markets of Indochina (*Banker* June 1993: 29; *FEER* 31 December 1992: 73–4). In launching the offshore banking facilities, the Thai government intended to turn Bangkok into a regional funding centre for economic development in Indochina and to promote economic ties between Thailand and Indochina [*Asian Wall Street Journal* (*AWSJ*) 28 February 1995; Wibulsawasdi 1992).

The launch of the BIBF was also motivated by policy-makers' desire to increase the range and availability of capital for industrial expansion and infrastructural works at home. In fact, the BIBF was not an offshore banking facility in a strict sense because out–out operations or pure offshore banking activities ran parallel to out–in transactions. The idea of adopting a mixture of these two types of transactions was to allow BIBF banks to mobilise funds abroad for re-lending to Thailand as well as to Indochina. Given that domestic savings lagged far behind investment, demand for foreign funds maintained such a high level that out–in far exceeded out–out transactions. The bulk of initial BIBF operations took the form of lending not to the liberalising economies of Indochina but to customers in Thailand itself. By early 1996, out–in lending accounted for more than 65 per cent of BIBF business and almost 17 per cent of overall domestic credit (BOT 1996: 18).

Although there was a strong economic case for the launch of the BIBF, political considerations on the part of financial authorities also seem to have played an important role. Thailand had been able to keep its domestic banking sector closed to foreign entry despite strong political pressure at bilateral and multilateral levels. The imminent completion of the GATT Uruguay Round of talks on financial services liberalisation in 1993, however, was likely to deprive financial authorities of the luxury of procrastinating on entry deregulation. Thailand, as signatory to the GATT agreement, would be obliged to commit itself to opening its financial system to substantial foreign participation. Governments of Thailand's major trading partners also continued to press this agenda bilaterally. The USA, in particular, used the threat of sanctions against

Thailand's exports as a lever to press for greater market access (*BP* 2 January and 8 November 1993).

By allowing foreign banks to engage in offshore banking activities, the Thai authorities intended to ease political pressure and to show that they were responding to GATT demands. At the same time, they were able to avoid exposing domestic banks to *full* foreign competition: the BIBF was formulated in such a way that it enabled the BOT to dictate the terms and conditions on which foreign banks were to be permitted into the domestic financial market. Foreign BIBF banks without full branches in Thailand were only allowed to operate foreign exchange lending, and were denied access to the whole range of banking and non-banking financial businesses. Although they intended to promote competition within the domestic banking sector, financial leaders were understandably keen to control entry deregulation and to ensure that foreign competition against local banks would not be excessive and detrimental to financial stability.

The private banking community as a whole did not oppose the move for a number of reasons. In the first place, the tax incentives of the BIBF were structured in such a way that they tempered foreign competition against local banks.[7] Furthermore, the fact that Thai banks stood to benefit from the BIBF in many ways muted their opposition to greater foreign presence in the domestic banking sector. The BIBF enabled local commercial banks to mobilise more foreign funds at lower cost; low-cost funds mitigated competition among banks for depositors, depressing deposit rates and widening the interest rate spreads. Not only did the BIBF enhance foreign banks' access to cheap sources of foreign funds, it also broadened their scope of operations in international banking business, particularly in foreign exchange lending and trade financing for non-residents. As foreign BIBF banks had a limited scope of operations, Thai banks could thus enjoy these benefits without excessive exposure to foreign competition.

### New bank entry: would competition prevail?

Although a half-hearted concession to foreign demands to open the financial system, the BIBF did provide foreign banks with a springboard to obtaining full branch licences. Shortly after obtaining the BIBF licences, many foreign banks approached the BOT about the possibility of establishing full branches. They were also aggressive in securing diplomatic support from their home governments for their efforts to lower entry barriers. In early and mid-1994, the USA and Japan pressed the Thai government to fulfil its obligations under the GATT agreement by fully deregulating bank entry restrictions (*BP* 19 January 1994; *Nation* 12 July 1994).

External political pressure was important but was unlikely to have any significant impact without fundamental changes in the official orientation. Despite the BOT's efforts to promote greater competition in the financial system in the 1980s, private banks continued to collude on lending rates and other service charges.[8] This not only undermined the positive effects of interest rate liberalisation but also impeded the improvement of financial system efficiency. Moreover, ownership concentration continued to be the source of managerial malpractices and fraudulent activities. Domestic banking problems, as well as external pressures, eventually prompted financial authorities to move to lift competitive restraints. During the second half of 1994, senior BOT and Finance Ministry officials worked on a deregulation plan, the key component of which was to grant more than ten commercial banking licences to qualified domestic and foreign institutions. Five to seven of these licences would be issued to foreign banks currently operating the BIBF; the others would be awarded to local industrial groups and finance companies.

Although changes in financial leaders' policy orientation were significant, they were insufficient to explain the move to open the domestic banking sector. Deregulation might have been impossible without a steadily strengthened group of commercial banks and their growing confidence in their capacity to operate in an increasingly open financial system. In the early and late 1980s, local industrialists and foreign bankers failed to enter the Thai banking sector, not only because the BOT intended to protect weak local banks but also because private bankers strongly opposed deregulation for fear of having to compete directly with new entrants, especially foreign ones. The gathering momentum of financial liberalisation since the late 1980s enabled Thai commercial banks increasingly to strengthen their ability to contend with new rivals.

Most critically, abolition of the requirement that commercial banks should hold government bonds in order to open new branches enabled them to expand aggressively across the country. The average annual rate of local branch expansion increased sharply from 4 per cent in the 1980s to over 8 per cent in the early 1990s; more than one-third of their 3,200 branches were opened during 1990–94 (*BP* 13 April 1995; Tara Siam 1994a: 87–8). As a result of this rapid expansion, all prime locations for establishing new bank branches in the Bangkok metropolitan area and provinces were taken up by Thai commercial banks. Furthermore, banks expanded rapidly into a wide range of new fee-based businesses in the late 1980s and early 1990s, when financial authorities permitted them to broaden their activities. Moreover, foreign exchange decontrol and the inauguration of the BIBF enhanced their access to low-cost foreign funds. This, combined with the increasingly widened scope of operations, helped the banking sector to achieve a high level of profits (Leightner and Lovell 1998; Tara Siam 1994a: 142–6).

When financial authorities announced their plan to open up the way for new entries in the domestic banking sector in early 1995, this did not generate grave concern among private bankers. Given their long lead-time in developing their infrastructure of branch networks, most of them appeared to believe that new entrants would not be able to compete directly with them in the area of full service retail banking . Expanding into the mass market of retail banking entailed such large investments in capital and human resources that it would be very hard for new entrants to catch up with existing banks (*Banker* April

1995: 75–8; *FEER* 9 March 1995: 63). Even in the wholesale banking business, where competitive pressure tended to be most acute, Thai commercial banks, particularly the big ones, seemed fully capable of maintaining their market position by dint of their longstanding customer relationships, newly acquired expertise in merchant and investment banking and enhanced access to cheap foreign funds.

While financial authorities seemed willing to open up the domestic banking sector, new licences were highly costly to applicants. New foreign entrants would face extensive operational restrictions and were asked to bring a minimum of US$80 million in fresh capital into Thailand (*Asiamoney* July/August 1995: 48–51). Mainly because of the tough entry conditions, only twelve foreign BIBF banks without full branches took part in the bidding for new licences (*EIUCR-Thailand* 1st Quarter 1996: 27; *Nation* 2 February 1996). The qualifying conditions required of domestic applicants for banking licences were even harsher. Successful applicants were required to have at least 10 billion baht in total assets, establish their headquarters in the provinces outside the Bangkok metropolitan area and operate in a dispersed ownership structure (*Nation* 21 June 1995). New banks to be established under such high capital requirements and so many operational constraints would find it hard to gain a foothold in the local banking sector, let alone to compete with incumbent players.

The granting of ten new banking licences in late 1996 did not have any immediate impact on the structure of the banking sector. While the stiff qualifying conditions deterred many potentially strong contenders, the restrictive operating rules and huge investments in start-up operations made it hard for the new banks to establish themselves rapidly on the local financial market. The requirement that the new banks should locate their headquarters outside Bangkok was a major impediment to their business expansion, making it less cost-effective to tap large pools of funds and to establish client bases in the capital, where the bulk of industrial and financial activities was concentrated. More importantly, given that efficient retail banking required a very large commitment in terms of capital and human resources, the new entrants were expected to focus on wholesale banking and to operate only a limited number of branches in the first few years. By virtue of their extensive branch networks and long-standing client relations, existing banks were able to maintain their dominant position in the financial system.

## Conclusions

In Thailand, external shocks and associated financial difficulties precipitated the adoption of important reform measures, particularly in the early to mid-1980s. Pressure leading to continuous financial liberalisation was also brought to bear by foreign governments and international financial organisations such as the World Bank and the IMF, as well as by changes in the domestic political landscape. Despite these impetuses, which were broadly similar to those in Korea, Thailand's financial liberalisation differed in both approach and outcomes.

The Thai government was generally inclined towards the removal of direct financial controls, while consistently refusing to open up the way to new entry in the banking sector. It placed greater emphasis on strengthening the role of commercial banks in product diversification and financial development but took a cautious approach to broadening the business scope of NBFIs; while maintaining a fairly liberal foreign exchange regime, it further lifted the remaining capital controls and liberalised the domestic financial market. This distinctive reform approach led to speedier interest rate liberalisation and foreign exchange and capital decontrol but aided the persistence of the oligopolistic banking structure and the relatively slow growth of the NBFI sector.

The structure of private preference formation partly explains Thailand's pattern of reform strategies and outcomes. As the case study has amply shown, major private interests centred around the banking community supported foreign exchange liberalisation and the removal of direct controls over financial prices and credit allocation but opposed entry deregulation and functional de-segmentation in favour of the NBFIs. The main reasons why private bankers were largely able to have their policy preferences projected into the reform process were their strong and coherent organisational capabilities, their dominant position in the financial system and their close relationships with financial authorities, particularly the BOT. These institutional factors that bolstered the lobbying power of private bankers dented the ability of Thai industrialists to act on their own interest in financial liberalisation and rendered them largely passive in the face of policy changes.

Thailand's distinctive liberalisation pattern, as opposed to that of Korea, also reflected the political and economic interests of financial authorities and the institutional structure on which they were based. The Thai financial authorities, specifically the BOT, favoured the removal of direct financial controls and the deregulation of foreign exchange controls with a view to improving the efficiency of financial institutions and development prospects. However, the BOT objected to rapid entry deregulation and expansion of NBFI business scope, fearing that this would destabilise the financial system and compromise its regulatory responsibilities. While incorporating the policy preferences of private bankers, the interests of central bankers reflected the long-established tradition of financial conservatism. The BOT was generally able to assert its interests in the reform process mainly because of its dominant authority *vis-à-vis* line ministries and politicians on macro-economic policy. These institutional features enabled central bankers to continue exercising significant controls over the direction of Thai financial reform, despite the growing economic policy influence of political parties in the late 1980s and early 1990s.

# 6    Liberalisation differences

## Focused comparison

Chapters 4 and 5 have presented case studies of financial liberalisation in Korea and Thailand. The first section of this chapter compares the empirical evidence on liberalisation approaches and outcomes displayed in those chapters. The second section develops a more complete explanation of the differences between the two countries. The purpose is not to recapitulate the analysis of the case chapters but to conduct focused comparison of the dependent variables and to highlight the application of the explanatory variables to the case studies.

### Comparing liberalisation patterns

Table 6.1 summarises cross-country differences in liberalisation approaches and outcomes. Korea adopted a highly gradual and piecemeal approach to interest rate deregulation. The government maintained strict control over financial prices during most of the 1980s. It was only towards the end of the decade that the government launched its first comprehensive programme of interest deregulation – only to abandon it when macro-economic conditions proved unfavourable. While a revised plan in 1991 envisaged a multistage interest rate liberalisation to be implemented over the next 5 years, serious efforts to free the main interest rates were not made until the mid-1990s.

While the Korean government was reluctant to loosen its grip on financial prices and credit allocation, it adopted a more liberal position on the deregulation of entry barriers. From the early 1980s onwards, Korea began to open up the way for new entry into essentially all sectors of the financial system. In the mid-1980s, restrictions on branch opening by domestic banks and non-bank financial institutions (NBFIs) were relaxed considerably to allow financial institutions greater discretion in setting up their branch networks. Foreign participation in the domestic banking sector was generally permitted, and foreign bank branches enjoyed considerable freedom in their operations and management.

Thailand began to reorient interest rate policy towards a freer and more flexible mode of operation in the early 1980s, when financial authorities confined themselves to setting ceiling rates and encouraged banks to adjust the

*Table 6.1* Cross-country differences in reform approaches and outcomes

| Korea | Thailand |
|---|---|
| *Reform approaches* | |
| A highly gradual approach towards interest rate liberalisation and preferential credit reduction; a more liberal position on entry barrier deregulation; differential regulatory treatment in favour of NBFIs with regard to business expansion and functional desegmentation; belated and selective approach towards foreign exchange and capital decontrols | A more rapid and comprehensive approach towards interest rate reform and removal of direct controls over bank credit allocation; a highly restrictive policy on entry deregulation; more emphasis on business expansion of banks at the expense of that of NBFIs; swifter move towards foreign exchange and capital liberalisation sequenced ahead of some domestic reform measures |
| *Reform outcomes* | |
| Rigid interest rate structures and a higher share of preferential loans in total domestic credit; increased entry of new domestic and foreign banks; rapid growth of NBFIs as opposed to the weakened position of banking institutions; continued and selective controls over external financial transactions and a low level of financial policy openness | Less rigid interest rate structures and a lower and declining share of mandated loans in total domestic credit; restricted entry of new domestic and foreign banks; continued dominance of commercial banks and much slower growth in the NBFI sector; greatly relaxed controls over capital mobility and a higher level of financial internationalisation |

Note
NBFI, non-bank financial institution.

actual levels of each interest rate independently. During much of the 1980s, the central bank rarely intervened in the setting of interest rates. From the second half of the decade, the process of interest rate liberalisation accelerated in Thailand. Between mid-1989 and early 1992, the government deregulated virtually all types of deposit and loan rates. Although the Bank of Thailand (BOT) attempted to impose the minimum retail rate scheme in late 1993, this was aimed at increasing financial pricing transparency, promoting competition and mitigating the oligopolistic structure of the banking sector.

One of the most striking differences in financial reform approaches between the two countries is that Thailand constantly restricted new bank entry and the branching of foreign banks while relaxing direct control over financial prices and credit allocation. Throughout the overall process of financial liberalisation until late 1996, the government effectively excluded newcomers from the domestic banking sector; it also severely limited the number of foreign banks and prevented those that did operate from entering the field of branch banking. Although financial authorities deregulated entry barriers into the NBFI sector in the late 1970s, they moved quickly to close the door and reduced the number of existing institutions after entry deregulation created serious regulatory problems in the early and mid-1980s.

In terms of relative emphasis given to the operational freedom and business expansion of banks and NBFIs, Korea and Thailand differed even more dramatically. Along with the programme of bank privatisation in the early 1980s, the Korean Finance Ministry abolished the system of directives designed to control the operations and management of commercial banks. But it never intended to allow banks to function as truly independent, privately run institutions and had exercised, at least by the early 1990s, considerable influence over the appointment of senior bank managers and business operations concerning credit allocation, investment activities and portfolio management. By contrast, NBFIs, which had traditionally enjoyed greater freedom in deposit mobilisation and significant immunity from mandatory reserve requirements and policy loan obligations, had restrictions on entry criteria, branch opening and their use of assets further reduced.

The differential regulatory treatment of banks and NBFIs was also visible in the expansion of their scope of financial services and product offerings. In its efforts to liberalise competitive restraints, the Korean government, specifically the Finance Ministry, tended to give NBFIs policy favours to the disadvantage of banks. NBFIs were generally allowed to expand into new areas of financial business before their bank rivals were permitted to do so, and even to encroach upon the territory of commercial banks. Only when the rapid expansion of NBFI business activities eroded the intermediation role of banks and affected the conduct of monetary and industry policies did the Ministry move to broaden the business scope of banks. But it stopped short of allowing banks to expand their service offerings when their market share improved and NBFIs complained about increased competitive pressure.

In Thailand, as in Korea, the government permitted financial institutions to broaden and diversify their business operations as part of its financial reform programme. But the Thai government invariably gave more attention to the banking system when removing regulatory barriers. From the early 1980s, Thai banks began to expand rapidly into many areas of non-banking financial business, often at the expense of NBFIs' market share. While financial authorities also allowed non-bank intermediaries to broaden their service offerings, they did so cautiously and even grudgingly. A recurrent pattern was that NBFIs were permitted to engage only in those banking businesses in which banks had been operating for years and had therefore achieved a dominant position.

Finally, the two countries followed different sequences of internal and external financial liberalisation. Korea moved to deregulate foreign exchange and capital restrictions long after having undertaken partial but important reform measures on the domestic side. By contrast, Thailand, which had maintained relatively relaxed controls over its international financial transactions, further liberalised remaining controls while lifting direct restrictions on interest rates and credit allocation. Neither country seemed to follow clearly delineated sequencing for financial liberalisation. While Korea had privatised commercial banks and relaxed entry restrictions before liberalising its foreign exchange regime, there was no significant difference, in terms of timing and direction, between interest rate deregulation and capital decontrols; the government adopted equally gradual and tardy approaches in these two reform areas. Thailand had kept its domestic financial market closed to new entry even after making considerable headway in foreign exchange and capital decontrols.

It may not be surprising that the differing approaches adopted by Korea and Thailand to financial reforms led to different outcomes in the major areas of liberalisation. In Korea, the halting and piecemeal approach to interest rate liberalisation and continued government intervention in the setting of financial prices resulted in bank interest rates remaining rigid and unresponsive to changing market conditions. This manifested itself not only in the large gap between bank interest rates and corporate and government bond yields, generally regarded as close approximations to free market rates, but also in the lack of change in bank interest rates for years on end, despite appreciable shifts in the level of inflation, as shown in Table 6.2. Interest rates in Thailand were more responsive to expectations about economic conditions, particularly following the removal of all interest rate controls after the late 1980s.

With regard to entry deregulation, Korea achieved much quicker progress than Thailand. In Korea, continued deregulation of entry barriers into the banking sector saw nationwide commercial banks increase from merely five in 1981 to fifteen in 1996; the ten provincial commercial banks brought the total number of commercial banks to twenty-five. During the same period, no single new commercial bank was allowed to establish in Thailand, and the total number of domestic banks, standing at fifteen, had remained unchanged for the past 30 years. Although the government licensed three commercial banks in early 1997, this was unlikely to transform the existing oligopolistic structure of the Thai banking sector, as the new banks were slow in commencing operations and found it difficult to compete with the incumbent banks.

Furthermore, the Korean government also made speedier progress in opening up the domestic banking sector to foreign entry. Foreign bank branches in Korea had increased to seventy-seven by the end of 1996, from thirty-seven in 1981. In Thailand, by contrast, the government was extremely reluctant to open the way to new foreign banks. For almost 20 years until late 1996, when seven foreign banks were allowed to establish branches, the Thai banking sector had been virtually closed to new foreign entry. Equally important, existing foreign banks in Korea enjoyed more operational freedom than those in Thailand. They could each establish more than one branch, tap deposits directly from the public, join the local association of bankers and obtain access to Bank of Korea (BOK) rediscounting facilities. Foreign bank branches in Thailand faced more restrictions in those aspects.

Perhaps the most striking difference in financial reform outcomes between the two countries is that Korean NBFIs witnessed much stronger growth than their Thai counterparts, as shown in Table 6.3. Granted greater freedom than banks in their operations and more policy favours in their business expansion, Korean NBFIs developed so rapidly that the shares of their deposits and loans as a percentage of the total began to overtake those of banking institutions in the mid-1980s and they achieved a dominant position within the financial

*Table 6.2* Trend of major interest rates in Korea and Thailand (percentages), 1982–95

| Period | One-year time deposit | General bank loan | Corporate bond yields | Government bond yields | Money market rates | Consumer price index |
|---|---|---|---|---|---|---|
| *Korea* | | | | | | |
| 1982 | 10.9 | 12.5 | 19.3 | 17.4 | 14.2 | 7.3 |
| 1983 | 8.0 | 10.0 | 14.4 | 13.1 | 13.0 | 3.6 |
| 1984 | 9.1 | 10.6 | 13.6 | 14.3 | 11.4 | 2.2 |
| 1985 | 10.0 | 11.5 | 13.4 | 13.6 | 9.4 | 2.5 |
| 1986 | 10.0 | 11.5 | 13.3 | 11.6 | 9.7 | 2.8 |
| 1987 | 10.0 | 11.5 | 12.9 | 12.4 | 8.9 | 3.5 |
| 1988 | 10.0 | 11.5 | 12.8 | 13.0 | 9.6 | 7.2 |
| 1989 | 10.0 | 11.5 | 15.7 | 14.7 | 13.3 | 5.6 |
| 1990 | 10.0 | 11.5 | 13.3 | 15.0 | 14.0 | 8.6 |
| 1991 | 10.0 | 11.5 | 13.4 | 16.5 | 17.0 | 9.7 |
| 1992 | 10.0 | 11.5 | 16.0 | 15.1 | 14.3 | 7.3 |
| 1993 | 8.5 | 9.5 | 12.6 | 12.1 | 12.1 | 4.8 |
| 1994 | 8.5 | 9.5 | 12.9 | 12.3 | 12.5 | 6.2 |
| 1995 | 8.8 | 9.0 | 13.8 | 12.4 | 12.5 | 4.5 |
| *Thailand* | | | | | | |
| 1982 | 12.5 | 19.0 | – | 13.9 | 14.9 | 5.2 |
| 1983 | 12.5 | 17.5 | – | 11.1 | 12.2 | 3.8 |
| 1984 | 12.5 | 19.0 | – | 12.4 | 13.6 | 0.9 |
| 1985 | 11.0 | 19.0 | – | 12.1 | 13.5 | 2.4 |
| 1986 | 7.3 | 15.0 | – | 9.1 | 8.1 | 1.9 |
| 1987 | 7.3 | 15.0 | – | 7.5 | 5.9 | 2.5 |
| 1988 | 8.6 | 15.0 | – | 7.5 | 8.7 | 3.8 |
| 1989 | 9.5 | 15.0 | – | 8.1 | 9.8 | 5.4 |
| 1990 | 14.3 | 19.0 | – | 10.6 | 12.7 | 6.0 |
| 1991 | 10.5 | 19.0 | – | 10.8 | 10.6 | 5.7 |
| 1992 | 8.5 | 16.3 | – | 10.8 | 7.1 | 4.1 |
| 1993 | 8.6 | 14.5 | – | 10.8 | 6.5 | 3.4 |
| 1994 | 9.3 | 14.4 | – | 10.8 | 7.1 | 5.1 |
| 1995 | 10.6 | 16.3 | – | 10.8 | 10.3 | 5.8 |

Sources: Bangkok Bank (*Commercial Banks in Thailand*, various issues), Bank of Korea (*The Korean Economy*, 1996; *Financial Statements Analysis*, various issues; *Monthly Bulletin*, various issues) and IMF (*International Financial Statistics Yearbook* 1997: 516–17, 806–7).

sector in the early and mid-1990s. While Thai NBFIs also grew more rapidly than banking institutions, this paled into virtual insignificance in comparison with the more vigorous development of their Korean counterparts.

The final major area of financial liberalisation in which differences in reform outcomes are explored is that of foreign exchange and capital decontrol. One way in which to compare reform outcomes in this area is to examine the degree of capital mobility or the extent of integration between domestic and world financial markets in Korea and Thailand. Perhaps the most straightforward method to measure the degree of capital mobility is to look at the size of capital flows between domestic and international economies or the value of

*Table 6.3*  Market shares of financial institutions in Korea and Thailand (percentages), 1975–95

|  | 1975 | 1980 | 1985 | 1990 | 1995 |
|---|---|---|---|---|---|
| **Korea** | | | | | |
| *Deposits* | | | | | |
| Commercial banks | 54.6 | 43.8 | 31.4 | 25.9 | 22.8 |
| Specialised banks | 24.3 | 26.4 | 22.3 | 16.6 | 9.2 |
| NBFIs | 21.1 | 29.8 | 46.3 | 57.5 | 68.0 |
| *Loans* | | | | | |
| Commercial banks | 47.2 | 39.6 | 34.4 | 29.9 | 28.3 |
| Specialised banks | 25.9 | 25.0 | 24.4 | 19.5 | 14.6 |
| NBFIs | 26.9 | 35.4 | 41.2 | 50.6 | 57.1 |
| **Thailand** | | | | | |
| *Deposits* | | | | | |
| Commercial banks | 74.1 | 70.6 | 73.9 | 74.9 | 68.6 |
| Government institutions | 13.1 | 11.6 | 10.8 | 9.9 | 7.6 |
| NBFIs | 12.8 | 17.8 | 15.3 | 15.2 | 23.8 |
| *Loans* | | | | | |
| Commercial banks | 70.9 | 69.5 | 75.0 | 74.7 | 68.5 |
| Government institutions | 7.1 | 8.8 | 6.8 | 5.4 | 6.6 |
| NBFIs | 22.0 | 21.7 | 18.2 | 19.9 | 24.9 |

Sources: Bank of Korea (*Economic Statistics Yearbook*, various issues), Vajragupta and Vichyanond (1999: 46), Vichyanond (1994: 6–15) and Wibulswasdi (1995: 12).

Note
NBFI, non-bank financial institution.

capital transactions in the balance of payments expressed as a share of gross domestic product (Montiel 1993). The results obtained by using this method, as recorded in Table 6.4, indicate that Thailand had a higher level of financial integration with the world economy than Korea, and suggest that the former achieved greater financial openness.

However, this method and other similar but more sophisticated ones suffer from various methodological problems.[1] The main problems, as they are more relevant to the central concern of this study, are that these methods do not *directly and completely* reflect changes in the direction of a country's foreign exchange and capital regime. This is because the degree of an economy's financial integration with the rest of the world is a function not only of government policy on capital controls, but also of transaction and information costs in financial asset trading, exchange risks and economic and political stability (or instability). Such variables may have substantial impact on the degree of capital mobility irrespective of changes in the regulatory regime governing foreign exchange and capital transactions.

In view of the above, a method that is directly indicative of changes in government policies and rules on foreign exchange and capital transactions would be more suitable to the present purposes of this study. Haggard and

Maxfield (1996) have devised such a method or a coding scheme in their recent attempt to measure and compare the openness of international financial policy in several newly industrialising economies.[2] On the basis of the information contained in the International Monetary Fund's (IMF) annual reports on exchange arrangements and restrictions, the degree of financial policy openness in the two countries can be compared, using the Haggard–Maxfield coding index, and the results are reported in Table 6.5. It is clear from Table 6.5 that, although both countries moved towards greater foreign exchange and capital liberalisation, Thailand had a higher level of financial policy openness, implying that it achieved more rapid progress in deregulating its external financial transactions.

## Explaining liberalisation differences

The previous section has described and compared the different patterns of financial policy reform in terms of approaches and outcomes – the dependent variables of this study – for Korea and Thailand. This section links these different patterns to the theoretical discussion, conducted in Chapters 2 and 3, about private preferences for, and public-sector interests in, financial policy and reform and about the institutional arrangements through which these

*Table 6.4*   Ratios of gross capital flows to GDP in Korea and Thailand (yearly averages), 1981–95

| Period | Korea | Thailand |
|---|---|---|
| 1981–83 | 5.8 | 6.1 |
| 1984–86 | 5.5 | 6.7 |
| 1987–89 | 5.1 | 7.1 |
| 1990–92 | 5.5 | 10.8 |
| 1993–95 | 8.4 | 14.0 |

Sources: The data are taken from the International Monetary Fund's (IMF) *Balance of Payments Yearbook*. The sum of all capital inflows and outflows is divided by two and converted into the won and baht by using the exchange rates recorded in the IMF's *International Financial Statistics Yearbook*. This is then divided by gross domestic product (GDP) figures reported in the same yearbook.

*Table 6.5*   Index of international financial policy openness in Korea and Thailand (yearly averages), 1981–95

| Period | Korea | Thailand |
|---|---|---|
| 1981–83 | 5 | 7 |
| 1984–86 | 5 | 7 |
| 1987–89 | 5 | 8 |
| 1990–92 | 6 | 9 |
| 1993–95 | 7 | 10 |

Sources: Figures for Korea during 1981–90 are taken from Haggard and Maxfield (1996: 45). Figures for Thailand during 1981–95 and those for Korea in the 1991–95 period are calculated on the basis of information provided by the International Monetary Fund (IMF) (*AREAER*, various issues).

preferences and interests are articulated and asserted. Table 6.6 highlights the causal linkages between institutional variations of financial policy-making and differences in reform approaches and outcomes in Korea and Thailand.

## Sectors, private preferences and societal constraints

The institutional structure of private preference formation and articulation strongly affected the pattern and direction of interest rate liberalisation and preferential credit reduction. In Korea, the chaebols were consistently opposed to interest rate liberalisation, fearing that they would be subjected to fluctuating and higher interest rates. They also vigorously resisted the discontinuation of policy loans, on which they relied to maintain their international competitiveness and to expand and diversify their business lines at lower credit risk.

The high level of industrial concentration within the large-business sector provided the chaebols, represented by the Federation of Korean Industries (FKI), with institutional resources to organise effective collective action and

*Table 6.6* Institutional variations and corresponding reform approaches and outcomes

| Korea | Thailand |
| --- | --- |
| *Institutional structures of the private sector and the state* | |
| The highly concentrated industrial sector *vis-à-vis* the more pluralistic banking sector, close but asymmetrical bank–chaebol ties and extensive chaebol–NBFI links enabled private preference formation to be dominated by the chaebols; the subordinate position of the BOK and the hegemonic status of finance/industry ministries preordained the assertion of government interests and facilitated the articulation of chaebol preferences | The oligopolistic banking sector *vis-à-vis* the more competitive industrial sector, extensive bank control over NBFIs and relatively limited finance–industry ties enabled private preference articulation to be dictated by private bankers; the more independent status of the BOK and its alliance with the Finance Ministry ensured the domination of central bankers' interests in the reform process and eased the way for private bankers to project their preferences into centres of financial policy |
| *Reform approaches and outcomes* | |
| The complementarity and compromise of chaebol preferences and government interests led to a gradual move towards interest rate reform and preferential credit reduction, rapid progress in entry barrier deregulation, robust growth of the NBFI sector and a tardy approach to foreign exchange liberalisation and selective controls over capital flows | The interest coalition between central and private bankers underpinned by the institutional structures made financial reform oriented towards a swifter approach to interest rate liberalisation and less rigid interest rates, restricted entry of new domestic and foreign banks, the repressed growth of the NBFI sector and more rapid progress in foreign exchange and capital decontrols |

Note
NBFI, non-bank financial institution; BOK, Bank of Korea.

to develop the capacity over the state to advance their interests. Equally important, the fact that a dominant part of the national economy was tied to the performance of the chaebols gave them a powerful source of leverage over financial policy. Throughout the 1980s, the chaebols and the FKI were able to delay and even to block efforts to free interest rates and reduce policy loans. It was not until the early 1990s, when chaebol firms came to depend more on direct financing, that they began to show more tolerance towards deregulated financial prices. Nevertheless, the chaebols pressed for government intervention whenever market interest rates became unpalatable to them.

In Thailand, Federation of Thai Industries (FTI) leaders and business firms lodged only weak protests against the government's efforts first to reorient interest rate policy to a freer and more flexible mode of operations and then to deregulate financial prices in the 1980s. Political demands by Thai industrialists for policies that would direct preferential credit to the manufacturing sector were feeble and ineffective throughout this period. The Thai manufacturing sector, distinguished by its low level of industrial concentration, invariably faced collective action problems in attempting to organise effectively to achieve its policy goals. The FTI had particular difficulty representing and articulating sectoral preferences on such macro-economic issues as interest rate policy, which bore upon broad private interests but required concentrated political resources to accomplish successful lobbying.

Private-sector preferences on interest rate and credit policies were dominated by those of Thai private bankers. This was mainly because of their strong and effective organisational capacity, which resulted from a highly concentrated banking sector, and because of the long-established close relations between private and central bankers. It was true that Thai commercial banks, long accustomed to government guidance on interest rate determination, needed time to adapt themselves to a more liberalised business environment. But private bankers in general favoured interest rate deregulation: the recovery of the autonomous right to set financial prices was what they had long desired. Also, Thai banks were less concerned than their Korean counterparts about adverse effects of interest deregulation on the performance of manufacturers, as they were not closely linked with each other in terms of bank loans to industry and holdings of corporate equities.

In both Korea and Thailand, private-sector preferences also influenced government policy on the deregulation of entry barriers. The Korean government's more liberal position on opening up the domestic banking sector to new entry partly reflected the chaebols' economic and political interests. The establishment of new domestic commercial banks provided big business with the opportunity to own and control those banks in order to meet its rapidly increasing capital needs more flexibly and, more important, to gain financial and political independence from the state. The chaebols also welcomed new foreign entrants, which brought investment funds with them and enhanced chaebol firms' access to cheap overseas financing. The institutional structure of private preference formation, in which the chaebols' interests prevailed by dint of their strong organisational capacity and their weighty position in the national economy, neutralised the opposition to the deregulation of entry barriers by Korean banks.

In Thailand, commercial banks shaped private preferences towards entry deregulation; the interests of private bankers rather than those of industrial manufacturers influenced the policy behaviour of financial officials. Thai private bankers' strong and persistent resistance to the competitive pressures associated with entry deregulation repeatedly frustrated attempts by industrialists and other potential entrants to get into the lucrative banking sector, and kept the domestic financial market long closed to new foreign entry. Despite the fact that Thai manufacturers were expected to benefit from the establishment of more domestic commercial banks and foreign bank branches, they found their demands frequently muted by the countervailing interests of powerful private bankers. FTI leaders failed to get their preferences projected into the centres of financial policy, mainly because they had difficulty gaining access to the policy processes of the Thai financial authorities.

The impact of the different institutional settings of private preference formation in Korea and Thailand was most discernible in functional de-segmentation and the growth of NBFIs. In Korea, the rapid liberalisation of competitive restraints and institutional segments in general, and the impressive growth of the NBFI sector in particular, were partly due to the fact that big business owned and controlled most NBFIs and that chaebol firms relied increasingly upon NBFIs for investment funds. FKI leaders always stood behind NBFIs' demands for greater operational autonomy and further expansion of their business scope; influential business figures even lobbied for policy favours on behalf of their NBFI subsidiaries.

Thai commercial banks were much better positioned to act on their policy preferences for functional de-segmentation owing to the institutional structure of intra-sector relations in the financial community. Within the Thai finance and securities industries, which accounted for more than 90 per cent of total assets of the NBFI sector, nearly half of the companies were affiliated with banks. Although these affiliates were independently operated, they generally had bank representatives sitting on their boards of directors; many of their key executives had earned their spurs within banks and were understood to take overall direction from bank owners and managers. Moreover, bank-affiliated finance and securities firms relied heavily upon commercial banks for technological support, staff reinforcement and capital back-up.

This peculiar intra-sector relationship split and weakened the otherwise unified demand for the rapid expansion of NBFI business boundaries: bank affiliates always remained aloof and indifferent whenever independent firms raised such demands. This, coupled with the more pluralistic structure of the Thai NBFI sector, dented the organisational capacities of leading non-bank financial business associations. The whole sector was not organisationally cohesive enough to counteract the efforts of powerful commercial banks to prevent rapid NBFI expansion into banking business. Further, as commercial banks were allowed to engage in more non-banking financial services, they began to lose interest in promoting the growth of their non-bank affiliates that had originally been established to evade regulatory barriers.

Finally, the slow and selective nature of capital decontrols in Korea partly reflected the economic interests of the chaebols. While they welcomed the opportunity to gain direct access to foreign financing and more freedom to operate abroad, the chaebols opposed the move to liberalise foreign direct investment (FDI) activities at home because they had developed a stake in the policies that had long kept foreign investors at bay. Also, given their strong desire to maintain ownership control over their family-dominated enterprises, the chaebols had profound qualms about unrestrained foreign entry into the domestic market that would dilute that control. Equally important was their fear that rapid capital account opening would put upward pressure on the exchange rate and weaken their export performance; this remained an important concern among the large-business sector throughout the 1980s.

In Thailand, local industrialists favoured deregulation of capital restrictions that enhanced their direct access to new sources of foreign financing and facilitated their expansion into overseas markets. However, unlike the chaebols, which generally disapproved the rapid entry of foreign investors, at least during the 1980s, Thai business firms did not oppose and even welcomed such entry. The difference was attributable to the fact that Thai business firms, which received little credit support from the government and borrowed from banks largely at commercial rates, relied relatively heavily upon foreign capital inflows as an important part of their investment needs. The reliance on foreign funds made Thai industrialists more willing to bear the potential costs of increased foreign competition.

The lack of industrial opposition to capital decontrols reinforced the long-standing preferences of Thai private bankers for unrestricted flows of international capital. With the exception of the deregulation of entry barriers to foreign banks, Thai commercial banks and the Thai Bankers' Association (TBA) were enthusiastic advocates of the liberalisation of the country's external financial transactions because of all the benefits that banks expected to reap from such liberalisation. Private bankers' strong organisational capacities and their dominant position in the financial system, and indeed in the Thai economy, ensured that their preferences would prevail over possible dissenting voices within the private sector. Equally important, the close relationship between the private banking community and the BOT provided an efficient conduit through which those preferences could be translated relatively easily into the policy process.

### Public-sector interests, state institutions and policy choices

In Korea, the piecemeal pattern of interest rate liberalisation admittedly was consonant with the chaebols' strong preferences; but it also reflected government interests in maintaining financial controls. In the first place, the development model based on the heavy use of repressed interest rates and subsidised credit to promote industrial growth was well entrenched in the economic bureaucracy, particularly in the ministries of finance and of trade and industry. Concerned that interest deregulation and preferential credit reduction would impair the export performance and international competitiveness of Korean industry, financial bureaucrats were reluctant to push for rapid liberalisation. Furthermore, continued interest rate and credit controls reflected Finance Ministry officials' desire to maintain their regulatory power, particularly *vis-à-vis* central bankers. Finally, politicians intended to exploit continued financial controls to dispense political patronage, seek financial donations from the business sector and secure bases of coalition support.

The BOK was more concerned about the perennial adverse effects of repressed interest rates and the lavish use of policy loans on monetary management and the soundness of the banking sector. Central bankers supported interest rate liberalisation and preferential credit reduction in order to contain inflationary pressure and to improve the financial position of commercial banks. However, they were generally unable to act on their institutional interests and policy objectives in the reform process because of the BOK's subordination to the government on macro-economic issues. In addition, the powerful status of the ministries of finance and of trade and industry, which had closer relations with the industrial constituency and were more sensitive to its needs and demands, eased the way for the chaebols to translate their preferences into interest rate and credit policies.

In Thailand, the central bank was able to define and pursue its own reform strategies in the area of interest rate liberalisation by virtue of its wide authority over financial policy. Long-standing policy objectives emphasising a stable currency and low inflation were embedded in the BOT's policy-making process. When the rigid structure of domestic interest rates threatened achievement of these objectives against the backdrop of adverse external economic changes in the early and mid-1980s, central bankers moved fairly swiftly to reorient interest rate policy towards a more liberal mode of management. They had initially opted for a more gradual pace of liberalisation in order to give private banks time to adjust to a more competitive environment and to ensure that their essential prudential responsibilities would not be compromised.

While the Korean government moved cautiously to lift direct interest rate and credit controls, it seemed more willing to promote competition in financial services by lowering entry barriers. Reluctant to remove direct financial control, the Finance Ministry saw entry deregulation as an alternative route by which to promote efficiency and competition within the banking sector. The establishment of more commercial banks was also intended to rejuvenate the ability of the banking industry to mobilise investment funds, which was constantly weakened under the combined effects of interest rate repression, government intervention and the rapid growth of NFBIs.

The Korean government also adopted a relatively permissive policy stance on the deregulation of entry barriers to foreign banks. Its position stemmed, in the first instance, from the fact that the presence of foreign banks contributed to the inflow of foreign capital – directly in the form of their operating funds and swap transactions and indirectly in their support for local business firms importing foreign finance. Furthermore, while the need to license more foreign bank branches to introduce foreign capital declined in the mid- and late 1980s, when Korea had large current account surpluses, continued entry deregulation was regarded as providing an important stimulus to the development of the Korean banking industry. Finally, the Finance Ministry, which bore the brunt of increased political pressure from the American government to lower entry barriers during this period, was more inclined to open up the way for foreign participation.

The BOK seemed less interested in using entry deregulation to achieve industry policy purposes, but more worried about the constant arrival of new domestic and foreign entrants. On the one hand, central bankers had deep misgivings that the intensified competition associated with entry deregulation would threaten the stability and solvency of domestic banks, particularly when many of them had increasingly shaky financial positions in the 1980s. On the other hand, they also feared that the greater presence of foreign banks, which had open banking practices and wide international linkages, would be more difficult to regulate. The institutional structure of financial policy-making within the state, however, made it virtually impossible for central bankers to oppose the policy preferences of Finance Ministry bureaucrats.

In Thailand, by contrast, the more independent status of the BOT led to different approaches to, and outcomes of, entry deregulation. The BOT invariably emphasised the solvency of the banking sector over industrial investment and economic expansion as its policy priorities. While more disposed towards the removal of direct interest rate and credit control, Thai central bankers adamantly refused to issue new licences for additional domestic or foreign banks. They were concerned that increased competition following entry deregulation would weaken the fragile position of smaller banks and create regulatory problems. This stability-oriented stance, often shared by senior Finance Ministry officials, sustained the concentrated structure of the Thai banking sector.

In functional de-segmentation, the impact of different government interests on reform approaches and outcomes was substantial. As mentioned earlier, the Korean government, specifically the Finance Ministry, tended to give more policy favours to NBFIs rather than to banks in its attempt to remove competitive restraints and regulatory barriers. The Finance Ministry was reluctant to grant banks genuine operational freedom, mainly because it wanted to use the banking system to control financial prices and credit allocation, promote the country's industrial development and discipline the behaviour of big business. These interests in continued financial control prompted Finance Ministry officials to opt to nurture the growth of NBFIs by giving them more leeway to determine their financial prices and by allowing them to operate under less strict regulations.

Korean central bankers had other interests in functional de-segmentation than those of Finance Ministry officials. While intending to maintain strict regulatory surveillance over banks, they were eager to strengthen the position of the banking sector for three reasons. First, the fragile banking sector impeded the effective conduct of monetary policy, as banks provided the important channel through which direct as well as indirect monetary control instruments were deployed. Second, Korean banks, many of which had dwindling ability to mobilise savings, were saddled with huge non-performing assets and operated on an increasingly weak capital base – they had to rely heavily upon preferential central bank funds for lending operations. This caused a severe drain on the BOK's reserves and plagued it with chronic operating deficits. Third, the BOK, as statutory supervisor of commercial banks, had the legal responsibility to maintain the stability and sound development of the banking sector. Again, Korean central bankers found it hard to translate their interests into policy outcomes because of the BOK's subordinate status.

In Thailand, the more powerful position of the BOT ensured that central bankers' interests in functional de-segmentation, heavily biased in favour of the banks, would prevail in the policy-making process. The BOT relied upon commercial banks not only for monetary policy implementation, but also for the development of the financial system, mainly because banks were the largest and most important institutions in the Thai financial sector. Central bankers intended to further strengthen the position of banks so that they would be able to fulfil these functions more effectively. Furthermore, the BOT often used functional de-segmentation as an instrument for soliciting support from private banks, and permitted them to diversify into new business areas in exchange for their co-operation in the pursuit of its policy objectives.

Public-sector interests and state institutions also played an important part in accounting for differences in the pattern of foreign exchange and capital decontrol. In Korea, the government had a strong stake in foreign exchange and capital controls. Its desire to preserve policy-making autonomy aside, the Finance Ministry wanted to maintain such controls as an instrument not only for macro-economic management and industry policy purposes, but also for structuring its relations with the economy and society. Strict capital controls, particularly on the inflow side, were designed to restrain foreign competitors and to direct foreign capital inflows to facilitate industrial development. Also, financial policy-makers feared, particularly during the 1980s, that unrestrained inflows of foreign funds would put upward pressure on the exchange rate and therefore jeopardise the country's export growth.

The Finance Ministry's desire to maintain its dominant status in the financial policy-making process reinforced these economic and political motives for the continuation of capital controls. Foreign exchange and capital decontrol was likely to make it difficult for the Finance Ministry to continue overseeing all the areas of foreign exchange policies in that such decontrols would diversify and expand the country's international financial transactions in both structure and scale. This would entail the hand-over of some foreign financial policy authority from the Ministry to the BOK or at least the sharing of that authority between the two institutions, given that the BOK had more monetary specialists, stronger policy expertise and more intimate knowledge of foreign exchange markets. Finance Ministry bureaucrats, however, were consistently reluctant to do so, slowing down the reform of Korea's foreign exchange and capital regime.

In Thailand, financial authorities were more inclined to move towards foreign exchange and capital decontrols, although they also realised the possible impact of greater capital mobility on their policy-making autonomy. As mentioned earlier in this section, an important motive for maintaining capital control in Korea was closely related to the conduct of industrial policy. In Thailand, by contrast, foreign financial and industrial policies were largely separated from each other. The government did not attempt to rely on capital control for containing foreign competition, directing foreign funds to selected sectors or promoting industrial development; as a consequence, it had less interest in restricting capital movements. This increased the ability of the Thai financial authorities to withdraw from regulatory involvement in foreign exchange and capital operations when they perceived it to be necessary to deal with external economic changes and political pressures.

Weak interests in maintaining strict capital control also derived from the hands-off attitude towards financial management that was well established within the BOT and the Finance Ministry. Financial technocrats heading these two institutions tended to share the basic policy-making rules associated with the long-standing tradition of financial conservatism and economic liberalism. This ideological orientation favoured necessary but minimal control over capital movements as well as non-intervention in the financial market. Moreover, central bankers were more disposed towards decontrols because they hoped that increased exposure to foreign markets would force greater fiscal and monetary discipline on the expansionist politicians who came to occupy the top echelons of the economic bureaucracy with the opening up of Thai politics in the late 1980s.

# Part III

# The political economy of financial crisis

# 7 Financial crisis in Korea and Thailand

The process of market liberalisation in Korea and Thailand took a dramatic twist during late 1997, when the two countries, like many of their neighbours, were stricken hard by the worst-ever economic crisis in the post-war history of East Asian economic development. In the thick of the crisis, Korea and Thailand were both caught in a spiral of massive capital flight, plunging stock prices and collapsing local currencies. The financial market turmoil was quickly transmuted into a crisis of the real economy that manifested itself in soaring interest rates, repressed industrial investments and outright recession. In connection with these economic woes, unemployment rose to an unprecedented high and the income of the non-agricultural labour force decreased sharply, leading to social instability and even political unrest.

Following the theoretical framework developed in this study, this chapter conducts a comparative analysis of the financial crisis in Korea and Thailand. It does not intend to provide comprehensive accounts of what occurred in the two countries during the 1997–98 period, as such accounts can be found in more synoptic studies.[1] The major purpose is to examine how the crisis broke out in the two countries, with specific reference to the institutional analysis of their financial reform experiences offered in the previous chapters. The argument to be developed is that the failed course of market liberalisation and the institutional structures that underpinned the policy process played catalytic roles in the build-up and final outbreak of the crisis in Korea and Thailand.[2] While the two countries were hit equally hard by the financial shocks, these largely undifferentiated shocks had different causes in each country; the common financial crisis originated in divergent liberalisation patterns and stemmed from dissimilar institutional deficiencies.

## The Thai experience

Popular analyses of the financial crisis in Thailand have converged on the combined effects of external imbalances, the rigid exchange rate regime and structural problems in the financial sector as the major driving forces behind the development of the crisis. While an emphasis on these factors is not misplaced, it is incomplete and superficial; some of these factors are actually the manifestations rather than the fundamental causes of the financial turmoil in Thailand. As will be shown below, financial sector difficulties resulted primarily from the poorly regulated liberalisation process, which in turn reflected the political constraints on financial policy. Equally, the flawed financial and exchange rate mechanisms were a function of the emerging institutional handicaps of macro-economic management. Taken together, institutional weaknesses and reform failures played crucial roles in the build-up and eruption of the crisis in Thailand.

## The unfolding of the financial crisis

Economic difficulties in Thailand had been brewing for some time prior to July 1997, evidenced in the gradual decline in export growth and steady increase in current account deficits. The worsening external imbalances were attributable to a slump in the international market for labour-intensive manufactured goods and, more importantly, to the rigid maintenance of the pegged exchange rate regime and the related problems of overvaluation. In an attempt to reduce domestic demands for imports, monetary authorities imposed limits on credit extension and raised interest rates. Tight monetary policies appeared to have run counter to their desired objectives, however, in that they artificially strengthened the baht and sucked in large capital inflows. To maintain the dollar peg in the face of such inflows, the Bank of Thailand (BOT) had to further tighten the money supply. This encouraged domestic borrowers to turn to overseas financial markets for cheaper credit and attracted foreign investors to seek higher yields in Thailand, when investment opportunities were less profitable in Japan and Europe, because of low real interest rates and declining returns on financial assets (Nidhiprabha 1999; Warr 1998).

Had Thailand not undertaken significant capital account liberalisation, it would probably have been able to stem rapid capital inflows, and tight monetary policies might have helped to improve the external position. As mentioned in Chapter 5, from the late 1980s onwards, financial authorities removed restrictions on capital movements with a view to turning Bangkok into a regional financial hub. The centrepiece of Thailand's efforts to achieve these objectives was the establishment of the Bangkok International Banking Facilities (BIBF) in early 1993. Through the BIBF, local and foreign banks could borrow in foreign currencies from abroad for on-lending in Thailand. Between 1990 and 1996, the annual inflow of foreign funds jumped from 7 per cent to 14 per cent of gross domestic product (GDP), and the total external debt, the bulk of which was incurred by the private sector, increased steadily (Table 7.1).

In Thailand, foreign capital inflows were a defining feature of the pattern of economic development; the country's economic boom in the late 1980s benefited from infusions of Japanese capital. Although a large share of foreign funds had formerly come as more stable direct investment, in the early and mid-1990s inflows were predominantly in the form of portfolio investment into

*Table 7.1* External debt in Thailand, 1990–96

|  | 1990 | 1992 | 1994 | 1996 |
|---|---|---|---|---|
| Total external debt as percentage of GDP | 32.80 | 37.51 | 33.31 | 50.05 |
| Short-term debt as percentage of total external debt | 29.63 | 35.22 | 60.67 | 52.41 |
| Short-term debt as percentage of foreign reserves | 62.55 | 72.34 | 99.48 | 99.69 |

Source: Adapted from Corsetti *et al.* (1999: Tables 23, 24 and 26).

Note
GDP, gross domestic product.

the stock market and loans to financial institutions and corporate firms, as shown in Figure 7.1. More critically, a large and growing portion of borrowed foreign funds were short-term debts during the first half of the 1990s (Table 7.1). The rapid build-up of short-term debts into Thai financial and corporate sectors made them vulnerable to the risks of abrupt capital flow reversals. That vulnerability was aggravated by the fact that much foreign borrowing was not hedged as a precaution against currency devaluation and that short-term loans were often used to finance long-term industrial projects (Lauridsen 1998: 1576–7; Parker 1998: 11–12).

Not only did a dominant share of capital inflows come as more volatile short-term funds, but also such inflows, and indeed the lending of domestic financial institutions, shifted away from the export and agriculture sectors towards consumer financing, marginal loans for stock traders and, in particular, property development. Table 7.2 indicates that bank loans extended to personal consumption, services, finance and real estate business increased, whereas those to agricultural, export and manufacturing activities decreased or stagnated. The increase in the share of total loans extended by all financial institutions for non-productive investments was likely to be much larger

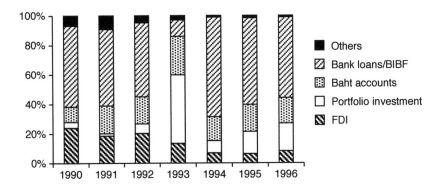

*Figure 7.1*   Private capital inflows in Thailand, 1990–96.

Source: Bank of Thailand (*Annual Report*, various issues; *Quarterly Bulletin*, various issues).

*Table 7.2* Bank lending by sector in Thailand (percentages), 1986–95

|  | 1986 | 1988 | 1990 | 1992 | 1994 | 1995 |
|---|---|---|---|---|---|---|
| Manufacturing | 22.8 | 25.8 | 25.1 | 23.7 | 23.5 | 25.8 |
| Wholesale/retail trade | 23.2 | 18.9 | 17.6 | 17.0 | 18.3 | 17.8 |
| Real estate | 3.8 | 6.3 | 11.9 | 11.5 | 10.9 | 9.4 |
| Personal consumption | 8.8 | 10.3 | 10.6 | 12.3 | 13.3 | 12.3 |
| Agriculture | 7.2 | 6.6 | 6.7 | 6.2 | 4.6 | 3.7 |
| Services | 5.2 | 5.7 | 6.1 | 7.3 | 8.1 | 7.8 |
| Banking/financial business | 6.1 | 6.4 | 5.1 | 6.1 | 6.2 | 8.0 |
| Exports | 9.1 | 8.3 | 6.1 | 5.4 | 5.0 | 4.3 |
| Construction | 5.6 | 4.3 | 4.0 | 4.1 | 4.2 | 4.4 |
| Imports | 5.9 | 5.3 | 4.6 | 4.0 | 3.2 | 3.3 |
| Public utilities | 1.7 | 1.6 | 1.7 | 1.9 | 2.4 | 2.6 |
| Mining | 0.6 | 0.5 | 0.5 | 0.5 | 0.4 | 0.6 |

Source: Bangkok Bank (*Commercial Banks in Thailand*, various issues).

because many non-bank financial institutions' (NBFIs) lending operations were less subject to regulation. Both market analyses and academic studies put the exposure of commercial banks and finance companies in real estate at a very high level – ranging from 25 per cent to 40 per cent of their total outstanding loans [Bello 1998: 428; *Far Eastern Economic Review* (*FEER*) 25 September 1997: 48; Reisen 1999: Table 4].

As massive funds were poured into the stock and property markets, the characteristics of a bubble economy became increasingly apparent in early 1995: prices on stock and real estate skyrocketed without reflecting the reality of corporate performance. Towards the end of 1994, the authorities sensed the emergence of asset bubbles and began to restrict bank lending to the purchase of empty land plots and the construction of golf courses and luxury condominiums (BOT 1996: 6). Private bankers were able to get around such restrictions, however, by claiming that loans that were actually extended to buy property or equity shares would be used to expand manufacturing and export activities. Moreover, finance companies, which were allowed more latitude in their lending operations and faced no such limitations, continued extending loans to stock traders, property developers and house buyers.

This reckless speculative investment in real estate led to a huge property glut in late 1995 (*Economist* February 1997: 90). The glut was aggravated in 1996 when the slowdown in economic growth appreciably dented the buying power of the middle and upper classes. As financial institutions tried to reduce their exposure to the troubled property market, the supply of credit started to fall rapidly. Coupled with high interest rates, this led to the bankruptcy of many property developers (*FEER* 6 March 1997: 49). Revelations that the real estate sector was on the rocks and that financial institutions were horribly exposed to the sector heavily affected the perceptions of foreign investors in Thailand. As a prominent indicator of concern, the stock market index moved downwards from late 1995 as foreigners began to sell their holdings of Thai stocks. The index kept on falling during the first half of 1996, and then plummeted from the middle of the year; by early 1997, the stock market had lost more than half of its total value (Vajragupta and Vichyanond 1999: 44–5).

The crash of the property and stock markets was soon translated into a serious crisis in the financial sector. The first sign of trouble was the June 1996 collapse of the Bangkok Bank of Commerce (BBC), with an enormous load of $3 billion of non-performing assets. Then, in February 1997, Finance One, the country's largest finance company, was taken over by a commercial bank on account of its severe liquidity problems. In June, the Thai authorities shut down sixteen finance companies that were lumbered with bad loans and became technically insolvent. The wrecked financial institutions had all their capital bases damaged by the sharp fall of stock prices, huge defaults on property loans and the rapid withdrawal of foreign funds (*Banker* May 1997: 70–1; *FEER* 14 November 1996: 80–1, 27 March 1997: 69).

The collapse of the BBC and Finance One was the first clear indication that many Thai financial institutions, heavily exposed to the battered property and stock markets, were now in deep trouble. Foreign creditors which had lent to these institutions soon discovered that their clients carried a huge load of bad assets.[3] Sharp export slumps and worsening external accounts in 1996 made them deeply concerned about the ability of the Thai private sector to repay the massive foreign debts. Under the circumstances, foreign sources began to call in their loans to Thai banks and finance companies. Domestic companies, many of which had not hedged their foreign exchange exposures, also started selling the baht for dollars as a precaution against a possible devaluation. The result was an increasing downward pressure on the value of the baht. Currency speculators took advantage of this situation and attacked the baht in late 1996 and early 1997.

In mid-1997, speculation intensified with growing evidence of the increasing fragility of financial institutions, mounting foreign debt and swelling current account deficits. This quickly overwhelmed the determination of financial authorities to defend the exchange rate, leading to unpegging of the baht and massive depreciation in early July. Following the devaluation, Thai banks and finance companies saw their foreign debts multiply. More than 40 billion short-term dollar loans borrowed by the private sector would fall due within the next 12 months. The BOT, which had squandered tens of billions of dollars in an ultimately futile bid to maintain the peg, now had alarmingly low foreign reserves and was in no position to act as a lender of last resort. The government had no choice but to approach the International Monetary Fund (IMF) for financial assistance (*Economist* 26 July 1997: 66; *FEER* 31 July 1997: 59).

### Financial liberalisation and structural problems

As noted above, high domestic interest rates were partly responsible for the rapid infusion of foreign capital, particularly short-term loans, into Thailand. Had financial authorities exercised adequate controls over capital movements, disparities between domestic and overseas interest rates might not have resulted in massive inflows of volatile foreign funds. In fact, even after Thailand began to remove most restrictions on capital mobility in the late 1980s and early 1990s, it still held short-term capital flows on a tight leash, in order to minimise the costs of capital account liberalisation. The launch of the BIBF, however, rendered this policy objective virtually unattainable, as it changed the composition of capital inflows and contributed to the hazardous growth of short-term external debts.

The establishment of the BIBF opened the door to greatly expanded transnational banking activities and enhanced the access of Thai financial institutions to external funds. While foreign creditors, attracted by higher returns and seemingly bright growth prospects in Thailand, were eager to lend, demand-side factors were also at play. Thai banks used the BIBF channels to acquire foreign funds at an interest rate 4–5 per cent lower than domestic funds; low-cost foreign funds helped to mitigate competition among banks for depositors, depressing deposit rates and widening the interest rate spreads. In the meantime, the new foreign BIBF banks competed with one another to project themselves as significant players by expanding their loan portfolios in an attempt to obtain the few licences available to operate full banking services in Thailand (Phongpaichit and Baker 1998: 98).

Aware of the negative effects of the rapid inflows of foreign funds, the Thai financial authorities had initially intended the BIBF to bring in more long-term funds for industrial development and to engage mainly in out–out lending activities. Intense lobbying on the part of private bankers to seek quick benefits through overseas borrowing (Overholt 1999: 1013–14), however, overwhelmed the financial authorities' ability to contain BIBF operations within their original policy parameters. As indicated in Table 7.3, BIBF operations were heavily skewed towards out–in lending activities. This not only contributed to the growing accumulation of external debts, but also aggravated the maturity structure of these debts, for the foreign funds borrowed via the BIBF were predominantly in the form of short-term loans.

While the launch of the BIBF resulted in massive inflows of short-term funds, failure to reform the oligopolistic structure of the Thai banking sector and to reduce its high level of ownership concentration also contributed to financial system problems. In the first place, Thai banks were not self-regulatory in that normal checks and balances among shareholders, directors and managers were lacking, mainly because those holding such positions tended to be either the same persons or members of the same families (Alba *et al.* 1998; Traisorat 2000: ch. 2). The lack of internal controls provided scope for managerial irregularities. The problem was particularly conspicuous where restrictions were circumvented on the extension of credit to shareholders and directors as well as affiliated businesses. Complex and personal cross-ownership and interlocking directorates enabled major shareholders and directors to finance their or their favoured clients' business undertakings, many of which neither had sufficient collateral nor were economically feasible. Such financing often clustered around a few areas, such as stock trading and property development.

*Table 7.3* BIBF lending and foreign liabilities of banks in Thailand, 1993–96

|  | 1993 | 1994 | 1995 | 1996 |
|---|---|---|---|---|
| Out–in lending as percentage of total BIBF lending | 98.10 | 81.90 | 56.83 | 62.60 |
| Short-terms loans as percentage of total out–in lending | – | 83.61 | 86.19 | 65.70 |
| BIBF lending as percentage of total external debts | – | 27.92 | 33.31 | 34.45 |
| Foreign liabilities of banks (US$ billion) | 25.59 | 44.63 | 79.62 | 85.15 |
| Banks' ratio of foreign liabilities to assets | 7.57 | 8.58 | 8.23 | 11.99 |
| Banks' short-term debts as percentage of foreign liabilities | – | 65.34 | 69.65 | 78.13 |

Sources: Adapted from Corsetti *et al.* (1999: Table 28), Khoman (2000: Table 4.3) and Krongkaew (1999: Table IV).

Note
BIBF, Bangkok International Banking Facilities.

Furthermore, the governance problems that derived from concentrated ownership and management also manifested themselves in the general lack of transparency of business operations in the Thai financial sector. In Thailand, as in other East Asian countries, the operations of traditional family-controlled businesses were based on informal networks of personal relationships and contacts rather than on formal contract-enforcement institutions. These informal networks intrinsically contributed to the systematic obscuring of financial and corporate accounts and activities by banks and finance companies (*FEER* 16 April 1998: 54–5; MacDonald 1998). The lack of corporate transparency, in turn, provided the cover under which Thai financial institution managers were able to beat restrictions on intra-affiliate lending, engage in highly risky transactions and even commit criminal activities without regulatory authorities knowing the true nature and full extent of these problems.

Ensconced in the protected sector, bank managers and shareholders paid little attention to the soundness of their institutions, specifically capital adequacy.[4] Despite rapid expansion of their business scope, they rarely mobilised their own funds, but relied instead upon deposits and borrowed funds for their lending operations. Furthermore, oligopolistic banks tended to follow high-risk, high-return strategies in their lending and investment activities, largely because of the problem of moral hazard. These institutions, which maintained the lion's share of total financial assets, capitalised upon the belief that the government would bail them out to prevent systemic meltdown if their risk-taking behaviour landed them in rough water. The result was serious overinvestment in, and excessive exposure to, such volatile activities as real estate development and stock trading. All this inevitably increased the overall vulnerability of banks when economic conditions turned hostile. These problems were clearly revealed in the mismanagement and eventual collapse of a dozen finance companies and the BBC just prior to the crisis (*Asiaweek* 31 July 1998: 31–9, 47–9; Phongpaichit and Baker 1998: 105–10).

Imprudent lending and risk-taking behaviour, specifically on the part of Thai finance companies, also stemmed from the biased approach towards functional de-segmentation. The differential regulatory treatment of banks and NBFIs led to two interrelated developments in the behaviour of the latter, both of which proved detrimental to their financial position. First, largely aided by favourable regulatory policies, Thai banks were able to mobilise low-cost funds, undertake a wider range of financial services and offer more attractive loan packages. They thus managed to lure primary borrowers away from finance companies and maintain a much stronger customer base in both retail and wholesale markets. Operating at a competitive disadvantage, finance companies, especially those that were not affiliated with banks, were often forced to take in those clients turned down by banks, many of whom had poor cash flows, shaky capital structures and risky investment portfolios. When economic difficulties gripped the country over the 1996–97 period, these clients bore the brunt, and many went under, bringing their creditors down with them.

Second, faced with competitive restraints, many large finance companies scrambled to establish themselves as big players in the domestic financial system, in the hope that they would be awarded full banking licences and compete with banks on a level playing field (Leightner 1999a; Warr 1998: 60). The desire to expand rapidly caused finance companies to seek quick and high returns with a short payback period. With the property and stock markets booming during the early to mid-1990s, real estate and share price speculation became their favoured lending and investment options. In late 1994, knowing that financial authorities would soon issue new banking licences, large finance companies began to compete to extend loans to property developers and build up their presence in the stock market in a desperate effort to be among the lucky recipients. Although finance companies did expand more rapidly during this period, much of that growth resulted from their excessive involvement in the property and stock markets (Leightner 1999b). When these markets collapsed, they found themselves saddled with a crippling load of non-performing assets.

A final aspect of Thai financial liberalisation that gave rise to financial sector problems, particularly fund misallocation, was the lax enforcement of regulatory rules. Although the Thai financial authorities had been worried about reckless lending by banks and finance companies to the risky and unproductive sectors before the crisis, and had indeed taken measures to restrict such lending, these measures tended to be weak, piecemeal and largely ineffective. Financial policy had then focused on deregulation rather than on the strengthening of supervisory control. In the late 1980s and early 1990s, the BOT reduced, as part of its liberalisation efforts, constraints on financial institutions' asset portfolio management to give them more latitude in their lending operations. Regulations on compulsory credit extension to such priority sectors as small and medium-sized enterprises, agriculture and exports were relaxed to such an extent that they became virtually non-binding (Vichyanond 1995: 360).

Popular accounts have attributed the regulatory failure to the lack of sufficient rules and supervisory expertise on the part of financial authorities or to hasty financial liberalisation without a compensating system of regulatory control. These accounts appear to have missed an important point. The early 1980s financial crisis in Thailand provided the spur for attempts to overhaul its system of prudential regulation; further efforts were made to tighten controls over banks and finance companies in the mid-1980s. The regulatory reforms endowed financial authorities, specifically the BOT, with wide-ranging legal powers and supervisory instruments (BOT 1992: 300–2; Johnston 1989). The sequencing of financial reforms in Thailand also seemed to follow the 'conventionally right' wisdom: prudential regulations had been strengthened before controls over the financial sector were relaxed (Fane 1998; Vichyanond 1995).

The problem was not so much that of technical deficiencies or wrongly sequenced reform measures as that of ineffective implementation of existing regulatory rules. Several political and institutional factors appear to have been important in accounting for the inefficacy of rule enforcement. As noted earlier in this section, the oligopolistic structure of the Thai banking sector remained largely intact despite official attempts to increase the level of competition. Most financial institutions were family controlled and closely linked in various ways to other businesses owned by the major shareholders and managers of the same institutions. Ownership and management concentration led to inadequate information disclosure and opaque business procedures, not only making it easier for banks and finance companies to dodge lending restrictions, but also complicating the BOT's efforts to assess the quality of their asset portfolios and to implement an efficient strategy for prudential regulation.

The traditional regulatory practices of the BOT, heavily based on moral suasion, also compromised its supervisory responsibility. In financial regulation, as in the monetary policy-making process, the central bank often persuaded banks to follow policies that it believed were in the interests of the financial system. Conducted mainly through consultations on an informal basis, moral suasion had no legal backing and usually left the practical implementation of official policies to the discretion of banks themselves (Traisorat 2000: 77–8). This instrument might have been effective prior to the late 1980s, when the BOT could back up its policy directives by threats to restrict branch opening and business scope or by promises to grant private bankers regulatory favours associated with direct financial controls. Market liberalisation weakened the ability of the BOT to use these 'carrots and sticks' and reduced the effectiveness of its moral suasion. Thai central bankers, however, continued using informal means to obtain compliance, despite the fact that their advice was increasingly ignored.

Finally, the efficacy of rule enforcement was undermined by the tendency on the part of central bankers to exercise supervisory forbearance (Nukul Commission Report 1998: para. 429–34). The reason partly lay with their dependence upon the private financial community for achieving important policy objectives. Time and again, they were unable to resist the temptation to relax regulatory standards as a way of securing support and co-operation from private bankers. Such considerations, for instance, made the BOT weaken the definition of banks' risk assets in 1986 and ease restrictions on their investment in non-bank businesses in 1987 and on their holdings of foreign liabilities in 1992. This might have sent the wrong signals to the private financial community and encouraged unscrupulous managers to engage in illegal activities in defiance of regulatory rules.

## Weakened institutions and policy mismanagement

While the ineffectively executed market reform gave rise to the various structural problems in the Thai financial sector, several institutional weaknesses that began to emerge in the early 1990s allowed the financial sector problems to persist and contributed directly to policy mismanagement. More specifically, these weaknesses were reflected in the diminished influence of central bankers within the financial community, increasingly strained relations between the BOT and the Finance Ministry and growing politicisation of macro-economic policy-making processes. Combined, they led to the flawed line of exchange rate management and impaired financial sector governance.

Political democratisation and financial liberalisation, which began to gain momentum in the late 1980s, changed the relative status of central bankers and private financiers. Most critically, the independence of the central bank came under threat as the number of claimants on the financial policy-making process increased and as politicians wielded growing influences on macro-economic issues. While central bankers' policy-making power was on the wane, private financiers saw their political space expanding against the backdrop of intensifying democratisation. During the early to mid-1990s, the successive cabinets from Chuan Leekpai to Chavalit Yongchaiyut fielded economic teams largely staffed by prominent private bankers. As some of its members now became key policy-makers themselves, the private banking community gained another, perhaps more effective, avenue to centres of official policy.

Equally important, financial liberalisation undercut the central bank's capacity to shape the behaviour of private financiers. Interest rate reform gave private banks greater latitude in determining domestic financial prices and in affecting the effectiveness of monetary policy; functional de-segmentation removed constraints on their asset management and allowed them to expand into a wider range of business activities; capital decontrol enhanced their access to foreign funds and opened up opportunities for them to operate in a much broader business environment. As private bankers benefited enormously from these reform measures, policy rewards to them for their compliance with

financial controls, many of which were eliminated in the liberalisation process, paled by comparison and became largely irrelevant. With their economic
autonomy on the rise, private financiers were more assertive with their policy
stance and less submissive to the dictates of the central bank.

While private bankers came to depend less on the BOT for policy largess and
preference articulation, central bankers, if anything, remained more reliant
upon their private counterparts than ever before for two important reasons.
As liberalisation made financial markets and transactions more complex
in structure and extensive in scale, financial technocrats faced a growing
number of new and unfamiliar policy and regulatory issues. They thus had
to turn increasingly to financial institutions for more accurate and detailed
information about ever-changing market conditions and for the effective use
of market-oriented monetary instruments. Moreover, central bankers needed
to mobilise the political support from private bankers to buttress their position, particularly when politicians were challenging the authority of the BOT.
All this rendered central bankers more responsive to the interests of private
bankers, despite the danger of subjecting financial policy to their distributive
demands.

The weaknesses of macro-economic institutions also resulted from the
increasingly problematic relationship between the BOT and the Finance Ministry. From its formative years, the BOT had developed a partnership with the
Finance Ministry, primarily on the basis of similar institutional histories and
policy interests. This close relationship began to disintegrate during Pramual
Sabhavasu's tenure as finance minister under Chatichai Choonhavan in the
early 1990s, as discussed in Chapter 5. Relations between the two institutions
came under further strain during the Chuan administration over the 1993–95
period. The finance minister intruded into policy areas previously reserved for
central bankers, and even made efforts to increase the power of the Finance
Ministry over financial policy *vis-à-vis* that of the BOT (Unger 1998: 99–100).
During the succeeding Banharn government, the rivalry between the BOT
and the Finance Ministry became more overt and their relations were at the
lowest ebb. Handpicked by Banharn, the new finance minister seemed willing
to defer to the wishes of his political master, and quickly became embroiled in
struggles and controversies with financial technocrats (*Nation* 29 May 1996).

With the Finance Ministry becoming more politicised, the ideological and
institutional underpinnings of its relationship with the BOT eroded. During
this period, frequent rifts between the two arose over many important policy
issues, ranging from inflation control, fiscal management, entry deregulation
and financial sector supervision. When the finance minister could not get his
way in these rifts, he either sacked the BOT governor or turned to his own
team of advisors, and broke away from the long-established practice of decid-
ing major policy issues together with central bankers. As a result, distrust
and confrontation gradually replaced the tradition of close consultation and
co-ordination between the BOT and the Finance Ministry. The weakening of

co-operative arrangements between the two key institutions hampered the effectiveness of overall financial management and posed serious problems to the maintenance of disciplined macro-economic policies.

As mentioned in Chapter 3, the political and economic independence of the BOT stemmed not so much from legal and formal dimensions as from informal, socio-political processes. The two most important aspects of such processes had been the influence of the BOT within the broad financial community and the policy alliance between central bankers and Finance Ministry officials. With the BOT's authority over private financiers diminishing and its relations with the Finance Ministry growing sour, the fundamental base of central bank independence began to shake. These changes, coupled with the rising leverage of politicians on macro-economic issues, reduced the policy-making autonomy of central bankers and prompted them to find ways to shore up their weakened positions. Instead of seeking legal amendments to enhance the statutory independence of the central bank, however, its leaders opted for politicking, bringing the institution ever closer to the murky politics of Thailand.

This deplorable situation surfaced during Vijit Supinit's tenure as BOT governor in the mid-1990s. Observers from both within Thailand and without opined that Vijit's governorship was characterised by his penchant for cultivating links with powerful figures and for resorting to political schemes to achieve his policy goals. Apparently enjoying no strong support from the financial community but increasingly constrained by partisan pressures, Vijit intended to use political influences to secure his position in the policy process (*FEER* 21 May 1998: 62–4; *Nation* 7 March 1996; Phongpaichit and Baker 1998: 118–21). The intention made him disposed to accommodate the interests of politicians and their constituencies at the expense of the prestige and integrity of the BOT. This was evident in Vijit's $400 million rescue effort to prop up the stock market in late 1995, in order to bail out well-connected investors; in his unsavoury use of political trickeries with which to fire his deputy, who was known to have clashed with Vijit over the stock market rescue package and other policy issues; and in his failure to move against the BBC, which lent massive public funds to influential politicians [*Bangkok Post Economic Review* (*BPER*) 2 July 1996: 35; *FEER* 27 February 1997: 51; *Nation* 9 January 1996].

The weakened status of the BOT was also attributable to several organisational problems within the institution itself. These were reflected, first and foremost, in the emergence of factions within the BOT; factionalism spawned distrust, resentment and even conflicts among senior BOT officials. Further, for some years prior to the financial crisis, the BOT had seen the number of its hierarchical levels swell and its organisational structure become more complex, creating a widening gap between those at the top and those at the bottom of the structure. Combined with factional activities, this led to hindered information flows, co-ordination difficulties and growing red tape. Finally, promotion tended to go by seniority rather than by merit, resulting in the declining motivation and morale of employees and the ineffective use of their wisdom and knowledge [*Asiamoney* February 1997: 11–28; *Bangkok Post* (*BP*) 3 May 1998; Siamwalla 1997].

The above-mentioned institutional changes – the diminished influence of the BOT within the financial community, strained BOT–Finance Ministry relations and the associated decline of central bank independence – came together during the mid-1990s to produce serious problems of financial policy management. Surely, some of these changes were partly to blame for the persistence of perverse liberalisation processes that led to various financial sector weaknesses? Shifts in the balance of power in favour of private bankers and the dented ability of the BOT to control the behaviour of financial institutions contributed to the misallocation of foreign funds and the failure to enforce regulatory rules strictly. But the weakening of macro-economic institutions had its direct negative influence on the handling of financial sector weaknesses and the conduct of exchange rate policy.

As noted earlier, the first clear sign of severe problems in the Thai financial sector emerged in mid-1996, when the BBC crashed under an immense load of non-performing loans. The debacle of the BBC stemmed from years of mismanagement and fraudulent activities on the part of its senior executives. The BOT had been aware of the fraud and the violation of regulatory rules at the bank since the early 1990s, but its attempts at tackling these malpractices were dilatory and ineffective. As a result, the BBC ran into serious trouble and became technically bankrupt in late 1995. Although the central bank mobilised nearly US$7 billion from its Financial Institutions Development Fund (FIDF) to keep the BBC afloat, the financial position of the bank was so debilitated that it was beyond rehabilitation. The BOT was eventually forced to take over the debt-stricken bank in May 1996, when it collapsed and its management absconded from the country [*BPER* 31 December 1996: 18–20; *Economist Intelligence Unit Country Report* (*EIUCR*)-*Thailand* 1st Quarter 1996: 26–7].

On the surface, the BBC scandal shows how concentrated ownership structures led to poor corporate governance and resulting financial weaknesses. Like many other Thai commercial banks, the BBC had been founded to service family interests and was controlled by a handful of banking families. Under the cover of complex cross-ownership, the management extended massive credits to interrelated businesses and politicians heavily engaged in property development and stock speculation and doctored documents to conceal staggering bad assets. Problems at the BBC and the inability of financial authorities to deal with them effectively, however, had deeper causes than merely ownership and managerial concentration. More important for the purposes of this chapter is that the collapse of the BBC revealed the emerging institutional weaknesses of financial sector management.

In Thailand, the central bank and Finance Ministry shared the responsibility for safeguarding the soundness of the financial sector, although the former had more authority over operational matters. Effective regulation was thus contingent upon the smooth co-ordination between the two institutions. In the early to mid-1990s, when growing fragility of the Thai financial sector put a premium on such co-ordination, relations between the two were strained. BOT governor Vijit and finance minister Tarrin were often locked into policy disputes with each other. In the aftermath of the BBC crash, Tarrin insisted that he had not been kept fully informed of problems at the BBC, while Vijit complained that he had never received timely feedback even though he had reported BBC irregularities to the Finance Ministry (*FEER* 21 May 1998: 62; *Nation* 22 February 1998). The weakening of co-operative ties between the BOT and the Ministry compromised regulatory effectiveness and partly resulted in a failure to nip the BBC trouble in the bud. This contrasts sharply with the resolution of the financial crisis in the mid-1980s, when the BOT governor and finance minister teamed up to restructure ailing financial institutions and reform the regulatory system.

The BBC saga also indicates the declining capacity of the BOT to exercise its supervisory functions independently of political influences. The BBC had served many well-connected and powerful clients in the public and private sectors. As later revealed in press reports, between 1992 and 1995 the bank lent a colossal US$2.8 billion to influential politicians and senior financial officials, much of which had no collateral or was backed by overvalued land (*Nation* 24 August 1998 and 3 September 1998). Being the beneficiaries of large loans from the BBC, these politicians and officials were suspected to be among those pressing the BOT to grant the bank preferential treatment and to provide rescue funds to keep it solvent. In a published interview, Vijit hinted that opposition from prominent figures in the ruling coalition had overwhelmed central bankers' resolve to move in on the BBC (*FEER* 21 May 1998: 63).

The institutional handicaps of financial sector management ran much broader than just the failure to tackle the BBC malfeasance. At the heels of the BBC debacle, Finance One, suffering from serious liquidity problems, was on the brink of collapse. Its distress epitomised the woes of Thai finance companies, many of which were lumbered with weighty non-performing loans resulting in large part from their overexposure to the troubled property and stock markets. In March 1997, the financial authorities introduced a few measures to shore up the sector. They ordered Finance One to merge with the Thai Danu Bank and encouraged weak finance companies to be absorbed into commercial banks; the FIDF injected more than US$1.5 billion into these wrecked finance companies in the face of runs by panicky investors. Meanwhile, all financial institutions were asked to raise their provisions for bad debts and nine finance companies were instructed to increase their capital to fully cover doubtful loans (*Banker* May 1997: 70–1).

It should be noted that the measures announced were moderate and fell short of a wholesale approach to restructuring the sector. This might have reflected the concerns of financial officials that more radical measures would provoke opposition. Their concerns proved not to be misplaced: the implementation of the moderate measures was politically unattainable. Ministers from the Chart Pattana Party, the second largest in the coalition government, were major shareholders in some of the weakest finance companies and strongly resisted the remedial action against these companies. They even demanded that the leading officials responsible for formulating the restructuring measures should be sacked (*FEER* 29 May 1997: 15; Lauridsen 1998: 1581–2). Eager to hold his shaky multiparty government together, Prime Minister Chavalit refused to take decisive action. Confronted with powerful resistance, financial technocrats backed down and seemed to be at a loss while the Thai financial sector slid into deep crisis.

The weakened institutional capacity of financial officials, particularly those at the central bank, assumed significance beyond its impact on policy-making efficiency. While the collapse of the BBC and Finance One in quick succession bolstered negative assessments of the Thai financial system, the BOT's inability to restructure the ailing banks and finance companies dealt a heavy blow to business confidence. Although the BOT tried to reassure the markets that most Thai financial institutions were healthy and solvent, investors appeared to lose faith in the credibility of central bankers. Throughout the first half of 1997, foreign investors quickened their steps to withdraw from Thailand, and many Thai companies and individuals also moved increasingly to US dollars. The result was that the value of the baht increasingly came under downward pressure.

Just as central bankers had lost the battle with politicians over financial sector restructuring, they fared little better in their efforts to handle the foreign exchange problem. The Thai financial authorities had maintained the fixed exchange rate regime since the mid-1980s. During the early to mid-1990s, the pegged regime produced a variety of macro-economic difficulties: the perverse cycle of tight monetary policy, rapid capital inflows, the real appreciation of the baht and repressed export growth. With severe problems in the financial sector unsolved and the country sliding into economic gloom in late 1996 and early 1997, the exchange rate was subjected to repeated speculative onslaughts. Market conditions clearly indicated that the continued maintenance of the dollar peg was not a sustainable strategy. The BOT, however, rejected the alternative to defending the baht, despite the fact that it had been aware of the incompatibility between free capital movements and the fixed exchange rate regime, and that the overvalued baht had resulted in growing external disequilibria.

From the perspective of central bankers, devaluation could rarely be a good policy option, particularly when economic conditions were unsettled and market sentiments were downcast. They expected the macro-economic problems to be short-term ones and to be smoothed over without resorting to drastic policy changes (Doner and Ramsay 1999: 186). Moreover, it was feared that devaluation might fail to improve external imbalances not only because of the rapid growth in imports spurred by strong domestic demand, but also because of the slump in export markets for labour-intensive manufactured goods. As global demand for many of Thailand's exports was sluggish during the 1990s, Thai financial policy-makers worried that devaluation would only inflict unnecessary damage on the already fragile economy if it failed to increase export competitiveness.

Throughout late 1996 and early 1997, when the dollar peg became increasingly unsustainable, prominent macro-economists from outside the BOT demanded a more flexible exchange rate policy and the devaluation of the baht. In the face of reality, even some central bankers began to question the wisdom of the baht defence strategy (*BPER* 30 June 1998). Their voices could barely be heard, however, above the clamours for the continuation of the peg from private financiers and their political allies. By the end of 1996, commercial banks, finance companies and their industrial clients had carried over US$60 billion dollars of foreign debts. Devaluing the baht would have immediately increased their debt-servicing burden, which was largely dollar denominated, and landed many of them on the rocks. They therefore lobbied hard against the devaluation of the baht (*FEER* 27 March 1997: 67–8; Phongpaichit and Baker 1998: 121–3).

Political pressures, together with the dire economic consequences of devaluation, made it difficult for central bankers to unpeg the baht. During the early months of 1997, the development of the financial crisis in Thailand came to a critical juncture. In early April, the US credit-rating agency Moody's downgraded the long-term foreign currency debt ceilings of Thailand, while consistent downward pressure on the baht raised the spectre of imminent devaluation. As local companies and foreign investors all betted against the baht, the currency suffered its heaviest assault in the middle of May. Although there was a clear and pressing need for effective action on the exchange rate front, senior BOT officials, for the above-mentioned reasons, remained indecisive.

To head off speculative attacks on the baht, the central bank had to spend foreign reserves to prop up the exchange rate. As came to light later, it spent US$9 billion on the spot market and committed another US$23 billion in forward contracts out of its US$39 billion reserves during the first 5 months of 1997 (*FEER* 4 September 1997: 60). While exchange market intervention was within the mandatory authority of the BOT, it seemed to be odd that it had almost exhausted the country's foreign reserves without the knowledge of the Finance Ministry – the other key state institution of foreign financial policy (*Nation* 10 February 1998). As the BOT and Finance Ministry drifted away from close co-operation during this period, they did not care to consult and monitor each other in the exchange policy-making process, with disastrous consequences for the national economy. This is in marked contrast to their close partnership in the mid-1980s, which had contributed to the successful adjustment of exchange rate policy and subsequent export boom.

The empirical analysis has clearly shown that the emerging weaknesses in macro-economic institutions produced serious problems of financial policy management. Some scholars have interpreted the Thai crisis as a result of the divided political structure, emphasising the way in which the fragmented party system and individualised electoral rules bred government instability and hindered decisiveness in the policy process (Haggard and MacIntyre 1998: 386–7; MacIntyre 1999). While not intending to underrate the explanatory value of political structure, this study argues that in the 1990s the Thai party and electoral systems remained as weak and the government as unstable as in the 1980s. These structural problems had stronger negative effects on economic outcomes, mainly because macro-economic agencies had weaker control over financial policy. The inability of the Thai government to respond effectively to the crisis situation stemmed from its weakened internal structure. A focus on party and electoral variables tends to miss a primary causal factor.

## The travails of Korea

As the Thai economy was collapsing in a dramatic fashion over the summer of 1997, the financial crisis began to build to a climax in Korea. Many of the crisis symptoms appeared to be similar: rapid inflows of foreign capital, a remarkable growth in bank lending to essentially speculative ventures and unproductive industrial projects and crippling financial sector weaknesses. The crisis in Korea, however, had its own individual causes, primarily reflecting the specific approaches and outcomes of financial liberalisation and the distinctive political and institutional features of Korean financial policy processes.

### The build-up and outbreak of the financial crisis

In Korea, as in Thailand, the financial crisis was preceded by the emergence of economic difficulties, manifestly evidenced in the dwindling export growth and growing current account deficits in the early to mid-1990s. The export slowdown was partly attributable to high labour costs in Korea. Combined with the failure to move into a more advanced industrial structure, this led to the gradual loss of the international competitiveness of Korean manufacturers. Furthermore, the trend of export slump that resulted from the structural problems was reinforced by unfavourable changes in world market conditions. These were mainly reflected in increased competition from low-cost producers and in a world-wide collapse of the prices for memory chips, which accounted for a large portion of Korean exports (Harvie 2000; Woodall 1998).

The current account deficits were financed by foreign capital inflows, attracted by Korea's successful track record and high domestic interest rates. Coupled with expanded overseas borrowings by Korean financial institutions and firms, the capital influx resulted in the steady accumulation of foreign debts. As indicated in Table 7.4, the country's total foreign debts nearly trebled between 1993 and 1996, growing at an average of 31.3 per cent per annum. More significantly, the proportion of short-term debt with maturity of less than 1 year to total foreign debts increased sharply, specifically over the 1995–96 period. As a consequence, the ratio of short-term debt to the country's foreign reserves hit a dangerously high level.

Emerging difficulties in the external sector were only a necessary condition for the eruption of the financial crisis in Korea. As shown in several studies (Baliño and Ubide 1999; Borensztein and Lee 1999; Chang 1998), the macro-

*Table 7.4* Foreign debt in Korea, 1993–96

|  | 1993 | 1994 | 1995 | 1996 |
|---|---|---|---|---|
| Total foreign debt (US$ billion) | 44.10 | 56.97 | 79.00 | 111.00 |
| Total foreign debt as percentage of GDP | 14.18 | 14.32 | 23.80 | 28.40 |
| Short-term debt as percentage of total foreign debt | 25.85 | 25.47 | 51.60 | 50.20 |
| Short-term debt as percentage of foreign reserves | 60.31 | 54.06 | 171.45 | 203.23 |

Sources: Adapted from Corsetti *et al.* (1999: Tables 23, 24 and 26) and Harvie (2000: Table 5.3).

Note
GDP, gross domestic product.

economic parameters involving GDP growth, price inflation and fiscal position indicated broad strength over the first half of the 1990s. Even the growing external imbalances, with the exception of the deteriorating debt maturity structure, were by no means excessive compared with both the benchmarks set by the World Bank and the previous crisis situation in Korea during the early 1980s. While the worsening external accounts certainly raised market doubts about Korea's ability to repay its foreign debts, what directly triggered the collapse of confidence was mounting weaknesses in the corporate and financial sectors.

Corporate weaknesses manifested themselves partly in the poor perform-ance of Korean firms. As illustrated in two comparative studies of corporate profits in East and Southeast Asia (Claessens *et al.* 1998; Pomerleano 1998), profitability in Korea not only showed a declining trend over time during much of the 1990s, but also was much lower in comparison with the other East Asian newly industrialising economies (NIEs).[5] The structural causes of low profitability might have related to ownership concentration in fam-ily-controlled chaebol firms and the associated managerial malpractices and weak corporate governance (Claessens *et al.* 1998). The immediate reasons for the depressed profits of the corporate sector rested with the fact that Korean manufacturers were being squeezed between high and rising labour costs at home and intensifying competition and unfavourable changes in international markets.

To counteract the effects of declining corporate profits, Korean firms, specifically the chaebols, undertook a major investment expansion (Haggard and Mo 2000; Woodall 1998). However, this investment boom apparently went awry in several ways. Much of the investment was clustered around a few industries such as electronics, automobiles and petrochemicals, whose viability tended to be precarious because of their susceptibility to external economic shocks. Chaebol firms, accustomed to investing for gaining and expanding market shares rather than for improving efficiency, gave little thought to the productivity of their capital investment (Bello 1998: 430–2; Park 1998). The quality of investment in the Korean manufacturing sector, as measured by the incremental capital-to-output ratio (the higher the ratio, the lower investment quality), increased from 350 per cent in 1987–89 to 510 per cent in 1993–95 (Radelet and Sachs 1998: 40).

To sustain the high level of capital investment, the corporate sector needed huge amounts of financing. Diminishing corporate profits meant that the bulk of that financing had to come from external sources. As chaebol firms were reluctant to raise equity capital for fear of diluting their ownership structures, however, they resorted to indirect financing or debt funding garnered from both local and foreign sources. Table 7.5 shows that in 1985–97 the corporate sector relied upon domestic and foreign borrowings for a high and rising share of their external funds. Greater dependence upon indirect financing aggravated the already fragile financial structure of Korean firms. As indicated in Table 7.6, the debt–equity ratios of the Korean manufacturing sector in general and of the chaebols in particular increased steadily, and their level of leverage was much above that of their counterparts in many Asian NIEs.

Highly leveraged capital structure, which had long typified industrial development in Korea, rendered chaebol firms vulnerable to sudden unfavourable changes in economic conditions. But their vulnerability was exacerbated in the mid-1990s: a substantial share of their newly incurred debt was short-term external debt. By the end of 1996, short-term external debt accounted for nearly 30 per cent of total corporate debt in Korea, the highest among all the East and Southeast Asian economies affected by the financial crisis (Claessens *et al.* 1998: 13). Growing indebtedness and worsening debt maturity, together with overcapacity and poor investment returns, left the financial position of Korean firms greatly debilitated. As these problems interacted with the sharp export slump in 1996 to cut their export revenues and profits, they suffered severe liquidity difficulties, and many began to default on their maturing debts. In 1996–97, the average number of corporate failures per month increased by

*Table 7.5*  Sources of external funds raised by the Korean corporate sector (percentage of total external financing), 1985–97

|  | 1985–89 | 1990–94 | 1995 | 1996 | Mid-1997 |
|---|---|---|---|---|---|
| *Indirect financing* | 36.0 | 39.0 | 31.8 | 31.3 | 50.1 |
| Banks | 19.8 | 17.3 | 14.9 | 15.7 | 24.6 |
| NBFIs | 16.2 | 21.7 | 17.0 | 15.6 | 25.5 |
| *Direct financing* | 42.8 | 42.6 | 48.1 | 47.0 | 26.8 |
| Stocks | 23.7 | 15.9 | 14.4 | 11.3 | 6.4 |
| Corporate bonds | 12.3 | 21.2 | 15.3 | 16.9 | 15.4 |
| Commercial paper | 6.8 | 5.5 | 16.1 | 17.5 | 2.9 |
| *Overseas borrowings* | 1.7 | 3.4 | 8.4 | 10.2 | 10.3 |
| *Others* | 19.8 | 15.3 | 11.7 | 11.5 | 13.0 |

Sources: Adapted from Bank of Korea (1995: Table 59) and Baliño and Ubide (1999: Table 3).

Note
NBFI, non-bank financial institution.

*Table 7.6*   Corporate leverage in Korea and other East Asian newly industrialised economies (NIEs) (percentage, arithmetic means), 1988–96

|  | 1988 | 1990 | 1992 | 1994 | 1996 |
|---|---|---|---|---|---|
| *Korea* |  |  |  |  |  |
| Listed firms | 282.0 | 310.5 | 337.3 | 353.0 | 354.5 |
| Top 30 chaebols | 484.0 | – | 398.2 | 389.4 | 386.5 |
| *Other East Asian NIEs (listed firms)* |  |  |  |  |  |
| Hong Kong | 183.2 | 178.3 | 183.5 | 227.3 | 155.9 |
| Indonesia | – | – | 209.7 | 166.1 | 187.8 |
| Malaysia | 72.7 | 101.0 | 62.7 | 99.1 | 117.6 |
| The Philippines | – | – | 118.6 | 114.8 | 128.5 |
| Singapore | 76.5 | 93.9 | 85.6 | 86.2 | 104.9 |
| Taiwan | – | – | 88.3 | 89.4 | 80.2 |
| Thailand | 160.2 | 215.9 | 183.7 | 212.6 | 236.1 |

Sources: Adapted from Claessens *et al.* (1998: Table 6), Corsetti *et al.* (1999: Table 7), *KT* (23 September 1989: 10) and Nam *et al* (1999: Table VII-10).

nearly 50 per cent (Hahm 1999: 117). More significantly, six chaebols went bankrupt or filed for court protection during the first 7 months of 1997.

The traumatic collapse of so many chaebols brought to the fore problems in the banking and financial sectors. Increasing defaults and failures in the corporate sector with which Korean banks and NBFIs had close relations landed many of these institutions in deep distress. The position of financial institutions, particularly banks, had always been fragile in Korea, but it suffered further deterioration in the early to mid-1990s. Two indicators of the poor profitability of banks, compared with that of foreign bank branches operating in Korea, were low and decreasing returns on assets and equity, as shown in Table 7.7. Likewise, their capital base, as measured by the capital–asset ratio, weakened substantially during the same period. Some NBFIs, specifically merchant banks that were highly exposed to chaebol firms, saw their balance sheets being adversely affected to an even greater extent (Hahm and Mishkin 2000: 16–17).

Just when the Korean banking sector became increasingly weak, interactions with the potentially unstable international financial markets were enhanced. Taking advantage of large differentials between domestic and overseas interest rates and the availability of abundant cheap capital in Asian markets in the mid-1990s, local banks and foreign bank branches brought in massive foreign funds. As a consequence, their external liabilities soared and their exposure to international short-term debts remained dangerously high (Table 7.7). Commercial and merchant banks lent heavily to chaebol firms without carefully screening industrial projects and monitoring corporate performance. In the mean time, they used borrowed foreign funds to invest in real estate markets and to buy local and foreign securities in an essentially speculative way (Park 1998: 16; Wade 1998: 1543). This wanton lending and investment behaviour contributed to a rapid accumulation of serious weaknesses in the banking sector.

*Table 7.7* Main indicators of financial institution soundness in Korea, 1993–97

|  | 1993 | 1994 | 1995 | 1996 | 1997 |
|---|---|---|---|---|---|
| *Profitability (percentage, means)* | | | | | |
| Return on assets | | | | | |
|   Twenty Korean banks | 0.45 | 0.42 | 0.32 | 0.26 | –0.93 |
|   Foreign bank branches | – | 1.32 | 1.17 | 1.53 | 3.89 |
| Return on equity | | | | | |
|   Twenty Korean banks | 5.90 | 6.09 | 4.19 | 3.80 | –14.18 |
|   Foreign bank branches | – | 10.96 | 10.28 | 12.51 | 34.79 |
| *Asset position (percentage, means)* | | | | | |
| Bank capital to asset ratio | | | | | |
|   Twenty Korean banks | 4.41 | 4.55 | 3.98 | 3.52 | 2.26 |
| Non-performing loan ratio | | | | | |
|   Korean financial authorities | 7.40 | 5.80 | 5.20 | 4.10 | 6.00 |
|   Jardine Fleming/JP Morgan | – | – | – | 8.00 | 16.00 |
| *External liabilities* | | | | | |
| Total external liabilities(US$, billions) | | | | | |
|   Deposit money banks | 6.55 | 10.94 | 18.94 | 26.71 | – |
|   Merchant banks | 1.45 | 1.82 | 3.87 | 5.94 | – |
| Short-term liabilities as percentage of total | | | | | |
|   Deposit money banks | 64.42 | 78.92 | 77.23 | 73.32 | – |
|   Merchant banks | 20.90 | 35.93 | 50.77 | 53.69 | – |

Sources: Adapted from Baliño and Ubide (1999: Table 5), Corsetti *et al.* (1999: Tables 20 and 22) and Hahm and Mishkin (2000: Tables 3, 4 and 6).

Banking weaknesses were quickly turned into a banking crisis in early to mid-1997, when the slumps in the real estate and stock markets cut down the asset value of banks. These difficulties, together with rising bankruptcies among small and medium-sized enterprises as well as chaebol firms, significantly damaged the asset position of banking institutions and swelled their already burgeoning problem-loan portfolios. The share of total non-performing assets in the combined outstanding loans of the commercial banking sector, calculated in different ways, was shown to have reached a perilously high level by the end of 1997 (Table 7.7). The expanding size of delinquent loans considerably reduced the net assets and capital adequacy of banks, rendering some of them technically insolvent.

Devastating corporate failures and the crippling weaknesses of banks stunned local and international business circles. Worries about the country's financial and economic environment began to affect the perceptions of foreign businesses in Korea from early 1997 onwards. Foreign investors sold their holdings of Korean stocks and reduced their local currency deposits, unloading trillions of won for US dollars. The won thus came under strong downward pressure. In an attempt to restore market confidence, financial authorities selectively rescued the troubled chaebols and supplied trillions of won to the wrecked banks through open-market operations. In September, the minister of finance and economy announced that the government would not allow any banks to fail and would guarantee repayments of their external debts (*Banker* October 1997: 47; *FEER* 31 July 1997: 57–8).

Given the magnitude of the problem, however, these *ad hoc* efforts lacked credibility, and were inadequate to tackle the root causes of mounting corporate and banking difficulties. Shortly after the Kia Group defaulted on its US$310 million loans on 15 July 1997, market sentiments were further depressed and speculative capital outflows intensified. At the same time, the eruption of the Thai financial crisis made foreign creditors take a closer look at the Korean situation. They soon discovered that the problems that had sparked the Thai meltdown were present or even worse in Korea: overstretched and highly indebted chaebols, fragile banks saddled with swelling bad loans, massive short-term foreign debts, growing external imbalances and the shaky ability of the private sector to repay its debts. In early August 1997, Standard & Poor's downgraded the local and foreign currency debt ratings of major Korean banks. From late September, the won began to tumble as immense foreign capital fled the country.

Between early October and mid-November 1997, the won lost more than 30 per cent of its value against the US dollar. The interest payment burden on the country's massive foreign debts now became crushing. Local financial and corporate borrowers, already weighed down by plunging profits and soaring non-performing loans, found it extremely hard to service some US$60 billion external debts that would mature in less than a year. The central bank, which had dumped its dollar reserves in an eventually futile attempt to defend the peg, had no foreign funds with which to help the cash-strapped financial institutions. As the exchange rate depreciated sharply and the domestic currency costs of servicing foreign debts mounted, foreign creditors, who already had investments and loans worth hundreds of billions of dollars in Korea, were reluctant to extend new loans or roll over existing loans. With the spectre of national default looming large, the government called in the IMF for a bailout in late November 1997.

## Market liberalisation and private-sector weaknesses

It is plain from the above analysis that, although external imbalances set the stage for the financial crisis in Korea, mounting problems in the corporate and financial sectors played crucial roles in the collapse of investor confidence, the rapid outflow of capital and the drastic fall of the won. The key causal factors that contributed to the accumulation of the private-sector problems were the incoherent approach to market liberalisation and the associated negative effects on financial system stability.

One important precursor of the financial crisis in Korea was the excessive growth of short-term external debts in the financial and corporate sectors. The massive inflow of short-term funds, and indeed foreign capital in general, was partly induced by Korea's economic boom in the late 1980s and by expectations of continued boom on the part of foreign creditors. Worried about rising inflationary pressures in the early 1990s, financial authorities tried to sterilise capital inflows, raising interest rates on domestic deposits and widening the interest differentials between Korean and foreign credit markets. Combined with the heavily managed exchange rate regime, this encouraged Korean financial institutions to intermediate actively between foreign lenders and domestic borrowers and caused chaebol firms to source cheaper industrial financing abroad.

Important as these factors were, the more fundamental reason for the rapid build-up of short-term external debts rested with the highly selective approach to capital decontrol. Although the Korean government was generally cautious with its attempts to open capital account transactions, it moved more rapidly to reduce limits on short-term foreign borrowings by domestic commercial and merchant banks and by the privileged chaebol firms. At the same time, it maintained restrictions on long-term foreign borrowings and on foreign direct investment, and gave foreigners only limited access to the bond market. As a consequence, longer term and more stable capital inflows accounted for a small proportion of total inflows (Hill and Athukorala 1998).

The increased exposure of Korean financial institutions to short-term external debts and foreign exchange risks also resulted from the biased approach to functional de-segmentation and the haphazard development of some NBFIs. Merchant banks were among the NBFIs that gained most from the differential regulatory treatment. Their development was further boosted between 1994 and 1996 when twenty-four finance companies were converted into merchant banks, drastically increasing their total number to thirty. Since merchant banks were allowed to engage in foreign exchange transactions, the very few NBFIs permitted to enter this business area, this deepened the linkages of the Korean financial sector with international financial markets. More significantly, as most merchant banks were affiliated with the chaebols, they were understandably keen to bring in short-term funds at the behest of their industrial owners, contributing to the worsening of debt maturity structures in the corporate and financial sectors.

Faced with the powerful alliance between the chaebols and their NBFI affiliates, Korean banks were unable to protect their business reserves from being encroached upon, constantly losing market shares to their non-bank rivals. From the late 1980s onwards, banks found themselves hemmed in by increasing competition from both domestic NBFIs and foreign bank branches. To break out of this extremely difficult situation, they reoriented their corporate strategies and focused on foreign exchange transactions, a financial activity that most NBFIs were barred from undertaking. Over the early to mid-1990s, Korean banks quickened their steps to open overseas branches and obtained expanded access to foreign funds. To establish themselves as dominant players in foreign loan intermediation and to win market shares in their rivalry with NBFIs, many banks were willing to borrow short abroad and lend long domestically, thereby taking risks that they might not ordinarily have contemplated.

The financial crisis in Korea had its origins not only in the influx of short-term external debts into the private sector, but also in the highly inefficient use of foreign funds. Large foreign capital inflows might not necessarily be a curse if the borrowed money could be allocated and used efficiently. In Korea, however, the financial system through which most foreign capital came in failed to do so. The bulk of foreign loans intermediated by commercial and merchant banks were either overinvested in chaebol-favoured industrial sectors with large surplus capacity and declining returns or ended up in their speculative ventures in real estate and stocks. As a result, the efficiency of credit allocation was low and declining in the early to mid-1990s. In a comprehensive study on the effects of credit policies in Korea during this period, Borensztein and Lee (1999) found that credit flows were not directed to the profitable sectors and that the favoured industries failed to improve their productivity.

The weak ability of banking institutions to allocate funds efficiently was mainly attributable to prolonged government intervention in their operations. Direct controls over financial prices and bank credit had long been the key instruments of the Korean government for spurring industrial development. Such controls were largely maintained long after full-scale financial liberalisation had been initiated in the late 1980s. Even during the mid-1990s, when most interest rates were deregulated and policy loans phased out, the government still imposed, through administrative guidance, various restrictions on the portfolio management of banks and did not allow them to have full autonomy in their lending activities.

While government intervention might have mitigated financial market failures and fuelled the industrialisation process, it rendered the Korean banking system underdeveloped and inefficient. During the earlier periods of pervasive financial repression, as the government had been extensively involved in credit allocation, bank managers had not developed any strong capacity for screening loans and assessing industrial projects and had become little more than functionaries for rubber-stamping official credit decisions. Although allowed greater discretion in allocating loans with the launch of financial reform, they were slow in changing their operational modes, established under the repressed financial regime. Furthermore, continued government involvement in the allocation of financial resources discouraged banks from improving their credit analysis and risk management skills. As a result, banks tended to base their lending decisions on the size or collateral of borrowing firms rather than on the expected returns of investment projects.

Partial and incomplete financial liberalisation also contributed to the persistence of the moral hazard problem in bank lending, which in turn hindered the emergence of a robust and independent banking sector. One of the lingering legacies of the state-directed financial system in Korea was that the government was potentially responsible for all bank losses and implicitly undertook to rescue the ailing industrial firms that claimed a large amount of credit. In this 'coinsurance scheme existing among government, banks and industry' (Smith 1998: 74), lending risks were minimal and banks often accommodated the financial needs of chaebol firms without conducting strict credit-worthiness checks. In the early to mid-1990s, heavy lenders to the large-business sector no doubt felt secure in their position, confident that the odds of default were slim and that financial authorities would bail them out as they had always done in the past.

For all these reasons, Korean financial institutions, particularly banks, had little incentive to restructure their problematic asset portfolios and to avoid their traditional but dubious chaebol clients. The result was that their lending behaviour remained largely unchanged long after the financial reform process had got under way. As a clear indicator of this situation, credit allocation was still heavily skewed towards the large-business sector, despite incessant government efforts to change it. By one account, the thirty largest chaebols received an annual average of 33.1 per cent of total corporate borrowing (including bank, non-bank and foreign loans and debt securities) over the 1986–95 period and 40.3 per cent in 1996 (Borensztein and Lee 1999: Table 5). Credit concentration in the poorly performing chaebols exposed banks to excessive investment risks and saddled their balance sheets with growing delinquent debts.

Favoured access to financial institution credit encouraged the chaebols to continue to rely heavily upon indirect financing for their industrial expansion. This also made it possible for them to maintain broad ownership and managerial controls over their family business networks, leading to concentrated decision-making processes, weak corporate governance and ineffective internal monitoring mechanisms for investment activities. Benefiting from implicit government support and the abundant supply of domestic and foreign loans, chaebol firms went on a borrowing binge and kept sinking money into capital-intensive manufacturing ventures. Between 1993 and 1996, nearly 70 per cent of the annual increase in corporate investment in Korea was financed by borrowed funds (Pomerleano 1998: Table 4). With enormous financial resources at their disposal, the chaebols continued expanding into businesses out of their core competencies, in order to strengthen their market position and to stay ahead of the competition. This expansionary behaviour overstretched chaebol firms and made them susceptible to external shocks. When such shocks hit the Korean economy in 1996–97, many floundered in depressed cash flows and severe illiquidity.

One may ask why the Korean government allowed huge short-term external debts to build into the economy and financial institutions to lend heavily to chaebol firms, given that they had grave destabilising effects and were in large part culpable for private-sector weaknesses. Apart from the flawed line of financial market liberalisation depicted above, the lax enforcement of prudential rules bears much of the blame. In Korea, domestic financial deregulation and capital account liberalisation were not matched by sustained and consistent efforts to establish an effective institutional framework of regulation and supervision. While financial authorities initiated some institutional and regulatory reforms during the late 1980s and early 1990s, these tended to be partial in scope and inefficient in implementation (Baliño and Ubide 1999).

Comparative assessments of financial regulation have given Korea lower scores on the quality of prudential supervision (Baliño and Ubide 1999; Reisen 1999; Smith 1998). When most restrictions on foreign borrowing were lifted in the mid-1990s, stringent rules were not in place to limit the exposure of financial institutions to foreign exchange risk. Nor were adequate controls exercised over the maturity structures of their external liabilities. Furthermore, the regulations concerning credit risk concentration were slack and ineffectively implemented, facilitating the allocation of credit to the large-business sector.[6] Even the fact that overexposure to the ruined chaebol firms severely damaged the asset position of many commercial and merchant banks did not evoke sufficient remedial action by financial regulators. Part of the reason rested with the fact that the standards for loan classification and provisioning against losses were low and permissive.[7]

In Korea, the inefficacy of prudential regulation is about technical deficiencies as much as about political and institutional constraints on the formulation and enforcement of supervisory rules. One such constraint was that commercial banks were supervised by the central bank whereas specialised banks and NBFIs operated under the supervision of the Ministry of Finance. This fragmented system complicated the execution of regulatory duties, particularly when banks and NBFIs encroached upon each other's business areas, and resulted in the development of risky practices among financial institutions. More significant, the long-running conflicts between the Bank of Korea (BOK) and the Ministry of Finance/the Ministry of Finance and Economy over the extended rights to supervise financial institutions undermined the government's efforts to establish a more unified regulatory system and to make its modes of prudential regulation more compatible with a more liberalised environment.

Concomitant with the fragmented system of financial regulation was the differential regulatory treatment of banks and NBFIs. Reflecting the asymmetrical power relations between finance and industry and between the BOK and the Ministry of Finance, the lack of uniform supervisory standards made the implementation of existing prudential rules ineffective. While the normal operations of commercial banks were subject to credit controls, exposure limits and liquidity requirements, their trust accounts, which were separate from banking operations but managed as one legal entity, were largely immune from these regulations. As a result, banks often used their trust accounts to evade regulatory rules. Moreover, supervision of many NBFIs was much laxer in terms of foreign exchange exposure, credit extension and liquidity management. So lax actually that the authorities were not aware until too late of the rapid growth of their external debts, reckless lending to chaebol firms and large maturity discrepancies (Chang 1998: 1558).

Regulatory weaknesses, derived from the state institutional failures, were complicated by the organisational deficiencies of the private sector. Korean banks, which tied a dominant percentage of their assets to the large-business sector, had strong incentives to continue providing the chaebols with fresh loans. Together with the moral hazard problem associated with implicit government support, this encouraged banks to dodge official limits on credit allocation and to lend heavily to chaebol firms. Similarly, the chaebols' ownership control over NBFIs, specifically merchant banks, also contributed to regulatory problems. Merchant banks often exploited close inter-corporate relations to increase their foreign exchange exposure and to channel short-term external funds to the related subsidiaries of their parent companies (Hahm and Mishkin 2000: 22–3). Intra-affiliate ties rendered opaque the financial transactions between NBFIs and their chaebol owners and made it difficult for regulatory authorities to monitor the borrowing and lending operations of NBFIs.

### Institutional deficiencies and policy failures

As made clear in the above, the poorly managed financial liberalisation played a direct role in the build-up of the various structural weaknesses in the corporate and financial sectors. The unsuccessful liberalisation process heightened the institutional deficiencies of the Korean political economy: the increasing capture of public policy by the powerful chaebols, the unruly relations between the large-business sector and financial industry, the subordinate position of the BOK and inter-bureaucratic conflicts. These deficiencies also exerted a powerful negative influence on the policy environment – an influence that produced serious problems of financial management through the lead-up period to the crisis. More specifically, they undermined the ability of the government to handle corporate failures and exchange rate policy, further compounding the loss of market confidence in Korea.

The first clear signs of the economic crisis in Korea came during the early months of 1997, when several chaebols ran into deep financial trouble, as noted earlier in the previous subsection. In its efforts to tackle the chaebol failures, however, the government adopted a selective and inconsistent approach: it let some crippled firms go under while bailing the others out, if only temporarily. Underlying this approach was a combination of several economic and political factors. In the first place, the chaebols, such as Hanbo and Sammi, that were left to fail were clearly second-tier business groups in terms of assets, sales and number of employees. Equally, they owed relatively modest debts to Korean banks and were not well known to international creditors. By contrast, the chaebols rescued by the government-orchestrated bank support, particularly Kia Motors, were leading manufacturing conglomerates with an international reputation.

Furthermore, the downfall of Hanbo and Sammi in quick succession in early 1997 sent a shock wave throughout the business community both at home and abroad. Foreign financial institutions that had lent heavily to the Korean corporate sector were alarmed at their traumatic collapse. This was not so much because they were unaware of the problems of the wrecked chaebol firms as because the Korean government, which had invariably supported the chaebols in time of trouble, now let some of them go under so easily. Following the Hanbo debacle, foreign creditors, realising that Korea was not so secure a credit risk as previously assumed, became reluctant to lend or roll over existing loans (*KH* 2 and 5 February 1997). To prevent the international credibility of the Korean economy being further damaged, the government had little choice but to support the other ailing chaebols that fell into financial distress at the heels of the Hanbo and Sammi collapse.

Economic factors aside, political considerations also accounted for the selective bailout. Nowhere was this more clearly demonstrated than in the government's decision to let Hanbo fail but to keep Kia afloat. The Hanbo failure was not an ordinary corporate bankruptcy and was turned quickly into a political scandal. It implicated some of President Kim Young-Sam's political allies and, above all, his son, who had been bribed to secure huge loans for the failed group (*Banker* April 1997: 75; *KT* 25 January 1997). In the circumstances, any official rescue efforts would have been interpreted as attempts to conceal the true extent of the scandal. In fact, the Kim government was accused of undertaking a perfunctory initial inquiry in order to whitewash itself in the affair (*EIUCR-Korea* 2nd Quarter 1997: 17). In the case of Kia, not only did its senior executives appear to have clean hands but the firm itself had a better public image, mainly because it was the only non-family-owned chaebol in Korea. In the wake of Kia's default on its debts, sixty-eight civic groups formed an 'Alliance to Rescue Kia' (*FEER* 31 July 1997: 58). Public support seemed to make it difficult for the government not to bail out the car manufacturer.

The incoherent approach to handling the corporate crisis sent contradictory messages to foreign creditors. While some foreign financial institutions were astonished to see the Korean government allow Hanbo and Sammi to collapse, the broad international business community perceived the development in a positive light: the non-interventionist stance appeared to signal the intention of financial leaders to put an end to the implicit co-insurance scheme that had produced gaping weaknesses in the economy. They expected Korean policy-makers to seize the opportunity for reform created by the crisis and to push ahead with the long-overdue restructuring of the corporate and financial sectors (*FEER* 13 February 1997: 53). Their expectations were, however, quickly betrayed by the Korean government's decision to save the other ailing chaebols from bankruptcy. This policy U-turn caused confusion among foreign creditors and significantly marred the credibility of official economic policy.

Another major source of discouragement to foreign investors and creditors was that the government failed in its indecisive and clumsy efforts to restructure the rescued chaebol firms, specifically Kia Motors (Haggard and Mo 2000: 210–12; Mo 2001). After Kia was pulled back from the brink of bankruptcy, the creditor banks agreed to give the company a 2-month breathing space to change its organisational structure. Among the many restructuring measures, Kia planned to reduce the number of group subsidiaries, sell redundant property and cut down the workforce. In return for these measures, Kia wanted its debts to be rescheduled. While the creditor banks, led by Korea First, were willing to reschedule Kia's debts to avoid its complete collapse, the government opposed the request and demanded the resignation of Kia's top management. Senior Kia executives, however, refused to step down and had no intention of following through with their restructuring plan. The two sides thus reached a deadlock.

The recalcitrant attitude of the Kia management aside, the deadlock reflected significant differences between political leaders and bureaucrats with regard to the chaebol rescue. With the presidential election imminent, Kim Young-Sam and his personal staff cajoled economic ministers to support the distressed chaebols in order to apply political balm to soothe public worries about the flagging economy (*FEER* 6 November 1997: 65). On the other hand, the economic bureaucracy under the leadership of Kang Kyung-Shik, deputy prime minister-cum-minister of finance and economy, maintained that the government should rely on market forces to sort out the Kia problem. Beneath this *laissez-faire* rhetoric, however, lay the true intentions of key economic policy-makers. During the 1990s, the Korean car market was plagued by growing overcapacity. Economic officials planned to consolidate the industry by reducing the car manufacturers to two or three giant firms. Equally, Kang, who had close ties with Samsung Motors, mainly through his previous efforts to help the firm to enhance its market position, had personal interests in turning Kia over to its major rival (Moon and Rhyu 2000: 93–4).

In their attempts to pursue their own interests, the chaebol management, political elites and economic bureaucrats held on to their own positions, refused to make any concessions and failed to find an effective solution to the Kia problem (Moon and Mo 1998). While these powerful actors were locked into a tug-of-war with each other, the unsettled predicament of Kia was wreaking havoc on the Korean financial market and economy. Although the government finally decided to put Kia on court receivership and turned the firm into a public enterprise, the 3-month policy stalemate over the restructuring of Kia caused irreparable damage. The international financial community was appalled at the inconsistent and ineffective way in which the government had handled the corporate failures. During September and October 1997, shares on the Seoul exchange nose-dived to their lowest levels in the decade, as foreign investors disposed of their stock holdings. At the same time, with enormous funds flowing out of Korea, the won came under rising pressure.

This was a crucial juncture in the development of the financial crisis in Korea. Clearly, there was an urgent need for an effective realignment of foreign exchange rate policy with widespread concerns among local and foreign businesses about the country's growing corporate and financial vulnerability. Actually, market pressures for the devaluation of the won began to increase as early as late 1996, from the deteriorating current account balance. While the Korean government had been willing to devalue the won to maintain export competitiveness in the past, it was now reluctant to take any decisive and effective measures. The basic factors that prevented the timely devaluation of the won derived from the political and institutional constraints of Korean economic management – the very constraints that led to the mishandling of the corporate failures.

Dominant private-sector actors formed one important source of opposition to the devaluation. During the 1996–97 period, the corporate and financial sectors were carrying massive and swelling foreign debts. Devaluing the won would have immediately increased their debt-servicing burden and wrecked their profits and balance sheets. Although the export earnings of the chaebols dwindled with the rising won, these costs were more than offset by the windfall profits that they obtained from borrowing foreign funds at lower interest rates. This appeared to change their preferences for exchange rate policy and rendered them disposed to a strong domestic currency. Commercial and merchant banks, which had channelled most foreign funds to the large-business sector, were as much concerned about the impact of devaluation on the fortunes of their chaebol clients as they were concerned about theirs. Together, the chaebols and banks formed an anti-devaluation alliance and lobbied hard against any attempts to devalue.

The Ministry of Finance and Economy (MOFE), which traditionally had close ties with the big-business community and was increasingly penetrated by its rent-seeking activities, found itself only too ready to accommodate the demands of the chaebols and their financial subsidiaries. Political pressures from dominant societal actors aside, economic officials, who were grappling with the unprecedented corporate failures throughout the first half of 1997, feared that devaluation would bring down more debt-stricken chaebol firms and, with them, financial institutions. Furthermore, the Kim government, which had come to power with a mandate to pursue price stability but failed to achieve the policy objective consistently, was eager to avoid cost-push inflation that might follow the devaluation of the won. This consideration took on more political importance, particularly when the presidential election was drawing near.

As the chaebols, bureaucrats and politicians had high stakes in the direction of exchange rate policy, opposition to the downward adjustment of the won was formidable. The government made comprehensive efforts to maintain the managed exchange rate against the US dollar, despite the fact that the strategy was increasingly unsustainable. Shortly after the outbreak of the financial crisis in Thailand in mid-1997, speculative assault on the won began to intensify. The BOK warned the government of the danger of an impending foreign exchange crisis and called for devaluation. Its warning and policy proposal were easily brushed aside, however, owing to the subordinate position of the BOK. Senior MOFE bureaucrats twisted the arms of central bankers to hold up the value of the won (*Economist* 22 November 1997: 93; *FEER* 2 April 1998: 15). Between June and November, the BOK lost US$12.2 billion in the spot market and US$7 billion in forward contract commitments in its attempts to defend the won (Park 1998: 16).

The won was indefensible, however. In late October and early November, the currency suffered its heaviest attacks, as foreign and local investors were all betting against it. Just as the crisis situation in Korea reached its critical moment, financial policy was thrown into disarray by the fierce bureaucratic battles over amendments to the central bank law between the BOK and the MOFE (*KT* 23 May 1997; Mo 2001). While Kang Kyung-Shik, deputy prime minister in charge of the MOFE, engaged in intense legislative manoeuvres to push through the bill that would deprive the BOK of its supervisory authority, central bankers took to the streets, fighting the bill and demanding more independence. The decade-long conflicts between the two institutions, which had undermined financial policy and reform, now prevented the government from responding to the unfolding crisis in a decisive manner.

Although the advice of central bankers began to break through in the face of the plunging won in early November 1997, it was too late to reverse the exchange rate policy. Had the government cut loose from the heavily managed exchange regime in early 1997, the won would have depreciated to a new equilibrium and external accounts might have been improved. Had financial authorities floated the won at the time of initial speculative attacks, they could have prevented the disastrous gambles on the currency market and the country might have been able to avoid the near-default situation in late November. The grave decisional mistakes on the exchange rate front were not merely policy misjudgements; they reflected the institutional deficiencies of Korean economic policy-making. These rendered the government incapable of either tackling the crippling financial problems in the private sector or managing and containing the foreign exchange crisis.

# 8    Findings, lessons and implications

The previous chapter has examined how the financial crisis built up and unfolded in Korea and Thailand. It has explored the causal relationship between poorly regulated financial liberalisation and the crisis by sketching different crisis symptoms and specific financial difficulties in each country and illustrating the impact of financial reform patterns and institutional structures on the development of these symptoms and difficulties. This final chapter summarises the major empirical findings that have emerged from the previous chapter, and reflects on the implications of these findings for financial policy-making and national economic governance in Korea, Thailand and other East Asian economies.

## Empirical findings and policy lessons

The financial crisis in Korea and Thailand occurred against the backdrop of wide regional and global economic instabilities. The two countries also experienced similar problems in the corporate and financial sectors. The external and economic factors alone, however, cannot explain why Korea and Thailand suffered in mid- to late 1997. Some other economies in the region, such as the Philippines, Singapore and Taiwan, were either able to escape the financial turmoil largely unscathed or were subjected to less economic destruction (Chu 1999; Haggard 2000: 126–38; Noland 2000). To have a more complete understanding of the causes of the financial crisis and to account for the variation across different national settings, therefore, one needs to look at internal factors and to see how domestic political and institutional factors affect financial policy processes and responses to the crisis.

The basic argument developed in the previous chapter has been that the financial crisis in Korea and Thailand had important endogenous origins. As summarised in Table 8.1, domestic institutional deficiencies and associated political constraints had important bearings on how the crisis developed and was managed. In the two countries, severe weaknesses in the corporate and financial sectors resulted primarily from the failed course of market reform, which in turn reflected the organisational and political structures of financial policy. Equally, the same set of institutional and political constraints that had

*Table 8.1* Institutional failures and financial crisis in Korea and Thailand

## Korea

*Institutional deficiencies and political constraints*: increasing chaebol capture of policy-making processes; close and unruly industry–finance ties; subordinate position of BOK; inter-bureaucratic conflicts

*Reform policy mistakes*: selective capital decontrols; uneven deregulation of competitive restraints; continued government intervention in banking operations; failure to establish an effective regulatory system

*Corporate and financial sector problems*: excessive growth of short-term external debts; misallocation of funds; declining corporate profits; highly leveraged capital structures; mounting non-performing bank assets

*Policy gridlock and crisis mismanagement*: ineffective efforts to handle corporate failures; inability to rectify flawed exchange rate policy

*Triggers of the crisis*: growing external imbalances; massive chaebol bankruptcies; collapse of investor confidence

## Thailand

*Institutional deficiencies and political constraints*: growing capture of public policy by private financiers; strained BOT–Finance Ministry relations; decline of BOT status; increasingly politicised macro-economic policy processes

*Reform policy mistakes*: ill-advised establishment of the BIBF; loose control over banks' external transactions; failure to transform the oligopolistic banking structure; biased approach towards functional desegmentation; lax enforcement of regulatory rules

*Financial sector weaknesses*: mounting foreign debts, massive fund misallocation; excessive exposure to property business and stock trading; growing managerial malpractices; severe moral hazard problems; deterioration of bank balance sheets and asset position

*Financial policy mismanagement*: ineffective efforts to restructure ailing financial institutions; flawed line of exchange rate management

*Triggers of the crisis*: serious external imbalances; financial institution failures; loss of investor confidence

Note
BIBF, Bangkok International Banking Facilities; BOK, Bank of Korea; BOT, Bank of Thailand.

impaired financial liberalisation contributed directly to exchange rate policy mismanagement and to the inability of the governments to tackle mounting corporate and financial difficulties in the period prior to the outbreak of the crisis.

What do these empirical findings suggest about efficient economic policy-making in East Asia in general and in Korea and Thailand in particular? In the wake of the Asian financial crisis, economists vied with each other to offer policy prescriptions for future crisis prevention, focusing on the importance of correct liberalisation sequence, appropriate exchange rate regimes and effective regulatory standards. While an emphasis on these technical issues is certainly not misplaced, it is inadequate and even superficial. As clearly revealed in the previous chapter, the fundamental reasons why the Korean and Thai governments persisted in their flawed financial policies had deep institutional roots. This point has also been emphasised in some theoretical and empirical studies on the causal relationship between domestic institutional structures and economic policy mismanagement in a wider range of the crisis countries (Haggard 1999; Henderson 1999; Kim 2000b; MacIntyre 2001).

The role of institutions has occupied the proscenium in the recent literature on governance. While scholars have not reached a consensus on the connotation of the term,[1] they have all concurred that the design of institutions has significant implications for coherent policy-making and implementation and for the efficient organisation of resources for development – the core ingredients of national economic governance. Institutions take many forms and impinge on policy-making efficiency and economic outcomes in different ways.[2] The major findings derived from this study suggest the importance of a specific set of socio-political institutions, namely business–government relations, organisational features of the private sector, bureaucratic structures and democratic mechanisms. It is weaknesses in these institutional configurations that produced serious policy failures and contributed to the onset of the financial crisis.

As discussed in the previous chapters, state economic agencies in both Korea and Thailand had close and reciprocal relations with big industrialists and private bankers. The intimate business–government relationship provided the opportunities for business control over the policy agenda and for particularistic rent-seeking. In Korea, the well-connected chaebols gained continued access to preferential credit, protection from foreign competition, windfall profits from external borrowings and other sorts of rent through the politicised process of financial reform. By the same token, Thai private bankers, who had a direct entrée to centres of financial policy through their close ties with the Bank of Thailand (BOT), were able to oppose the competitive pressures associated with both domestic and capital account liberalisation and to maintain the policies that guaranteed them oligopolistic profits.

Rent-seeking activities on the part of dominant private actors also negatively affected the conduct of financial policy. As the governments were responsive more to narrower constituencies than to broad public interests, they had difficulties implementing coherent reform policies that would benefit the economy and society at large. Throughout the liberalisation process, the chaebols in Korea and private financiers in Thailand constantly sought policy outcomes that protected their vested interests but led to serious reform errors. Equally important, Korea and Thailand could not realign exchange rates with changing market conditions in a timely manner, mainly because politicians and economic bureaucrats became captives of the private sector through collusive ties. For similar reasons, the governments failed to restructure ailing corporate and financial firms, aggravating the various problems in the private sector and setting the stage for the crisis.[3] The overly close ties between government officials and private business have also been identified as an important source of policy failures and financial vulnerability in Indonesia and Malaysia (Haggard 2000: 38–45).

The close interactions between the public and private sectors were previously identified as a defining feature of the development experiences in Korea and Thailand, as well as in the other East Asian newly industrialised economies (NIEs), that contributed to economic growth. In Korea, business–government collaborations enhanced economic performance by facilitating information flows between economic officials and firms, promoting trust between public and private actors, generating business confidence and encouraging firms to take on risky but technologically advanced investments (Evans 1998: 74–8; Schneider and Maxfield 1997: 6–15; Wade 1990: 284–9). In Thailand, the close alliance between central and private bankers helped to maintain the virtues of financial conservatism, formulate coherent macro-economic policy and foster sustained growth (BOT 1992; Doner and Unger 1993). The degeneration of business–government relations into a major political liability was in large part attributable to deficiencies in the other institutions identified above.

The ability of the Korean chaebols and Thai private bankers to obtain access to, and growing control over, policy processes stemmed from the substantial increase in their organisational capabilities. The main source of this organisational strength was the spectacular concentration of their industrial structure – the direct result of deliberate government efforts to achieve specific industrial and financial policy goals, as discussed in the previous chapters. The high degree of industrial concentration enhanced the capacity of big industrialists and private bankers to overcome collective action problems and increased the leverage that these powerful private actors had *vis-à-vis* state actors. Earlier studies on the behaviour of oligopolistic industries in developing countries suggested potential negative implications of concentration for business–government relations and for economic policy (Granovetter 1994; Leff 1979b). This study and other studies based on wider national settings (see Haggard 2000: 21–4) confirm that major business groups could translate their oligopolistic power into political capital and use it to their particular advantage at the expense of overall social welfare.

Furthermore, large and concentrated industrial and financial firms were able to wield their influence over government policy from their sheer weight in the national economy. Chaebol firms had dominant positions across the modern sector of the Korean economy. In Thailand, commercial banks had considerable control over the entire financial system and many other economic sectors. The fact that the performance of the national economy was closely tied to the fortunes of these industrial and financial groups shifted the balance of power towards private actors, and had constraining effects on policy choice and implementation. All this undercut the patterns of business–government relations that had contributed to growth and weakened the ability of the governments to carry out effective and timely policy decisions at the time of the financial crisis.

Another organisational feature of the private sector that played a role in the crisis is high levels of ownership concentration. Prominent studies on corporate governance propose that concentrated ownership may lead to weak management and poor performance despite its purported potential benefits (Grossman and Hart 1986; Shleifer and Vishny 1996). As noted in the previous chapter, the concentrated structure of ownership in Korean chaebol firms and Thai private banks resulted in the lack of checks and balances among major shareholders, directors and managers, who were closely related to each other through family ties. Weak internal controls created the scope for managerial malpractices, irregularities and even criminal activities. Cross-national research set in the other crisis economies, such as Indonesia and Malaysia, further confirms that ownership concentration encouraged firms to engage in risky investments and gave family-based owners excessive power to pursue their own interests. This undermined the important mechanisms of shareholder protection, and led to the build-up of severe weaknesses in the corporate and financial sectors [Asian Development Bank Institute (ADBI) 1999; Johnson *et al.* 1999; Khan 1999].

Concentrated ownership was responsible not only for poor corporate governance, but also for regulatory failures in both Korea and Thailand. Many empirical analyses of the Asian financial crisis emphasise deficiencies of regulation as being central to its onset. While there can be little doubt that regulatory failures sprang in part from the incompatibility between old regulatory regimes and new liberalised environments, they also had political and institutional causes. Apart from the problematic designs of regulatory agencies, which will be discussed below, complicated and opaque inter-affiliate relations, typically associated with corporate ownership concentration, created monitoring and regulatory difficulties for financial authorities. Chaebol owners were able to exploit their control over a large number of industrial and financial firms to channel foreign funds into speculative ventures or affiliated companies. In Thailand, ownership concentration in the financial sector impeded information disclosure and obscured business transactions, making it easy for banks to dodge regulatory rules but difficult for the BOT to exercise its supervisory functions.

Organisational deficiencies in the private sector thus had a powerful negative impact on the economic policy environment – an impact that vitiated business–government interactions, facilitated particularistic rent-seeking, generated poor systems of corporate governance and undermined the efficiency of government policy. If the organisation of private business contributed to the crisis, however, it was also the way that state institutions were structured internally. Previous studies on the political economy of growth in East Asia focused on the importance of a cohesive, competent and independent bureaucracy in offsetting rent-seeking interests and ensuring growth-oriented policies (Evans 1995; Haggard 1994; Johnson 1987; Leipziger and Thomas 1993; Wade 1990). However, empirical evidence presented in this study shows that the Korean and Thai governments no longer tallied with this modal view. Indeed, it was weakened state institutions that bore the majority of the blame for serious policy failures and the financial crisis.

In the first place, the internal structure of the state in Korea and Thailand became increasingly divided and fragmented. Key state economic agencies in both countries did not possess the structural cohesiveness to pursue collective goals, and lacked the sense of corporate purposes previously contained in the developmental ideology in Korea and in the tradition of financial conservatism in Thailand. This produced co-ordination problems and bred inter-bureaucratic conflicts, hindering decisiveness in the policy process and effective responses to the unfolding crisis. Moreover, conflictual inter-agency relations created the opportunity for big industrialists and private financiers to penetrate the state apparatus and to influence the policy agenda. This was especially true where different state agencies attempted to mobilise social support in their rivalries with each other and therefore became more responsive to distributive demands from dominant private actors.

Furthermore, Korean and Thai economic bureaucrats did not appear to have any high level of technical competence to formulate sound financial policies and to manage the crisis situation. In Korea, the implementation of financial reforms was so inconsistent and incoherent that they often worked at cross-purposes and led to various policy problems. In Thailand, financial technocrats failed to align domestic reform with capital account liberalisation and to fully assess the negative effects of Bangkok International Banking Facilities' (BIBF) operations. In both countries, effective regulatory regimes were not established in line with more liberalised financial markets, displaying, among other things, the lack of adequate information and technical expertise on the part of regulators. Equally important, when the crisis began to grip the economy, the Korean and Thai governments were unable to carry out efficient restructuring measures to phase out delinquent firms and to restore market confidence; nor were they capable of correcting exchange policy mistakes decisively.

Finally, the emerging weaknesses in the internal state structure, together with the rising influence of private business, weakened the capacity of economic bureaucrats to pursue their policy goals independently of political pressures. In Korea, key economic line ministries found it increasingly difficult to insulate themselves from business groups, and the central bank tried in vain to change its subordinate status. Similarly, Thai financial technocrats saw their policy authority being challenged by private financiers and politicians. As the position of state economic and regulatory agencies remained weak or weakened, efficiency-enhancing business–government ties deteriorated into corruptive and rent-seeking networks, giving disastrous consequences for financial policy and for the management of systemic corporate distress. In Singapore and Taiwan, by contrast, the relatively high degree of political independence on the part of financial and regulatory authorities contributed to the effective conduct of policies, enabling the two economies to withstand the deadly impact of the contagion (Chu 1999; *FEER* 2 April 1998: 10–14; Zhang 2002 and forthcoming).

These institutional deficiencies did not develop in isolation from changes in the broad political context in Korea and Thailand. During the late 1980s, the transition to democracy in the two countries, as elsewhere in the region, altered the political landscape and the institutional setting of economic policy-making. Dominant private actors seized growing control over political resources through political parties and parliamentarian processes, and asserted themselves more aggressively in public affairs. Liberal democratic arrangements increasingly subjected economic bureaucrats to competing distributive claims and eroded the institutional underpinnings of their policy-making independence. The government thus found it increasingly difficult to shape development strategies in isolation from ever-stronger distributive demands.

In fact, several newly democratised NIEs, including Korea and Thailand, were hit so hard by the Asian financial crisis that scholars have been pondering on whether democratisation played any role (Blondel *et al.* 1999; Clark 2000; Haggard 1999: 31–4). As illustrated in the previous chapter, business influences on policy processes and inter-bureaucratic conflicts hindered decisive and effective policy responses and contributed to market uncertainty in Korea and Thailand. An examination of a wider range of the crisis and non-crisis economies, however, would suggest that there was no systematic correlation between democratisation and the financial crisis. Authoritarian regimes, particularly Indonesia, fared no better than democratic governments; some democratic societies, such as Taiwan, managed to escape the turmoil largely unscathed. The fact that more democracies seemed to be embroiled in the crisis was most likely to be the result of their economic structure rather than their political system: democratic polities tended to have more open economies, and hence greater exposure to the vagaries of international markets.

Economic governance in Korea and Thailand did not decline with democratisation *per se* but was undermined by the incongruity of existing institutional configurations with democratic processes. In both Korea and Thailand, rules and norms required for the effective functioning of democracy were not fully developed, and the transition from authoritarian rule to democratic governance was not completely achieved (Godement 1999; Harris forthcoming; Moon and Kim 2000). Despite the emergence of political pluralism, politicians, bureaucrats and big business continued dominating economic policy, largely to the exclusion of broad social forces. This left the position of powerful industrialists and financiers unchallenged by competing groups and subjected government policy to their particularistic demands. Moreover, democratisation did not seem to have resulted in much change in the behaviour of state and business actors. Opaque customs and collusive ties concealed policy processes and business transactions from public eyes, defying the rule of law and creating scope for corruption and other socio-economic malpractices (Haggard 1999; Moon and Mo 1998).

In sum, there is ample evidence that the financial crisis in Korea and Thailand was a manifestation of crippling weaknesses in the particular set of socio-political institutions. These weaknesses were reflected in rent-oriented business–government ties, in oligopolistic industrial organisation and concentrated corporate ownership, in growing fragmentation and inter-agency rivalry within the state and in immature democratic structures. They facilitated extensive private penetration of the state apparatus, compromised the ability of government officials to act independently and impaired the coherence and effectiveness of economic policy.

## Implications for institutional reforms

Institutional failures and their powerful negative effects have heightened the need for reforming the modes and structures of economic governance in the crisis countries. Neo-classical political economists have long argued that the best way to ensure the public interest-driven policy agenda and to mitigate the tendency for state–society interactions to degenerate into rent-seeking activity is to reduce the discretionary authority of the state and to resort to market means of resource allocation (see Buchanan *et al.* 1980; Krueger 1974). Market-oriented solutions, while providing a potential political route through which to restructure business–government relations, cannot be divorced from the need to reform the institutional structures of the private sector and the state. Although there are strong incentives for private actors and groups to seek policies that would enhance their particularistic interests, they must possess the necessary organisational capability to translate their incentives into policy outcomes. As illustrated in the previous chapters, the ability of Korean chaebols and Thai private bankers to project their demands into policy processes hinged in part upon their concentrated industrial structure. Corporate restructuring is thus likely to hold the key to the transformation of the problematic public–private nexus.

In the wake of the crisis, the Korean government under the new leadership of Kim Dae June announced sweeping reforms to reduce industrial concentration. They focused on the rationalisation of the corporate structure of the chaebols through the forced swaps of subsidiaries and the reduction of overlapping investments and production capacity. For a similar purpose, the government also bolstered the anti-trust and fair trade acts and prohibited any new cross-investment and inter-subsidiary debt guarantees (Kim 1999: 490–3; Woo-Cumings 1999a: 130–3). In Thailand, the reformist Chuan Leepai government continued with the competitive reorganisation of the banking sector by allowing in more local and foreign players. In fact, the dominant position of incumbent banks was weakened as much by the crisis itself as by government policies (Hewison 2000: 203–5; Phongpaichit and Baker forthcoming). In Indonesia and Malaysia, the governments adopted a comprehensive programme of financial restructuring, economic reforms and changes to the legal framework governing banking and corporate operations (Haggard 2000: ch. 4; Hamilton-Hart 2000).

In Korea and Thailand, as in the other East Asian NIEs, efforts to restructure the corporate and financial sectors were also directed at the problem of ownership concentration, which produced poor corporate governance and impeded the effective functioning of regulatory systems. The Korean government was singularly insistent on cutting down chaebol families' ownership controls by formulating a number of forceful reform measures designed to enhance the supervisory role of outside directors and strengthen the rights of minority shareholders (Jung 1999: 83–4). Realising the ineffectiveness of previous regulations in disbursing bank ownership, the Thai financial authorities took two different tacks. They raised the ceiling on foreign stock ownership and enforced re-capitalisation requirements, both intended to dilute control of financial institutions by dominant family interests (Traisorat 2000: 156–7).

Corporate restructuring, which was launched in the aftermath of the financial crisis, has been an on-going process, and it is therefore difficult to foresee its ultimate impact. It looks quite certain, however, that the restructuring, if implemented fully as planned, would change the structure of industrial organisation and corporate ownership in the Korean chaebols and Thai banks. But the fundamental reform of the organisational structures and governance modes that have been so deeply embedded in the specific political economies of East Asia is no easy job. While the governments were able to overcome political opposition and initiate corporate reforms thanks to the magnitude of the crisis and powerful external pressures, they might have had difficulty persisting with the reforms. On the one hand, corporate restructuring, much of which was mandated by the International Monetary Fund (IMF), had a heavy dose of Anglo-American capitalism and raised the question of whether it could be implanted into the unique social and cultural milieux of East Asia. On the other hand, whatever the crisis countries accomplished with corporate and financial reforms stood at risk of modification or even reversal. This is mainly because the institutional and ideological configurations that underpinned the previous pattern of financial and corporate operations appeared to be capable of defying pressures for convergence towards neo-liberal practices (Nesadurai 2000; Robison forthcoming).

Corporate restructuring is only a partial solution for corruptive business–government ties; to reorient public–private networks towards collective goals rather than particularistic rent-seeking entails the reform of state institutions. The approach towards such reform may constitute three different but interrelated elements. The first element concerns the importance of a Weberian bureaucracy and the resulting coherence of the state. In governments with Weberian features, bureaucrats are meritocratically recruited and enjoy a distinctive and rewarding status; private actors have little opportunity to seek rents because meritocracy and long-term career rewards commit bureaucrats to pursue corporate interests (Evans 1995: 10–13, 1998: 70–4). Two influential World Bank studies (1993: 174–9, 1997: 92–6) also found that merit-based recruitment and promotion practices help to foster an *esprit de corps*, prevent intra-bureaucratic conflicts and build internal cohesion.

Key Korean economic ministries and Thai macro-economic agencies, specifically the BOT, were previously held up as the paragons of Weberian institutions. They became increasingly incompetent, weak and even corrupt over the 1990s. This was partly because rising opportunities in the private sector eroded the material base of the distinctive status of government officials, partly because the ever-enlarging gap between public and private salaries lured many competent technocrats away and partly because neo-liberal ideologies and reforms that denied the economic role of the state diminished the incentives to work in the state apparatus (Evans 1995: 228–34; McVey 1992). To improve their capability and effectiveness, the Korean and Thai governments may not need to look to other countries for role models: they have the experience of building well-functioning bureaucracies. What they need to do is to resuscitate the principles of meritocratic recruitment, promotion by merit criteria and adequate rewards for participation in the government.

The second element is that meritocratic bureaucrats would have to be equipped with policy instruments that can be used to control private-sector behaviour and to achieve macro-economic and regulatory objectives. Economic deregulation and financial liberalisation have deprived the governments of a repertoire of direct instruments and administrative tools previously deployed for such purposes. These instruments and tools cannot possibly be re-deployed, however, because of various political and economic constraints, both at home and abroad. This has left economic bureaucrats with little choice but to develop and employ indirect, market-oriented policy instruments with which to manage exchange rates, control the money supply and supervise financial institutions. The innovative and effective use of these instruments would constitute a crucial precondition for the restoration of state capacity.

Coherent economic policy requires not only meritocracy and technical sophistication on the part of bureaucrats, but also the capacity to limit the play of particularistic interests and to restrain distributive claims on policy processes. The political mechanism through which the state can obtain such capacity is to grant policy-making autonomy to economic agencies. The observation that independent state institutions are crucial to overall economic performance is well known, and the traumatic experiences of East Asia in the financial crisis have only too clearly heightened the theoretical underpinnings of the normative arguments on institutional insulation from political pressures.[4] In the wake of the crisis, Korea, Indonesia and Thailand effected important legislative changes to strengthen the status of economic and regulatory agencies, particularly the central banks.

Reform of state institutions along these lines would be no mean task, because it could be a time-consuming process and could encounter considerable political opposition. But this should not diminish the potential advantages of successful reform and implications for economic governance. There has been no lack of historical examples in which today's established industrial countries succeeded in having built professional bureaucratic systems. More important, economic development in Korea, Thailand and other Asian NIEs benefited from their previous efforts to transform weak bureaucratic structures. Moreover, the practices of corruption and patronage, at least in the key state economic institutions, are not so ingrained in Korea and Thailand as in many other developing countries. Thus, the reform may not involve drastic changes in the fundamental way that governments act but may require higher levels of institutional innovations in line with the changing domestic and international landscapes.

The final component of institutional reform in post-crisis East Asia is to change the manner in which democracy is practised. As discussed above, the failure to consolidate the democratisation process contributed to extensive business penetration of the state and created serious policy failures. The heart of the problem is that industrialists and private financiers became so powerful that they virtually turned private–public networks into rent-seeking avenues. One possible solution to the problem, as suggested by Biddle and Milor (1997) and Evans (1997), would be to counteract the influence of dominant private actors by including a broader range of social groups in policy processes and by establishing a more encompassing form of state–society relations. Inclusion of more social groups, particularly those whose interests are different from those of business actors, is likely to prevent the policy agenda from being captured by particularistic interests and to keep business–government ties oriented towards efficiency-enhancing activities.

There have been traditional concerns about the political feasibility of this solution. Competing social groups, for instance, may face collective action problems and are therefore unable to counterbalance the weight of the business sector. Inclusion of more social groups is likely to breed more distributive coalitions and impair effective policy. Empirical evidence that emerges from several important studies appears to cast doubts on the validity of these concerns (Campos and Nugent 1999; McCallum and Blais 1987; Unger and van Waarden 1999). They suggest that the expansion of interest groups associated with democratisation does not necessarily constitute a threat to growth-oriented policies, and that the relative organisational strength of business *vis-à-vis* other social groups may not prove problematic if the state institutionalises the interactive process that gives civil society, labour unions and private firms equal opportunities for input and oversight.

The more participatory approach towards the state–society nexus is obviously at odds with opaque policy-making modes and creates strong pressures for transparency. Transparency, a form of information exchange in policy processes and business operations, significantly decreases the incentives for private rent-seeking by making such actions more easily observed and therefore more costly (Biddle and Milor 1997: 283–4; Schneider and Maxfield

1997: 9). Moreover, transparency in public policy, through dissemination of rules and criteria, can reduce market uncertainty, enhance policy credibility and stimulate economic growth (Lensink *et al.* 1999). Transparency cannot emerge by itself, however; its development is contingent upon deliberate state efforts to introduce open policy-making systems, promote the role of media as a check on government and institutionalise public–private ties in the form of corporatist bodies (Haggard 1999: 37–8). These efforts can facilitate open negotiations over income distribution and provide incentives for different economic agents to monitor each other and to bide by the negotiated rules (Campos 1993; Campos and Root 1996: 99–105; World Bank 1995).

The lack of transparency in government policy and corporate affairs was one of the major factors that allowed many East Asian economies to be savaged by the financial turmoil. The crisis pushed their governments to make decision-making and business systems less opaque and more open in their conduct, mainly by establishing new regulations and laws (Jayasuriya 2000). The emphasis on legal and technical issues, while important, should not be separated from the efforts to build a more encompassing state–society network. Inclusion of more social groups in the network permits wider public access to the knowledge about government policy and business operations, generates incentives for mutual checks on network members and renders it more difficult and costly to seek non-transparent and narrow rent-oriented ties. To successfully embed transparency in its political and economic systems, therefore, East Asia would do well to socialise and institutionalise democratic reforms.

These four components of institutional reforms in the arenas of business–government relations, private-sector organisational structures, bureaucratic designs and democratic processes should be viewed as an integral effort to provide the sound structural foundations for national economic governance in East Asia. As made clear in the foregoing analysis, all four reform components are interrelated and interact closely with each other. The four components are likely to work at cross-purposes and to compromise each other's effectiveness unless reforms in all the arenas synchronise. The success of institutional reforms depends upon combining the four in an interactive way. Just as the financial crisis stemmed from the combined weaknesses in the four sets of socio-political institutions, comprehensive reform of these institutions holds out the prospects for crisis prevention and, more importantly, for economic recovery and development in a sustainable manner.

# Notes

## 1 Introduction

1   The traumatic results of Southern Cone experiences with financial liberalisation have generated a voluminous literature on the reasons for reform failures, for which macro-economic instability and inadequate banking supervision are generally blamed. For comparative discussions on this subject, see Corbo and de Melo (1985) and Dooley and Mathieson (1987).

2   Economists have undertaken some important comparative studies in this area – see Faruqi (1993), Patrick and Park (1994), Viksnins and Skully (1987) and Zahid (1995). The few comparative studies on the political economy of finance and financial reform in Northeast and Southeast Asia are Bernard (1997), Haggard *et al.* (1993b) and Lee and Haggard (1995).

3   The few studies that have emphasised political and institutional factors in their analyses of the causal relationship between financial liberalisation and crisis include Haggard (2000: 32–8), Weiss (2000) and Zhang (2002).

4   Although there is diversity within this broad perspective, neo-classical scholars have generally attributed the success of economic development, particularly in Northeast Asia, to the policy mix of liberal foreign trade regime, outward-looking development strategies, minimal price distortions and cautious macro-economic management. Among the many studies conducted along the neo-classical line of reasoning, those frequently cited include Balassa (1981), James *et al.* (1989), Krueger (1992) and Noland (1990). Critical discussions of the neo-liberal perspective include Amsden (1989, 1992), Bradford (1987), Haggard (1990), Henderson (1993), Wade (1990, 1993) and Weiss and Hobson (1995). The critics emphasise that the trade and industrial policy regime of the Northeast Asian newly industrialised economies (NIEs) was not so liberal and market oriented as neo-classical proponents claimed, and that government intervention contributed to rapid economic development in the NIEs.

5   The intellectual inspiration of neo-classical influences on the formulation of financial policies in the developing world comes mainly from the pioneering work of McKinnon (1974) and Shaw (1973). Their theoretical propositions have been applied to the prescriptive analysis of financial reform experiences in a wide range of developing countries. Prominent examples are Balassa (1990–91), Bascom (1994), Edwards (1984), Fry (1995) and McKinnon (1982, 1991).

6   The classical statements of the developmental state model can be found in Amsden (1989), Haggard (1990), Haggard and Moon (1983), Johnson (1987) and Wade (1990). The basic theoretical premise of the model can be traced to the works of such economic historians as Gerschenkron (1962), Hirschman (1958) and Landes (1969). While advancing different interpretations of the economic growth trajectories of nineteenth-century Europe and of the twentieth-century developing

world, they all stressed that the state played an indispensable role in establishing the necessary institutional environments for, and in overcoming structural impediments to, economic transformation and capitalist development.

7 It is far beyond the scope of this study to comprehensively evaluate the continued applicability of the developmental state model, particularly against political and economic development in East Asia during the 1980s and 1990s. Recent critical assessments of the model include Doner (1992), Kim (1993), Kang (1995), Moon and Prasad (1998) and Woo-Cumings (1999b).

8 This necessarily brief account of the party system approach may not do full justice to the diversity of different arguments and conceptual paradigms within this broad approach. For more comprehensive reviews of the various versions of party system theories, with particular respect to economic policy reform in the developing world, see Haggard (1997), Haggard and Kaufman (1995) and Haggard and Webb (1994).

9 It should be apparent that the explanatory approach developed in this study draws upon the insights of a prominent line of analysis in the comparative political economy literature. Zysman (1983) emphasises the institutional structures of finance–industry relations in his efforts to explore the dynamics of industrial transformation in Britain and France. Cox (1986) and others use a similar but modified approach to illustrate the way in which the state formulates and implements industrial investment policies through its relationship with the financial and industrial sectors of the economy in six leading advanced industrial societies. Hall (1984, 1986) stresses the organisation of three basic facets of the socio-economic structure of a nation – the state, capital and labour – in an institutional account of cross-country differences in British, French and German macro-economic, industrial and incomes policies. Destler and Henning (1989) and Henning (1994) analyse bank–industry ties and the organisation of state institutions that underlie exchange rate policy-making in Japan, Germany and the United States. In his comparative attempt to examine the monetary policy processes of large Organization for Economic Co-operation and Development (OECD) countries, Epstein (1992) focuses on capital–labour, finance–industry and central bank–government relationships for explanatory variables. More recently, this line of reasoning has been applied to the political analysis of economic policy-making and reform in developing countries, particularly newly industrialising economies in East Asia and Latin America (for prominent examples, see Frieden 1991a; Maxfield 1990, 1991; Weiss 1998). By examining national economic policies through the organisation of societal groups and the structures of state agencies, all these studies have theoretical underpinnings very much in common with a traditional method of socio-economic inquiry that focuses attention on the role of institutions. The explanatory value of this method has been rediscovered and extensively applied to empirical research in various disciplines (see March and Olsen 1989; Moe 1991; Moe and Caldwell 1994; North 1990; Steinmo *et al.* 1992; Williamson 1985, 1995).

10 The method, originally associated with the works of Eckstein (1975) and George (1979), has recently been employed and further refined in such important comparative policy studies as Friman (1990), Henning (1994) and Lukauskas and Minushkin (2000).

## 2 Interests, institutions and financial policy

1 Quinn (1997) and Williamson (forthcoming) are two important studies that illustrate the benefits as well as the costs of financial market reform, particularly capital account liberalisation.

2   Sectoral analyses are to be found in virtually all modern treatments of comparative political economy in both developed and developing countries. For classic statements, see Ferguson (1984), Frieden (1988, 1991a), Gourevitch (1986), Kaufman (1979) and Mamalakis (1969). The approach is applied explicitly and extensively in the political economy analysis of trade policy, prominent examples of which are McKeown (1984), Milner (1987) and Rogowski (1989).

3   In the analysis of private preference formation on market liberalisation, the proposition developed here privileges policy interests of big industrialists and financiers. The relevance of this reasoning to the politics of financial policy reform may be questioned. Several other sectors may also have potential interests in financial policy and reform. Savers suffer from deposit rate ceilings; small and medium-sized industrial firms are disfavoured by selective credit policies; and the general interests of agriculture are harmed by financial policy bias towards urban industrial sectors. For three different but interrelated reasons, however, the policy preferences of these sectors and actors tend to be muted in the financial policy-making process. In the first place, financial institutions and industrial groups normally have their own policy research departments which provide top corporate decision-makers with the capacity to analyse government policy changes and relate these changes easily to their tangible economic interests. Unlike financiers and big industrialists, individual savers, farmers and small manufacturers do not have sophisticated views about, and analytical insight into, the relationship between financial policy change and group interests (Krasner 1978: 65–6; Odell 1982: 347). Further, the incentive to engage in political action is weakened by their inability to determine what interests they may have at stake in the financial policy-making process. As their group interests are obscure, these sectors tend to be poorly motivated in pressing for sectoral demands on governments. Finally, even if individual savers and small industrialists could identify the effects of specific liberalisation measures on their economic interests, they are very unlikely to organise themselves effectively for group activities. This is mainly due to the fact that these social actors, who are typically dispersed and unorganised, encounter serious impediments to collective action (Haggard and Maxfield 1993b: 67).

4   A similar approach to mapping out private-sector preferences can be found in Destler and Henning (1989: 119–36) and Henning (1994: 22–8) for exchange rate policy; in Frieden (1991a: 19–22) for general economic policy and Frieden (1991b: 433–42) for financial integration; in Gourevitch (1986: 56–8) for trade and industry policies; in Haggard (1990: 35–42) for development strategies; in Haggard and Maxfield (1993a: 299–301, 1993b: 66–7, 1996: 38–40) for interest rate and credit policies and capital account liberalisation; and in Maxfield (1990: 24–6, 1991: 424–7) for monetary policy, foreign exchange controls and financial regulation.

5   This discussion is kept necessarily brief and therefore cannot do full justice to the width and depth of the Olsonian theorem. Since the publication of his two major books, Olson's theoretical arguments have been critically examined and extensively applied to empirical studies in various disciplines. Excellent examples of such critical examination and empirical application are Hardin (1982) and Margolis (1982).

6   Scholars who have adopted the dominance or structural approach to bank–industry relations owe an intellectual debt to Gerschenkron (1962) and Hilferding (1981). Both argued that bank participation in industry meant bank dominance. However, the former maintained that financial and industrial capital were becoming increasingly entwined in a tightly knit oligarchic network, and the latter held that the relationship between banks and industry was transitory.

7   Inflation behaves as a tax on money holdings if governments expand the stock of money to increase the general price level. It also behaves as a tax if public savers are forced to keep their money balances at the same level as rising inflation erodes

the values of these holdings. A simple numerical example may help to illustrate how rising inflation raises the tax on money holdings and hence inflation tax revenue. At 10 per cent inflation, for instance, the annual tax on money holdings is 9 per cent [derived from $t = p/(1 + p)$, where $t$ is annual tax rate and $p$ is price inflation rate per year], and at 20 per cent inflation the annual tax rate is 17 per cent. More detailed treatments of the relationship between price inflation and inflation tax revenue can be found in Ghatak (1995: 103–15) and McKinnon and Mathieson (1981).

8   Financial repression behaves as a tax and hence another source of government revenue when deposit rate ceilings imposed directly on depositors, high legal reserve requirements and obligatory holdings of low-yielding government securities by the private sector make financial assets yield net returns well below the world market interest rate. Giovannini and de Melo (1993: 959) estimate that the cross-country average tax revenue from financial repression is equal to about 2 per cent of gross domestic product (GDP) and 9 per cent of total government revenue for twenty-two developing countries over various periods between 1972 and 1987.

9   Quinn and Inclán (1997) find that left-wing governments in countries with skilled labour as their relative factor advantage tend to favour financial openness. This is mainly because the relative incomes of skilled workers, who are the major constituents of left-wing parties, will rise when financial liberalisation makes domestic prices compatible with world prices. They also find that right-wing governments in nations with internationally competitive industrial and financial firms tend to support capital decontrol, largely owing to the fact that the incomes of the business sector, members of which are generally the direct constituents of right-wing governments, are likely to rise when there are fewer restrictions on capital account transactions. The need to disaggregate the interests of governments in capital decontrol along partisan lines seems to be trivial when it comes to financial policy reform in developing countries. This is because unskilled labour predominates and business firms are generally internationally uncontested in most developing economies. Moreover, some other important cross-national studies suggest that partisan differences have little impact on the process of foreign exchange and capital decontrols in both developed and developing countries (Alesina *et al.* 1994; Grilli and Milesi-Ferretti 1995).

10   This causal linkage should be qualified by one caveat: the structure and development of the private banking community is but one factor that may affect the status of central banks. For instance, in Britain, Canada and Japan, where private financiers are strong and powerful, the position of central banks is relatively weak *vis-à-vis* other state agencies in policy-making processes. Generally, the linkage between central bank independence and the structure and health of private financial institutions tends to prevail in developing rather than in developed countries. The author is grateful to Geoffrey Underhill for drawing his attention to this issue.

## 3   Institutional variations in Korea and Thailand

1   The alternative ways to measure industrial concentration at the individual market level include the Herfindahl index, the Lorenz curve and the Gini coefficient. These are often used to measure monopoly power in relatively narrowly defined markets or market segments rather than the aggregate-level industrial concentration. As this study is mainly concerned with measuring the latter, the aggregate concentration ratio is more applicable. For a detailed discussion on the applicability of different measures of industrial and market concentration, see Clarkson and Miller (1982: 62–70).

2   The debate over the impact of Japanese colonialism on Korean development in general and on the growth of Korean entrepreneurship in particular has recently been renewed in academic circles. The prominent examples of empirical studies that have stressed the negative effects of Japanese colonialism and discontinuities between the colonial and post-war eras in terms of economic growth and entrepreneurial development are Fields (1995: ch. 2), Haggard (1990) and Haggard *et al.* (1991). The revisionist views that have emphasised the beneficial impact of Japanese colonial rule and greater continuities are to be found in, among other studies, Eckert (1991) and Kohli (1994). For a recent review of the debate and an attempt to reject the revisionist arguments, see Haggard *et al.* (1997b).

3   The Economic Planning Board (EPB) was dismantled in early 1995, as part of the Kim Young-Sam government's administrative reform. The major functional components of the EPB merged with the Finance Ministry, and the merged ministry was renamed the Ministry of Finance and Economy.

4   Some scholars may point out that the dominance of Chinese-origin entrepreneurs in Thai business made the government cautious about promoting the fortunes of industrial firms. It is true that in Thailand, as in many other Southeast Asian countries, ethnicity was at various times closely linked with the orientation of development strategy. In fact, the interventionist industrial policy of the post-1932 regime was largely designed to suppress the immigrant Chinese. Throughout the 1940s and 1950s, however, the anti-Chinese business stance was gradually submerged in the increasing importance of private capital accumulation and the dynamic growth of Chinese or Sino-Thai industrial capitalists (Phongpaichit and Baker 1995: ch. 4; Suehiro 1989: ch. 4). In the mean time, Chinese-origin entrepreneurs, and indeed the whole Chinese community, became well integrated into the Thai economic structure. Ethnicity is thus of little significance in accounting for the policy stance adopted by the Thai government after the 1950s. Moreover, unlike the manufacturing sector, the banking sector in Thailand was highly concentrated. Ethnicity-oriented interpretations obviously have difficulty in explaining this sectoral difference as the manufacturing and banking sectors were dominated by private actors of the same ethnic origins.

5   The Bank of Korea Law was amended four times in subsequent decades up to late 1997, with the last amendment made in 1982. Unless otherwise indicated, the following description is made with reference to the amended Act of 1982.

6   The ability of the BOT to restrict government borrowing and spending also derived from its direct and active role in the process of budgetary allocation and development planning. These prerogatives helped the BOT to ensure that long-term development strategies were consistent with its policy objectives and that government spending would not compromise monetary stability.

## 4   Financial liberalisation in Korea

1   Shareholding by the government in the five nationwide commercial banks had averaged 28 per cent of total equity share before the privatisation plan was implemented. The ten provincial commercial banks have been in private hands since they were established in the late 1960s and early 1970s.

2   The debt–equity ratio of manufacturing firms in Korea is much higher than that of several leading East Asian economies. During the 1980s, for instance, the ratio averaged 396.1 per cent in Korea compared with 338 per cent in Japan and 93 per cent in Taiwan (Fields 1995: 108).

3   To keep the privatised nationwide commercial banks out of the hands of the chaebols, the Finance Ministry restricted the maximum single personal or corporate shareholding to 10 per cent. But several leading chaebol groups managed

to beat the restriction and acquired controlling shares in the privatised banks through their non-bank financial institution (NBFI) subsidiaries and through family members of chaebol owners. As a consequence, the government intended to tighten restrictions on the maximum shareholding by the chaebols to 5 per cent. But this provoked strong opposition from the Federation of Korean Industries (FKI) and other organisations representing the interests of big business. As a compromise, the General Banking Act, which was amended in late 1982 to readjust restrictions on bank ownership, set the ceiling on maximum shareholding by any single person at 8 per cent.

4   The electoral system under Chun Doo-Hwan derived directly from the authoritarian Yushin system introduced by Park Chung-Hee and was based on a combination of a national list (national constituency) and two-member districts. One-third of the total seats in the National Assembly allocated to the national list were allotted by a proportional representation scheme through which the ruling party could capture the majority of these seats because the popular vote it received was proportionally higher than that received by opposition parties. Remaining seats were filled through two-member districts whose boundaries were gerrymandered to favour conservative voters in rural areas where the ruling party's power was rooted. For a concise discussion on the evolution of Korea's electoral and party systems, see Bedeski (1994).

5   For more than three decades up to 1993, it had been legal for Koreans to hold financial assets in banks and NBFIs and to conduct financial transactions under false names. While the false-name financial system attracted savings and even illicit funds into the organised financial sector, it encouraged tax evasion, financial fraud and other criminal activities. The system also made it difficult for monetary authorities to monitor the flow of funds between markets, institutions and business firms.

6   The chaebols' preferences might have played an important role in accounting for the Korean government's impressive record in trade liberalisation. In Korea, the import liberalisation ratio (the ratio of the number of items allowed to be imported without government approval to the total number of imported items) rose from 68 per cent in 1979 to 92 per cent in 1986 and to 98 per cent in 1992 (You 1992: 133). It is plausible to argue that more rapid progress in trade liberalisation reflected not so much the economic rationale of the sequencing theory as the institutional capacities that allowed policy-makers to pursue those economic reforms that were politically feasible.

7   Before this, foreigners had been allowed to invest indirectly in domestic capital markets through the Korea Fund and the Korea Europe Fund. While the former, which was listed on the New York Stock Exchange, issued equity shares to American and other foreign investors with which to finance the purchase of Korean stocks, the latter was based in London and served European investors.

8   Major NBFIs include development institutions, merchant banking corporations, mutual savings and finance companies, credit unions and mutual credit facilities, securities firms and leasing companies. Development institutions, whose funds are raised from government and foreign borrowings or the issuance of special bonds, provide medium- and long-term loans for the development of key sectors. The main business activities of merchant banking corporations are brokerage of foreign capital, trade in commercial papers issued by business firms, underwriting of securities sales, and investment and management consulting services. Mutual savings and finance companies mobilise funds through their mutual instalment savings and time deposits and specialise in providing financial services to households and small business firms (BOK 1995: 56–72).

9   The author is grateful to Chung-In Moon for having drawn his attention to how

the personal interests of Finance Ministry bureaucrats influenced their preferences for functional desegmentation.

10    It is beyond the scope and intention of this study to discuss, in a detailed manner, the various regulatory problems that the expansion of financial institutions' business operations generated in Korea. For a comprehensive discourse on the pros and cons of financial desegmentation and its implications for the regulation and supervision of financial institutions, see Nam (1994b).

## 5   Financial liberalisation in Thailand

1    For much of the post-war period, Thailand adopted the par value system with the baht maintained virtually at fixed parity with the US dollar. Pressure to devaluate the baht began to grow in early 1981, when the dollar appreciated sharply, increasing the value of the baht against the Japanese yen and major European currencies. This made Thai goods less competitive in European and Japanese markets and severely affected the country's export income. During the first half of 1981, Thai financial authorities twice reduced the value of the baht against the US dollar, once by 1.07 and once by 8.7 per cent. But this did little to improve Thailand's external imbalances. In late 1984, the central bank finally devalued the baht by 14.7 per cent, despite fierce opposition from the military and import-oriented enterprises whose interests were harmed by the devaluation. For detailed political economy analyses of changes in Thailand's exchange rate policy during this period, see Laothamatas (1992b), Phongpaichit (1992a) and Warr (1993).

2    During the economic distress of the early to mid-1980s, Thailand was hit by a series of finance company and commercial bank failures. From late 1983 to late 1984, fifteen finance and security companies collapsed and had their licences revoked by the authorities. Before the financial system could recuperate from this situation, the Asia Trust Bank encountered difficulties in late 1984 and later merged with the state-owned Krung Thai Bank. To prevent widespread loss of public confidence in the financial system, the authorities stepped in and rescued thirty-two other ailing finance companies and two commercial banks through a number of rehabilitation schemes. In the mean time, financial authorities initiated sweeping legal reforms to enhance their regulatory power in late 1985. Comprehensive discussions of Thailand's financial crisis and regulatory reforms can be found in Johnston (1989) and Sundaravej and Trairatvorakul (1989).

3    The BOT relaxed the foreign exchange position of commercial banks from 20 per cent of capital funds to 40 per cent, so that banks could use their foreign exchange holdings to invest in foreign countries in order to boost their revenue. Banks were also allowed to swap government bonds that had been issued earlier at higher interest rates and that had not yet matured with new bonds based upon current market prices. The bond swap measure would enable banks to earn more income immediately in the form of premiums from such swaps.

4    The August 1984 lifeboat scheme represented a major effort by financial authorities to rescue ailing finance companies in the early 1980s. Participation in the scheme was voluntary but subject to the condition that the financial position of participating companies was deemed recoverable and that they accept direct BOT involvement in their management.

5    Out–out operations involve taking foreign-currency deposits or loans from foreign countries and lending the funds thus obtained to foreign countries, and taking baht deposits or loans from foreign countries and lending the baht funds in foreign countries. Out–in transactions take place when foreign-currency deposits and loans derived from foreign countries are lent to Thailand. Bangkok International Banking Facilities (BIBF) licencees can also operate a limited number of offshore

banking businesses related to trading financing, foreign exchange and financial advisory and consulting services. For a detailed discussion about the operations and regulatory framework of the BIBF, see *Asiamoney* (March 1993: 54–6).

6 A primary distortion in Thailand's pattern of development, which intensified in the 1970s, was the extreme concentration of industrial and commercial activities in the Bangkok metropolitan area and the rapidly growing gap between urban and rural income largely as a consequence of that concentration. From the late 1970s onwards, successive Thai administrations tried to rectify this distortion and to spread wealth to rural areas. See Phongpaichit (1992b) for a comprehensive discussion on the issue.

7 Although financial authorities reduced corporate income tax from 30 per cent to 10 per cent and waived the 3.3 per cent specific business and municipality tax for BIBF operations, they still levied 10 per cent withholding tax on out–in transactions. This tax, although applied to all BIBF operators, had a major loophole that discriminated against foreign institutions. Whereas foreign BIBF banks were subject to the withholding tax on funds raised abroad, Thai banks were exempted because they brought outside funds into the country through their overseas branches, which were considered part of the same legal entity as their domestic branches. Moreover, another 10 per cent tax was imposed on repatriation of profits earned by foreign BIBF banks. Both taxes increased the cost of BIBF business for foreign banks and placed them at a disadvantage *vis-à-vis* their Thai counterparts (*Nation* 3 June 1993 and 16 August 1993).

8 As one important effort to consolidate and promote the positive effects of interest rate liberalisation, financial authorities introduced the minimum retail rate (MRR) in October 1993. Based on the average cost of deposits, the MRR was intended to be a reference rate by which commercial banks set their lending rates for retail customers. To ensure that banks' retail rate really reflected the actual cost of their funds, the BOT required them to disclose details of their MRR formulation to financial authorities and the public (interviews, Bangkok, 14 and 25 March 1997; *Nation* 26 October 1993).

## 6 Liberalisation differences: focused comparison

1 The other two measurement techniques also frequently used to examine the degree of capital mobility in developed and developing countries look at saving–investment correlations and interest rate parity conditions. It is far beyond the scope of this study to explore the conceptual bases of these two and other measurement techniques, as well as the methodological and empirical problems associated with their use. See Kim (1995) and Montiel (1993) for comprehensive discussions.

2 The Haggard–Maxfield coding index measures the openness of international financial policy in four areas of foreign exchange and capital transactions: international operations of domestic and foreign commercial banks; payments for financial services and repatriation of capital; portfolio investment and private borrowing; and foreign direct investment. The coding index is based on a four-point scale from 0 to 3, allowing the index to vary from the least open score of 0 (a score of 0 in all four policy areas) to the most open score of 12 (a score of 3 in all the four areas). A country will get the least open score of 0, for instance, if it does not permit private banks to engage in foreign transactions, subjects all payments for financial services to government approval, allows no inward or outward portfolio investment and imposes strict and extensive controls over foreign direct investment. The most open score of 12 will be given to a country if it allows substantial freedom for international operations by banks, imposes no control over payments for financial services, permits inward and outward portfolio investment and overseas borrowing and places very limited restrictions on the

operations of foreign investors. A fuller explanation of the coding rules for the four policy areas can be found in Haggard and Maxfield (1996: 63–4).

## 7  Financial crisis in Korea and Thailand

1  There is a growing number of comprehensive accounts, particularly economic analyses, of the financial crisis in Korea (Chang 1998; Hahm and Mishkin 2000; Harvie 2000; Kim 1999) and in Thailand (Khoman 2000; Krongkaew 1999; Nidhiprabha 1999; Warr 1998). Studies that focus on political dimensions as explanations of the causes of the crisis are exemplified in Doner and Ramsay (1999), Haggard and Mo (2000), Henderson (1999) and Hewsion (2000).

2  This argument sets itself apart from one dominant set of interpretations that has held internal and real economy factors culpable for the financial turmoil in East Asia in general and in Korea and Thailand in particular (Kaminsky and Reinhart 1999; Krugman 1998; Reisen 1999). It also represents an attempt to overcome the limitations of another set of perspectives that has attributed the extent and depth of the crisis to external factors (Feldstein 1998; Radelet and Sachs 1998; Wade and Veneroso 1998; Winters 2000).

3  By the end of 1996, the Thai commercial banking sector had accumulated a large and rising amount of non-performing assets. According to one widely quoted source, the share of such assets in the total loan outstanding stood at 13 per cent in Thailand, compared with 4 per cent in Singapore, 4 per cent in Taiwan and 10 per cent in Malaysia (Corsetti *et al.* 1999: Table 21).

4  Capital adequacy can be measured in different ways. One of the most widely used measures is the ratio of total capital funds to risk-weighted assets (CARs). The Basel Committee on Banking Supervision, established under the auspices of the Bank for International Settlements, recommends that the CARs should be at least 8 per cent for banks. As non-performing loans damage the capital base of banks, provisions for such loans are often used as a supplementary measure of capital adequacy. For more detailed expositions on capital adequacy and on the pros and cons of its various measures, particularly as they are applied to financial regulation in developing countries, see Caprio and Honohan (1999) and Fane (1998).

5  In these two studies, profitability is measured differently. Claessens *et al.* focus on the real rate of return on assets in local currency, calculated at the firm level as earnings before interest and taxes in local currency over total assets minus the annual inflation rate in the country, and on the return on assets in US dollars, adjusted for the effects of currency movements. Pomerleano (1998) uses the return on equity, calculated as net earnings after taxes over share capital and reserves, and the return on capital employed, derived from net profit before interest and taxes over share capital and long-term loans.

6  The revision of the General Banking Act in 1994 set the limits for single borrowers at 15 per cent of a bank's equity capital for loans and 30 per cent for guarantees. Banks that could not comply with these regulations were given a very generous phase-in period of 3 years. Merchant banks were allowed to lend to a single borrower up to 150 per cent of their equity capital. See Bank of Korea (1995: 140–62) for a fuller description of the relevant rules.

7  In Korea, non-performing loans were defined as loans that had been in arrears for more than 6 months, compared with a standard definition of 3 months in many Organization for Economic Co-operation and Development (OECD) and developing countries. Bad loans were defined as the portion of non-performing loans not covered by collateral. In many cases, however, only bad loans were reported as non-performing, overstating the soundness of the Korean banking sector (see Baliño and Ubide 1999).

## 8 Findings, lessons and implications

1  This is not the place to discuss the concept of governance in a detailed manner, but it may be possible to get some flavour of the connotation of governance by briefly looking at how it has been defined in several influential studies. The World Bank (1992: 52) defines the term as the manner in which power is exercised in the management of a country's economic and social resources for development. In a similar but more specific way, Kaufmann *et al.* (1999: 1) characterise governance as the traditions and institutions by which authority in a country is exercised. Clague (1997), Haggard (1999) and Williamson (1995) emphasise the process of governance as the design of economic, social and political institutions for making collective decisions on economic policy and development.

2  See Haggard (1999) for a succinct discussion of different strands of literature that focus on the role of market, social and political institutions in economic policy-making and national governance. Recent studies have also attempted to transcend the disciplinary divides and examined the overall impact of institutions in their various dimensions (Burki and Perry 1998; Campos and Nugent 1999).

3  The private capture of public policy processes and its powerful negative effects are also emphasised as one crucial causal factor of the Asian crisis in, for instance, Haggard (2000: 15–46), Moon and Rhyu (2000) and Zhang and Underhill (forthcoming). For a more general and theoretically oriented discussion of the real and potential dangers of private capture in the domain of financial and monetary governance, see Underhill (2000).

4  The traditional concern that delegation from politicians to autonomous technocrats would contravene democratic accountability may be overdrawn (see Friedman 1962 and 1986 for classic discussions). There are mechanisms which allow politicians to exercise effective control over bureaucrats and to restrict undue political influences on economic policies at the same time. For more detailed analysis of these mechanisms and of how they help to achieve the right balance between independence and accountability, see Campos and Root (1996: 153–71) and Haggard (1999: 38–40).

# Bibliography

## Books and articles

Advanced Research Group (ARG) (1990–91) *Thailand Company Information*, Bangkok: ARG.

Aghevli, Bijan and Jorge Marquez-Ruarte (1985) 'A Case of Successful Adjustment: Korea's Experience during 1980–84', Occasional Paper 39. Washington, DC: The International Monetary Fund.

Ahn, Chung-Si (1990) 'Political Transition and Economic Policy-making in South Korea', in John W. Langford and K. Lorne Brownsey (eds) *Economic Policy-Making in the Asia-Pacific Region*. Halifax, NS: The Institute for Research on Public Policy.

Ahn, Chung-Si and Hoon Jaung (1999) 'South Korea', in Ian Marsh, Jean Blondel and Takashi Inoguchi (eds) *Democracy, Governance, and Economic Performance: East and Southeast Asia*. Tokyo: United Nations University Press.

Aizenman, Joshua and Pablo E. Guidotti (1994) 'Capital Controls, Collection Costs, and Domestic Public Debt', *Journal of International Money and Finance* 13 (1): 41–54.

Akyüz, Yilmaz (1991) 'Financial Liberalisation in Developing Countries: A NeoKeynesian Approach', Discussion Paper 36. Geneva: the United Nations Conference on Trade and Development.

Alba, Pedro, Stijn Claessens and Simeon Djankov (1998) 'Thailand's Corporate Financing and Governance Structures: Impact on Firms' Competitiveness', Policy Research Working Paper 2003. Washington, DC: The World Bank.

Alba, Pedro, Leonardo Hernandez and Daniela Klingebiel (1999) 'Financial Liberalisation and the Capital Account: Thailand, 1988–97', Policy Research Working Paper 2188. Washington, DC: The World Bank.

Alesina, Alberto (1994) 'Political Models of Macro-economic Policy and Fiscal Reforms', in Stephan Haggard and Steven B. Webb (eds) *Voting for Reform: Democracy, Political Liberalisation, and Economic Adjustment*. New York: Oxford University Press.

Alesina, Alberto and Lawrence H. Summers (1993) 'Central Bank Independence and Macro-economic Performance: Some Comparative Evidence', *Journal of Money, Credit and Banking* 25 (2): 151–62.

Alesina, Alberto and Guido Tabellini (1989) 'External Debt, Capital Flight and Political Risk', *Journal of International Economics* 27: 199–220.

Alesina, Alberto, Vittorio Grilli and Gian Maria Milesi-Ferretti (1994) 'The Political Economy of Capital Controls', in Leonardo Leiderman and Assaf Razin (eds) *Capital Mobility: The Impact on Consumption, Investment and Growth*. New York: Cambridge University Press.

Ames, Barry (1987) *Political Survival: Politicians and Public Policy in Latin America*. Berkeley, CA: University of California Press.

Amsden, Alice H. (1989) *Asia's Next Giant: South Korean and Late Industrialisation*. New York: Oxford University Press.

Amsden, Alice H. (1992) 'A Theory of Government Intervention in Late Industrialisation', in Louis Putterman and Dietrich Rueschemeyer (eds) *State and Market in Development: Synergy or Rivalry?* Boulder, CO: Lynne Rienner.

Amsden, Alice H. and Yoon-Dae Euh (1993) 'South Korea's 1980s Financial Reforms: Good-bye Financial Repression (Maybe), Hello New Institutional Restraints', *World Development* 21 (3): 379–90.

Andrews, David M. (1994) 'Capital Mobility and State Autonomy: Toward a Structural Theory of International Monetary Relations', *International Studies Quarterly* 38 (3): 193–218.

Arrow, Kenneth (1985) 'Informational Structure of the Firm', *The American Economic Review* 75 (2): 303–7.

*Asia Year Book* (various issues) Hong Kong.

Atkinson, Michael M. and William D. Coleman (1985) 'Corporatism and Industrial Policy', in Alan Cawson (ed.) *Organised Interests and the State*. London: Sage.

Balassa, Bela (1981) *The Newly Industrialising Countries in the World Economy*. New York: Pergamon Press.

Balassa, Bela (1990–91) 'Financial Liberalisation in Developing Countries', *Studies in Comparative International Development* 25 (4): 56–70.

Baliño, Tomás J. T. and Angel Ubide (1999) 'The Korean Financial Crisis of 1997 – A Strategy of Financial Sector Reform', IMF Working Paper WP/99/28. Washington, DC: The International Monetary Fund.

Banaian, King, Leroy O. Laney and Thomas D. Willet (1986) 'Central Bank Independence: An International Comparison', in Eugenia Froedge Toma and Mark Toma (eds) *Central Bankers, Bureaucratic Incentives, and Monetary Policy*. New York: Kluwer.

Bangkok Bank (various issues) *Commercial Banks in Thailand*, Bangkok: Research Department, Bangkok Bank.

Bascom, Wilbert O. (1994) *The Economics of Financial Reform in Developing Countries*. London: Macmillan.

Beck, Nathaniel (1988) 'Politics and Monetary Policy', in Thomas D. Willett (ed.) *Political Business Cycles*. Durham, NC: Duke University Press.

Becker, Gary S. (1983) 'A Theory of Competition among Pressure Groups for Political Influence', *Quarterly Journal of Economics* 98 (3): 371–400.

Bedeski, Robert E. (1994) *The Transformation of South Korea: Reform and Reconstitution in the Sixth Republic under Roh Tae Woo, 1987–1992*. London: Routledge.

Bello, Walden (1998) 'East Asia: on the Eve of the Great Transformation?' *Review of International Political Economy* 5 (3): 424–44.

Bello, Walden and Stephanie Rosenfeld (1990) *Dragon in Distress: Asia's Miracle Economies in Crisis*. London: Penguin Books.

Bernard, Mitchell (1997) 'Globalisation, the State and Financial Reform in the East Asian NICs: The Cases of Korea and Taiwan', in Geoffrey R. D. Underhill (ed.) *The New World Order in International Finance*. London: Macmillan.

Biddle, Jesse and Vedat Milor (1997) 'Economic Governance in Turkey: Bureaucratic Capacity, Policy Networks and Business Associations', in Sylvia Maxfield and Ben Ross Schneider (eds) *Business and the State in Developing Countries*. Ithaca, NY: Cornell University Press.

Blondel, Jean (1999) 'The Role of Parties and Party Systems in the Democratisation Process', in Ian Marsh, Jean Blondel and Takashi Inoguchi (eds) *Democracy, Governance and Economic Performance: East and Southeast Asia*. Tokyo: United Nations University Press.

Blondel, Jean, Takashi Inoguchi and Ian Marsh (1999) 'Economic Development v. Political Democracy', in Ian Marsh, Jean Blondel and Takashi Inoguchi (eds) *Democracy, Governance, and Economic Performance: East and Southeast Asia*. Tokyo: United Nations University Press.

Bloomfield, Arthur I. (1952) *Report and Recommendations on Banking in South Korea*. Seoul: The Bank of Korea.

Bloomfield, Arthur I. and John P. Jensen (1963) *Banking Reform in South Korea*. Seoul: The Bank of Korea.

Bonbright, James C. (1961) *Principles of Public Utility Rates*. New York: Columbia University Press.

Booth, Anne (1999) 'Initial Conditions and Miraculous Growth: Why is South East Asia Different from Taiwan and South Korea?', *World Development* 27 (2): 301–21.

Borensztein, Eduardo and Jong-Wha Lee (1999) 'Credit Allocation and Financial Crisis in Korea', IMF Working Paper WP/99/20. Washington, DC: The International Monetary Fund.

Bowie, Alasdair and Danny Unger (1997) *The Politics of Open Economies: Indonesia, Malaysia, the Philippines, and Thailand*. Cambridge, UK: Cambridge University Press.

Bradford, Colin I. (1987) 'Trade and Structural Change: NICs and Next Tier NICs as Transitional Economies', *World Development* 15 (3): 299–316.

Brown, Ian (1975) 'The Ministry of Finance and the Early Development of Modern Financial Administration in Siam, 1885–1910'. PhD Dissertation, London University.

Brown, Ian (1988) *The Elite and the Economy in Siam, 1890–1920*. Singapore: Oxford University Press.

Buchanan, James M., Robert D. Tollison and Gordon Tullock (eds) (1980) *Toward a Theory of Rent-Seeking Society*. College Station, TX: Texas A&M University Press.

Burdekin, Richard C. K. and Leroy O. Laney (1988) 'Fiscal Policy-making and the Central Bank Institutional Constraint', *Kyklos* 41 (4): 647–62.

Burki, Shahid Javed and Guillermo E. Perry (1998) *Beyond the Washington Consensus: Institutions Matter*. Washington, DC: The World Bank.

Campos, Edgardo (1993) 'Insulation Mechanisms and Public Sector–Private Sector Relations', in *The Institutional Foundations of High-Speed Growth in the High-Performing Asian Economies, Part I*. Washington, DC: The World Bank.

Campos, Edgardo and Hilton Root (1996) *The Key to the Asian Miracle: Making Shared Growth Credible*. Washington, DC: Brookings Institution.

Campos, Nauro F. and Jeffrey B. Nugent (1999) 'Development Performance and the Institutions of Governance: Evidence from East Asia and Latin America', *World Development* 27 (3): 439–52.

Caprio, Gerard and Patrick Honohan (1999) 'Restoring Banking Stability: Beyond Supervised Capital Requirements', *Journal of Economic Perspectives* 13 (4): 43–64.

Cardoso, Fernando Henrique and Enzo Faletto (1979) *Dependency and Development in Latin America*. Berkeley, CA: University of California Press.

Cargill, Thomas F. and Michael M. Hutchison (1990) 'Monetary Policy and Political Economy: the Federal Reserve and Bank of Japan', in Thomas Mayer (ed.) *The Political Economy of American Monetary Policy*. Cambridge, UK: Cambridge University Press.

Castells, Maunel (1992) 'Four Asian Tigers with a Dragon Head: A Comparative Analysis of the State, Economy and Society in the Asian Pacific Rim', in Richard P. Appelbaum and Jeffrey Henderson (eds) *States and Development in the Asian Pacific Rim*. London: Sage.

Chaiyasoot, Naris (1995) 'Industrialisation, Financial Reform and Monetary Policy', in Medhi Krongkaew (ed.) *Thailand's Industrialisation and its Consequences*. New York: St. Martin's Press.

Chang, Ha-Joon (1998) 'Korea: The misunderstood Crisis', *World Development* 26 (8): 1555–61.

Cheng, Tun-Jen (1990) 'Political Regimes and Development Strategies: South Korea and Taiwan', in Gary Gereffi and Donald L. Wyman (eds) *Manufacturing Miracles: Paths of Industrialisation in Latin America and East Asia*. Princeton, NJ: Princeton University Press.

Cho, Dong-Sung (1984) 'Incentives and Restraints: Government Regulation of Direct Investments between Korea and the United State', in Karl Moskowits (ed.) *From Patron to Partner: The Development of U.S.–Korean Business and Trade Relations*. Lexington, NY: Lexington Books.

Cho, Soon (1994) *The Dynamics of Korean Economic Development*. Washington, DC: Institute for International Economics.

Cho, Yoon-Je (2001) 'The Role of Poorly Phased Liberalisation in Korea's Financial Crisis', in Gerard Caprio, Patrick Honohan and Joseph E. Stiglitz (eds) *Financial Liberalisation: How Far? How Fast?* Cambridge, UK: Cambridge University Press.

Cho, Yoon-Je and David C. Cole (1992) 'The Role of the Financial Sector in Korea's Structural Adjustment', in Vittorio Corbo and Sang-Mok Suh (eds) *Structural Adjustment in a Newly Industrialising Country: The Korean Experience*. Cambridge, MA: Harvard University Press.

Cho, Yoon-Je and Joon-Kyung Kim (1995) 'Credit Policies and the Industrialisation of Korea', World Bank Discussion Paper 286. Washington, DC: The World Bank.

Choi, Byung-Sun (1987) 'Institutionalising A Liberal Economic Order in Korea: the Strategic Management of Economic Change', PhD Dissertation, the Kennedy School of Government, Harvard University.

Choi, Byung-Sun (1989) 'The Changing Conception of Industrial Policy-making in Korea', *The Korea Journal of Policy Studies* 4: 17–43.

Choi, Byung-Sun (1993) 'Financial Policy and Big Business in Korea: the Perils of Financial Regulation', in Stephan Haggard, Chung H. Lee and Sylvia Maxfield (eds) *The Politics of Finance in Developing Countries*. Ithaca, NY: Cornell University Press.

Choi, Yearn-Hong and Lee Yearn-Ho (1995) 'Political Reform and the Government–Business (Chaebôl) Relationship in South Korea', *Korea Observer* 26: 39–61.

Choonhavan, Kraisak (1984) 'The Growth of Domestic Capital and Thai Industrialisation', *Journal of Contemporary Asia* 14 (2): 135–46.

Christensen, Scott (1991) 'The Politics of Democratisation in Thailand: State and Society since 1932'. Unpublished manuscript, Thailand Development Research Institute, Bangkok, Thailand.

Christensen, Scott (1992) 'The Public Policy Process and Political Change in Thailand: A Summary of Observations', *TDRI Quarterly Review* 7: 21–6.

Christensen, Scott, David Dollar, Ammar Siamwalla and Pakorn Vichyanond (1993) *Thailand: The Institutional and Political Underpinnings of Growth*. Washington, DC: The World Bank.

Chu, Yun-Han (1989) 'State Structure and Economic Adjustment of the East Asian Newly Industrialising Countries', *International Organisation* 43 (4): 647–72.

Chu, Yun-Han (1999) 'Surviving the East Asian Financial Storm: The Political Foundation of Taiwan's Economic Resilience', in T. J. Pempel (ed.) *The Politics of the Asian Economic Crisis*. Ithaca, NY: Cornell University Press.

Chuansomsook, Suntichai (1983) 'Demand for and Supply of Commercial Bank Loan: Sectoral Analysis', MA Thesis, Thammasat University.

Chung, Un-Chan (1988) 'Capital Liberalisation in Korea' *Pacific Focus* 3: 173–85.

Claessens, Stijn, Simeon Djankov and Larry H. P. Lang (1998) 'Corporate Growth, Financing, and Risks in the Decade before East Asia's Financial Crisis', Policy Research Working Paper 2017. Washington, DC: The World Bank.

Clague, Christopher (1997) 'The New Institutional Economics and Economic Development', in Christopher Clague (ed.) *Institutions and Economic Development: Growth and Governance in Less-Developed and Post-Socialist Countries*. Baltimore, MD: The Johns Hopkins University Press.

Clark, Cal (2000) 'Modernisation, Democracy, and the Developmental State in Asia: A Virtuous Cycle or Unraveling Strands?', in James F. Hollifield and Calvin Jillson (eds) *Pathways to Democracy: The Political Economy of Democratic Transitions*. New York: Routledge.

Clarkson, Kenneth W. and Roger LeRoy Miller (1982) *Industrial Organisation: Theory, Evidence, and Public Policy*. New York: McGraw-Hill.

Cole, David C. and Yung Chul Park (1983) *Financial Development in Korea, 1945–1978*. Cambridge, MA: Harvard University Press.

Cole, David C. and Betty F. Slade (1991) 'Reform of Financial Systems', in Dwight H. Perkins and Michael Roemer (eds) *Reforming Economic Systems in Developing Countries*. Cambridge, MA: Harvard Institute for International Development.

Cole, William S., Somboon Suksamran and Gary S. Merritt Suwannarat (1990) 'Political Economy of Thailand: An Analysis of Recent Thai Development'. Unpublished policy paper, The USAID, Bangkok, Thailand.

Coleman, William and Wyn Grant (1984) 'Business Associations and Public Policy', *Journal of Public Policy* 4 (3): 209–35.

Collyns, Charles (1983) 'Alternatives to the Central Bank in the Developing World', Occasional Paper 20. Washington, DC: The International Monetary Fund.

Coolidge, T. Jefferson (1981) 'The Realities of Korean Foreign Investment Policy', *Asian Affairs* 12: 370–85.

Corbo, Vittorio and Jaime de Melo (1985) 'Liberalisation with Stabilisation in the Southern Cone of Latin America: Overview and Summary', *World Development* 13 (8): 863–6.

Corden, W. M. (1967) 'The Exchange Rate System and Taxation of Trade', in T. H. Silcock (ed.) *Thailand: Social and Economic Studies in Development*. Canberra: Australian National University Press.

Corsepius, Uwe and Bernhard Fischer (1988) 'Domestic Resource Mobilisation in Thailand: A Success Case for Financial Deepening', *The Singapore Economic Review* 33 (2): 1–20.

Corsetti, Giancarlo, Paolo Pesenti and Nouriel Roubini (1999) 'What Caused the Asian Currency and Financial Crisis?', *Japan and the World Economy* 11 (3): 305–73.

Cox, Andrew (1986) 'The State, Finance and Industry Relationship in Comparative Perspective', in Andrew Cox (ed.) *State, Finance, and Industry: A Comparative Analysis of Post-War Trends in Six Advanced Industrial Economies*. New York: St. Martin's Press.

Cukierman, Alex (1992) *Central Bank Strategy, Credibility, and Independence: Theory and Evidence*. Cambridge, MA: The MIT Press.

Dalla, Ismail and Deena Khatkhate (1995) *'Regulated Deregulation of the Financial System in Korea'*, World Bank Discussion Paper 292. Washington, DC: The World Bank.

Daniels, Philip (1992) 'Industrial Policy', in Martin Harrop (ed.) *Power and Policy in Liberal Democracies*. New York: Cambridge University Press.

Deane, Marjorie and Robert Pringle (1994) *The Central Banks*. London: Hamish Hamilton.

Destler, I. M. and C. Randall Henning (1989) *Dollar Politics: Exchange Rate Policymaking in the United States*. Washington, DC: Institute for International Economics.

Deyo, Frederic (1987) 'Coalition, Institutions, and Linkage Sequencing – Toward a Strategic Capacity Model of East Asian Development', in Frederic C. Deyo (ed.) *The Political Economy of the New Asian Industrialism*. Ithaca, NY: Cornell University Press.

Doner, Richard F. (1988) 'Weak State – Strong Country? The Thai Automobile Case', *The Third World Quarterly* 10 (4): 1542–64.

Doner, Richard F. (1991) 'Approaches to the Politics of Economic Growth in Southeast Asia', *The Journal of Asian Studies* 50 (4): 818–49.

Doner, Richard F. (1992) 'Limits of State Strength: Toward an Institutionalist View of Economic Development' *World Politics* 44 (3): 398–431.

Doner, Richard F. and Gary Hawes (1995) 'The Political Economy of Growth in Southeast and Northeast Asia' in Manochehr Dorraj (ed.) *The Changing Political Economy of the Third World*. Boulder, CO: Lynne Rienner.

Doner, Richard F. and Anek Laothamatas (1994) 'Thailand: Economic and Political Gradualism', in Stephan Haggard and Steven Webb (eds) *Voting for Reform: Democracy, Political Liberalisation, and Economic Adjustment*. New York: Oxford University Press.

Doner, Richard F. and Ansil Ramsay (1999) 'Thailand: From Economic Miracle to Economic Crisis', in Karl D. Jackson (ed.) *Asian Contagion: the Causes and Consequences of a Financial Crisis*. Boulder, CO: Westview Press.

Doner, Richard F. and Daniel Unger (1993) 'The Politics of Finance in Thai Economic Development', in Stephan Haggard, Sylvia Maxfield and Chung Lee (eds) *The Politics of Finance in Developing Countries*. Ithaca, NY: Cornell University Press.

Dooley, Michael P. (1996) 'A Survey of Literature on Controls over International Capital Transactions', *IMF Staff Papers* 43 (4): 630–87.

Dooley, Michael and Donald Mathieson (1987) 'Financial Liberalisation in Developing Countries', *Finance and Development* 24 (3): 20–34.

Duriyaprapan, Chittima and Mathee Supapongse (1996) 'Financial Liberalisation: Case Study of Thailand', paper presented to the 12th Pacific Basin Central Bank Conference, Singapore, 18–20 November.

Easterly, William and Patrick Honohan (1990) 'Financial Sector Policy in Thailand: A Macro-economic Perspective', Working Paper 440. Washington, DC: The World Bank.

Eckert, Carter J. (1991) *Offspring of Empire: The Koch'ang Kims and the Colonial Origins of Korean Capitalism, 1976–1945*. Seattle, WA: University of Washington Press.

Eckert, Carter J. (1993) 'The South Korean Bourgeoisie: A Class in Search of Hegemony', in Hagen Koo (ed.) *State and Society in Contemporary Korea*. Ithaca, NY: Cornell University Press.

Eckstein, Harry (1975) 'Case Study and Theory in Political Science', in Fred I. Greenstein and Nelson W. Polsby (eds) *Handbook of Political Science*, Vol. VII. Reading, MA: Addison-Wesley.

Edwards, Sebastian (1984) 'The Order of Liberalisation of the External Sector in Developing Countries', *Princeton Essays in International Finance No. 156*. International Finance Section, Department of Economics, Princeton University.

Elgie, Robert and Helen Thompson (1998) *The Politics of Central Banks*. London: Routledge.

Epstein, Gerald A. (1992) 'Political Economy and Comparative Central Banking', *Review of Radical Political Economics* 24: 1–30.

Epstein, Gerald A. and Thomas Ferguson (1984) 'Monetary Policy, Loan Liquidation, and Industrial Conflict: The Federal Reserve and the Open Market Operations of 1932', *Journal of Economic History* 44 (4): 957–83.

Epstein, Gerald A. and Herbert Grintis (1992) 'International Capital Markets and the Limits of National Economic Policy', in Tariq Banuri and Juliet B. Schor (eds) *Financial Openness and National Autonomy: Opportunities and Constraints*. Oxford: Clarendon Press.

Epstein, Gerald A. and Juliet B. Schor (1990a) 'Macropolicy in the Rise and Fall of the Golden Age', in Stephen A. Marglin and Juliet B. Schor (eds) *The Golden Age of Capitalism: Reinterpreting the Postwar Experience*. Oxford: Oxford University Press.

Epstein, Gerald A. and Juliet B. Schor (1990b) 'Corporate Profitability as a Determinant of Restrictive Monetary Policy: Estimates for the Postwar United States', in Thomas Mayer (ed.) *The Political Economy of American Monetary Policy*. Cambridge, UK: Cambridge University Press.

Epstein, Gerald A. and Juliet B. Schor (1992) 'Structural Determinants and Economic Effects of Capital Controls in OECD Countries', in Tariq Banuri and Juliet B. Schor (eds) *Financial Openness and National Autonomy: Opportunities and Constraints*. Oxford: Clarendon Press.

Euh, Yoon-Dae and James C. Baker (1990) *The Korean Banking System and Foreign Influence*. London: Routledge.

Evans, Peter (1995) *Embedded Autonomy: States and Industrial Transformation*. Princeton, NJ: Princeton University Press.

Evans, Peter (1997) 'State Structures, Government–Business Relations, and Economic Transformation', in Sylvia Maxfield and Ben Ross Schneider (eds) *Business and the State in Developing Countries*. Ithaca, NY: Cornell University Press.

Evans, Peter (1998) 'Transferable Lessons? Re-examining the Institutional Prerequisites of East Asian Economic Policies', *The Journal of Development Studies* 34 (6): 66–86.

Fane, George (1998) 'The Role of Prudential Regulation', in Ross H. McLeod and Ross Garnaut (eds) *East Asia in Crisis: From Being a Miracle to Needing One?* London: Routledge.

Faruqi, Shakil (ed.) (1993) *Financial Sector Reforms in Asian and Latin American Countries*. Washington, DC: The World Bank.

Feldstein, Martin (1998) 'Refocusing the IMF', *Foreign Affairs* 77 (2): 20–33.

Ferguson, Thomas (1984) 'From Normalcy to New Deal: Industrial Structure, Party Competition, and American Public Policy in the Great Depression', *International Organisation* 38: 41–94.

Fields, Karl J. (1995) *Enterprise and the State in Korea and Taiwan*. Ithaca, NY: Cornell University Press.

Fischer, Bernhard (1993) 'Impediments in the Domestic Banking Sector to Financial Opening', in Helmut Reisen and Bernhard Fischer (eds) *Financial Opening: Policy Issues and Experiences in Developing Countries*. Paris: OECD.

Frankel, Jeffrey A. (1992) 'The Recent Liberalisation of Korea's Foreign Exchange Markets and Tests of U.S. versus Japanese Influence', *Seoul Journal of Economics* 5: 1–29.

Frieden, Jeffry A. (1988) 'Sectoral Conflict and Foreign Economic Policy, 1914–1940', *International Organisation* 42 (1): 59–90.

Frieden, Jeffry A. (1991a) *Debt, Development, and Democracy: Modern Political Economy and Latin America, 1965–1985*. Princeton, NJ: Princeton University Press.

Frieden, Jeffry A. (1991b) 'Invested Interests: the Politics of National Economic Policies in a World of Global Finance', *International Organisation* 45 (4): 426–51.

Friedman, Milton (1962) 'Should there be an Independent Monetary Authority?' in Leland B. Yeager (ed.) *In Search of a monetary Constitution*. Cambridge, MA: Harvard University Press.

Friedman, Milton (1986) 'Monetary Policy: Theory and Practice', in Eugenia F. Toma and Mark Toma (eds) *Central Bankers, Bureaucratic Incentives, and Monetary Policy*. New York: Kluwer.

Friman, H. Richard (1990) *Patchwork Protectionism: Textile Trade Policy in the United States, Japan, and West Germany*. Ithaca, NY: Cornell University Press.

Fry, Maxwell (1986) 'Financial Structure, Financial Regulation, and Financial Reform in the Philippines and Thailand, 1960–1984', in Hang-Sheng Cheng (ed.) *Financial Policy and Reform in Pacific Basic Countries*. Lexington, NY: Lexington Books.

Fry, Maxwell (1995) *Money, Interest, and Banking in Economic Development*, 2nd edn. Baltimore, MD: The Johns Hopkins University Press.

Fry, Maxwell, Charles A. E. Goodhart and Alvaro Almeida (1996) *Central Banking in Developing Countries*. London: Routledge.

von Furstenberg, George M. (1980) 'Inflation, Taxes, and Welfare in LDCs', *Public Finance* 35 (2): 700–10.

Galbis, Vicente (1986) 'Financial Sector Liberalisation under Oligopolistic Conditions and a Bank Holding Company Structure', *Savings and Development* 2: 117–41.

George, Alexander L. (1979) 'Case Studies and Theory Development: The Method of Structured, Focused Comparison', in Paul Gordon Lauren (ed.) *Diplomacy: New Approaches in History, Theory, and Policy*. New York: The Free Press.

Gerschenkron, Alexander (1962) *Economic Backwardness in Historical Perspective*. Cambridge, MA: Harvard University Press.

Ghatak, Subrata (1995) *Monetary Economics in Developing Countries*. London: St. Martin's Press.

Giovannini, Alberto and Martha de Melo (1993) 'Government Revenue from Financial Repression', *The American Economic Review* 83 (4): 953–63.

Girling, John (1996) *Interpreting Development: Capitalism, Democracy, and the Middle Class in Thailand*. Ithaca, NY: Cornell University Southeast Asia Programme.

Glasberg, Davita Silfen (1989) *The Power of Collective Purse Strings: The Effects of Bank Hegemony on Corporations and the State*. Berkeley, CA: University of California Press.

Godement, François (1999) *The Downsizing of Asia*. New York: Routledge.

Goodhart, Charles (1988) *The Evolution of Central Banks*. Cambridge, MA: The MIT Press.

Goodman, John B. (1992) *Monetary Sovereignty: The Politics of Central Banking in Western Europe*. Ithaca, NY: Cornell University Press.

Goodman, John B. and Louis W. Pauly (1993) 'The Obsolescence of Capital Controls? Economic Management in an Age of Global Markets', *World Politics* 46 (3): 50–82.

Gourevitch, Peter (1986) *Politics in Hard Times: Comparative Responses to International Economic Crises*. Ithaca, NY: Cornell University Press.

Grajdanzev, Andrew J. (1944) *Modern Korea*. New York: The John Day Company.

Granovetter, Mark (1994) 'Business Groups', in Neil J. Smelser and Richard Swedberg (eds) *The Handbook of Economic Sociology*. Princeton, NJ: Princeton University Press.

Grilli, Vittorio and Gian Maria Milesi-Ferretti (1995) 'Economic Effects and Structural Determinants of Capital Controls', *IMF Staff Papers* 42 (3): 517–51.

Grilli, Vittorio, Donato Masciandaro and Guido Tabellini (1991) 'Political and Monetary Institutions and Public Policies in the Industrial Countries', *Economic Policy: A European Forum* 13: 341–93.

Grossman, Sanford and Oliver Hart (1986) 'The Costs and Benefits of Ownership: A Theory of Vertical and Lateral Integration', *Journal of Political Economy* 94 (4): 691–719.

de Haan, Jakob and Willem J. Kooi (2000) 'Does Central Bank Independence Really Matter? New Evidence for Developing Countries Using a New Indicator', *Journal of Banking & Finance* 24 (4): 643–64.

Haggard, Stephan (1990) *Pathways from the Periphery: The Politics of Growth in the Newly Industrialising Countries*. Ithaca, NY: Cornell University Press.

Haggard, Stephan (1994) 'Business, Politics and Policy in Northeast and Southeast Asia', in Andrew MacIntyre (ed.) *Business and Government in Industrialising Asia*. St Leonards, NSW: Allen & Unwin.

Haggard, Stephan (1997) 'Democratic Institutions, Economic Policy, and Development', in Christopher Clague (ed.) *Institutions and Economic Development: Growth and Governance in Less-Developed and Post-Socialist Countries*. Baltimore, MD: The Johns Hopkins University Press.

Haggard, Stephan (1999) 'Governance and Growth: Lessons from the Asian Economic Crisis', *Asian-Pacific Economic Literature* 13 (2): 30–42.

Haggard, Stephan (2000) *The Political Economy of the Asian Financial Crisis*. Washington, DC: Institute for International Economics.

Haggard, Stephan and Tun-Jen Cheng (1987) 'State and Foreign Capital in the East Asian NICs', in Frederic C. Deyo (ed.) *The Political Economy of the New Asian Industrialism*. Ithaca, NY: Cornell University Press.

Haggard, Stephan and Robert R. Kaufman (1992) 'The Political Economy of Inflation and Stabilisation in Middle-Income Countries', in Stephan Haggard and Robert R. Kaufman (eds) *The Politics of Economic Adjustment: International Constraints, Distributive Conflicts and the State*. Princeton, NJ: Princeton University Press.

Haggard, Stephan and Robert R. Kaufman (1995) *The Political Economy of Democratic Transitions*. Princeton, NJ: Princeton University Press.

Haggard, Stephan and Andrew MacIntyre (1998) 'The Political Economy of the Asian Economic Crisis', *Review of International Political Economy* 5 (3): 381–92.

Haggard, Stephen and Sylvia Maxfield (1993a) 'Political Explanations of Financial Policy in Developing Countries', in Stephen Haggard, Chung H. Lee and Sylvia Maxfield (eds) *The Politics of Finance in Developing Countries*. Ithaca, NY: Cornell University Press.

Haggard, Stephen and Sylvia Maxfield (1993b) 'The Political Economy of Capital Account Liberalisation', in Helmut Reisen and Bernhard Fisher (eds) *Financial Opening: Policy Issues and Experience in Developing Countries*. Paris: OECD.

Haggard, Stephen and Sylvia Maxfield (1996) 'The Political Economy of Financial Internationalisation in the Developing World', *International Organisation* 50 (1): 35–68.

Haggard, Stephan and Jongryn Mo (2000) 'The Political Economy of the Korean Financial Crisis', *Review of International Political Economy* 7 (2): 197–218.

Haggard, Stephen and Chung-In Moon (1983) 'The South Korean State in the International Economy: Liberal, Dependent or Mercantile?' in J. G. Ruggie (ed.) *The Antinomies of Interdependence*. New York: Columbia University Press.

Haggard, Stephen and Chung-In Moon (1990) 'Institutions and Economic Policy: Theory and a Korean Case Study', *World Politics* 42 (2): 210–37.

Haggard, Stephen and Chung-in Moon (1993) 'The State, Politics, and Economic Development in Postwar South Korea', in Hagen Koo (ed.) *State and Society in Contemporary Korea*. Ithaca, NY: Cornell University Press.

Haggard, Stephen and Steven B. Webb (1994) 'Introduction', in Stephen Haggard and Steven B. Webb (eds) *Voting for Reform: Democracy, Political Liberalisation and Economic Adjustment*. New York: Oxford University Press.

Haggard, Stephen, Byung-Kook Kim and Chung-In Moon (1991) 'The Transition to Export-led Growth in South Korea: 1954–1966', *The Journal of Asian Studies* 50 (4): 850–73.

Haggard, Stephen, Richard N. Cooper and Chung-In Moon (1993a) 'Policy Reform in Korea', in Robert H. Bates and Anne O. Krueger (eds) *Political and Economic Interactions in Economic Policy Reform: Evidence from Eight Countries*. Oxford: Basil Blackwell.

Haggard, Stephan, Chung H. Lee and Sylvia Maxfield (eds) (1993b) *The Politics of Finance in Developing Countries*. Ithaca, NY: Cornell University Press.

Haggard, Stephan, Richard N. Cooper, Susan Collins, Choongsoo Kim and Sung-Tae Ro (1994) *Macro-economic Policy and Adjustment in Korea, 1970–1990*. Cambridge, MA: Harvard Institute for International Development.

Haggard, Stephan, Sylvia Maxfield and Ben Ross Schneider (1997a) 'Theories of Business and Business–State Relations', in Sylvia Maxfield and Ben Ross Schneider (eds) *Business and the State in Developing Countries*. Ithaca, NY: Cornell University Press.

Haggard, Stephan, David Kang and Chung-In Moon (1997b) 'Japanese Colonialism and Korean Development: A Critique', *World Development* 25 (6): 867–81.

Hahm, Joon-Ho (1999) 'Financial System Restructuring in Korea: The Crisis and Its Resolution', in Seiichi Masuyama, Donna Vandenbrink and Chia Siow Yue (eds) *East Asia's Financial Systems: Evolution and Crisis*. Singapore: Institute of Southeast Asian Studies and Tokyo: Nomura Research Institute.

Hahm, Joon-Ho and Frederic S. Mishkin (2000) 'Causes of the Korean Financial Crisis: Lessons for Policy', NBER Working Paper 7483. Cambridge, MA: National Bureau of Economic Research.

Hall, A. Peter (1984) 'Patterns of Economic Policy: An Organisational Approach', in Stephen Bornstein, David Held and Joel Krieger (eds) *The State in Capitalist Europe: A Casebook*. London: George Allen & Unwin.

Hall, A. Peter (1986) *Governing the Economy: The Politics of State Intervention in Britain and France*. London: Polity Press.

Hamilton-Hart, Natasha (2000) 'Indonesia: Reforming the Institutions of Financial Governance?', in Gregory W. Noble and John Ravenhill (eds) *The Asian Financial Crisis and the Architecture of Global Finance*. Cambridge, UK: Cambridge University Press.

Hardin, Russell (1982) *Collective Action*. Baltimore, MD: The Johns Hopkins University Press.

Harris, Stephen (forthcoming) 'Korea and the Asian Crisis: The Impact of the Democratic Deficit and OECD Accession', in Geoffrey R. D. Underhill and Xiaoke Zhang (eds) *International Financial Governance under Stress: Global Structures versus National Imperatives*. Cambridge, UK: Cambridge University Press.

Harvie, Charles (2000) 'The Korean Financial Crisis: Is Bail-out a Solution?' in Tran Tan Hoa and Charles Harvie (eds) The *Causes and Impact of the Asian Financial Crisis*. London: Macmillan.

Hawes, Gary and Hong Liu (1993) 'Explaining the Dynamics of the Southeast Asian Political Economy: State, Society, and the Search for Economic Growth', *World Politics* 45 (3): 629–60.

Helleiner, Eric (1994) *States and the Reemergence of Global Finance: From Bretton Woods to the 1990s*. Ithaca, NY: Cornell University Press.

Henderson, Jeffrey (1993) 'The Role of the State in the Economic Transformation of East Asia', in Chris Disxon and David Drakakis-Smith (eds) *Economic and Social Development in Pacific Asia*. London: Routledge.

Henderson, Jeffrey (1999) 'Uneven Crises: Institutional Foundation of East Asian Economic Turmoil', *Economy and Society* 28 (3): 327–68.

Henning, C. Randall (1994) *Currencies and Politics in the United States, Germany, and Japan*. Washington, DC: Institute for International Economics.

Hewison, Kevin J. (1981) 'The Financial Bourgeoisie in Thailand', *Journal of Contemporary Asia* 11 (4): 395–412.

Hewison, Kevin J. (1985) 'The State and Capitalist Development in Thailand', in Richard Higgott and Richard Robinson (eds) *Southeast Asia: Essays in the Political Economy of Structural Change*. London: Routledge.

Hewison, Kevin J. (1987) 'National Interests and Economic Downturn: Thailand', in Richard Robison, Kevin Hewison and Richard Higgott (eds) *Southeast Asia in the 1980s: The Politics of Economic Crisis*. Sydney: Allen & Unwin.

Hewison, Kevin J. (1988) 'Industry Prior to Industrialisation: Thailand', *Journal of Contemporary Asia* 18 (4): 389–411.

Hewison, Kevin J. (1989) *Bankers and Bureaucrats: Capital and the Role of the State in Thailand*. Monograph Series 34. New Haven, CT: Yale University Southeast Asia Studies.

Hewison, Kevin J. (2000) 'Thailand's Capitalism before and after the Economic Crisis', in Richard Robison, Mark Beeson, Kanishka Jayasuriya and Hyuk-Rae Kim (eds) *Politics and Markets in the Wake of the Asian Crisis*. London: Routledge.

Hibbs, Douglas A. (1977) 'Political Parties and Macro-economic Policy', *The American Political Science Review* 71 (4): 1467–87.

Hilferding, Rudolf (1981) *Finance Capital: A Study of the Latest Phase of Capitalist Development*. London: Routledge & Kegan Paul.

Hill, Hal and Prema-chandra Athukorala (1998) 'Foreign Investment in East Asia: A Survey', *Asian-Pacific Economic Literature* 12 (2): 23–50.

Hirschman, Albert O. (1958) *The Strategy of Economic Development*. New Haven, CT: Yale University Press.

Ikenberry, G. John (1986) 'The Irony of State Strength: Comparative Responses to the Oil Shocks in the 1970s', *International Organisation* 40 (1): 105–37.

Ingram, James C. (1955) *Economic Change in Thailand Since 1850*. Stanford, CA: Stanford University Press.

Ingram, James C. (1971) *Economic Change in Thailand, 1950–1970* (an expanded edition). Stanford, CA: Stanford University Press.

International Business Research Co. (IBRC) (1991) *Million Baht Business Information*, Bangkok: IBRC.

Ireland, Alleyne (1926) *New Korea*. New York: E. P. Dutton.

James, William, Seiji Naya and Gerald Meier (1989) *Asian Development: Economic Success and Policy Lessons*. Madison, WI: University of Wisconsin Press.

Jayasuriya, Kanishka (2000) 'Authoritarian Liberalism, Governance and the Emergence of the Regulatory State in Post-Crisis East Asia', in Richard Robison, Mark Beeson, Kanishka Jayasuriya and Hyuk-Rae Kim (eds) *Politics and Markets in the Wake of the Asian Crisis*. London: Routledge.

Jeong, Kap-Young (1994) 'Industrial Policy and Market Concentration in Korea', *Korean Social Science Journal* 20: 59–72.

Johnson, Chalmers (1982) *MITI and Japanese Miracle*. Stanford, CA: Stanford University Press.

Johnson, Chalmers (1987) 'Political Institutions and Economic Performance: The Government–Business Relationship in Japan, South Korea, and Taiwan', in Frederic C. Deyo
(ed.) *The Political Economy of the New Asian Industrialism*. Ithaca, NY: Cornell University
Press.

Johnson, Simon, Peter Boone, Alasdair Breach and Eric Friedman (1999) 'Corporate
Governance in the Asian Financial Crisis, 1997–98', Unpublished manuscript,
Cambridge, MA: The MIT.

Johnston, R. Barry (1989) 'Distressed Financial Institutions in Thailand: Structural Weaknesses, Support Operations and Economic Consequences', Working paper WP/89/4.
Washington, DC: The International Monetary Fund.

Johnston, R. Barry (1991) 'Sequencing Financial Reform', in Patrick Downes and Reza
Vaez-Zadeh (eds) *The Evolving Role of Central Banks*. Washington, DC: The International
Monetary Fund.

Jones, Leroy P. and Il Sakong (1980) *Government, Business, and Entrepreneurship in Economic
Development: The Korean Case*. Cambridge, MA: Harvard University Press.

Jung, Ku-Hyun (1995) 'Changing Business–Government Relations in Korea', *Journal of
Far Eastern Business* 1 (3): 98–112.

Jung, Ku-Hyun (1999) 'Asian Economic Crisis and Corporate Restructuring', *Korea
Focus* 7 (3): 77–90.

Kahler, Miles (1990) 'Orthodoxy and its Alternatives: Explaining Approaches to Stabilisation and Adjustment', in Joan M. Nelson (ed.) *Economic Crisis and Policy Choice: the Politics
of Adjustment in the Third World*. Princeton, NJ: Princeton University Press.

Kahler, Miles (1992) 'External Influence, Conditionality, and the Politics of Adjust-
ment', in Stephan Haggard and Robert R. Kaufman (eds) *The Politics of Economic
Adjustment: International Constraints, Distributive Conflicts and the State*. Princeton, NJ:
Princeton University Press.

Kaminsky, Graciela L. and Carmen M. Reinhart (1999) 'The Twin Crises: The Causes
of Banking and Balance-of-Payments Problems', *The American Economic Review* 89
(3): 473–500.

Kang, David C. (1995) 'South Korean and Taiwanese Development and the New
Institutional Economics', *International Organisation* 49 (3): 555–87.

Kang, David C. (2002) 'Bad Loans to Good Friends: Money Politics and the Developmental State in South Korea', *International Organisation* 56 (1): 177–207.

Kaufman, Robert R. (1979) 'Industrial Change and Authoritarian Rule in Latin America:
A Concrete Review of the Bureaucratic–Authoritarian Model', in David Collier (ed.)
*The New Authoritarianism in Latin America*. Princeton, NJ: Princeton University Press.

Kaufman, Robert R. (1985) 'Democratic and Authoritarian Responses to the Debt Issue:
Argentina, Brazil and Mexico', *International Organisation* 39 (3): 473–503.

Kaufman, Robert R. and Barbara Stallings (1989) 'Debt and Democracy in the 1980s:
The Latin American Experience', in Barbara Stallings and Robert R. Kaufman (eds)
*Debt and Democracy in Latin America*. Boulder, CO: Westview Press.

Kaufmann, Daniel, Aart Kraay and Pablo Zoido-Lobatón (1999) 'Governance Matters',
Policy Research Working Paper 2196. Washington, DC: The World Bank.

Khan, Haider A. (1999) 'Corporate Governance of Family Businesses in Asia', Working
Paper 3. Tokyo: Asian Development Bank Institute.

Khoman, Sirilaksana (2000) 'The Asian Financial Crisis and Prospects for Trade and
Business with Thailand', in Tran Tan Hoa and Charles Harvie (eds) *The Causes and
Impact of the Asian Financial Crisis*. London: Macmillan.

Kim, Byong Kuk (1965) *Central Banking Experiment in a Developing Economy: Case Study of Korea*. Seoul: The Korean Research Centre.

Kim, Eun Mee (1993) 'Contradictions and Limits of a Developmental State: With Illustrations from the South Korean Case', *Social Problems* 40 (2): 228–49.

Kim, Dohyung (1999) 'IMF Bailout and Financial and Corporate Restructuring in the Republic of Korea', *The Developing Economies* 37 (4): 460–513.

Kim, Hyuk-Rae (2000a) 'The Viability and Vulnerability of Korean Economic Governance', *Journal of Contemporary Asia* 30 (2): 199–220.

Kim, Hyuk-Rae (2000b) 'Fragility or Continuity? Economic Governance of East Asian Capitalism', in Richard Robison, Mark Beeson, Kanishka Jayasuriya and Hyuk-Rae Kim (eds) *Politics and Markets in the Wake of the Asian Crisis*. London: Routledge.

Kim, Kwang Suk and Michael Roemer (1979) *Growth and Structural Transformation*. Cambridge, MA: Harvard University Press.

Kim, Kyong-Dong (1976) 'Political Factors in the Formation of the Entrepreneurial Elite in South Korea', *Asian Survey* 16 (5): 465–77.

Kim, Kyung-Soo (1995) 'International Capital Mobility: Causes, Measurements and Consequences – A Survey', in Rudiger Dornbusch and Yung Chul Park (eds) *Financial Opening: Policy Lessons for Korea*. Seoul: Korea Institute of Finance.

Kim, Pyung Joo (1994) 'Financial Institutions', in Lee-Jay Cho and Yoon Hyung Kim (eds) *Korea's Political Economy: An Institutional Perspective*. Boulder, CO: Westview.

Kim, Young-Jong (1986) *Bureaucratic Corruption: The Case of Korea*. Seoul: The Chomyung Press.

King, Daniel E. (1996) 'Thailand in 1995: Open Society, Dynamic Economy, Troubled Politics', *Asian Survey* 36 (2): 135–41.

King, Daniel E. (1997) 'Thailand in 1996: Economic Slowdown Clouds Year', *Asian Survey* 37 (2): 160–6.

King, Daniel E. (1999) 'Thailand', in Ian Marsh, Jean Blondel and Takashi Inoguchi (eds) *Democracy, Governance, and Economic Performance: East and Southeast Asia*. Tokyo: United Nations University Press.

Kiriwat, Ekamol (1993) 'Financial Sector Reform: Thailand', in Shakil Faruqi (ed.) *Financial Sector Reforms in Asian and Latin American Countries: Lessons of Comparative Experience*. Washington, DC: The World Bank.

Kohli, Atul (1994) 'Where do High Growth Political Economies Come From? The Japanese Lineage of Korea's "Developmental State"', *World Development* 22 (9): 1269–93.

Kong, Tat Yan (1995) 'From Relative Autonomy to Consensual Development: The Case of South Korea', *Political Studies* 63 (4): 630–44.

Koo, Bohn-Young (1985) 'The Role of Direct Investment in Korea's Recent Economic Growth', in Water Galensen (ed.) *Foreign Trade and Investment: Economic Development in the Newly Industrialising Asian Countries*. Madison, WI: University of Wisconsin.

Koo, Bon-Ho (1993) 'Industrial Policy and Financial Reforms in Korea', in Shakil Faruqi (ed.) *Financial Sector Reforms in Asian and Latin American Countries*. Washington, DC: The World Bank.

Koo, Hagen and Eun Mee Kim (1992) 'The Developmental State and Capital Accumulation in South Korea', in Richard P. Appelbaum and Jeffrey Henderson (eds) *States and Development in the Asian Pacific Rim*. London: Sage.

Krasner, Stephen D. (1978) 'United States Commercial and Monetary Policy: Unravelling the Paradox of External Strength and Internal Weakness', in Peter Katzenstein (ed.) *Between Power and Plenty: Foreign Economic Policies of Advanced Industrial States*. Madison, WI: The University of Wisconsin Press.

Krongkaew, Medhi (1999) 'Capital Flows and Economic Crisis in Thailand', *The Developing Economies* 37 (4): 395–416.

Krueger, Anne O. (1974) 'The Political Economy of the Rent-Seeking Society', *The American Economic Review* 64 (3): 291–303.

Krueger, Anne O. (1992) *Economic Policy Reform in Developing Countries*. Oxford: Basil Blackwell.

Krugman, Paul (1998) 'What Happened to Asia?', at <http://web.mit.edu/krugman/www/DISINTER.htm>

Kuo, Cheng-Tian (1995) *Global Competitiveness and Industrial Growth in Taiwan and the Philippines*. Pittsburgh: University of Pittsburgh Press.

Kurzer, Paulette (1988) 'The Politics of Central Banks: Austerity and Unemployment in Europe', *Journal of Public Policy* 7: 21–48.

Landes, David (1969) *The Unbound Prometheus: Technological Change and Industrial Development in Western Europe from 1750 to the Present*. Cambridge, UK: Cambridge University Press.

Laothamatas, Anek (1992a) *Business Associations and the New Political Economy of Thailand: From Bureaucratic Polity to Liberal Corporatism*. Boulder, CO: Westview Press.

Laothamatas, Anek (1992b) 'The Politics of Structural Adjustment in Thailand: A Political Explanation of Economic Success', in Andrew MacIntyre and Kanishka Jayasuriya (eds) *The Dynamics of Economic Policy Reform in Southeast Asia and the Southwest Pacific*. Singapore: Oxford University Press.

Lauridsen, Laurids S. (1998) 'The Financial Crisis in Thailand: Causes, Conduct and Consequences?' *World Development* 26 (8): 1575–91.

Lee, Chong-Sik and Hyuk-Sang Sohn (1994) 'South Korea in 1993: the Year of the Great Reform', *Asian Survey* 34 (7): 1–9.

Lee, Chung H. (1992) 'The Government, Financial System, and Large Private Enterprises in the Economic Development of South Korea', *World Development* 20 (2): 187–97.

Lee, Chung H. (1995) *The Economic Transformation of South Korea: Lessons for the Transition Economies*. Paris: Development Centre, OECD.

Lee, Chung H. and Stephan Haggard (1995) 'Introduction: Issues and Findings', in Stephan Haggard and Chung H. Lee (eds) *Financial Systems and Economic Policy in Developing Countries*. Ithaca, NY: Cornell University Press.

Lee, Yeon-ho (1996) 'Political Aspects of South Korean State Autonomy: Regulating the Chaebôl, 1980–93', *The Pacific Review* 9 (2): 149–79.

Leeahtam, Pisit (1991) *Thailand's Economic Adjustment in the 1980s: From Crisis to Double Digit Growth*. Bangkok: Dokya.

Leff, Nathaniel H. (1978) 'Industrial Organisation and Entrepreneurship in the Developing Countries: the Economic Groups', *Economic Development and Cultural Change* 26 (4): 661–75.

Leff, Nathaniel H. (1979a) 'Entrepreneurship and Economic Development: The Problem Revisited', *Journal of Economic Literature* 17: 46–64.

Leff, Nathaniel H. (1979b) '"Monopoly Capitalism" and Public Policy in Developing Countries', *Kyklos* 32 (4): 718–38.

Leightner, Jonathan E. (1999a) 'Globalisation and Thailand's Financial Crisis', *Journal of Economic Issues* 33 (2): 367–73.

Leightner, Jonathan E. (1999b) 'The Achilles' Heel of Thailand's Financial Market', in Tsu-Tan Fu, Cliff J. Hunang and C. A. Knox Lovell (eds) *Economic Efficiency and Productivity Growth in the Asia-Pacific Region*. Cheltenham: Edward Elgar.

Leightner, Jonathan E. and C. A. Knox Lovell (1998) 'The Impact of Financial Liberalisation on the Performance of Thai Banks', *Journal of Economics and Business* 50: 115–31.

Leipziger, Danny M. and Peter A. Petri (1994) 'Korean Industrial Policy: Legacies of the Past and Directions for the Future', in Lee-Jay Cho and Yoon Hyung Kim (eds) *Korea's Political Economy: An Institutional Perspective*. Boulder, CO: Westview.

Leipziger, Danny M. and Vinod Thomas (1993) *Lessons of East Asia: An Overview of Country Experience*. Washington, DC: The World Bank.

Lensink, Robert, Hong Bo and Elmer Sterken (1999) 'Does Uncertainty Affect Economic Growth? An Empirical Analysis', *Weltwirtschaftliches Archiv* 135 (3): 179–396.

Lew, Seok-Jin (1992) 'Bringing Capital Back In: A Case Study of South Korean Automobile Industrialisation'. Unpublished PhD Dissertation, Yale University.

Lindblom, Charles E. (1977) *Politics and Markets: The World's Political-Economic Systems*. New York: Basic Books.

Luedde-Neurath, Richard (1984) 'State Intervention and Foreign Direct Investment in South Korea', *IDS Bulletin* 15 (2): 18–25.

Luedde-Neurath, Richard (1988) 'State Intervention and Export-Oriented Development in South Korea', in Gordon White (ed.) *Developmental States in East Asia*. London: Macmillan.

Lukauskas, Arvid and Susan Minushkin (2000) 'Explaining Styles of Financial Market Opening in Chile, Mexico, South Korea, and Turkey', *International Studies Quarterly* 44 (3): 695–723.

McCallum, John and André Blais (1987) 'Government, Special Interest Groups, and Economic Growth', *Public Choice* 54: 3–18.

MacDonald, Scott B. (1998) 'Transparency in Thailand's 1997 Economic Crisis: The Significance of Disclosure', *Asian Survey* 38 (7): 688–701.

MacIntyre, Andrew (1993) 'Indonesia, Thailand, and the Northeast Asian Connections', in Richard Higgott, Richard Leaver and John Ravenhill (eds) *Pacific Economic Relations in the 1990s: Cooperation or Conflict?* Sydney: Allen & Unwin.

MacIntyre, Andrew (1994) 'Business, Government and Development: Northeast and Southeast Asian Comparisons', in Andrew MacIntyre (ed.) *Business and Government in Industrialising Asia*. Sydney: Allen & Unwin.

MacIntyre, Andrew (1999) 'Political Institutions and the Economic Crisis in Thailand and Indonesia', in T. J. Pempel (ed.) *The Politics of the Asian Economic Crisis*. Ithaca, NY: Cornell University Press.

MacIntyre, Andrew (2001) 'Institutions and Investors: The Politics of the Economic Crisis in Southeast Asia', *International Organisation* 55 (1): 81–122.

MacIntyre, Andrew J. and Kanishka Jayasuriya (1992) 'The Politics and Economics of Economic Policy Reform in Southeast Asia and the Southwest Pacific', in Andrew J. MacIntyre and Kanishka Jayasuriya (eds) *The Dynamics of Economic Policy Reform in Southeast Asia and the Southwest Pacific*. Singapore: Oxford University Press.

McKeown, Timothy J. (1984) 'Firms and Tariff Regime Change: Explaining the Demand for Protection', *World Politics* 36 (2): 215–33.

McKinnon, Ronald I. (1974) *Money and Capital in Economic Development*. Washington, DC: Brookings Institution.

McKinnon, Ronald I. (1982) 'The Order of Economic Liberalisation: Lessons from Chile and Argentina', in Karl Brunner and Allen Meltzer (eds) *Economic Policy in a Changing World*. Amsterdam: North-Holland.

McKinnon, Ronald I. (1991) *The Order of Economic Liberalisation: Financial Control in the Transition to a Market Economy*. Baltimore, MD: The Johns Hopkins University Press.

McKinnon, Ronald I. and Donald J. Mathieson (1981) 'How to Manage a Repressed

Economy', *Princeton Essays in International Finance No. 145*. Princeton, NJ: International Finance Section, Department of Economics, Princeton University.

McVey, Ruth (1992) 'The Materialisation of the Southeast Asian Entrepreneur', in Ruth McVey (ed.) *Southeast Asian Capitalists*. Ithaca, NY: Cornell University Southeast Asia Programme.

Mamalakis, Markos J. (1969) 'The Theory of Sectoral Clashes', *Latin American Research Review* 4 (3): 9–46.

Management Efficiency Research Institute (MERI) (1985) *Korea's Fifty Major Business Groups*, Seoul: MERI.

March, James G. and Johan P. Olsen (1989) *Rediscovering Institutions: the Organisational Basis of Politics*. New York: Free Press.

Mardon, Russell (1990) 'The State and the Effective Control of Foreign Capital: The Case of South Korea', *World Politics* 43 (1): 111–38.

Margolis, Howard (1982) *Selfishness, Altruism and Rationality: A Theory of Social Choice*. Cambridge, UK: Cambridge University Press.

Mathieson, Donald J. and Liliana Rojas-Suárez (1993) 'Liberalisation of Capital Account: Experiences and Issues', Occasional Paper 103. Washington, DC: the International Monetary Fund.

Mathieson, Donald J. and Liliana Rojas-Suarez (1994) 'Capital Controls and Capital Account Liberalisation in Industrial Countries', in Leonardo Leiderman and Assaf Razin (eds) *Capital Mobility: the Impact on Consumption, Investment and Growth*. New York: Cambridge University Press.

Maxfield, Sylvia (1990) *Governing Capital: International Finance and Mexican Politics*. Ithaca, NY: Cornell University Press.

Maxfield, Sylvia (1991) 'Bankers' Alliances and Economic Policy Patterns: Evidence from Mexico and Brazil', *Comparative Political Studies* 23 (4): 419–58.

Maxfield, Sylvia (1994) 'Financial Incentives and Central Bank Authority in Industrialising Nations', *World Politics* 46 (4): 556–88.

Milner, Helen (1987) 'Resisting the Protectionist Temptation: Industry and the Making of Trade Policy in France and the United States During the 1970s', *International Organisation* 41 (4): 639–65.

Mintz, Beth and Michael Schwartz (1986) 'Capital Flows and the Process of Financial Hegemony', *Theory and Society* 15 (1–2): 77–101.

Mo, Jongryn (2001) 'Political Culture and Legislative Gridlock: Politics of Economic Reform in Precrisis Korea', *Comparative Political Studies* 34 (5): 467–92.

Moe, Terry M. (1991) 'Politics and the Theory of Organisation', *Journal of Economics and Organisation* 7: 106–29.

Moe, Terry and Michael Caldwell (1994) 'The Institutional Foundations of Democratic Government: A Comparison of Presidential and Parliamentary Systems', *Journal of Institutional and Theoretical Economics* 150: 171–95.

Montiel, Peter J. (1993) 'Capital Mobility in Developing Countries: Some Measurement Issues and Empirical Estimates', Policy Research Working Paper 1103. Washington, DC: The World Bank.

Moon, Chung-In (1988) 'The Demise of a Developmentalist State? Neoconservative Reforms and Political Consequences in South Korea', *Journal of Developing Societies* 4: 67–84.

Moon, Chung-In (1994) 'Changing Patterns of Business–Government Relations in South Korea', in Andrew MacIntyre (ed.) *Business and Government in Industrialising Asia*. Sydney: Allen & Unwin.

Moon, Chung-In (1995) 'Globalisation: Challenges and Strategies', *Korea Focus* 3 (3): 62–75.

Moon, Chung-In (1996) 'Democratisation and Globalisation as Ideological and Political Foundations of Economic Policy', paper presented at a workshop on Democracy and the Korean Economy organised by the Hoover Institution, Stanford University, 2 July.

Moon, Chung-In and Song-min Kim (2000) 'Democracy and Economic Performance in South Korea', Larry Diamond and Byung-Kook Kim (eds) *Consolidating Democracy in South Korea*. Boulder, CO: Lynne Rienner.

Moon, Chung-In and Rashemi Prasad (1998) 'Networks, Politics, and Institutions', in Steve Chan, Cal Clark and Danny Lam (eds) *Beyond the Developmental State: East Asia's Political Economies Reconsidered*. London: Macmillan.

Moon, Chung-In and Sang-young Rhyu (2000) 'The State, Structural Rigidity, and the End of Asian Capitalism: A Comparative Study of Japan and South Korea', in Richard Robison, Mark Beeson, Kanishka Jayasuriya and Hyuk-Rae Kim (eds) *Politics and Markets in the Wake of the Asian Crisis*. London: Routledge.

Moran, Michael (1981) 'Finance Capital and Pressure-Group Politics in Britain', *British Journal of Political Science* 11 (4): 381–404.

Moran, Michael (1984) 'Politics, Banks and Markets: An Anglo-American Comparison', *Political Studies* 32 (2): 173–189

Moran, Michael (1990) 'Financial Markets', in James Simmie and Roger King (eds) *The State in Action: Public Policy and Politics*. London: Pinter.

Mousny, André (1964) *The Economy of Thailand: An Appraisal of A Liberal Exchange Policy*. Bangkok: Social Science Association Press of Thailand.

Muscat, Robert J. (1994) *The Fifth Tiger: A Study of Thai Development Policy*. Armonk, NY: M. E. Sharpe.

Muscat, Robert J. (1995) 'Thailand', in Stephan Haggard and Chung H. Lee (eds) *Financial Systems and Economic Policy in Developing Countries*. Ithaca, NY: Cornell University Press.

Nam, Chang-Hee (1995) 'South Korea's Big Business Clientelism in Democratic Reform', *Asian Survey*, 35 (4): 357–366.

Nam, Il Chong, Joon-Kyung Kim, Yeongjae Kang, Sung Wook Joh and Jun-Il Kim (1999) 'Corporate Governance in Korea', paper presented to the OECD/KDI conference on Corporate Governance in Asia, Seoul, 3–5 March.

Nam, Sang-Woo (1986) 'Korea's Stabilisation Efforts Since the Late 1970s', in Kim Joong-woong (ed.) *Financial Development Policies and Issues*. Seoul: Korea Development Institute.

Nam, Sang-Woo (1994a) 'Korea's Financial Reform since the Early 1980s', in Gerard Caprio Jr, Izak Atiyas and James A. Hanson (eds) *Financial Reform: Theory and Experience*. Oxford: Oxford University Press.

Nam, Sang-Woo (1994b) 'Institutional Reform of the Korean Financial System', in Lee-Jay Cho and Yoon Hyung Kim (eds) *Korea's Political Economy: An Institutional Perspective*. Boulder, CO: Westview.

Nam, Sang-Woo (1995) 'Korea's Financial Markets and Policies', in Shahid N. Zahid (ed.) *Financial Sector Development in Asia*. Hong Kong: Oxford University Press.

Nelson, Joan M. (1990) 'Introduction: the Politics of Economic Adjustment in Developing Nations', in Joan M. Nelson (ed.) *Economic Crisis and Policy Choice: the Politics of Adjustment in the Third World*. Princeton, NJ: Princeton University Press.

Nelson, Joan M. (1992) 'Poverty, Equity and the Politics of Adjustment', in Stephan

Haggard and Robert R. Kaufman (eds) *The Politics of Economic Adjustment*. Princeton, NJ: Princeton University Press.

Nembhard, Jessica Gordon (1996) *Capital Control, Financial Regulation, and Industrial Policy in South Korea and Brazil*. London: Praeger.

Nesadurai, Helen E. S. (2000) 'In Defence of National Economic Autonomy? Malaysia's Response to the Financial Crisis', *The Pacific Review* 13: 73–114.

Nidhiprabha, Bhanupong (1999) 'Economic Crises and the Debt-Deflation Episode in Thailand', in H. W. Arndt and Hal Hill (eds) *Southeast Asia's Economic Crisis: Origins, Lessons, and the Way Forward*. New York: St. Martin's Press.

Noble, Gregory (1987) 'Contending Forces in Taiwan's Economic Policymaking', *Asian Survey* 27 (6): 683–704.

Noland, Marcos (1990) *Pacific Basin Developing Countries: Prospects for the Future*. Washington, DC: Institute for International Economics.

Noland, Marcus (2000) 'The Philippines in the Asian Financial Crisis', *Asian Survey*, 40 (3): 401–12.

Noll, Roger G. (1985) 'Government Regulatory Behaviour: A Multidisciplinary Survey and Synthesis', in Roger G. Noll (ed.) *Regulatory Policy and the Social Sciences*. Berkeley, CA: University of California Press.

Nordhaus, William D. (1975) 'The Political Business Cycles', *Review of Economic Studies* 42: 169–90.

Nordlinger, Eric A. (1981) *On the Autonomy of the Democratic State*. Cambridge, MA: Harvard University Press.

North, Douglass C. (1990) *Institutions, Institutional Change and Economic Performance*. New York: Cambridge University Press.

Nukul Commission Report (1998) *Analysis and Evaluation on Facts Behind Thailand's Economic Crisis*. Bangkok: Nation Multimedia Group.

Odell, John S. (1982) *U.S. International Monetary Policy: Markets, Power and Ideas as Sources of Change*. Princeton, NJ: Princeton University Press.

Olson, Mancur (1965) *The Logic of Collective Action: Public Goods and the Theory of Groups*. Cambridge, MA: Harvard University Press.

Olson, Mancur (1982) *The Rise and Decline of Nations: Economic Growth, Stagflation, and Social Rigidities*. New York: Yale University Press.

Osborne, Dale K. (1976) 'Cartel Problems', *The American Economic Review* 66 (5): 835–44.

Overholt, William H. (1999) 'Thailand's Financial and Political Systems', *Asian Survey* 39 (6): 1009–35.

Park, Won-Am (1996) 'Financial Liberalisation: The Korean Experience', in Takatoshi Ito and Anne O. Krueger (eds) *Financial Deregulation and Integration in East Asia*. Chicago, IL: University of Chicago Press.

Park, Yung Chul (1993) 'The Role of Finance in Economic Development in South Korea and Taiwan', in Alberto Giovannini (ed.) *Finance and Development: Issues and Experience*. Cambridge, UK: Cambridge University Press.

Park, Yung Chul (1994) 'Korea: Development and Structural Change of the Financial System', in Hugh T. Patrick and Yung Chul Park (eds) *The Financial Development of Japan, Korea, and Taiwan: Growth, Repression, and Liberalisation*. New York: Oxford University Press.

Park, Yung Chul (1998) 'Investment Boom, Financial Bust: The Crisis in Korea', *Brookings Review* 16 (3): 14–17.

Park, Yung Chul and Dong Won Kim (1994) 'Korea: Development and Structural Change of the Banking System', in Hugh T. Patrick and Yung Chul Park (eds) *The Financial*

*Development of Japan, Korea and Taiwan: Growth, Repression, and Liberalisation*. New York: Oxford University Press.

Park, Yung Chul and Won-Am Park (1993) 'Capital Movement, Real Asset Speculation, and Macro-economic Adjustment in Korea', in Helmut Reisen and Bernhard Fisher (eds) *Financial Opening: Policy Issues and Experience in Developing Countries*. Paris: OECD.

Parker, Stephen (1998) 'Out of the Ashes?: Southeast Asia's Struggle through Crisis', *Brookings Review* 16 (3): 10–13.

Patrick, Hugh T. and Yung Chul Park (eds) (1994) *The Financial Development of Japan, Korea and Taiwan: Growth, Repression and Liberalisation*. Oxford: Oxford University Press.

Peltzman, Sam (1976) 'Toward a More General Theory of Regulation', *The Journal of Law and Economics* 19: 211–40.

Phagaphasvivat, Somjai (1990) 'Thai–American Relations: Trade in Services', in Clark D. Neher and Wiwat Mungkaudi (eds) *U.S.–Thailand Relations in a New International Era*. Berkeley, CA: Institute of East Asian Studies, University of California.

Phongpaichit, Pasuk (1980) 'The Open Economy and Its Friends: The "Development" of Thailand', *Pacific Affairs* 53 (3): 440–60.

Phongpaichit, Pasuk (1992a) 'Technocrats, Businessmen, and Generals: Democracy and Economic Policymaking in Thailand', in Andrew MacIntyre and Kanishka Jayasuriya (eds) *The Dynamics of Economic Policy Reforms in Southeast Asia and the Southwest Pacific*. Singapore: Oxford University Press.

Phongpaichit, Pasuk (1992b) 'Social Consequences of Economic Restructuring in Thailand', Development Paper 15. Bangkok: The United Nations Economic and Social Commission for Asia and the Pacific.

Phongpaichit, Pasuk (1996) 'The Thai Economy in the Mid-1990s', *Southeast Asian Affairs*. Singapore: Institute for Southeast Asian Studies.

Phongpaichit, Pasuk and Chris Baker (1995) *Thailand Economy and Politics*. Oxford: Oxford University Press.

Phongpaichit, Pasuk and Chris Baker (1996) *Thailand's Boom!* Chiang Mai: Silkworm Books.

Phongpaichit, Pasuk and Chris Baker (1998) *Thailand Boom and Bust*. Chiang Mai: Silkworm Books.

Phongpaichit, Pasuk and Chris Baker (2000) *Thailand's Crisis*. Singapore: Institute of Southeast Asian Studies.

Phongpaichit, Pasuk and Chris Baker (forthcoming) 'Crisis Consequences: Lessons from Thailand', in Geoffrey R. D. Underhill and Xiaoke Zhang (eds) *International Financial Governance: Global Structures versus National Imperatives*. Cambridge, UK: Cambridge University Press.

Pocmontri, Isorn (1980) 'The Impact of Central Banking on Monetary Policy of Thailand: 1930–1955', manuscript. Essex: University of Essex.

Polanyi, Karl (1957) *The Great Transformation: The Political and Economic Origins of Our Time*. Boston, MA: Beacon.

Pomerleano, Michael (1998) 'The East Asia Crisis and Corporate Finances: The Untold Micro Story', Policy Research Working Paper 1990. Washington, DC: The World Bank.

Posen, Adams S. (1993) 'Why Central Bank Independence does not Cause Low Inflation: There is no Institutional Fix for Politics', in Richard O'Brien (ed.) *Finance and the International Economy*. New York: Oxford University Press.

Posner, Richard A. (1974) 'Theories of Economic Regulation', *Bell Journal of Economics and Management Science* 5: 335–58.

Przeworski, Adam and Michael Wallerstein (1988) 'Structural Dependence of the State on Capital', *American Political Science Review* 82 (1): 11–29.

Quinn, Dennis P. (1997) 'The Correlates of Change in International Financial Regulation', *American Political Science Review* 91 (3): 531–51.

Quinn, Dennis P. and Carla Inclán (1997) 'The Origins of Financial Openness: A Study of Current and Capital Account Liberalisation', *American Journal of Political Science* 41 (3):771–813.

Radelet, Steven and Jeffrey D. Sachs (1998) 'The East Asian Financial Crisis: Diagnosis, Remedies, Prospects', *Brookings Papers on Economic Activity* 1: 1–90.

Reisen, Helmut (1999) 'Domestic Causes of Currency Crises: Policy Lessons for Crisis Avoidance', *IDS Bulletin* 30 (1): 120–33.

Remmer, Karen (1986) 'The Politics of Economic Stabilisation: IMF Standby Programs in Latin America, 1954–1984', *Comparative Politics* 19 (1): 1–24.

Rhee, Jong-Chan (1994) *The State and Industry in South Korea: the Limits of the Authoritarian State*. London: Routledge.

Ro, Sung-Tae (1993) *Korea's Monetary Policy (1962–1992)*. Seoul: First Economic Research Institute.

Robison, Richard (1989) 'Structures of Power and the Industrialisation Process in Southeast Asia', *Journal of Contemporary Asia* 19 (4): 371–97.

Robison, Richard (forthcoming) 'The Politics of Financial Reform: Re-Capitalising Indonesia's Banks', in Geoffrey R. D. Underhill and Xiaoke Zhang (eds) *International Financial Governance under Stress: Global Structures versus National Imperatives*. Cambridge, UK: Cambridge University Press.

Rogowski, Ronald (1989) *Commerce and Coalitions: How Trade Affects Domestic Political Alignments*. Princeton, NJ: Princeton University Press.

Rozental, Alek A. (1970) *Finance and Development in Thailand*. New York: Praeger

Rueschemeyer, Dietrich and Peter B. Evans (1985) 'The State and Economic Transformation: Toward an Analysis of the Conditions Underlying Effective Intervention', in Peter B. Evans, Dietrich Rueschemeyer and Theda Skocpol (eds) *Bringing the State Back In*. Cambridge, UK: Cambridge University Press.

Sakong, Il (1993) *Korea in the World Economy*. Washington, DC: Institute for International Economics.

Samudavanija, Chai-Anan (1971) 'The Politics and Administration of the Thai Budgeting Process', PhD Dissertation, University of Wisconsin.

Sanittanont, Sura (1973) 'Exchange Rate Experience and Policy in Thailand Since World War II', in Herbert G. Grubel and Theodore Morgan (eds) *Exchange Rate Policy in Southeast Asia*. Lexington, NY: Lexington Books.

Schneider, Ben Ross and Sylvia Maxfield (1997) 'Business, the State, and Economic Performance in Developing Countries', in Sylvia Maxfield and Ben Ross Schneider (eds) *Business and the State in Developing Countries*. Ithaca, NY: Cornell University Press.

Scott, John (1986) *Capitalist Property and Financial Power: A Comparative Study of Britain, the United States, and Japan*. New York: New York University Press.

Shafer, D. Michael (1994) *Winners and Losers: How Sectors Shape the Developmental Prospects of States*. Ithaca, NY: Cornell University Press.

Shaw, Edward S. (1973) *Financial Deepening in Economic Development*. New York: Oxford University Press.

Shin, Roy W. (1991) 'The Role of Industrial Policy Agents: A Study of Korean Intermediate Organisations as a Policy Network', *Pacific Focus* 6 (2): 49–64

Shleifer, Andrei and Robert W. Vishny (1996) 'A Survey of Corporate Governance',

NBER Working Paper 5554. Cambridge, MA: National Bureau of Economic Research.

Siamwalla, Ammar (1997) 'Can a Developing Democracy Manage its Macro-economy? The Case of Thailand', *TDRI Quarterly Review* 12 (4): 3–10.

Sibunruang, Atchaka (1986) 'Industrial Development Policies in Thailand', manuscript. Bangkok: Thailand Development Research Institute.

Silcock, T. H. (1967) 'Money and Banking', in T. H. Silcock (ed.) *Thailand: Social and Economic Studies in Development*. Canberra: Australian National University Press.

Simmons, Beth A. (1996) 'Rulers of the Game: Central Bank Independence during the Interwar Years', *International Organisation* 50 (3): 407–43.

Singh, Ajit and Javed Hamid (1992) 'Corporate Financial Structures in Developing Countries', Technical Paper 1. Washington, DC: International Finance Corporation.

Sithi-Amnuai, Paul (1964) *Finance and Banking in Thailand: A Study of the Commercial System, 1888–1963*. Bangkok: Bangkok Bank Limited.

Skidmore, Thomas E. (1977) 'The Politics of Economic Stabilisation in Postwar Latin America', in James M. Malloy (ed.) *Authoritarianism and Corporatism in Latin America*. Pittsburgh, PA: Pittsburgh University Press.

Smith, Heather (1998) 'Korea', in Ross H. McLeod and Ross Garnaut (eds) *East Asia in Crisis: From being a Miracle to Needing One?* London: Routledge.

Snitwongse, Kusuma (1994) 'Thailand in 1993: Politics of Survival', *Asian Survey* 34 (2): 147–52.

Song, Byung-Nak (1997) *The Rise of the Korean Economy*. Hong Kong: Oxford University Press.

Stallings, Barbara (1990) 'The Role of Foreign Capital in Economic Development', in Gary Gareffin and Donald Wyman (eds) *Manufacturing Miracles: Paths of Industrialisation in Latin America and East Asia*. Princeton, NJ: Princeton University Press.

Stallings, Barbara (1992) 'International Influence on Economic Policy: Debt, Stabilisation, and Structural Reform', in Stephan Haggard and Robert R. Kaufman (eds) *The Politics of Economic Adjustment: International Constraints, Distributive Conflicts and the State*. Princeton, NJ: Princeton University Press.

Steinmo, Sven, Kathleen Thelen and Frank Longstreth (eds) (1992) *Structuring Politics: Historical Institutionalism in Comparative Analysis*. New York: Cambridge University Press.

Stigler, George J. (1974) 'Free Rider and Collective Action: An Appendix to Theories of Economic Regulation', *Bell Journal of Economics and Management Science* 5: 359–65.

Stiglitz, Joseph E. (1989) 'Financial Markets and Development', *Oxford Review of Economic Policy* 5: 55–68.

Stiglitz, Joseph E. and Andrew Weiss (1981) 'Credit Rationing in Markets with Imperfect Information', *The American Economic Review* 71 (3): 393–410.

Stone, Alan (1977) *Economic Regulation and Public Interest: the Federal Trade Commission in Theory and Practice*. Ithaca, NY: Cornell University Press.

Suehiro, Akira (1989) *Capital Accumulation in Thailand, 1855–1985*. Tokyo: The Center for East Asian Cultural Studies.

Suehiro, Akira (1992) 'Capitalist Development in Postwar Thailand: Commercial Bankers, Industrial Elite and Agribusiness Groups', in Ruth McVey (ed.) *Southeast Asian Capitalists*. Ithaca, NY: Cornell University Southeast Asia Programme.

Suehiro, Akira (1993) 'Family Business Reassessed: Corporate Structure and Late-starting Industrialisation in Thailand', *The Developing Economies* 31 (4): 378–407.

Suksamran, Somboon (1990) 'Socio-Political and Cultural Constraints on the Decision-making Process in Thailand', in Samart Chiasakul and Mikimasa Yoshida (eds) *Thai Economy in the Changing Decade and Industrial Promotion Policy*. Tokyo: Institute of Developing Economies.

Sundaravej, Tipsuda and Prasarn Trairatvorakul (1989) 'Experiences of Financial Distress in Thailand', Working paper 283. Washington, DC: The World Bank.

Sussman, Oren (1991) 'Macro-economic Effects of a Tax on Bond Interest Rates', *Journal of Money, Credit and Banking* 23: 239–48.

Tara Siam Business Information (1994a) *Thai Commercial Banking Sectoral Study 1994*. Bangkok: Tara Siam Business Information.

Tara Siam Business Information (1994b) *Thai Finance Company Sectoral Study 1994*. Bangkok: Tara Siam Business Information.

Taylor, Lance (1983) *Structuralist Macro-economics: Applicable Models for the Third World*. New York: Basic Books.

Titman, Sheridan and Roberto Wessels (1988) 'The Determinants of Capital Structure Choice', *The Journal of Finance* 43 (2): 1–19.

Tivakul, Aroonsri and Pongpanu Svetarundra (1993) 'Financial Innovation and Modernisation of the Thai Financial Market', *Bank of Thailand Quarterly Bulletin* 33 (4): 21–46.

Traisorat, Tull (2000) *Thailand: Financial Sector Reform and the East Asian Crisis*. The Hague: Kluwer Law International.

Tufte, Edward (1978) *Political Control of the Economy*. Princeton, NJ: Princeton University Press.

Underhill, Geoffrey R. D. (2000) 'The Public Good versus Private Interests in the Global Monetary and Financial System', *International and Comparative Corporate Law Journal* 2 (3): 335–59.

Unger, Daniel (1993) 'Government and Business in Thailand', *Journal of Northeast Asian Studies* 12 (3): 66–88.

Unger, Daniel (1998) *Building Social Capital in Thailand: Fibers, Finance, and Infrastructure*. Cambridge, UK: Cambridge University Press.

Unger, Brigitte and Frans van Waarden (1999) 'Interest Associations and Economic Growth: A Critique of Mancur Olson's Rise and Decline of Nations', *Review of International Political Economy* 6 (4): 425–67.

Vajragupta, Yos and Pakorn Vichyanond (1999) 'Thailand's Financial Evolution and the 1997 Crisis', in Seiichi Masuyama, Donna Vandenbrink and Chia Siow Yue (eds) *East Asia's Financial Systems: Evolution and Crisis*. Singapore: Institute of Southeast Asian Studies and Tokyo: Nomura Research Institute.

Vichyanond, Pakorn (1994) *Thailand's Financial System: Structure and Liberalisation*. Bangkok: Thailand Development Research Institute.

Vichyanond, Pakorn (1995) 'Financial Sector Development in Thailand', in Shahid N. Zahid (ed.) *Financial Sector Development in Asia*. Hong Kong: Oxford University Press.

Viksnins, George and Michael T. Skully (1987) 'Asian Financial Development: A Comparative Perspective of Eight Countries', *Asian Survey* 27 (5): 535–551.

Vogel, Ezra F. (1991) *The Four Little Dragons: The Spread of Industrialisation in East Asia*. Cambridge, MA: Harvard University Press.

Wade, Robert (1985) 'East Asian Financial Systems as a Challenge to Economics: Lessons from Taiwan', *California Management Review* 27 (4): 106–27.

Wade, Robert (1990) *Governing the Market: Economic Theory and the Role of Government in East Asian Industrialisation*. Princeton, NJ: Princeton University Press.

Wade, Robert (1992) 'East Asia's Economic Success: Conflicting Perspectives, Partial Insights, Shaky Evidence', *World Politics* 44 (2): 270–320.

Wade, Robert (1993) 'Managing Trade: Taiwan and South Korea as Challenges to Economics and Political Science', *Comparative Politics* 26 (2): 147–67.

Wade, Robert (1998) 'The Asian Debt-and-Development Crisis of 1997–?: Causes and Consequences', *World Development* 26 (8): 1535–53.

Wade, Robert and Frank Veneroso (1998) 'The Asian Crisis: The High Debt Model versus the Wall Street–Treasury–IMF Complex', *New Left Review* 228: 3–22.

Wallerstein, Immanuel (1976) 'Semi-peripheral Countries and the Contemporary World Crisis', *Theory and Society* 3 (4): 461–83.

Wallerstein, Immanuel (1979) *The Capitalist World Economy: Essays by Immanuel Wallerstein*. New York: Cambridge University Press.

Warr, Peter G. (1993) 'The Thai Economy', in Peter G. Warr (ed.) *The Thai Economy in Transition*. Cambridge, UK: Cambridge University Press.

Warr, Peter G. (1998) 'Thailand', in Ross H. McLeod and Ross Garnaut (eds) *East Asia in Crisis: From being a Miracle to Needing One?* London: Routledge.

Waterbury, John (1989) 'The Political Management of Economic Adjustment and Reform', in Joan Nelson (ed.) *Fragile Coalitions: The Politics of Economic Adjustment*. New Brunswick, NJ: Transaction.

Weiss, Linda (1998) *The Myth of the Powerless State: Governing the Economy in a Global Era*. Cambridge, UK: Polity Press.

Weiss, Linda (2000) 'Developmental States in Transition: Adapting, Dismantling, Innovating, not "Normalising"', *The Pacific Review* 13 (1): 21–55.

Weiss, Linda and John M. Hobson (1995) *States and Economic Development: A Comparative Historical Analysis*. Cambridge, UK: Cambridge University Press.

Whitley, Richard (1992) *Business Systems in East Asia: Firms, Markets, and Societies*. London: Sage.

Wibulswasdi, Chaiyawat (1986) 'The Formulation and Implementation of the Monetary Policy: the Thai Monetary Experience during 1983–1984', *Bank of Thailand Quarterly Bulletin* 26 (3): 27–44.

Wibulswasdi, Chaiyawat (1987) 'Thai Experience in Economic Management during 1980–87', *Bank of Thailand Quarterly Bulletin* 27 ( 3): 31–46.

Wibulswasdi, Chaiyawat (1992) 'Thailand as a Regional Financial Center in the Year 2000', paper presented at an international conference on Business Opportunities under the Thai SEC organised by Center for Capital Market Studies and the Stock Exchange of Thailand, 2–4 December.

Wibulswasdi, Chaiyawat (1995) 'Strengthening the Domestic Financial System', *Papers on Policy Analysis and Assessment* (Bank of Thailand): 1–12.

Wibulswasdi, Chaiyawat and Orasa Tanvanich (1992) 'Liberalisation of the Foreign Exchange Market: Thailand's Experience', *Bank of Thailand Quarterly Bulletin* 32 (4): 25–37.

van Wijnbergen, Sweder (1983) 'Interest Rate Management in LCDs', *Journal of Monetary Economics* 12: 433–52.

Williams, John T. (1990) 'The Political Manipulation of Macro-economic Policy', *American Political Science Review* 84 (3): 767–95.

Williamson, Oliver E. (1985) *The Economic Institutions of Capitalism*. New York: Free Press.

Williamson, Oliver E. (1995) 'The Institutions and Government of Economic Development and Reform', *Proceedings of the World Bank Annual Conference on Development Economics 1994*. Washington, DC: The World Bank.

Williamson, John (forthcoming) 'Costs and Benefits of Financial Globalisation: Concepts, Evidence and Implications', in Geoffrey R. D. Underhill and Xiaoke Zhang (eds) *International Financial Governance under Stress: Global Structures versus National Imperatives*. Cambridge, UK: Cambridge University Press.

Wilson, Graham K. (1990) *Business and Politics: A Comparative Introduction*, 2nd edn. London: Macmillan.

Winters, Jeffrey A. (2000) 'The Financial Crisis in Southeast Asia', in Richard Robison, Mark Beeson, Kanishka Jayasuriya and Hyuk-Rae Kim (eds) *Politics and Markets in the Wake of the Asian Crisis*. London: Routledge.

Woo, June-En (1991) *Race to the Swift: State and Finance in Korean Industrialisation*. New York: Columbia University Press.

Woo-Cumings, Meredith (1999a) 'The State, Democracy, and the Reform of the Corporate Sector in Korea', in T. J. Pempel (ed.) *The Politics of the Asian Economic Crisis*. Ithaca, NY: Cornell University Press.

Woo-Cumings, Meredith (1999b) 'Introduction: Chalmers Johnson and the Politics of Nationalism and Development', in Meredith Woo-Cumings (ed) *The Developmental State*. Ithaca, NY: Cornell University Press.

Woodall, Pam (1998) 'A Survey of East Asian Economies', *The Economist* 7 March.

Woolley, John T. (1977) 'Monetary Policy Instrumentation and the Relationship of Central Banks and Governments', *The Annals of the American Academy of Political and Social Science* 434: 151–73.

Woolley, John T. (1984) *Monetary Politics: The Federal Reserve and the Politics of Monetary Policy*. Cambridge, UK: Cambridge University Press.

Woolley, John T. (1985) 'Central Banks and Inflation', in Leon N. Lindberg and Charles S. Maier (eds) *The Politics of Inflation and Economic Stagnation: Theoretical Approaches and International Case Studies*. Washington, DC: The Brookings Institution.

Woolley, John T. (1994) 'The Politics of Monetary Policy: A Critical Review', *Journal of Public Policy* 14 (1): 57–85.

Yoo, Seong Min (1994) 'Issues and Reforms in Korea's Industrial and Trade Policies', in Lee Jay Cho and Yoon Hyung Kim (eds) *Korea's Political Economy: An Institutional Perspective*. Boulder, CO: Westview.

You, Jong S. (1992) 'Trade and Financial Liberalisation Policies in Korea: An Uncoordinated Effort', *The Korean Economic Review* 8 (1): 131–42.

Zahid, Shahid N. (ed.) (1995) *Financial Sector Development in Asia*. Hong Kong: Oxford University Press.

Zhang, Xiaoke (2002) 'Domestic Institutions, Liberalisation Patterns, and Uneven Crises in Korea and Taiwan', *The Pacific Review* 15 (3): 375–408.

Zhang, Xiaoke (forthcoming) 'Political Structures and Financial Liberalisation in Pre-crisis East Asia', *Studies in Comparative International Development*.

Zhang, Xiaoke and Geoffrey R. D. Underhill (2002) 'Private Capture, Policy Failures and Financial Crisis: Evidence and Lessons from Korea and Thailand', in Geoffrey R. D. Underhill and Xiaoke Zhang (eds) *International Financial Governance under Stress: Global Structures versus National Imperatives*. Cambridge, UK: Cambridge University Press.

Zysman, John (1983) *Governments, Markets, and Growth: Financial Systems and the Politics of Industrial Change*. Ithaca, NY: Cornell University Press.

# Newspapers and magazines

*Asiamoney*
*Asian Finance*
*The Asian Wall Street Journal*

*Asiaweek*
*The Banker* (London)
*Bangkok Bank Monthly Review*
*The Bangkok Post*
*The Bangkok Post Economic Review*
*Business Korea*
*The Economist*
*Economist Intelligence Unit Country Report*
*The Far Eastern Economic Review*
*The Financial Times* (London)
*Korea Business World*
*The Korea Herald*
*The Korea Times*
*The Nation* (Bangkok)
*Southeast Asia Business*


## Publications by official sources

Asian Development Bank Institute (ADBI) (1999) 'Corporate Governance in Asia', ADBI Executive Summary Series No. S15/00. Tokyo: Asian Development Bank Institute.
Bank of Korea (various years) *Annual Report*, Seoul.
Bank of Korea (various issues) *Money and Banking Statistics* (in Korean), Seoul.
Bank of Korea (various years) *Economic Statistics Yearbook*, Seoul.
Bank of Korea (various issues) *Financial Statements Analysis*, Seoul.
Bank of Korea (1983, 1985, 1990, 1995) *Financial System in Korea*, Seoul.
Bank of Korea (1991, 1993) *Foreign Exchange System in Korea*, Seoul.
Bank of Korea (1996) *The Korean Economy*, Seoul.
Bank of Korea (various issues) *Monthly Bulletin*, Seoul.
Bank of Korea (1997) *The Present Conditions and Competition Strategies of Korean Commercial Banks' Subsidiaries* (in Korean), Seoul.
Bank of Thailand (various years) *Annual Report*, Bangkok.
Bank of Thailand (1992) *50 Years of the Bank of Thailand: 1942–1992*, Bangkok.
Bank of Thailand (various issues) *Quarterly Bulletin*, Bangkok.
Bank of Thailand (1996) *Supervision Report, 1996*, Bangkok.
Economic Planning Board (various years) *Korea Statistical Yearbook*, Seoul.
International Monetary Fund (various years) *Annual Report on Exchange Arrangement and Exchange Restrictions (AREAER)*, Washington, DC.
International Monetary Fund (various years) *Balance of Payments Yearbook*, Washington, DC.
International Monetary Fund (various years) *International Financial Statistics Yearbook*, Washington, DC.
International Monetary Fund (1998) *World Economic Outlook*, Washington, DC.
National Statistical Bureau of Korea (various issues) *Major Statistics of the Korean Economy*, Seoul.
Thai National Statistical Office (various issues) *The Industrial Survey*, Bangkok.
United Nations (various years) *Economic and Social Survey of Asia and the Pacific*.
United Nations (various years) *World Economic and Social Survey*.
World Bank (1986) *Korea: Managing the Industrial Transition*, Washington, DC.

World Bank (1992) *Governance and Development*. Washington, DC: The World Bank.
World Bank (1993) *The East Asian Miracle: Economic Growth and Public Policy*. New York: Oxford University Press.
World Bank (1995) *Governance: The World Bank's Experience*. Washington, DC.
World Bank (1997) *World Development Report 1997: The State in a Changing World*. New York: Oxford University Press.
World Bank (various issues) *World Debt Tables*, Washington, DC.

# Index

accountability 203n4
Act on the Undertaking of Finance
  Business, Security Business, and
  Credit Foncier Business 59
administrative guidance 174
aggregation 27, 28
Agricultural Bank 50, 62
agro-industry 92
*amakudari* 95
Anand Panyarachun 115
appreciation 90, 101, 165
arbitrage 27, 38, 109; capital account
  opening and 27
Asia Trust Bank 111, 200n2
Asian financial crisis 4, 6; *see also*
  financial crisis
Association of Finance Companies 126
Association of Securities Companies 126

baht 108, 117, 152, 155, 165, 166, 200n1
Bangkok 105, 114, 115, 123, 124, 127,
  132
Bangkok Bank 49
Bangkok Bank of Commerce 155, 157–8,
  162, 163, 164
Bangkok International Banking
  Facilities 106, 117, 128–30, 152, 156,
  187; and capital inflows 152–4; and
  financial crisis in Thailand 152–4,
  156; major operations of 200–1n5;
  taxation scheme of 201n7
Bangkok Metropolitan Bank 51
Banharn Silapa-archa 127
Bank of Ayudhya 51
Bank of Chosen 60–1
Bank for International Settlements
  202n4
Bank of Korea: appointments 57;
  authority over monetary policy

58–9; economic independence 58–60;
  financing of government deficits
  60; Monetary Board 56; origin and
  evolution of 60–4; policy objectives 57;
  political independence 57–8; relations
  with Finance Ministry 98, 145, 180–1;
  supervisory authority 59, 176
Bank of Korea Act 56, 198n5
bank privatisation 77, 81, 136
Bank of Thailand: appointments 57–8;
  authority over monetary policy 58–9;
  Court of Directors 56; diminished
  authority of 67–8, 160–7; economic
  independence 58–60; financing of
  government deficits 60, 198n6; policy
  objectives 57; relations with Finance
  Ministry 65–6, 86–7, 105, 128,
  146–8, 160–7; relations with private
  financiers 66–7, 159–60, 160–7;
  supervisory authority 59
Bank of Thailand Act 56
banking families 49, 163
bankruptcy 92, 93, 154, 171, 178
Bloomfield, Arthur 61
bond market(s) 101
Brazil 41
Britain *see* United Kingdom
bureaucratic polity 127
business associations 11–2
business–government relations 38,
  86, 184, 192; and economic policy-
  making 38–9; and financial crisis
  184–5
business groups 44

Cambodia 107
capital account liberalisation 26–7, 37,
  89–91, 96, 97, 100–3, 136–7, 152;
  and financial crisis 152–4, 172–3; *see*

*also* foreign exchange and capital decontrol

capital adequacy 157, 171; measurement of 202n4

capital–asset ratio 170, 171

capital controls 2, 26, 37, 87, 90, 103

capital flight 3, 151

capital-intensive industries 175

capital investment 168, 169

capital market(s) 52, 89, 90, 101, 102

capital mobility 26, 37, 120, 138, 156

capital–output ratio 169

capital structure 158, 169

cash flow 158

central bank(s) 14, 33; functions of 33; interests in financial policy and liberalisation 34–8; policy-making autonomy of 33, 38; relations with governments 33–4; relations with private financial community 39–40; supervisory responsibilities of 39

central bank independence 14, 87, 162, 163; definition of 33–4; and financial policy 34; and private preference articulation 34, 38–41

central bank reform 61, 191

central bankers 14, 34, 77, 160, 162; preferences for financial policy and liberalisation 34–8; relations with private bankers 34, 39–40

chaebols 44, 46, 74–5, 80, 82, 84, 91–2, 98, 99, 168, 177; bankruptcy 177–8; industrial structure of 44–5; growth of 45–7; policy influence 76–7, 85–6, 91–3, 141–4, 184–5

Chart Pattana Party 164

Chart Thai Party 114, 121, 127

Chatichai Choonhavan 113, 161

Chavalit Thanachanan 115, 120, 121, 125

Chavalit Yongchaiyut 127, 160

China 60

Cho, Soon 93

Chuan Leekpai 127, 160, 189

Chun, Doo-Hwan 75

Chung, Ju-Yung 85

Citibank 122

Citizens National Bank 82

Civil and Commercial Code 109

civil society 97

clientelism 11

coalition(s) 14, 28, 46, 96, 119, 120, 127, 128, 145, 164, 192

collateral 156, 164

Commercial Banking Act 59

commercial banks 49, 50, 51, 52–5, 77, 81, 94, 100, 108, 110, 114, 117, 119, 124, 131, 136, 137, 143, 154, 166, 170, 173; relations with NBFIs 158

commercial papers 79, 91, 169

concentration ratio 44

Congress 90

constituency 37, 114, 118, 127, 162

construction 154

convergence 190

corporate debentures 79, 91, 92

corporate restructuring 189–90

CP group 54

corruption 96, 97, 99, 127, 189, 192

Council of Economic Ministers 114

credit-rating agency 166

cross-ownership 163

curb market(s) 23, 63, 75, 78, 84, 93

Currency Reserve Act 57

current account 101; deficits 152, 155, 167; transactions 101

Daewoo Shipbuilding and Heavy Machinery Company 92

Dai-ichi Ginko 60

debt(s) 102, 107, 119, 152, 157, 167; external 153, 155, 156, 157, 166, 167, 172, 180; maturity profile of 156, 157, 167–8, 169; short-term 153, 155, 156, 157, 167, 169–70

democracy 83, 86, 188

Democratic Justice Party 78, 83, 96

Democratic Liberal Party 96

Democratic Party 127

democratisation 96, 98, 127, 128, 160, 188, 192; and economic policy-making efficiency 188–9

dependency paradigm 9

deposit rates 91, 100, 109, 110, 120, 135, 156; *see also* interest rates

deregulation of entry barriers 2, 23–4, 26, 36, 81–3, 130–2, 135

devaluation 108, 153, 155, 165, 166, 179, 200n1

development institutions 199n8

developmental state model 5, 194–5n6; criticisms of 9–12; and economic development 9

direct financing 23, 169

Donghwa Bank 99

East Asian NIEs 1, 5, 27, 41, 85, 123,
168, 185, 190
economic crisis 74, 106, 151
Economic Planning Board 46, 59, 63, 74,
75, 93, 98
electoral cycle 35; and economic policy
35–6
Exchange Control Act 117
exchange rate 90, 151, 152, 160, 163,
165; and financial crisis 151, 165–7,
197–81; multiple 117
export-led strategy 54, 100, 123
export-oriented industries 31, 54, 119

factionalism 162
Fair Trade and Anti-monopoly Act 96
Federal Reserve System 61
Federation of Bank and Financial
Workers Union of Thailand 124
Federation of Korean Industries 53–4,
78, 81, 85, 90, 91, 93, 94, 99, 141
Federation of Thai Industries 55, 142,
143
fee-based income 120, 122, 125, 131
finance companies 2, 53, 55, 82, 108,
111, 123, 125, 126, 131, 143, 154, 155,
157, 164, 166; business activities of
199n8; competition with commercial
banks 158
finance–industry ties 14, 30, 195n9,
196n6; and cross-sector collective
action 30–2; in Korea 51–3; and
private financiers' preferences
for financial policy 30–1; and
structural problems 176–7; in
Thailand 54–5
finance ministries 14, 33, 38, 40;
relations with central banks 33;
supervisory responsibilities of 39–40
Finance One 155, 164
financial crisis 2, 151, 159, 166, 167, 169,
172, 182
financial institutions 39, 40, 41, 76, 84,
95, 100, 105, 109, 113, 122, 124, 128,
153; lending to high-risk sectors
154–5
Financial Institutions Development
Fund 163, 164
Financial Institutions Lending Rate Act
109, 122
financial liberalisation 1, 3–4, 73, 76,
84, 87, 96, 97, 98, 101, 105, 131;
approaches to 2–3, 134–7; and

financial crisis 4, 15, 151–81, 182–4;
sequencing of 3, 73, 136–7, 159
financial openness 138–9; measurement
of 139–40, 201n1, 201n2
financial reform *see* financial
liberalisation
financial regulation(s) 39, 175
financial repression 5–6, 35, 38, 174,
197n8
financial sector 5–6, 29, 30, 114;
preferences for financial market
liberalisation 25–7; relations with
industrial sector 30–2
financial system 73, 84, 87, 93, 97, 99,
108, 113, 114, 115, 125, 129, 132, 144,
158, 186
financiers 14, 25, 30, 39, 41, 160, 166,
187, 188
foreign banks 82–3, 114, 122, 123, 124,
129, 130, 135, 137, 152
foreign capital 38, 82, 118, 167, 172, 174
Foreign Capital Deliberation
Committee 59, 88
Foreign Capital Inducement Act 59, 88
foreign creditors 155, 156, 172, 178
foreign direct investment(s) 101, 103,
123, 144, 152, 153, 173
foreign exchange and capital decontrol
2, 24–5, 26–7, 36–7, 76, 87–91, 101,
116–20, 128, 136–7; and financial
crisis 152–4
Foreign Exchange Control Act 59, 88, 90
foreign investment trusts 102
foreign investors 87, 88, 101, 102, 116,
119, 144, 152, 154, 165, 166, 171, 178,
179
foreign reserves *see* international
reserves
France 41
free riding 28, 29
functional de-segmentation 2, 24, 26, 36,
124–7, 136, 137–8, 146, 158, 160; and
financial crisis 158, 173

General Agreement on Tariffs and
Trade 85, 97, 113, 123, 129
General Banking Act 59, 94, 95, 199n3,
202n6
General System of Preferences 123
global market integration 113
Gourevitch, Peter 28
governance 160, 184, 189; corporate
163, 168, 175, 186, 190; definition of

203n1; financial sector 160; national economic 184–9
government(s) 14, 145, 167; interests in financial policy and liberalisation 34–8, 144–8; intervention in financial markets 5, 174, 194n4; relations with central banks 14, 33–4; ties with private sector 38–41

Hanbo 177
Heavy and Chemical Industrialisation 46, 74
high-technology industries 80–1, 92
Hong Kong 170
Hyundai 85

import-substituting industrialisation 62
indirect financing 23, 169
Indochina 105, 113, 119, 129
Indonesia 170, 185, 186
Industrial Bank of Chosen 60–1, 62
industrial concentration 29, 142, 185, 197n1; and collective action 29, 185; in Korea 44–51, 185; measurement of 197n1; in Thailand 44–51, 185
Industrial Finance Corporation of Thailand 48, 112
industrial investment 36
industrial ministries 34, 36, 41
industrial policy 36, 77
industrial sector 22, 29, 30; preferences for financial policy and liberalisation 22–5; relations with financial sector 30–2
industrial structure 14, 28, 185; and collective action 28–9; in Korea 44–9; in Thailand 44–9
industrialists 14, 22, 30, 40, 41, 111, 112, 114, 122, 142, 144, 187, 188
inflation 35, 39, 67, 74–5, 84, 92, 101, 106, 109, 114, 117, 122, 161, 180; taxes 35, 196–7n7
information costs 29, 139
infrastructure 112, 115
inter-corporate relations 30–2; *see also* finance–industry ties
interlocking directorates 30, 156
International Monetary Fund 1, 64, 76, 108, 120, 132, 140, 155, 172; and corporate reforms 190
international reserves 116, 117, 166
internationalisation 88
interest rate(s) 91, 92, 93, 94, 99, 100,

105, 108, 109, 115, 120, 121, 125, 137, 152, 155, 167; ceilings 108, 110, 120; liberalisation 2, 22–3, 25, 35, 77, 84, 91–3, 97, 98–100, 120–2, 131, 134–5; spreads 156
investment banking 125, 132
Investment Promotion Act 117

Japan 41, 116, 130, 152
Jardine Fleming 171
Jensen, John 61
joint ventures 123
JP Morgan 171

Kamchorn Sathirakul 115
Kang, Kyong-Shik 78, 179
Kia Group 172, 178
Kim, Dae-Jung 84, 189
Kim, Jae-Ik 78
Kim, Young-Sam 73, 84, 96, 97, 100, 101, 179
King Chulalongkorn 64, 65
KorAm Bank 82
Korea: bank–NBFI ties 53–4; central bank–government relations 55–68; chaebol–government relations 85–6; deregulation of entry barriers 81–3; developmental state in 9–12; evolution of financial system 50–1; finance–industry relations 51–3; financial crisis in 167–81; financial liberalisation 73–104; foreign exchange and capital decontrol 87–91; functional de-segmentation in 93–6; industrial structure 44–5; interest rate deregulation in 77–9, 91–3, 98–100; National Assembly 83, 86, 87, 95; organisation of financial sector 49–51; pattern of financial liberalisation 2–3; reduction of preferential credit in 79–80
Korea Development Bank 50, 62
Korea Development Institute 90
Korea Federation of Banks 54, 81, 83, 94
Korea Foreign Exchange Bank 82
Korean War 50, 52, 61
Krung Thai Bank 49, 200n2

labour-intensive 80, 113; industries 80, 113; manufactured goods 152, 165
Laos 113
leasing 125
legal reserve requirements 25, 40

lender of last resort 39–40, 47, 75, 155
lending rates 91, 115, 120, 130; *see also*
    interest rates
leverage 169
loan rates 109, 110, 122, 135
Liberal Party 45
lifeboat scheme 123, 200n4

Malaysia 3, 170, 185, 186
manufacturing sector *see* industrial
    sector
marginal loan(s) 153
Meiji Restoration 62
mercantilism 87; and capital controls
    87–8
merchant banking 132
merchant banks 2, 53, 170, 173, 202n6;
    business activities of 199n8
meritocracy 191
Mexico 41
middle class 127
minimum retail rate 201n8
Ministry of Finance and Economy 64, 98,
    176, 180, 198n3
monetary policy 33, 58–9, 76, 90, 95, 96,
    118, 152, 160, 165
Moody's 166
moral hazard 157, 174, 176; and risk-
    taking behaviour 157, 174–5
moral suasion 159

National Banking Bureau 65
National Economic and Social
    Development Board 114
National Investment Fund 46
negative-list system 90
negotiable certificates 91
neo-classical perspective 5, 194n4;
    criticisms of 6–7; and financial policy
    5–6
New Aspiration Party 127
non-bank financial institutions 2, 24, 26,
    27, 36, 53–5, 93–6, 103, 125, 133, 136,
    143, 154; lending to high-risk sectors
    154–5; relations with commercial
    banks 126–7, 143–4
non-performing assets 25, 155, 158, 171;
    in East Asian banking sectors 202n3;
    *see also* non-performing loans
non-performing loan(s) 163, 164, 172,
    202n4; Korean definition of 202–3n7;
    ratio 171
non-residents 117
Nukul Prachuabmol 109

offshore banking 128, 130
oligopolistic structure(s) 26, 27, 69, 111,
    189; of Thai banking sector 49, 108,
    128, 142, 156, 159
Olson, Mancur 28, 29
Organisation for Economic Co-operation
    and Development 37, 97, 100, 101,
    102
organisational structure 162
overvaluation 152; exchange rate policy
    and 152
ownership concentration 49, 108,
    163, 177, 186, 190; and corporate
    governance 186–7; and regulatory
    failure 186–7

Park, Chung-Hee 45, 46, 74
partisan cycle 35; and economic policy
    35
party-system approach 12, 195n8;
    criticisms of 13; to economic policy
    analysis 12–3
patronage 192
the Philippines, 170, 182
planning ministries 34, 36, 41
Polanyi, Karl 6
policy loans 46
political party 86, 107, 115, 119, 127,
    128, 188
political structure(s) 167, 182
portfolio investment 152, 153
portfolio management 93, 125, 136, 158,
    174
pound sterling 116
Pramual Sabhavasu 114, 120, 121, 124,
    161
preferential credit 2, 87; reduction of 2,
    23, 25–6, 35, 134
Prem Tinsulanonda 107
presidential commission for financial
    reform 97
Presidential Emergency Decree 63
Prince Viwatanajai 57
private bankers 109, 110, 111, 119, 131,
    133, 142, 143, 144, 160; relations with
    central bankers 38–40, 160–6, 197n10
private–public networks *see* business–
    government relations
private-sector preferences 13–4, 16,
    196n4; aggregation and articulation
    of 27–32, 196n3; for financial policy
    and liberalisation 22–7, 141–4; *see also*
    financial sector and industrial sector
property development 153, 154, 156, 163

proportional representation system
199n4
Provincial International Banking
Facilities 129
prudential regulation 93, 159;
weaknesses of 158–60, 175–7
public-sector interests 13, 15; in
financial policy and liberalisation 34–
8, 144–8; institutional determinants
of 34, 144–8; *see also* central banks
and governments
Puey Ungphakorn 67

ratio of debt to equity 78, 169
real estate 102, 117, 153, 154, 157, 158,
170, 171, 174
real-name financial transaction system
84, 96, 97, 101
re-capitalisation 190
regional financial centre 105, 113, 124
regulatory rules 158, 159, 163, 176
rent seeking 127, 180, 184, 186,
188, 190, 192; and policy-making
problems 184–5, 186–7
retail banking 131
return on assets 170, 171; measurement
of 202n5
return on equity 170, 171; measurement
of 202n5
Rhee, Syngman 45, 61
Roh, Tae-Woo 83, 85, 89, 92
Royal Decree Regulating the Affairs of
the Bank of Thailand 56

Sakong, Il 87
Samsung Motors 179
Sarit Thanarat 47, 118
saving(s) 124, 129
Second World War 65, 67, 116, 118
securities firms 2, 53, 95, 125
selective credit allocation 62
Shinhan Bank 82
short-term capital flows 37, 102
Siam Commercial Bank 49, 50
Siam Motors 54
Singapore 170, 182, 188
Sommai Hoontrakul 112
Sommi 177
Southern Cone countries 1, 194n1
specialised banks 50, 82
speculation 158, 163
Standard & Poor's 172
stabilisation programme 75, 108
state(s) 4, 6, 8, 189; autonomy 9;

capacity 10, 191; and economic
development 6, 9; institutions 10–1,
33, 182–4, 187–9, 190–1, and national
economic governance 189–93
state–society relations 192
stock market(s) 101, 102, 116, 117, 153,
154, 158, 162, 164, 171
stock trading 156, 157
Suchinda Kraprayoon 115
supervision 99, 200n10
supervisory forbearance 160
swap system 82
system-centred approach 5; criticisms
of 8–9; to economic policy analysis
7–8

Taiwan 3, 170, 182, 199
technocrats 114, 116, 118, 120, 128, 161,
187, 191
Thai Bankers' Association 55, 67, 108,
110, 111, 120, 124, 144
Thai Danu Bank 164
Thai Farmers' Bank 51
Thailand: bank–NBFI ties 55; central
bank–government relations 55–68;
deregulation of entry barriers in
111–2, 122–4, 130–2; evolution
of financial system in 50–1;
finance–industry relations 51–3;
financial crisis in 151–167; financial
liberalisation 105–33; foreign
exchange and capital decontrol in
116–20; functional de-segmentation
in 124–7; industrial structure 44–5;
interest rate deregulation 108–11,
120–2; organisation of banking
sector 49–51; pattern of financial
liberalisation 2–3;
Thailand Development Research
Institute 124
time-inconsistent preferences 35
trade liberalisation 199n6
trading companies 47
transparency 157, 192
trust accounts 176

Unification National Party 86
Union Bank of Bangkok 51
United Kingdom 30, 41, 65
United States 30, 41, 97, 123, 129, 130
US Trade Act 89
US Treasury Department 89, 90

vertical integration 47

Vietnam 113
Vietnam War 107
Vijit Supinit 162, 164

Washington consensus 1

Weberian bureaucracy 190
wholesale banking 132
won 89, 90, 101, 171, 179
World Bank 1, 76, 108, 117, 118, 123, 132, 168, 191